ADJUDICATION IN RELIGIOUS FAMILY LAWS

How do multireligious and multiethnic societies construct accommodative arrangements that can both facilitate cultural diversity and ensure women's rights? Based on a rich ethnography of legal adjudication of marriage and divorce across formal and informal arenas in Mumbai, this book argues that the shared adjudication model in which the state splits its adjudicative authority with religious groups and other societal sources in the regulation of marriage can potentially balance cultural rights and gender equality. In this model, the ideologically diverse lay, civic, and religious sources of legal authority construct, transmit, and communicate heterogeneous notions of the conjugal family, gender relations, and religious membership within the interstices of state and society. In so doing, they fracture the homogenized religious identities grounded in hierarchical gender relations within the conjugal family. The shared adjudication model facilitates diversity as it allows the construction of hybrid religious identities, creates fissures in ossified group boundaries, and provides institutional spaces for ongoing intersocietal dialog. In this pluralized legal sphere, individual and collective legal mobilization by women spurs law reform and paves the way toward formal and substantive gender equality.

Gopika Solanki is assistant professor of political science at Carleton University in Canada. She is the coauthor of *Journey from Violence to Crime: A Study of Domestic Violence in the City of Mumbai*. She has contributed articles to various journals and books.

CAMBRIDGE STUDIES IN LAW AND SOCIETY

Cambridge Studies in Law and Society aims to publish the best scholarly work on legal discourse and practice in its social and institutional contexts, combining theoretical insights and empirical research.

The fields that it covers are studies of law in action; the sociology of law; the anthropology of law; cultural studies of law, including the role of legal discourses in social formations; law and economics; law and politics; and studies of governance. The books consider all forms of legal discourse across societies, rather than being limited to lawyers' discourses alone.

The series editors come from a range of disciplines: academic law, socio-legal studies, sociology, and anthropology. All have been actively involved in teaching and writing about law in context.

Series Editors

Chris Arup
Monash University, Victoria

Martin Chanock
La Trobe University, Melbourne

Pat O'Malley
University of Sydney

Sally Engle Merry
New York University

Susan Silbey
Massachusetts Institute of Technology

Books in the Series

The World Trade Organization Knowledge Agreements
2nd Edition
Christopher Arup

Law and Nature
David Delaney

Constitutionalizing Economic Globalization: Investment Rules and Democracy's Promise
David Schneiderman

Law, Anthropology, and the Constitution of the Social: Making Persons and Things
Edited by Alain Pottage and Martha Mundy

Continued after Index

Adjudication in Religious Family Laws

CULTURAL ACCOMMODATION, LEGAL PLURALISM, AND GENDER EQUALITY IN INDIA

Gopika Solanki

Carleton University

CAMBRIDGE UNIVERSITY PRESS
Cambridge, New York, Melbourne, Madrid, Cape Town,
Singapore, São Paulo, Delhi, Tokyo, Mexico City

Cambridge University Press
32 Avenue of the Americas, New York, NY 10013-2473, USA

www.cambridge.org
Information on this title: www.cambridge.org/9781107006102

© Gopika Solanki 2011

This publication is in copyright. Subject to statutory exception
and to the provisions of relevant collective licensing agreements,
no reproduction of any part may take place without the written
permission of Cambridge University Press.

First published 2011

Printed in the United States of America

A catalog record for this publication is available from the British Library.

Library of Congress Cataloging in Publication data
Solanki, Gopika, 1970–
 Adjudication in religious family laws : cultural accommodation, legal pluralism,
and gender equality in India / Gopika Solanki.
 p. cm. – (Cambridge studies in law and society)
 Includes bibliographical references and index.
 ISBN 978-1-107-00610-2 (hardback)
 1. Domestic relations – India. 2. Religion and law – India. 3. Legal polycentricity –
India. 4. Justice, Administration of – India. I. Title. II. Series.
 KNS540.S64 2011
 346.5401′5–dc22   2010054306

ISBN 978-1-107-00610-2 Hardback

Cambridge University Press has no responsibility for the persistence or accuracy of URLs
for external or third-party Internet Web sites referred to in this publication and does not
guarantee that any content on such Web sites is, or will remain, accurate or appropriate.

To my Mother, and Bapuji
and the memory of Ba

Contents

List of Figures	*page* xvii
List of Tables	xix
Preface	xxi
Acknowledgments	xxv
Abbreviations	xxix
Glossary	xxxi

1	**Introduction**	1
	Who Shall Govern the Family? Outlining Two Approaches	5
	Research Questions	9
	Case Selection	9
	A General Outline of the Developments in the Indian Case	11
	The Study in the Indian Context	24
	The Context of Inquiry	25
	Research Site	29
	Methods	29
	Feminist Deliberations	31
	Sampling in State Courts	32
	Data Collection in State Courts	34
	Sampling and Data Collection in Informal Courts	35
	Organization of the Book	37

ix

2. **The Shared Adjudication Model: Theoretical Framework and Arguments**   41
   Introduction   41
   Theoretical Framework: State-Society Interactions at the Interface of Personal Laws   42
   Arguments   49
   The Indian Model: Juristic Diversity in the Legal Landscape   50
       Formal Legal Organizations and Actors: The Lower Courts   51
       Legal Organizations and Actors in Society: An Overview of Typologies, Structures, and Functions   52
       Formal Organizations   52
       The Doorstep Courts – Informal Associations, Groups, and Networks   55
       Individual Legal Actors   55
   Interactions between State and Societal Organizations and Actors   56
       The Question of Legal and Extralegal Authority and Accountability   56
   An Open-Ended Conception of State-Society Relations among Heterogeneous Legal Actors   60
   The Paradoxical Movement between State Laws and Societal Laws   60
       The Centralization of Law in the Formal Legal System   61
       Fragmentation and Societalization of Law in State Courts   63
       Centralization of Law in Informal Legal Forums   64
       The Decentralization of Law in Society   65
   Characterizing the Legal Landscape: Legal Flexibility, Fragmentation, and Change   66
       Dispelling Myths about Contesting Areas in Hindu and Muslim Personal Laws: Not So Different After All?   66
   Balancing Cultural Accommodation and Gender Justice   68
       Normative Heterogeneity and Cultural Accommodation: Making and Unmaking Religious Communities, the Conjugal Family, and Gender   69

CONTENTS

    Preventing the Ossification of the Boundaries of
        Religious Groups — 69
    Accommodating Intragroup Difference and Facilitating
        Intersocietal Dialog — 70
    Making and Unmaking the Conjugal Family — 72
  Hindu and Muslim Personal Laws and the Question of
    Gender Equality — 74
  Conceiving Agency and Its Limit — 78
    The Agency of Litigant Women — 78
    Individual Women's Agency: Forum Switching and
        Gender Justice — 79
    Structural Change through Individual Agency: Hindu
        and Muslim Women Litigants and Changes in
        Personal Laws — 80
    Envisaging Legal Change through Collective
        Socio-Legal Processes — 82
    Women's Transformative Collective Agency in
        Contouring the Socio-Legal Processes in Society — 83
    Women's Transformative Collective Agency: Everyday
        Processes of Adjudication and Visions of Change — 85
  The Question of Gender Equality in the Shared
    Adjudication Model — 88
  Conclusion — 89

3. **State Law and the Adjudication Process: Marriage, Divorce, and the Conjugal Family in Hindu and Muslim Personal Laws** — 91
  Introduction — 91
  The Functioning of the Family Court — 92
    An Overview of Cases Filed in the Family Court — 95
  The Disposal of Cases in the Family Court — 97
  The Nature of Justice in the Family Court: Consensual
    Rather than Adversarial? — 100
  Adjudication in Hindu and Muslim Personal Laws — 104
  Determining "Marriage" – Outlining Boundaries of the
    Community, Protecting Individual Rights — 104

Void and Voidable Marriages: Streamlining Family Laws and Protecting Individual Rights	109
The Provision of Restitution of Conjugal Rights and the Standardization of Hindu and Muslim Personal Laws	114
The Regulation of Polygyny under Hindu and Muslim Personal Laws	116
Divorce in Hindu and Muslim Personal Laws	120
Divorce under Muslim Personal Law: The Debate over Triple Talaq	131
Divorce under Muslim Personal Law: Issues in Statutory Divorce	137
Women and Property in Marriage and Divorce Laws	139
Legal Provisions Applicable to Hindu and Muslim Women under State Laws	139
Maintenance and Alimony under Hindu Personal Law	141
Muslim Women's (Protection of Rights on Divorce) Act 1986	145
Maintenance under Section 125 CrPC	151
Implementation of Maintenance Orders	158
Injunction for Property	162
Negotiating the Retrieval of Stridhan	168
Conclusion	172
4. **Making and Unmaking the Conjugal Family: The Administration of Hindu Law in Society**	175
Introduction	175
Caste Formation and Lawmaking among Meghwals	177
Migration to Mumbai and the Statist Construction of the "Caste"	178
Nationalist Movement, Naming the Community, and Attempts at Lawmaking	181
Exposure to Democratic Politics, Creating Structures of Governance, Constructing Identity through Laws	184
Democratizing Panchayats, Civic Awareness, and Law Reforms: From the Panch System to the Panchayat	187

Attempts at Repoliticization and the Conflict over Caste Constitution	189
The Decade of the 1990s: Consolidating the Caste Identity, Social Regulation, and Lawmaking	192
Summary of the Constitutional Provisions: Commonalities, Continuities, and Discontinuities	195
The Gendered Sphere among the Meghwals	198
Innovative Legal Process: Democratic Participatory Justice	200
Structure and Organization of the Meghwal Caste Panchayat	202
Process of Adjudication in the Meghwal Caste Panchayat and the Provision for Appeal	202
Similarities, Dissimilarities, and Hybridity in State Law and Nonstate Law	203
Who Is a Hindu, Who Is a Meghwal?	203
Consent	205
Differing Conceptions of Marriage and Divorce: Marriage as Fixed or Fluid?	209
Validity of Marriage	211
Procedural Aspects of Defining Valid Marriages	212
Divorce in Caste Laws	213
Economic Rights within Marriage and upon Divorce	216
Interactions between Diverse Societal Organizations and Actors	218
Contestations among Informal Legal Actors	218
Women's Organizations as Informal Forums of Justice: Implementing State Law without Litigation	220
Women's Organization as Moral Watchdogs: Women's Organizations and Caste Authorities	221
Bargaining for Women's Rights vis-à-vis the State and the Caste	222
The Caste Panchayat among the Sai Suthars	224
Internal Governance of Family Matters among the Sai Suthars	224

The Gendered Sphere among the Sai Suthars	227
Fragmented Caste Panchayat *and the Adjudication of the Family within the Caste*	229
The Caste Is the Public Sphere and the State Private	231
In the Shadow of State Law and Courts	232
Justice through "Other Means"	232
Women's Experiences in State Courts	233
Dual Patriarchies of the Family and the State	234
Struggles for Legal Autonomy in Family Matters among the Kutchi Visa Oswals (KVOs)	237
The KVOs and the History of Migration to Mumbai	238
Forming a Panchayat	239
Family, Capital, and Religio-Cultural Organization	242
Gendered Sphere within the Caste	244
Protecting the Good Woman: Denial of Divorce in the Family Court	245
Rubber-Stamping Informal Settlements	247
Social Movement around Marriage and Divorce – Reaction to State-Led Reforms	251
State-Society Encounters in Law: Comparison of Caste-Based Legal Forums	252
Other Societal Legal Bodies: Women's Organizations	254
Legal Actors in Society: Notaries, Lawyers, Middlemen	259
Leveraging Authority: Strongmen and Political Parties in the Adjudication of Hindu Law in Society	261
Conclusion	265
5. Juristic Diversity, Contestations over "Islamic Law," and Women's Rights: Regulation of Matrimonial Matters in Muslim Personal Law	**267**
Introduction	267
The Nature of Muslim Personal Law and the Classification of Legal Actors and Institutions in Societal Arena	268
Individual Legal Actors and "Private" Divorce	269

Interlawyer Negotiations	273
The Clergy	274
Strongmen	276
Organized Legal Bodies, Doorstep Courts, and Processes of Adjudication	278
The Administration of Muslim Personal Law in the Dar ul Qaza	278
Residential Committees	281
Civil Society and the Administration of Muslim Personal Law	284
The Doorstep Courts	290
Dispute Resolution among Organized Sects: The Khojas	292
Sociopolitical Changes in the Community between the 1950s and the 1990s	295
Family Laws among the Ithana Ashari Khojas	296
Interaction with Other Forums	298
The Question of Representation: Who Represents the Community?	300
Divergent Opinions on the Establishment of Religious "Courts"	302
Conflict and Convergence between Statutory Muslim Personal Law and Societal Laws	303
Agency and Its Constraints: Muslim Women's Rights in the Legally Plural Sphere	312
The Campaign around *Nikahnama*: Reforms from Within	316
Competing Ideologies and Interests among Socio-Legal Actors and Institutions	320
Conclusion	323
6. **Conclusion**	325
What Factors Would Bring About a Change in This Model?	333
The Shared Adjudication Model Compared to Other Proposals for Accommodating Communities and Ensuring Gender Equality	335

Discussing Law Reform in Personal Laws 343
Conclusion 346

Appendix 349
Bibliography 351
Index 387

Figures

2.1. **Dynamics of interaction: state laws and societal laws** *page* 61
3.1. **Comparison of percentages of cases filed under matrimonial remedies, cases filed under civil and criminal laws of maintenance for economic rights, and injunctions for suits** 96
3.2. **Number of cases filed and disposed (1990–1999)** 98
3.3. **The nature of disposal of cases in Family Court** 100

Tables

3.1. **Number of Cases Filed in the Family Court, Mumbai (1989–2001)** *page* 95
3.2. **Total Number of Cases Filed and Disposed in the Family Court, Mumbai (1990–2001)** 97
3.3. **Number of Litigants Interviewed** 104
4.1. **Accessing Diverse Adjudicative Forums under Hindu Law** 177

Preface

States and religious groups struggle to control the family in multireligious and multiethnic societies, and as a result, these societies face the challenge of constructing institutional arrangements that can facilitate equality *between* diverse ethno-religious groups and ensure gender justice *within* these groups. Responding to this issue, many postcolonial states have not enacted uniform civil laws to govern the family, but have adopted legal pluralism and arrived at accommodative agreements with religious groups in the regulation of the family. Scholars have argued that these states' recognition of religious family laws essentializes religious groups, fuels religious extremism, leads to interreligious conflict, and prevents the construction of the political community. Feminists add that states barter women's rights to accommodate religious groups and thus violate women's human rights in the family.

Drawing on these debates, this book addresses the questions: How do societies resolve the critical tension between cultural autonomy and gender equality in contestations around family law? How do they design group rights without cementing group boundaries? I turn to legal institutional arrangements adopted by postcolonial states to answer this question and study what I call the "shared adjudication model" adopted in India. The Indian state recognizes religious laws of Hindus and Muslims, and shares its adjudicative authority with internally heterogeneous religious communities and other societal sources in matters of marriage and divorce. This study offers an ethnographic account of how religious family law is produced, interpreted, and adjudicated in state courts as well as in multiple societal legal sites such as caste and sect councils, and informal legal sites such as mosques, "doorstep law courts," women's organizations, and lawyers' offices in Mumbai.

The central claim in this book is that cultural pluralism in recognition of religious family laws can facilitate gender equality in law and prevent the ossification of religious identities. Retaining the analytical fiction of demarcation between state and societal laws while focusing on state-society negotiations over the meanings of these boundaries, I argue that the Indian model creates an interpenetrative legal sphere governing the family, which facilitates the paradoxical movement of centralization and decentralization of law in which societal legal orders and actors infiltrate the formal legal system while state law is carried into society by societal legal agents, and thus, religious family law is generated in both the state and societal arena by heterogeneous actors. As a result, among Hindus and Muslims, plural legal actors imagine, construct, debate, shape, and regulate heterogeneous notions and models of the family, marriage, gender, and religion in state and societal legal sites. These ideologically diverse actors and institutions interact with one another and transmit, communicate, transform, or resist these plural versions of the family, gender, and religion across legal spheres. These processes allow cross-pollination of insights and enable the different meanings of Hinduness and Muslimness, of religious identities and belonging, of conjugality and cohabitation, of gender roles, and rights to flourish.

I contend that a plural legal system with shifting balance of authority between the state, internally fragmented religious communities, civic organizations, and women's movement at times undermines the state even as at other times it strengthens the state, and often checks violations of individual liberty. The book argues that the *shared adjudication* model adopted by the Indian state facilitates diversity, as it allows the construction of hybrid religious identities, fractures the "fixed" religious identities, and provides institutional spaces for ongoing intersocietal dialog between ethno-religious groups, civil society, and the state.

PREFACE

Gender equality in this model is complex, uneven, and negotiated – an outcome of localized struggles between various actors and bodies, requiring a bundle of strategies simultaneously. In this model, state-led reforms from above travel into and cross-fertilize with society-led reforms from below; doctrinal tensions and diverse interpretations of religious texts (including feminist readings) coexist with contestations around what constitutes customary law and traditions. Processes of public reason and deliberation between various stakeholders over normative value differences coexist with political negotiations, street action, and campaigns for law reforms. Individual and collective agency of women, despite its constraints, challenges, in millions of adjudicative sites, the gender inequality grounded and institutionalized in state and societal legal systems through legal mobilization, and offers alternatives for change, pushing for structural reforms from below.

These interactions between the lay, civic, and religious authorities are grounded in certain specific sociocultural and political developments. The implicit consensus between a majority of political parties over accommodation of group rights in the governance of the family, internally fragmented community elite who have displayed flexibility in discussing law reforms with the civil society and social movements, the Indian Women's Movement's multipronged approaches to legal reforms, active civic organizations, reformist judiciary, and the institutionalization of bargaining and accommodation as state craft are some conditions that underlie the shared adjudication model and enable structural change. This book contends that cultural pluralism and gender equality are not antithetical to one another, but can be harmonized, and the findings here are of significance to ongoing discussions on law reform and the designing of institutional arrangements in multicultural societies.

Acknowledgments

This book emerged out of my doctoral thesis in the Department of Political Science at McGill University in 2007, and I am grateful to a wide range of people who have made it possible. Fieldwork for me was the highlight of this endeavor – a productive, engaging phase – and I am immensely grateful to respondents who shared their experiences and stories. During the course of countless conversations, a broad range of people engaged with my research and offered insights; familiarized me with customs, laws, and procedures; invited me to celebrate rituals, festivals, and meetings; asked me about my politics and shared theirs; and offered me hospitality. I am very grateful to women litigants who took extra time from their packed daily routines to share their stories. In particular, I would like to thank various members and officials of the Meghwal *panchayat*. Pushpaben Waghela, Lalitbhai Waghela, and Vishrambhai Waghela accompanied me to interviews with various litigants, and I am deeply grateful to them for sharing their insights into the workings of the Meghwal *panchayat*. I also appreciate the help of Leeladharbhai Gadda, Kanubhai Galia, Bipinbhai Gohil, Mohammadbhai Habibali, Shirish Malde, Shirinben Maneckia, Iqbal Maniar, Harounbhai Musawala, Sushilaben Shah, and Yasmin Sheikh. I also would like to thank Mr. S.G. Tambe, Additional Registrar (Admin., Appellate Side) of the Bombay High Court, for facilitating the permission to access court records.

I would like to acknowledge Pratibha Jagtap and Vandana Nanaware of the Special Cell for Women, and to extend my thanks to Hasina Khan,

Naseem Sheikh, and Yasmin Sheikh from Awaz e Niswan for discussing individual cases and letting me accompany them in their field visits. In addition, I would like to acknowledge the struggles of many feminist groups, including Mumbai-based groups like Awaz e Niswan, the Forum Against Oppression of Women, Majlis, Stree Mukti Sanghatana, the Women's Centre, and the Women's Research and Action Group toward democratic, just, and equal families.

At McGill University, I owe first thanks to my advisor, Narendra Subramanian, for his patience and constructive comments. I am especially indebted to Alan Patten for his mentoring in the early stages of the doctoral program and for his consistent support. My reading course with Alan was instrumental in building the theoretical foundations of this project. Thanks are also due to Juliet Johnson and Hudson Meadwell for their support during key moments, and to my doctoral committee members, Jacob Levy and Khalid Medani, for their instructive questions. Rachel Sturman has been an important interlocutor and I am deeply grateful to her, to the anonymous reviewers, and the law and society series editors at Cambridge University Press for their invaluable advice, comments, and suggestions. More recently, at Carleton University, I would like to thank my colleagues, Vandna Bhatia, Chris Gabriel, Randall Germain, Radha Jhappan, and Laura Macdonald, for their supportive collegiality, and Nabarun Roy and Michael Spacek for research assistance. Many findings of this study were shared at various conferences, and I have benefited immensely from encouragement and the suggestions of Itty Abraham, Tani Barlow, Amrita Basu, Srimati Basu, Durba Ghosh, and Sylvia Vatuk. I would especially like to thank my editor at Cambridge University Press, John Berger, for believing in this project from the very beginning and for his quiet encouragement throughout the process.

Friends in Canada, India, and elsewhere have been invaluable in this pursuit. I have leaned on Giselle Amantea, Dolores Chew, Nimisha Dalal, Debjani Das, Arnika Fuhrmann, Geetanjali Gangoli, Sandhya Gokhale, Ramlath Kavil, Mrityunjoy Mohanty, Shree Mulay, Sandra

ACKNOWLEDGMENTS xxvii

Robinson, Evelyn Rodinos, Takeshi Sato, Fatima Seedat, Chayanika Shah, Daya Varma, and Peter White for their generosity and understanding. I would also like to thank Nasreen Chowdhory, Mustapha Ettobi, Prashant Keshavmurthy, and Spyro Kotsovilis for their warm solidarity; Manal Jamal for her stories and laughter; and Suranjan Weeraratne for many stimulating conversations.

My family has been a source of strength in every way. My brother Chetan Solanki kept me grounded with his love, empathy, and wit. Without him, it would have been impossible to finish this project. I would like to thank C.S. Mehta, Nandini and Dhiru Mehta, Shweta Patel, and Ashoka Valia for their support. I am grateful to Jethabhai Valia, Jyotsna and Harshad Valia, and Mohan Valia for their strength, care, and wisdom. Most of all, I would like to acknowledge my grandfather, Keshubhai Valia, whose work with vulnerable members of the society, including women, has inspired me. He cofounded and nurtured one of the first women's organizations in Saurashtra, and the central concerns of this book have been influenced by the numerous stories of women I have heard over the years. Similarly, I owe a deep personal debt to my grandmother, Ramaben, and to my mother, whose academic interests and support of women's rights have shaped my politics and research agendas over the years. This book is dedicated to my mother, Asha Valia, and to my grandparents, Ramaben Valia and Keshubhai Valia, for it all began with them and without them, this project would never have materialized.

Abbreviations

AIMPLB	All Indian Muslim Personal Law Board
BJP	Bhartiya Janata Party
BMC	Bombay Municipal Corporation (currently Municipal Corporation of Greater Mumbai)
CPI (M)	Communist Party of India (Marxist)
CrPC	Criminal Procedure Code
HAMA	Hindu Adoption and Maintenance Act 1956
HMA	Hindu Marriage Act 1955
IPC	Indian Penal Code
IWM	Indian Women's Movement
MWA	Muslim Women's (Protection of Rights on Divorce) Act 1986
OBC	Other Backward Classes
SC	Supreme Court
SP	Samajwadi Party
UCC	Uniform Civil Code

Glossary

Adivasi	Generic term to describe a tribes-person
Asmita	Dignity
Barots	Clan genealogists and poets
Bhailog	Local mafia
Burqa	Veil
Chamar/Chamhar	The name of an oppressed caste
Chawl	A residential building that is structured like barracks; each family has a room, but they share toilet facilities with others
Chhappaniyo dukal	The famine of 1856
Chowky	Beat office of the local police station
Dada	Strongman
Dargah	The site of the Muslim shrine
Dashavatar	The story of the ten reincarnations of the Hindu god Vishnu
Dher	Literally, animals. Derogatory name for an oppressed caste
Faisla	Decision
Faskh	Judicial dissolution of marriage for causes stipulated in Islamic law

The technical legal terms, especially in Islamic law, used here reflect their local usage in Urdu, Hindi, and/or local languages, and are not an exact transliteration from Arabic or Persian.

Fatwa	Legal opinion
Fiqh	The product of human understanding that sought to interpret and implement the Sharia
Ghar-gharna	Second marriage that is not ritualistically celebrated in public
Gharsansar	Domestic matters
Gnati	Caste
Hadith	Commentaries on the Quran
Holi	Spring festival
Homa	Invocation before the sacred fire
Iddat	A period of three months and ten days
Ijtihad	Interpretive science of juridical reasoning
Imambara	A locality in central Mumbai with a high concentration of Muslim families
Jamaat	Assembly, collective
Jamaatkhana	A council hall of the community
Kamadiya	Accountant
Khula	A form of divorce initiated by the wife
Khum	One-fifth of the savings of every individual
Lakh	One hundred thousand
Lok Adalat	People's court
Lok Sabha	The lower house of parliament
Madhabib	Classical schools of law
Mahar	The name of an oppressed caste
Mahila Aghadi	The women's wing of Shiv Sena, the Hindu right wing party
Mahila Mandal	A women's group
Mangalsutra	A necklace made of black beads worn by married Hindu women in India
Masjid	Mosque
Mehar	Dower
Melawala	A social gathering
Mohalla	Residential area

GLOSSARY

Mufti	Juriconsultant
Mukhi	Treasurer
Mulla	Religious teacher or leader
Muta	Temporary marriages contracted under the Shia law. This marriage does not create the right of inheritance between the husband and wife, but the children are legitimate and could inherit from both parents
Nats	Acrobats
Nawab	An aristocrat
Nikah	Marriage
Nikahnama	A marriage contract
Nyay Panchayat	Forum for justice
Panch	A group of five elders of the community
Panchayati Raj	Decentralized governance
Pateliyas	Middlemen
Pir	Sufi preceptor
Pooja	Prayer
Pucca	Made of cement
Qazi	Judge, officiating officer representing religious authority
Saakh	Social prestige
Samaj	Collective
Sanskar	Culture
Sapinda	Nearest heir or blood relative, connected by ties of consanguinity
Saptapadi	A ceremony in Hindu marriage that involves walking seven steps around the sacred fire
Sharia	The divine law
Shehnai	A traditional wind instrument made of metal
Sodchithi	Customary divorce
Stridhan	Gifts given to a married woman at the time of her marriage or during the course of her marriage

Sunna	The Prophet's deeds and teachings
Talaq	Divorce
Talaq ahasan	A single pronouncement of divorce made during a period of menstruation followed by sexual abstinence during *iddat*
Talaq e tafwid	Delegated divorce
Talaq hasan	Three pronouncements made during successive *tuhr*s during which time no sexual relations take place
Talaqnama	Deed of divorce
Talaq ul bidaat	Three pronouncements made during a single *tuhr* in one sentence or a single pronouncement made during a *tuhr* clearly indicating an intention to dissolve the marriage irrevocably
Tuhr	The period between menstrual cycles
Turis	Shehnai players
Vanakars	Weavers
Varghoda	The groom's party

1 Introduction

Multireligious, multiethnic, and culturally plural postcolonial societies debate over who should govern the family as states and religious groups struggle to regulate the family. There are several reasons why states and groups aim to regulate the conjugal family: States realize their liberal, secular projects by infiltrating and fashioning individual subjectivities. States also strive for social cohesion, the transmission of property (Glendon 1981, 1989), and the delegation of welfare responsibilities (Menski 2001). In addition, the regulation of family is often tied to the nation-building projects of states (Heuer 2005; Loos 2006; Woods 2004). Furthermore, the demarcation of kinship boundaries forms the basis of the state; it creates race, caste, and religious groups (Cott 2000; Loos 2006), and enables the state to perpetuate itself (Hanley 1989; Stevens 1999). Similarly, religious and cultural groups identify religious or customary laws as markers of group identity and seek autonomy to govern the family. Groups, too, seek to perpetuate themselves and attempt to impact upon or subvert the statist vision of the nation by regulating the family (Woods 2004; Yuval-Davis 1997).

In this context, the key question is whether states should adopt legal centralism[1] and enact uniform laws to govern the family, or provide

---

[1] Legal centralism is the idea that all law emanates from the state and is adjudicated and enforced by state institutions. Societal normative orders cannot generate "law" as it is distinguished by its efficacy "as a form of social control, institutional enforcement, precision, unity, self-consistency, and doctrinal elaboration" (Hart 1961; Tamanaha 1993; Woodman 1999, 12).

autonomy to religious or cultural groups through the adoption of legal pluralism.[2] States like Turkey, Thailand, and Ethiopia, which have not been officially colonized, have enacted uniform civil codes, though neither has been successful in wiping out legal pluralism on the ground.[3] Among postcolonial states, Tunisia has moved toward some form of centralized legal system and codified Islamic laws, but it has not transplanted or opted for a uniform civil code modeled along the lines of French, German, or Swiss civil codes. Similarly, Tanzania and Morocco have codified their various laws, and Morocco has abolished the autonomy of Berbers in the governance of the family.[4] Most other postcolonial states have opted to provide greater autonomy to ethno-religious groups in governance of the family.

For, the ongoing processes of state formation require that postcolonial states balance economic development, social cohesion, and political stability, as well as create national consciousness, by outlining shared meanings among their citizens through legislation, adjudication, and the enforcement of laws.[5] To serve these ends, the states seek to modernize

---

[2] The idea and the practice of legal pluralism (i.e., the coexistence of multiple systems of law) exist at many levels in time, space, and knowledge, and many competing versions of legal pluralism remain under discussion. Some scholars characterize the intermingling of suprastate law and official state laws, seen in the case of the European Union, as an example of legal pluralism. Others take different forms of official laws – administrative law (Arthurs 1985) and military law – at the level of the state to exemplify legal pluralism. Thus, the coexistence of different types of law within the realm of the state or between suprastate bodies and nation-states is seen as a typology of legal pluralism.

[3] The Turkish uniform code, though, has not succeeded completely in wiping out religious practices (Starr 1990; Yilmaz 2005). Ethiopia has also tried legal unification through codification, but the civil code was scrapped after the Socialist Revolution in 1974. There was widespread dissatisfaction with the civil code even before that because it enacted entirely new laws that were unfamiliar to the judges; problems of high illiteracy coupled with the survival of other laws made the exercise of codification a failure on the ground (Allott 1970; Hooker 1975; Menski 2006).

[4] These measures are all largely seen as a reaction against the colonial policies of legal pluralism (Menski 2006; Moors 2003).

[5] State formation in Western Europe was a gradual process involving the homogenization of population, secularization, territorial demarcation, the centralization of taxation, legal uniformity, and the monopolization of force (Tilly 1975, 1985). However,

key institutions such as the family and marriage, and shape ethnic, religious, sexual, and gender identities through law. However, postcolonial states are confronted with diverse societal groups that also seek to retain control over the governance of family laws,[6] which are seen as markers of community identities. As a result, most postcolonial societies evince ongoing negotiations between states and societal groups over the content of laws and the extent of community autonomy in the governance of the family.

The assertion of religious family laws as symbols of community identity by societal groups has many implications for women's rights within the family. Women are implicated in the conception of community, as women's productive, reproductive, and cultural labor is used to maintain and perpetuate religio-cultural communities. Their dress, behavior, appearance, and sexuality are controlled to define, separate, limit, and control group boundaries (Sapiro 1993; Shachar 2001; Yuval-Davis 1997). Also, these laws regulate the distribution of resources within the family and define women's rights to own, access, and control these resources (Mukhopadhyay 1998; Shachar 2001). Concerns about women's rights in the family are pivotal to the debates on the regulation of family laws.

---

state formation is a nonlinear process, and the recent trend has been toward decentralization and differentiation of the state (Warren 2003). The processes of state formation in postcolonial states have been diverse. In some cases, the "overdeveloped postcolonial state" (Alavi 1972) has followed policies of "authoritarian high modernism" to centralize authority, overcome local orders, and penetrate society (Scott 1998). However, a number of scholars have argued that postcolonial state formation was marked, not by zero-sum conflict between the state and other social groups, but by the incorporation and accommodation of local orders into the state (Barkey 1994; Corrigan and Sayer 1985; Hansen and Stepputat 2001; Nugent 1994; Shastri and Wilson 2001).

[6] Religious family laws are also called "personal laws" in India and I use these terms interchangeably. The term "personal laws" came into existence in colonial times as these were laws a person carried within across regions. Personal laws include laws governing group membership (determining who is a group member and defining the exit option in law through a change in group membership through conversion, marriage, voluntary subjection or negation). They also regulate intergroup interactions. Different states have evolved law regarding which areas (family laws or criminal laws) would be governed by group norms in which jurisdictions (geographical boundaries) (Hooker 1975).

The state-society contestations over the governance of the family have an impact on relationships between states and religio-cultural groups, as well as those within religio-cultural groups. For instance, the nonrecognition of Islamic religious laws has led to agitations for the recognition of Islamic laws in South Africa (Amien 2006; Moosa 2002). In India, the state's decision not to codify Muslim religious family law has been contested across religious boundaries by Hindu nationalists and secular modernists alike. In Malaysia, debates over the jurisdictional expansion of Islamic courts spearheaded by the UMNO (United Malays National Organization) government in the 1980s, and over the introduction of the *Hudud* (Islamic Criminal Codes) Bill by the right-wing PAS (Parti Islam Se-Malaysia) government in Kelantan in 1993, have been opposed by non-Malay parties representing the interests of other religious groups (Hamayotsu 2003; Ibrahim 2000; Kamali 2000; Peletz 2002). Indonesia has witnessed conflicts over expanding the scope of Sharia in different provinces (Bowen 2003; Butt 1999; Lev 1972; Lindsey 1999). The expansion of the Sharia in the northern part of Nigeria is one of the reasons for violence between Christians and Muslims in Nigeria and in Sudan. The question of reforming the Personal Law of Egyptian Copts has been a bone of contention between the church, the state, modernist proreform Muslims and Copts, and the antireform lobby comprising conservative Muslims and Copts (Afifi 1996).

State failure to recognize group claims can lead to conflicts, but states that adopt multicultural policies and recognize religious or customary laws are not necessarily exempt from these contestations, as public recognition is often unevenly circumscribed across religious, caste, and indigenous groups. The recognition of religious family laws also shapes and freezes religious and ethnic identities,[7] and these can also contribute to

---

[7] The argument that state-initiated policies of classification, categorization, and enumeration of the populace freeze group identities is made by numerous scholars (Corrigan and Sawyer 1985; Scott 1998). In the Indian context, the colonial state's legal policies and the postcolonial state's continuation of the system of religious family laws have eroded heterogeneous religious identities and marked boundaries between religious communities (Cohn 1996; Dirks 1992, 2001; Mukhopadhyay 1998; Pandey 1990).

intergroup rivalries. As a result, multireligious and multiethnic democracies face the challenge of constructing policies that can facilitate equality *between and among* diverse ethno-religious groups while ensuring gender equality *within* these groups in the matter of religious family laws.

Who Shall Govern the Family? Outlining Two Approaches

Two strands of theoretical debates inform the issue outlined previously. The first strand, which is society-centered, suggests group autonomy for cultural groups, especially minorities, in the regulation of the family. Chatterjee has argued for "strategic politics of difference" outside the domain of the state. He argues that cultural communities can refuse to be homogenized in the name of dominant reasonableness by developing an "inner democratic forum." The proceedings of this forum should follow codes of transparency, publicity, and representation (Chatterjee 1994). Discussing the nature of ethnic conflict in Sri Lanka, Scott has argued for the cultivation and institutionalization of cultural political spaces in which groups can "formulate their moral-political concerns … in the language of their respective traditions" (Scott 1999, 185). He has called for the creation of modalities through which communities can engage in intracultural dialog of mutual recognition and negotiate claims and counterclaims about the meaning of their traditions (Scott 1999). Although Scott's approach does not prevent reification of group boundaries and does not place gender equality at its center, it does reclaim the centrality of society-centered politics in his project.

In contrast, some proponents of state-centric arguments suggest that difference should be relegated to the private, societal sphere. For instance, Rawls has argued for an "overlapping consensus" in which a diversity of conflicting comprehensive doctrines would endorse the same political conception: justice as fairness in the public domain of culturally diverse, plural societies (Rawls 1996).[8] Thus, the Rawlsian project locates cultural

---

[8] Rawls's political liberalism has also been criticized for being grounded in universal reason. It has been argued that Rawls has failed to resolve the question of incommensurability of values in societies. Critics argue that Rawls's conception of political

difference in the private realm. Furthermore, cultural difference is almost seen as inessential – a matter of voluntary association. Following Rawls, many feminists and reformers suggest that the state should be the only locus of law in matters related to personal laws. For instance, feminists argue that cultural plurality can be privatized, pursued in forums other than the family law; thus, the demands for religious family law are illegitimate (Parashar and Dhanda 2008).

With regard to debates on the recognition and reforms of religious family laws, scholars argue that religious family laws cement group boundaries and do not reflect religious principles enshrined in classical laws (Phillips 2007). They also point out that the possibility of internal reform in religious laws is limited, as they are not compatible with equality guaranteed in national constitutions or universal rights enshrined in international human rights conventions. Feminists also resist the idea of cultural autonomy in family matters, as groups are imbued with patriarchal values and norms and violate the individual rights of women. Feminists have thus criticized states' adoption of cultural pluralism as states' privileging of group rights over women's rights in the family (An-Na'im 2002a; Cook 1994; Dhagamwar 1974, 1992; Jayal 2001; Joseph 1997; Kukathas 1992; Mahajan 2005; Moghadam 1994; Nussbaum 1995, 2000; Okin 1997, 2005; Parashar, 1992; Phillips 2003, 2004; Sangari 1995, 2003; Welchman 2004). Other state-centric proponents of cultural autonomy argue for special group rights for cultural communities, especially minorities. Young argues that liberalism creates a public sphere that is falsely universal, homogeneous, and abstract. This public realm excludes the voices, experiences, and perspectives of these groups from the formal public realm. She advocates special rights for disadvantaged groups and minorities (Young, 1989, 1990). Similarly, Kymlicka makes a case for three sets of group rights for minorities. These include special representation

liberalism exaggerates the degree of "overlapping consensus" in any society, that it poses rationalistic and legalistic solutions to deal with value pluralism, and that it creates an excessively formal public sphere that is emptied of political indeterminacy and contingencies (Gray 1995).

rights, self-governing rights, and polyethnic rights. He suggests differentiation between two kinds of rights: one that involves the claim of a group against its own members, and one that involves the group's claim against the larger society. He argues that liberalism can only accommodate the ideas of "freedom within groups" and "equality between groups" (Kymlicka 1995, 152). Spinner-Halev also supports group rights, but he argues against state intervention as it violates the group's right to shape its collective identity (Spinner-Halev 1994). These arguments have been criticized because these arrangements have led to the ossification of group boundaries, and they ignore intragroup hierarchies (Deveaux 2006; Kukathas 1992; Okin 1989; Phillips 1995, 2007). Scholars also suggest that the state should provide conditions in which reforms of religious family laws can be initiated (Bilgrami 1994; Deveaux 2000, 2006; Hallaq 2001, 2004, 2005). However, both state-centered and society-centered approaches maintain the critical tension between group autonomy and gender equality, and do not discuss how awarding group rights can prevent the ossification of community boundaries.

In the context of the regulation of family laws, feminists have sought to incorporate intragroup equality while assuring the accommodation of cultural groups by advocating a model to regulate the family. Shachar advocates the "joint governance" approach wherein the state and cultural groups split juridical authority in the regulation of family laws (Shachar 1998, 2001). The institutional arrangement advocated by Shachar segregates the demarcating function of family law, used to define group membership, from the distributive function that ensures the division of intrahousehold resources within the family. Shachar further suggests that demarcating aspects of family laws should fall under the purview of cultural groups while the distribution of property between family members would be governed by the state. According to Shachar, the bifurcated legal authority would give legitimacy to both the state and the group. Thus, juridical autonomy enjoyed by either the state or the cultural group in one sphere of family law is seen as a positive step to ensuring cultural accommodation while providing intragroup equality. Shachar also suggests that legal pluralist policies in several spheres prevent reification of group boundaries (Shachar 2001). Shachar's proposal directs us toward accommodative arrangements between states and societies that balance group rights with gender equality by adopting legal pluralism in the governance of the family. For the purpose of this study, I define legal pluralism as a policy in which the state recognizes and regulates nonstate laws.[9]

Yilmaz (2005) identifies six types of relationships between state and nonstate laws across a continuum. The set of legal arrangements across an imagined analytical spectrum would have legal centralist arrangements at one end and complete legal pluralism at the other extreme. Between the two extremes exist possibilities such as parallel systems of state and local laws, codification of local laws, partial recognition of local laws, and the incorporation of local actors into the state legal system (Yilmaz 2005, 25–26). Variants of Shachar and Yilmaz's proposals exist in many postcolonial societies: In practice, most postcolonial states accept the policy of cultural pluralism in the governance of the family and tailor different models of legal pluralism[10] to govern the family by sharing authority between states and sections of ethno-religious groups within the society. This book examines the nature of state-society interactions in the governance of the family, and it assesses its impact on the constructions of religious groups and gender relations within the family.

---

[9] I draw on Griffiths' definition of legal pluralism, which he defines as "that state of affairs, for any social field in which behaviour pursuant to more than one legal order occurs" (Griffiths 1986b, 2). Griffiths defines two types of legal pluralism: The strong variant is the one in which the state law is one among the body of laws, and the second is the one in which the state law identifies and orders nonstate laws (Woodman 1999). Drawing from Griffiths' definition, I adapt the second typology of his definition as it is compatible with a wide range of empirical cases.

[10] Crafting these arrangements requires that states make decisions regarding the recognition of tribunals applying group laws, as well as the possibility of reform in some areas under community authority, especially ones that are against the legal norms of modern states (Allott 1970; Derret 1963; Griffiths 1986b; Hooker 1975).

Research Questions

How do accommodative arrangements advocating cogovernance by state and society in legally plural societies impact the interactions between and within religious groups and other societal bodies? And how do they affect gender equality in the family?

What is the nature of state-society interactions in the adjudication of religious laws in legally plural societies?

Case Selection

Four typologies capture legally plural arrangements made by postcolonial states. Leaning toward extreme legal pluralism is the Lebanese case in which communities have complete autonomy in the governance of the family. In fact, the state does not recognize interreligious marriages (Joseph 2001). The second typology includes states such as South Africa and Botswana that recognize customary laws but not religious laws, and have allowed customary tribunals; states such as Bangladesh and Sri Lanka recognize both customary and religious laws, and allow customary courts. The third typology includes Israel, Malaysia, and Indonesia, which have institutionalized religious courts. The fourth typology leans toward legal centralism, drawn out in the case of Tanzania, which has attempted the codification of law through state-society interactions with local elites but has not accepted customary authority (Allott 1970, Menski 2006). This typology also includes states such as Tunisia, which has codified its laws, and Morocco, which has established a hegemonic Islamic law on different communities through codification. Following decolonization, Morocco abolished Berber customary laws and codified Islamic laws. The state allowed rabbinical courts to govern the Jews, but Christians are governed by Islamic laws except in matters related to repudiation (Moors 2003).

Most postcolonial states have witnessed contestations over the granting of cultural rights in the governance of religious family laws, but India is an important case to examine because all four possibilities are debated by a broad range of actors within the Indian context. In addition, I have chosen the Indian case because the Indian model of legal pluralism in recognition of religious family laws falls at the center of the spectrum of legally plural arrangements adopted by various states.

India has witnessed contestations between and within religious groups in the regulation of religious family laws. Furthermore, women's roles and rights in the family are terrains over which some of these arguments have been played out. The Indian state has crafted a broad range of accommodative arrangements to govern the family. The Indian state recognizes both religious and customary laws, and the nature of autonomy granted to groups is unevenly circumscribed across groups. The state does not establish religious or customary courts and retains the exclusive authority to enforce the distribution of property. The state has also enacted a secular law to govern interreligious marriages and provided an option to its citizens to opt out of religious laws. In addition, in the Indian case, the conflict over the governance of the family has been sharpest when it comes to the governance of marriage and divorce; in this matter, the Indian state has adopted what I call a model of *shared adjudication*, in which the state splits its adjudicative authority with social actors and organizations in the regulation of marriage and divorce among a section of religious and caste groups and other actors.[11] In doing so, the Indian state adopts what I call a *restrained autonomy* in the governance of the

---

[11] For instance, Section 29(2) of the Hindu Marriage Act 1955 allows customary divorce, and as such, both state courts and societal bodies act as legal agents in matters of marriage and divorce. This provision was meant to allow caste authorities to regulate customary divorce in castes that have historically practiced divorce, but my data show that many other societal agents also adjudicate in divorce under this provision. Muslim Personal Law in postcolonial India is based on local custom, Islamic laws, and precepts; customary laws are made by sect-based organizations, state-law enactments, and judicial precedent. The state courts administer the uncodified Muslim Personal Law as well as state-enacted laws. In general, state law recognizes uncodified Islamic laws when it comes to marriage and divorce but privileges statutory law in matters of maintenance and postdivorce financial settlement.

family; that is, the Indian state allows societal actors and institutions to govern marriage, but the state does not relinquish its authority to govern the family.

A General Outline of the Developments in the Indian Case

The state law of pluralism practiced in the Indian case is a result of colonial legacies as well as postcolonial policies adopted by the Indian state.[12] At the time of independence, there were overlapping jurisdictions

[12] In the period prior to colonization, the laws were divided as territorial laws, administered by the state (these included laws on taxation, treason, and certain criminal acts), and personal laws (which dealt with other matters) that were administered by community and caste councils, or *panchayats*. The laws were not fixed and were subject to change and different interpretations. Community boundaries were not rigid, and there were overlapping customs and laws among different Hindu and Muslim communities. The religious family laws emerged as a separate category of laws as a result of colonial policies. Cohn has also argued that the colonial project of documenting the governed populace and codification of Hindu and Muslim laws led to the emergence of separate religious family laws (Cohn 1996). The judges in state-established courts also borrowed from textual sources and sought opinions of Brahmins and Maulavis in the case of Hindu and Muslim laws, respectively. These processes privileged Brahminical and textual interpretations of religious law over customary usage and fixed religious laws and identities (Cohn 1996; Lata Mani 1990). According to Washbrook, during the early stages of British rule, the mercantilist state sought to consolidate the ownership of property and as a result, introduced changes in the civil and criminal laws. The laws introduced during this period were based on the philosophy of "possessive individualism," whereby the individual was freed from external controls that limited property and wealth through the market because at that time, in India, property was seen to be in the trust of the owner; the land was not seen as a commodity, and many rights over land were governed by communitarian rights. The state also established judicial courts and imported judges from England. However, as Washbrook points out, alongside the colonial state's attempts at developing public laws, there was also a hidden attempt to define the "private law" of the subjects. The philosophical underpinnings of the public law were to free the individual to join the market, but the basis of personal law was a vision of a society wherein the individual was subject to the customary laws and obligations of a community. Hence, family laws were the laws excluded from the state project of law reform (Washbrook 1981). Other scholars suggest that the colonial state created a myth of nonintervention in family matters of religious communities to ensure legitimacy; in reality, state courts routinely adjudicated matters of religious family laws (Sturman 2005).

in the category known as *family laws*. Formal jurisdiction in this area included laws enacted by the colonial state as well as the Constituent Assembly. The Princely states had their own laws and caste *panchayats* (councils), customary tribunals and religious clergy, too, ruled on family laws (Agnes 1999; Derret 1963, 1968; Galanter 1968; Nair 1996; Parashar 1992; Smith 1963).

Post independence, the Indian state sought to pursue economic development, social cohesion, and national unity. The decades of the 1950s, 1960s, and 1970s were hailed as the Indian state's success in achieving these goals. The Indian state's policies of linguistic federalism, secularism, affirmative action for the Scheduled Castes and Tribes, repression of secessionist movements, and a socialist planning process, along with reasonable economic growth in the first decade, contributed to relative harmony and peace between various mobilized groups in society (Brass 1994).

The issue of whether to enact a uniform civil code for all citizens was debated in the 1950s and came up again in the 1970s, within this ethos of a democratic resolution of difference. The thrust of the arguments in favor of the Uniform Civil Code was that the newly formed and slowly industrializing Indian state required the construction of a modern, political community. This in turn necessitated transferring people's particularistic attachments from their premodern communities to the nation-state. Questions of women's equality in the family and minority accommodation were other concerns informing these debates. However, there was opposition to this move by the state from different sections of all communities.

There were six parties taking part in the debate.[13] Between the 1950s and 1970s, the meaning of uniform civil code meant different things to the different groups. On the part of the state, a uniform civil code represented the conflict between an image of a unified political community and the practice of accommodation through bargaining and compromise implicit

---

[13] I have adapted the typology from Rudolph and Rudolph (2001, 36–68).

in the governance of a plural society. The Hindu right, which opposed the agenda of gender equality in the process of law reform, saw the Uniform Civil Code as a tool to construct a Hindu nation in which Muslims and other minorities would assimilate, and their identity markers would be erased. Modernists from both the Hindu and the Muslim communities saw the Uniform Civil Code as the actualization of the state's commitment to secularism and as a tool to foster national unity. The conservative and moderate sections of the minorities saw the Uniform Civil Code as a majoritarian device to ensure political assimilation. For the Indian Women's Movement, the Uniform Civil Code was seen to be synonymous with both the achievement of women's equality within the family and the abolition of premodern and backward community authority resistant to the ideals of women's equality (Everett 2001; Gandhi and Shah 1992; Mukhopadhyay 1998; Parashar 1992; Rudolph and Rudolph 2001).

The state conceded to the multicultural rule of law at this juncture to secure the support of the *adivasis* and the religious-cultural minorities. The state did not enact a uniform civil code[14] but added a proviso in the nonjusticiable Directive Principles of the Indian Constitution that the state should endeavor to enact a uniform civil code. In addition, the state reformed the law of the Hindu community but did not ensure women's equality in law.[15] Through the codification of Hindu law, the

---

[14] The Uniform Civil Code is applied to the Union Territory of Goa.

[15] The modernist lobby within the Congress Party, supported by the All India Women's Congress, which pushed the reformist agenda (Parashar 1992), and a modernist section of Hindus, were in favor of state-initiated reforms in religious matters, including personal laws (Chatterjee 1993, 1994). The Congress government faced resistance to reforms within the Hindu law by the Hindu nationalists, as well as by the conservative lobby within the Congress Party. The state's policy of reforming the Hindu law appeased the pro-reform lobby because it sent the message that the Indian state was serious about modernizing the majority Hindu community through law reform. The dilution of the content of Hindu laws and of the Special Marriage Act 1954 was meant to win over the antireform lobby (Derret 1963; Everett 2001; Parashar 1992; Smith 1963). The reforms within the Hindu law were not radical, and many of these "reformist" laws were versions of laws practiced in one form or another in different parts of India, including the princely states (Nair 1996). Scholars have also argued that there exists a pact between Hindu and

state constructed the category "Hindu" and subsumed Buddhists, Jains, Sikhs, and Scheduled Castes and Scheduled Tribes under this typology. The Hindu law legalized divorce, allowed intercaste marriage, permitted customary divorce,[16] recognized customary authority, and gave women limited inheritance rights. The Muslim Personal Law had been partially codified in the 1930s, resulting in two enactments: the Shariat Act 1937 and the Dissolution of Muslim Marriages Act 1939. In the face of opposition from minorities in the aftermath of the partition, the state did not reform religious family laws of minorities.[17] The state enacted the Special Marriage Act 1954 to govern interreligious marriages and thus provided a secular option for citizens.

The policy of the Indian state to leave Muslim laws largely uncodified has led the Hindu right to assert, time and again, that the minorities, especially Muslims who are the most visible opponents of the Uniform Civil Code, are not members of the political community (Chatterjee 1994). The policy has also led feminists and modernists to question the state's

  Muslim elites in which the Hindu elite do not interfere in matters related to recognition, codification, and reforms of Muslim personal laws, and in exchange, Muslims respect the cow-protection lobby among Hindus (Brass 1991).

[16] This move by the Indian state was a result of a pragmatic compromise between the conservatives who opposed legalization of divorce and the modernists who pushed for it. By doing so, the Indian state adopted a *shared adjudication* model in which the state and caste authority could adjudicate in customary divorce. This provision was supposedly to be limited to castes that traditionally allowed divorce. This provision was meant to appease the conservatives who were against legalizing divorce in the Hindu Marriage Act 1955 and who saw customary divorces as immoral practices of lower castes that should not be imitated or adopted by upper castes that prohibited divorce.

[17] During colonial rule, the nationalist elites had constructed the realm of the family as private, away from the intervention of the colonial state. Postindependence, the postcolonial state was deemed as a legitimate authority to intervene in this matter. However, in the aftermath of the partition, the Muslim elite used the same rhetoric to oppose unification or codification of Muslim laws (Chatterjee 1993, 1994). In response, the Indian state adopted the policy of accommodating minorities until they were ready to merge into a unified political community. It is also suggested that many Congress leaders were Hindus and could therefore push for reforms within the Hindu law. Another explanation is that the state reformed the Hindu law as a first step toward enacting a uniform code, and they hoped that other religious communities would reform their laws and perhaps accept a uniform civil code at their own pace (Derret 1963, 1968).

commitment to gender equality. Scholars argue that the policy of recognition of religious laws exists in opposition to freedom of religion and secularism (Bhargava 1998; Dhagamwar 1974; Galanter 1989; Parashar 1992).[18] And that the state policy had "fixed" religious laws and identities (Cohn 1987; Mukhopadhyay 1998).

The Indian state's project of national unity, social cohesion, and secularism has been strained since the late 1970s. Between 1975 and 1977, India went through a period of authoritarianism. The 1980s and 1990s saw an escalation of communal conflicts, the resurgence of majority fundamentalism, caste wars, and regional separatist movements (in Assam, Punjab, Darjeeling district of West Bengal, and Kashmir). All these have pointed to the Indian state's failure to achieve its goal of national unity (Brass 1994).

Debates over the Indian state's policy of legal pluralism had been muted until the 1970s,[19] but they gained momentum in the mid-1980s. In 1985, the Indian Supreme Court passed a judgment in the case of Shah Bano who had approached the court for maintenance after a divorce under Section 125 of the Code of Criminal Procedure 1973, which is

---

[18] For instance, in the case of *State of Bombay* v. *Appa*, the petitioner argued that under the system of religious laws, Muslims were allowed to contract polygynous marriages, whereas the practice was banned among Hindus. The petitioner stated that Hindus should not be disallowed polygynous marriages contracted to mitigate failure to produce a male heir, which was integral to the Hindu religion. The court opined that polygyny for reasons of producing a male heir was not central to Hindu religious practice, as adoption was allowed in Hinduism. The court also held that the state's commitment to secularism was compatible with incremental social reforms and that these social reforms could be undertaken by different religious communities at varying paces (see *State of Bombay* v. *Appa*, AIR Bombay 84 [1952]). See also *Srinivas Aiyar* v. *Saraswathi Ammal*, AIR [1952] Madras 193). (For a detailed discussion, see Jacobsohn 2003; Larson 2001; Menski 2003.)

[19] The issue was debated between 1972 and 1984, when the state attempted to introduce a uniform adoption bill. This was opposed by a section of *ulemas*, the clergy, as un-Islamic. In 1973, the state amended sections of the Criminal Procedure Code, and conservative Muslim leaders argued that divorced Muslim husbands should be exempted from the reach of Section 125 Criminal Procedure Code, as this section allowed divorced women across religious communities to file for maintenance. The law minister allowed a compromise. He suggested that a Muslim man who had paid a settlement to his wife after divorce could be exempted from Section 125 CrPC (Parashar 1992, 167).

uniformly applied across religious cleavages. Her husband argued that he was not obliged to pay her maintenance beyond the period of *iddat*, a period of three months and ten days, under Muslim Personal Law. The court awarded Shah Bano the maintenance but opined that the Indian state should enact a uniform civil code (*Mohammad Ahmed Khan* v. *Shah Bano Khan*, 1985, SC 945). This statement led to heated debates within the communities. The following assembly election saw the governing party's defeat in the state; this led the Congress government to pass the Muslim Women's (Protection of Rights on Divorce) Act 1986, which would govern the economic rights of divorced Muslim women.[20]

The developments after the Shah Bano case and the enactment of the Muslim Women's (Protection of Rights on Divorce) Act 1986 marked a critical moment in the trajectory of legal developments on this issue. The debate in the Shah Bano case moved beyond the question of the recognition of religious laws: The controversy also revolved around the degree and limit of recognition that could be granted to the Muslim community in matters of governance of the Muslim conjugal family. The debate raised the question of whether the Muslim community could ask for exemptions from provisions of uniform criminal laws.

The Indian Women's Movement, Muslim moderates and intelligentsia, secular modernists, as well as large sections of civil society protested against the state's enactment of the Muslim Women's (Protection of Rights on Divorce) Act 1986 in order to problematize the community's assertion of autonomy at the cost of women's rights within the family. The Hindu right gained considerable mileage from the Indian state's so-called appeasement of minorities by agreeing to their demands for increased

---

[20] The most common reason cited for this act of the Congress Party is linked to the decline in the Congress Party's support in the 1980s. To revive its sagging vote bank and to win over conservative Hindus, the Congress Party unlocked the doors of a temple devoted to the Hindu God Ram in a disputed site at Ayodhya, in North India. Following widespread criticism of this move, and in a desire to regain the support of Muslims, the Congress government backed Muslim conservative leaders' demands for more autonomy in matters related to personal laws following the Supreme Court's judgment in the Shah Bano case (see Hasan 1994).

group autonomy. The right has since further demonized the Muslim minority as backward, parochial, premodern, and resistant to the formation of a political community (Agnes 1999; Hasan 1994; Mukhopadhyay 1998; Parashar 1992; Sunder Rajan 2000). A small section of moderates saw the critical pitting of gender justice versus minority rights the Shah Bano case highlighted (Menon, 1998), and highlighted gender inequality in both Hindu and Muslim laws. For instance, Mukhopadhyay compared litigation processes in Hindu and Muslim laws of maintenance and inheritance that govern property rights of women, and argued that women's citizenship under religious laws is mediated by their membership in religious communities during adjudication, and that Hindu and Muslim women are dispossessed of their rights in law in different ways as a result. She also discussed the ideological double-bind for women's movement in India when it comes to the debate around the Uniform Civil Code. She argued that on the one hand, women's movement's demand for gender equality and a uniform civil code had forced them to share an ideological platform with the Hindu right; on the other hand, demands for multicultural accommodation were often hijacked by religious conservative forces that dilute feminist demands for gender equality. However, many feminist analyses of the laws after the Shah Bano case have highlighted the state's policy of privileging cultural accommodation at the cost of Muslim women's equality in the context of religious family laws. It was also argued that this policy has further sharpened the difference between the family laws of Hindus and those of Muslims, and that Muslim women are compromised by dual patriarchies: the community and the state.

The political landscape of the 1990s saw an unprecedented rise of the Hindu right, and the destruction of the Babri Mosque in December 1992 and the riots that followed changed the political landscape of the country. This period saw the Hindu nationalist party, the Bharatiya Janata Party (BJP) in three coalition governments – from May 16–28, 1996, in 1998–1999, and for a full term between 1999 and 2004. During the rule of the BJP-led coalition (1999–2004), more than 2,500 Muslims were killed in the state of Gujarat by Hindu fundamentalists, with the active abetment of the BJP-ruled state of Gujarat in western India in 2002. In the context of virulent and aggressive Hindu majoritarianism, and the demonizing of Muslims following the events of September 11, 2001, debates on a uniform civil code in the political landscape are muted but simmering below the surface.

Indian politics has become more fragmented since the late 1990s; the decade has seen the rise of ethnic and regional parties, and five coalition governments have ruled the country since 1989. The era of coalition politics has contained the Hindu right's core agenda of the Uniform Civil Code as an electoral issue. Understanding the centrality of the Uniform Civil Code to the ideology of the BJP, many other political parties have arrived at an implicit consensus on continuing the policy of recognition of religious family laws. In the 1990s, the women's wings of the left parties dropped their demand for a uniform civil code and built a consensus to engage with the minority communities for internal reforms. The Samajwadi Party also followed the policy of noninterference in matters of religious family law, and many other parties followed suit. The increased fragmentation of politics and competitive party politics would not push this issue on the agenda of other parties.

There were legislative changes in personal laws of Parsis and Christians during this time,[21] and the Hindu Succession (Amendment) Act 2005 has led to pro-women changes in the inheritance laws of Hindus since the Congress-led government returned to power in 2004.[22] While in power, the BJP did not attempt to enact a uniform civil code, but since

---

[21] Among the minorities, the personal law of the Parsi community was amended in 1991 at the behest of the Parsi elite. As a result, Parsi women obtained equal rights to inheritance under the amended law (Agnes 1999). The Christian community, too, had arrived at an agreement after wide-ranging discussions on changes in their personal laws (Agnes 2002; Jacob 1999; Subramanian 2004).

[22] The Hindu Succession (Amendment) Act 2005 removed inequalities in the inheritance of agricultural land and made Hindu women's right to inherit agricultural land equal to those of Hindu men across all states. The latter development is valuable, as states such as Delhi, Haryana, Himachal Pradesh, Jammu and Kashmir, Punjab, and Uttar Pradesh had enacted state-level tenurial laws that were gender-unequal. See Sonu Jain, "Women Didn't Receive Rights without Struggle," *Indian Express* (September 13, 2005).

INTRODUCTION 19

its defeat in national elections in 2004, Hindu nationalists have sought to reiterate their control over the family by virulently opposing religious conversions, interreligious and intercaste marriages, and upholding the Brahminical[23] family, which celebrates a rigid gender hierarchy within the family.[24] The Hindu right has a two-pronged approach to reshaping the family and defining religious community. In states that are governed by the BJP, the state has institutionalized extralegal practices to constrain parties from contracting interreligious and intercaste marriages.[25] In addition, the Hindu nationalists have turned to their cultural organizations and affiliates to enforce its vision of the Hindu family through Hindu militant organizations and private strongmen[26] across states. In general, the Muslim elite had been measured in their responses to these debates and in their public response to judicial exhortations for the

---

[23] The Hindu nationalists seek to enforce a gender-based division of labor within the family and advocate modesty in dress and appearance. Women's sexuality is strictly controlled, and Hindu women are warned against the lascivious intent of violent Muslim men (Basu 1995; Kapur and Cossman 1996).

[24] The Hindu nationalists hold supremacist, exclusivist, and paternalist notions of caste hierarchy. While "lower" castes are incorporated into the fold of the Hindu right, they are "sanskritized" (Jaffrelot 1998; Jenkins 2001; Shah 2001).

[25] For instance, in Gujarat, the ruling BJP party issued a circular requiring couples to furnish their parents' consent for the registration of marriage. This "rule" contravenes provisions of both the Hindu Marriage Act 1955 and the Special Marriage Act 1954. In 2003, succumbing to the propaganda of the Vishwa Hindu Parishad, a cultural affiliate of the BJP, the state government had made it mandatory to solemnize interreligious marriages only with the prior permission of district collectors. See Rathin Das, "Gujarat Marriage Fiat Tied in Knots," *Hindustan Times* (July 21, 2006).

[26] For instance, Babu Bajrangi, a BJP strongman, has forcibly "recovered" many Hindu women who marry Muslim men or men from other regions or castes. He and his cohort, with the help of the lower judiciary, kidnapped these women and forced them to divorce their husbands, after which they arranged their remarriage to Hindu men. See Basant Rawat, "VHP Crown for Gujarat Mob Leader," *The Telegraph*, Ahmedabad (February 28, 2004). Available at http://www.telegraphindia.com/1040229/asp/nation/story_2950417.asp. See also Dione Bunsha, "A Serial Kidnapper and his Mission," *The Hindu* 23, no. 25 (December 2006). Furthermore, the mobilizational strategies of the Hindu right entail the infiltration of the family through their cultural organizations, such as the RSS. This reorienting of RSS families into model families imagined by the Hindu ideologues is also one of the strategies used to change the ethos of the Hindu family (Sarkar 1995).

enactment of a uniform civil code.[27] Careful after the backlash generated in the aftermath of the Shah Bano case and politically preoccupied with fighting communal violence and the aggression of the Hindu right and the demonization of Islam from some quarters post–9/11, many sections of the Muslim community have turned to evolving internal mechanisms to regulate and reform Muslim Personal Law (Subramanian 2008).

In the aftermath of violence in Gujarat, most modernists have abandoned the idea of a uniform civil code, recognizing that such a move supports the Hindu nationalists' cry for a homogeneous public sphere dominated by majoritarianism values. For most Muslims and other minorities, any move toward enacting a uniform civil code represents an attempt to assimilate them into the political community against their wishes. Whereas some modernists continue to tie the uniform civil code to secular values (Narain 2001), others argue that the pursuit of incremental social justice through state-led reforms in religions is compatible with the Indian state's understanding of secularism (Mahmood 1993, 1997), and that the notion of "principled distance" permits different treatments of religious groups, which is compatible with the "ameliorative secularism" professed by the Indian state (Jacobsohn 2003, 285).[28]

Since the late 1970s, the outreach and influence of the Indian Women's Movement has increased substantively, and the number of civil society organizations has increased substantially since the 1990s. These have also emerged as a significant voice in matters of law reform (Subramanian 2008). The introduction of social legislation as a strategy for gender

---

[27] In the post–Shah Bano case era, the Muslim leadership has not reacted to provocative and anti-Muslim judgments, which is exemplified in the case of *Sarla Mudgal* v. *Union of India*, AIR [1995] SC 1531. In this case, the court was asked to rule whether a polygynous marriage of a former Hindu man contracted after conversion to Islam was valid. The court ruled that Hindu marriage undertaken under the Hindu Marriage Act 1955 could not be dissolved on the basis of a second marriage contracted after conversion to Islam. The judge also advised the enactment of the Uniform Civil Code to prevent such misuse of the law (see *Sarla Mudgal* v. *Union of India*, AIR [1995] SC 1531).

[28] There is no consensus on the reading of Indian secularism among scholars. For an excellent discussion of the Indian model of secularism in a comparative perspective, see Jacobsohn 2003.

equality within the family and in society has been an ongoing agenda of the Indian Women's Movement. Since the 1970s, in response to feminist campaigns on law reforms, the Indian state has amended rape law, banned female feticide, sex determination and sex preselection, introduced legislation to criminalize violence against women within the family (including dowry-related violence), prohibited dowry demands, and has evolved policies to deal with sexual harassment in the workplace. In addition, women's organizations have lobbied for the legal recognition of women's labor within the family as well as in the informal sector of economy[29] (Gandhi and Shah 1992; Gangoli 2006; Ray 1999). The Indian Women's Movement is also part of a broader peoples' movements for democratic reforms, minority rights, gay rights, environmental movements, movements against the communalization of politics and neoliberal economic reforms, and has transnational linkages with other social movements. The Indian Women's Movement has active links with women's wings of left-wing parties, trade unions, peoples' movements and NGOs working on a variety of issues, academic institutions (especially women's studies department and women's universities), other academic institutions, and professional associations such as the bar council and the press club (Gandhi and Shah 1992; Gangoli 2006; Ray 1999).

The Indian Women's Movement has debated the issue of the Uniform Civil Code throughout the 1990s. The Indian Women's Movement has painstakingly distanced its positions from the Hindu right's demand for a uniform civil code; it has reached a consensus on the need to support processes of intracommunity reforms, and it has evolved innovative strategies to work for gender justice without negating the criticality of the assertion of difference (Menon 1998; Sunder Rajan 2003). For instance, a section of the Indian Women's Movement has asked for a common civil code that is not modeled on the lines of the Hindu law but that places

---

[29] The Supreme Court bench has advised the parliament to determine the criteria to measure the economic and noneconomic value of housework to determine compensation in matrimonial and other laws. Available at http://www.deccanchronicle.com (accessed August 7, 2010).

gender justice at its center (Forum Against Oppression of Women 1996), while another section of the women's movement has argued for the disengagement from the law and the state because the state is inherently patriarchal (Anveshi Law Committee 1997). A section of civil rights groups has argued for the flexibility of the option to exit from personal laws to secular law (Working Group on Women's Rights 1996). However, the movement also points out that community processes are limited as religious laws are based on patriarchal premises. Since the Shah Bano case, leading feminists and academics have highlighted miscellany in various laws applicable to Muslims across India, and argued that economic rights of Muslim women are not protected in these laws (Agnes 1999; Ahmad 2003; Anveshi Law Committee 1997; Forum Against Oppression of Women 1996; Gangoli 1996; Menon 1998; Sangari 1995).

There are several points of convergence in these debates. With the exception of a few,[30] most scholars suggest that the Indian policy of legal pluralism has privileged group rights, especially the group rights of Muslims, over gender equality. It is conceded that women of all religious communities are denied equal rights in religious laws, but Muslim women are the most discriminated against in religious family laws, especially under laws governing divorce and maintenance upon divorce. In addition, some scholars suggest that since the Shah Bano case, the Indian state has not been able to intervene in reforms of Muslim religious family law.[31] It is also said that the state's policy has cemented group identities and widened the gap between the laws of Hindus and those of Muslims.

---

[30] A few scholars have established, through empirical research, that minority rights need not be entangled with women's rights, and that the Muslim Women's (Protection of Rights on Divorce) Act 1986 can be beneficial to women (Subramanian 2004, 2005; Vatuk 2005).

[31] Mahajan argues against the Indian state's intervention in reforms of Muslim Personal Law because it will generate an outcry against the "colonizing" state (Mahajan 2005). Mahajan's analysis underplays the history of state law developments in Muslim Personal Law. The Indian state has continued to intervene in Muslim Personal Law in the legislature and, more recently, in the adjudicative arena. Recently, the state has also refused to allow the establishment of parallel religious courts among Muslims – a demand that is occasionally raised by a small section of the Muslim clergy in India (*Outlook*, Web edition, available at http://www.outlookindia.com [accessed May 22, 2006]).

The dilemma in the Indian case is to tailor law reform that would balance both minority rights and women's rights.[32] Feminists see the processes of internal reforms as one such strategy but realize that their scope is often limited. Whereas the Anveshi Law Committee argues for reforms exclusively in the domain of society, proposals by Forum Against Oppression of Women and *Majlis* suggest piecemeal reforms in state laws as well as broadening the scope of law reform by deepening women's citizenship rights as means to unravel the knot between gender justice and minority rights. The Forum proposal argues for an extension of civic and social citizenship for women, asks for reform within the legal system, and demands the reconfiguration of the definition of the family by legalizing homosexual families and asking for the recognition of legal rights arising from cohabitation without marriage. Both the Forum and the *Majlis* argue for new laws on matrimonial property and call for the enhancement of women's economic rights in marriage. This strategy does not challenge the autonomy of the communities; rather, it provides women with economic rights within marriage (Agnes, 1999; Anveshi Law Committee 1997 Forum Against Oppression of Women 1996; Gangoli 1996; Menon 1998; Sunder Rajan 2003). However, both these proposals envisage change in the legislative domain, through statist interventions.

This book approaches the question by a different route, namely by focusing on state-society contestations in the adjudication of religious family laws. I pay analytical attention to the degree and nature of legal pluralism enshrined in the governance of marriage among Hindus and Muslims, and highlight the power and reach of state- and society-based sources of authority. These state-society negotiations to define and fashion the boundaries of religious groups' autonomous zones take place in two arenas: One is the legislative terrain in which changes take place either through the edicts of the state or in response to the demands of communities; the other is the process of adjudication, wherein law is produced (Zemans 1982). I turn to the micropolitics of adjudication in multiple legal forums because adjudicative sites are loci where laws are

---

[32] For a detailed discussion of this impasse, see Sunder Rajan 2003.

produced (Zemans 1982) and where law reforms take place through legal mobilization (Black 1973). These adjudicative processes bring to light the contestations over the nature and degree of community autonomy and gender equality within adjudicative processes. These reveal how individual litigants and adjudicators view marriage and the conjugal family, religious membership, and women's rights in law.

The Study in the Indian Context

The body of literature on religious family laws in India focuses on normative debates on group rights (Jayal 2001; Mahajan 2005; Nussbaum, 2000; Sunder Rajan 2000, 2003), legislative debates around personal laws, and analyses of legal precedents in religious family laws (Jaising 2000, Narain 2001, 2005; Parashar 1992). This literature also studies legal reasoning through the analysis of case judgments in state courts, especially in higher courts (Agnes 1999; Derret 1963, 1968; Galanter 1989; Mahmood 1991, 1997, 2002; Menski 2001; 2003; Sagade 1996). Both Mukhopadhyay and Sagade have studied the process of adjudication in matters related to marriage, divorce, maintenance, and inheritance among Hindu and Muslim women in lower courts (Mukhopadhyay 1998; Sagade 1996). In general, except for Mukhopadhyay, this body of literature does not take into account the nature of legal pluralism in the regulation of religious family laws, and it does not consider adjudication in informal legal forums. The anthropological literature on legal pluralism in India recognizes the prevalence of parallel community forums; much of this literature studies the adjudication process in rural India, but it does not focus on personal laws and does not discuss the concerns of gender justice in the regulation of family matters (Baxi 1985; Cohn 1965, 1987; Galanter 1989; Hayden 1999; Mendelsohn 1981; Moog 1991).

The theme of women's rights to matrimonial property under religious laws in formal courts has received the attention of some scholars (Mukhopadhyay 1998; Sagade 1996; Sturman 2005; Vatuk 2001, 2003). Scholars have also focused on the question of women's rights and, more generally, on access to property (Basu 1999, 2001; Sharma 1983). There have been several studies on women's access to, and control over, land rights (Agarwal 1994) and on Hindu widows' marginality in land rights under personal laws (Chen and Dreze 1992). However, few studies attend to the comparative constructions of matrimonial property in state courts and informal adjudicative bodies.

Among these few studies, Vatuk's work digresses from the trend of excessive focus on archival work. Vatuk has examined Muslim women's rights under laws related to marriage, divorce, and maintenance under Muslim Family Law in formal courts (Vatuk 2001, 2003) and in informal sites, focusing on the adjudication by the clergy (Vatuk 2005). Mukhopadhyay compares Hindu and Muslim women's claims to property in state and nonstate bodies and identifies the collusion of state and nonstate patriarchies in depriving women of their legal rights. Similarly, Erin Moore's ethnography, based on a Muslim woman's search for judicial alternatives to realize her rights, focuses on adjudication under Muslim Personal Law in both state courts and informal sect/caste councils in a village and in district court in Rajasthan (Moore 1998). Prem Chowdhry and Kriti Kapila have highlighted the role of political economy, state law, and discourses of modernity, individualism, and nationalism on changing marriage practices and laws in rural North India (Chowdhry 2004; Kapila 2004). Holden (2004) has studied customary divorces in Central India and has highlighted customary practices that benefit Hindu women more than state law, whereas Eckert (2005) has focused on the role of political parties as judicial actors. However, comparative studies of judicial processes under different personal laws in formal and informal courts of law in urban areas remain scarce.

The Context of Inquiry

I seek to examine the issue from a different entry point by focusing on neglected areas in both empirical and conceptual writings on religious family laws. I use the analytical framework of state-society relations to study the processes of adjudication in laws of marriage and divorce among Hindus and Muslims. In contrast to the existing body of work on religious family laws in the Indian context, I focus on the Indian state's model of legal pluralism in the regulation of the marital family and focus on the state's accommodative arrangement in the governance of marriage and divorce among Hindus and Muslims. I call this the *shared adjudication* model. To explain this model, I describe the specific arrangement between the state and communities that undergird this model. The Indian state shares adjudicative authority with both Hindus and Muslims in the regulation of marriage and divorce in Hindu and Muslim religious family laws, and determines the degree and extent of power sharing. For instance, societal laws that are repugnant to principles laid down by state law are not recognized by state courts, and the state reserves the right to be the final arbiter of law in cases of appeal. In addition, in principle, the state alone regulates the distribution of property in law. The nonstate agents who adjudicate divorce often finalize the quantum of maintenance and the division of matrimonial property as well. However, the state is the final arbitrator when it comes to disputes about the division of property in Hindu or Muslim family law.

How has the state split its authority with societal agents in regulation of marriage and divorce among Hindus? The Hindu law has been codified through the legislative process in postcolonial India. The Hindu Marriage Act 1955 governs Hindu marriages. Section 29(2) of the Hindu Marriage Act 1955 allows customary divorces in Hindu castes that traditionally practiced divorce. The majority of "customary" divorces are notarized, and lower courts do not routinely verify caste traditions in state courts. Customary divorces are scrutinized against the provisions and principles of the Hindu law when challenged in courts. Hindus belonging to castes that historically did not practice divorce are governed by state law and are required to approach state courts. In addition, parties who register their marriage under Hindu law are also required to dissolve the marriage in state courts. In practice, in addition to caste councils, individuals, civil society organizations, caste and sect councils, and informal bodies – what I call the *doorstep courts* – also intervene and regulate Hindu marriage.

The boundary of community autonomy among Hindus and Muslims is unevenly circumscribed. The Muslim religious family law is less codified than the Hindu law. Nevertheless, the state courts recognize some forms of customary or religious divorce and do not recognize others. In addition, state courts govern the division of property and maintenance under the Muslim religious family law. In practice, however, a variety of bodies and legal actors – sect councils, the doorstep courts, religious clergy, and individual actors – decide cases of Islamic divorce. Furthermore, the shared adjudication model is limited to regulation of marriage and divorce and is not applicable to adjudication in other aspects of religious family laws such as inheritance, adoption, and guardianship. It does not apply to adjudication in other civil or criminal laws in India.

Is the shared adjudication model a natural result of the weakness of the Indian state? For instance, Santos, in the context of Mozambique, suggests that the weakness of the state in Africa has led it to succumb to neoliberal globalization, and this in turn has led to the reemergence of traditional authorities as socio-legal actors, resulting in privatization of justice at the local levels. Thus, under the dual pressure at the suprastate and infrastate levels, the nation-state is transformed into a social field in which state and nonstate and local and transnational legal orders interact and merge with and confront one another (Santos 2006, 44). In the Indian context, scholars have argued that legal heterogeneity in India is merely due to a weak state that is captured by social elements. According to these scholars, the Indian state can be characterized as a "hollowed state" that steps back from its task of making public policy and creates a two-tier system of justice in which the poor have no choice but to opt for alternate forums and inefficient lower courts (Galanter and Krishnan 2003). Eckert has suggested that the Indian state can be classified as a "selective state" that strategically allows other political actors to access, influence, and act from within the state legal system. However, Eckert ignores a crucial distinction: The state does not share authority with societal actors in the governance of uniform criminal and civil law, but does so in the governance of the religious family law (Eckert 2006). I hold that the previously mentioned characterizations of the Indian state do not capture the functioning of the shared adjudication model, and maintain that this model is a pragmatic outcome, a result of political and cultural negotiations that took place between the national elite and the state in the 1950s over the question of accommodation of religious groups and regulation of marriage and divorce. The model recognizes customary autonomy over the regulation of marriage within the interstices of the state law but also restrains the autonomy of societal actors and outlines its boundaries. The model is crafted from above, but it has been creatively interpreted from below by a range of societal agents such as caste and sect groups, civil society, ethnic organizations, and individuals to chart their own socio-legal formations, forums, and laws. Adjudicative bodies such as civil society organizations, women's groups, women's wings of the left of the center political parties, and organizational offshoots of social movements are key sources of legal authority that contribute to ideological diversity in this model. Thus, both state and plural societal bodies and actors adjudicate in religious family laws of Hindus and Muslims. As a result, the questions about the meaning of religious membership, rights, and obligations within marriage are shaped and refashioned within state law and courts, as well as within informal bodies. I classify state and societal legal agents; I also analyze the interaction between official and unofficial laws and legal forums and discuss its impact on cultural pluralism and gender equality. I focus on adjudication in formal and informal legal forums, as these processes bring to light the plural constructions of the religious community and the marital family, and bring out the disagreements, conflict, and consensus over ideas of marriage and the rights and obligations of men and women within marriage in adjudication processes in plural legal locations. The term "adjudication" here refers to the processes of dispute resolution leading to an outcome in matters related to marriage and divorce. These processes are not always consensual and can take place in formal courts, informal arenas, or in both legal settings.

I limit my investigation to examining Hindu and Muslim personal laws around marriage, divorce, and maintenance because these are pitted against each other in the debates around religious family laws. In any case, the Indian state allows shared adjudication in cases of marriage and divorce under both Hindu and Muslim laws. I also include cases of maintenance during marriage and postdivorce because these have an impact on the economic rights of women within marriage and postdivorce, and these are linked to questions of marriage and divorce.

Research Site

I have chosen to locate the study in Mumbai, an urban metropolis in Maharashtra, in western India. One important reason for choosing Mumbai as a research site is that the study seeks to compare the traditional legal systems with the formal legal system of the state. The Family Court in Mumbai has existed since 1989 and is perceived to be one of the most efficient Family Courts in the country. The existence of community-based legal councils in a metropolis deserves attention, for the existence of parallel informal legal systems in a city like Mumbai, where the formal legal options, like the Family Court, are accessible and available, has implications for the questions at hand. Secondly, Mumbai was affected by communal riots in 1992–1993; it is also a stronghold of a Hindu fundamentalist party, the Shiv Sena, which, along with the BJP, has campaigned against the special exemption granted to minority Muslim community in matters of personal laws. In addition, women's groups and human rights groups from the city of Mumbai have been active in legal reforms and have initiated many discussions and countrywide debates on personal laws (see also Ray 1999).

Methods

Drawing from political and legal anthropology and feminist studies, I pay attention, not only to the law's intertwining with power and knowledge, but its role in reinforcing or countering gender/race/class hierarchy

(Cohn 1987, 1996; Comaroff 1981; Hirsch 1998; Lazarus-Black and Hirsch 1994; Scott 1998; Starr 1978, 1992; Starr and Goodale 2002). I also examine the formation of adjudicative forums, the unfolding of judicial processes, and their outcomes. I provide thickly descriptive accounts of the way in which state and nonstate legal actors incorporate, apply, or subvert state agendas. I also focus on the ways in which litigants and adjudicators use law, not only as a resource, but also as a tool to rework cultural meanings of the family, gender relations in the family, and religious membership (Peletz 2002). Historians studying legal developments in Islam see law as an outcome of discussions and communication between jurists and judges that precede judicial decisions and opinions (Hallaq 2001, 2005; Tucker 1998), and recently, scholars have turned to analyses of case records and courtroom processes in Islamic courts to assess how law is produced and women's rights shaped (Hirsch 1998; Moors 1996; Welchman 2000). I broaden the scope of this inquiry to include other legal actors – women's organizations, civil society organizations, state officials, and what I call doorstep courts, or informal committees and networks – as well as individual litigants to understand their contribution to lawmaking. I also study the organizational politics influencing judicial outcomes.

Although I have combined description with explanation, I have been alert to the politics of authoritative representation of empirical findings. I have attempted to capture *polyvocality* by interviewing different sections of religious and caste groups and of litigants. I have sought to represent their individual, nuanced, and contextualized positions on individual cases as well as on issues pertaining to religious family laws.

The judicial trends recorded in this chapter are not generalized on the basis of individual cases. The content analysis of legal records and judgments and interviews with litigants in cases of marriage and divorce revealed certain broad trends. For instance, the data showed that in the majority of cases of contested divorce, the Family Court does not grant divorce to male litigants if the divorce is strongly opposed by the wife. However, if no clear trend is evident, I have highlighted case details and represented them as cases with diverse circumstances and results. This is evident, for instance, in my record of various kinds of Islamic divorce in state and societal laws. In some other instances, I have highlighted trends and reported on the exceptions.[33]

Feminist Deliberations

I stepped into a familiar terrain with this project. As a member of the Forum Against Oppression of Women, I was involved in drafting the feminist proposal for gender-just laws entitled "Visions of Gender Just Realities." The Indian Women's Movement debated the issue of law reforms in 1996, and I participated in these discussions, holding the position that wide-ranging reforms in state law were the only means to achieve gender equality in law, though community-initiated internal reforms were necessary. My work as a feminist social worker at the Special Cell for Women and Children in Mumbai entailed negotiating with a number of community leaders and actors in working toward women's rights in law. While I learned to bargain and cooperate with community leaders for women's rights, I viewed them as opponents, for I saw religious and caste groups as inherently patriarchal.

However, during fieldwork, I found myself revisiting my previous assumptions as I conversed with various actors through my interviews, and witnessed the prevalence of diverse family forms, regulatory practices, and understandings of the family, marriage, and religious membership among Hindus and Muslims; these conversations challenged my previous assumptions. My understanding of the functioning of formal and informal forums and the nature of legality going beyond the realm of the state has shaped the change in my perceptions. The reworking of former ideological position in light of the empirical findings is evident in the central argument of this book.

---

[33] See, for instance, my discussion of cases of annulment filed in religious laws of Hindus and Muslims in the Family Court at Bombay.

My previous work helped me access a range of civil society organizations and state officials. However, accessing caste-based organizations and networks among Hindus was initially challenging, as some members saw their caste laws and practices as private and away from the gaze of the outsider. In the aftermath of the systemic state-sanctioned and large-scale violence against Muslims in Gujarat in 2002, my religious and regional identity as a Gujarati Hindu became salient when I sought to interview individuals from Muslim sects and religious organizations, many of whom were from Gujarat. I was screened and interviewed by group members among Hindus and Muslims, and while my politics and background as a social worker in a secular women's organization gave me a guarded entry into the "inner courtyards" of caste and sect organizations, interestingly, my essentialized identity allowed me greater access in unforeseen ways. During these interviews, I was invariably asked personal questions about my "family background," which always generated elaborate questions about my anthropologists parents' intercaste and, more importantly to my respondents, hypogamous marriage. My parents' marriage was exclaimed over and dissected: Some respondents were surprised or shocked when I assured them that my Gandhian grandparents on both sides accepted the marriage. This was dismissed as a social experimentation of "unworldly" academics. Interestingly, however, this made my caste and religious status fluid and malleable, and in the course of fieldwork, members of castes or sects belonging to Hindus and Muslims gave me their caste/sect identity by accepting me as "their own." I realized the shift when they began to refer to their caste laws (*amara kayda-kanoon*) as "our" caste laws (*apna kayda-kanoon*) during our conversations.

Sampling in State Courts

I have analyzed court records of cases filed under matrimonial laws of Hindus and Muslims. I have included cases resolved in lower courts, especially the Family Court, Mumbai, as only 5 percent of cases reach state high courts in India (Sagade 1996), and therefore, the largest number of cases are decided at this level. Section 22 of the Hindu Marriage Act 1955 forbids the publication of records of trial courts. Permission to access court records was granted to me by the Bombay High Court on condition of maintaining the confidentiality of sources, and as a result, names of parties and other identifiable details have been changed in the study. I have chosen to analyze recent judgments (January 2002 to January 2003) due to their easy accessibility.

By and large, cases of marriage and divorce in both Hindu law and Muslim law are processed in the Family Court in Mumbai. The Bombay High Court denied me permission to attend hearings in state courts – either the Family Court or the Metropolitan Magistrates' Court – as these are deemed private. However, I was allowed to interview litigants whose cases had been decided. I chose more recent cases for several reasons. For one, only the more recent judgments were stacked in piles in the Family Court's record room, and these were more accessible and reliable records from which to select the sample. Another reason concerned the intrusion into litigants' lives after a longer period of time. For instance, many litigants may have rebuilt their lives after the resolution of court cases and might be more reluctant to reengage with questions concerning previous court cases. Thirdly, choosing contemporary cases also gave me access to litigants who wished to move the Bombay High Court to appeal the judgments of the Family Court, and their reasons for doing so.

I have chosen to analyze these institutions through experiences of litigants and legal actors who were part of the process. The respondents were selected from recent court records of judgments given between June 2002 and January 2003 and that had no previous ties to each other in the sense that they did not share common lawyers or occupations and places of work or residence. I traced litigants from addresses available in court records. The initial sample was pared down as some respondents could not be traced – they had either changed residences or given addresses of distant relatives who had supported them through the legal process. Based on the information contained in court records,

I telephoned the respondents to secure appointments in cases where I could locate a number. I also contacted respondents through their lawyers or directly approached them at their residences. Some respondents previously selected had to be eliminated from the study, because many addresses were incorrect or difficult to trace. Some respondents could not be reached despite multiple attempts. Only two respondents refused to participate in the study.

Cases filed under the Muslim Women's (Protection of Rights on Divorce) Act 1986 are determined by the Metropolitan Magistrates' Court in Mumbai. It was not possible to sample cases from court records in this instance. There are no official statistics concerning the number of cases filed under the Muslim Women's (Protection of Rights on Divorce) Act 1986 because cases are not exclusively recorded under this section in the magistrates' court. Inquiries to court clerks about the nature of cases filed under this act showed that they were not aware of the existence of this act. I have sampled these cases through lawyers' records instead. The state law criminalized male homosexuality in 2002–2003,[34] and no cases of marriage between homosexual or transgender partners were adjudicated in state courts. However, I came across cases of homosexual marriages and unions in society and have discussed these in the context of societal adjudication.

Data Collection in State Courts

Most judicial analyses of case law in Hindu and Islamic laws in India are based on case records, but I soon found that judicial records, if taken at face value and by themselves, were insufficient and, at times, misleading

---

[34] The Section 377 of the Indian Penal Code 1860 criminalized male homosexuality in India. In July 2009, the Delhi High Court pronounced that the Section 377, IPC 1860 should be read down to exclude consensual sex between adults. (See *Naz Foundation (India) Trust v. Government of NCT, Delhi and Others. WP (C) No. 7455/2001*). This ruling has been appealed in the Supreme Court since 2009 and the matter is subjudice.

sources of data. Analyzing case records also meant being alert to the legal construction of a case through which litigants' experiences are converted into legally relevant language. During fieldwork, I learned to look for hidden data and discrepancies in case records.[35] For instance, I found that case records of cases of mutual-consent divorce bore almost no details of financial transactions through which one party "bought off" another. Besides, given that "fault" is the basis of contested divorce, proof of adultery was often "manufactured" in cases presented in courts. Respondents' financial details were routinely obfuscated in cases of maintenance. To overcome this, I have combined nonparticipant observation and open-ended interviews with the analysis of judicial records to understand factors that influence case proceedings.

I have conducted 120 interviews of cases of adjudication in formal courts. These interviews and nonparticipant observations gave me an insight into how society-based actors influence decisions of litigants and the final outcome of cases. In state courts, I also discussed the details of cases with lawyers and members of court staff (especially court clerks, peons, and record keepers). These interviews gave me insights into court procedures, the working of the legal system at the informal level, and "gossip" about lawyers, judges, prominent judicial cases, and "successful" strategies used by lawyers.

Sampling and Data Collection in Informal Courts

Sourcing of data and sampling cases from informal forums is challenging, because the registration of divorce in India is not centralized or compulsory. Another option available to me in this study was to sample cases from notaries' offices, as parties who operate the nonstate forums for divorce may often notarize their divorces. However, initial interviews with some key respondents (lawyers, women's rights activists, and social

---

[35] The issue of reading silences in legal processes through careful interdisciplinary research has been addressed by Peletz in the study of adjudication in Islamic courts in Malaysia (Peletz 2002).

workers) illuminated the fact that focusing on notarized divorce would not exhaust the range of categories. There are no official records on the number of divorces granted, and no list indicates numbers and types of legal actors and organizations who adjudicate in family laws. Initially, I approached more "visible" legal organizations – women's organizations, religious seminaries, and the clergy – and interviewed the litigants who had approached them. I then broadened my range to include newer actors.

I have chosen to study the processes of community formation and lawmaking among diverse caste, ethnic, and religious communities (Meghwals, Sai Suthars, Kutchi Visa Oswals, and Ithana Ashari Khojas). The castes and sects whose members I interviewed have not documented their histories. I have relied on oral histories and archival records to supplement and cross-check folklore about the history of migration and the evolution of caste-based organizations. To gain insights into the politics of caste- and sect-based socio-legal organizations, I attended weddings, intracaste social gatherings (*melawalas*), festivals, and religious rituals *poojas* (prayers). These informed my understanding of the everyday functioning of socio-legal organizations and helped me comprehend intragroup factionalism, corruption, and lobbying. I was informed of recent sensational cases of marriage and divorce, and I learned the meaning and experiences of social pressure: public shaming, ridicule, and social boycott.

It might be argued that aside from the Sai Suthar, each of them seem to be exceptional communities in a number of ways (a self-made community, a Jain community adjudicating under the Hindu law, a Muslim community that historically partially adjudicated under Hindu law, etc.). However as constructivist approaches to the construction of ethnic identity suggest, ethnic groups are products of human action and ideas. Every community is exceptional and is made and shaped by specific historical and socioeconomic processes; therefore, it is not useful to think of them in terms of exception and norm.[36]

---

[36] I would like to thank Rachel Sturman for her comments on this aspect.

When allowed, I have also attended adjudicative processes in informal forums. I attended case proceedings in caste councils, especially in the Meghwal caste council, Meghwal *panch*'s offices, and informal family adjudications among Meghwals and Sai Suthars and in what I call the doorstep courts. I accompanied social workers and activists in field visits with social workers from Awaz e Niswan, the Special Cell for Women and Children, the Stree Mukti Sanghatana, and Maholla Committees. To study the adjudication of Muslim family laws, I attended counseling and adjudication sessions in a clergy's office in a mosque, and sat in on proceedings in a religious organization housed in a local charitable trust's office. I have constructed sixty-five cases of adjudication in informal forums among Hindus and eighty-nine cases of adjudication in Muslim religious laws. Each case, where possible, includes a constellation of interviews with a set of respondents: husband, wife, and formal and/or informal legal actors who intervened in cases.

The nonparticipant observation and interviews brought out disagreements and conflict as well as consensus over ideas of marriage, rights, and the obligations of men and women within marriage in adjudication processes in plural legal locations. The process helped me understand how individual litigants or organizations challenged ideas of marriage and gender hierarchy enshrined and instantiated in state or nonstate laws and courts.

Organization of the Book

Whereas this chapter frames the backdrop of the case, Chapter 2 presents the analytical skeleton of the work: Drawing from the theory of state-society relations, I argue that the Indian state's model of shared adjudication, in which state and nonstate bodies adjudicate in the governance of marriage and divorce, points to an alternate route to facilitate diversity and ensure gender equality under certain conditions. I contend that this model enables the formation of several normative universes in formal and informal legal arenas; as a result, the statist constructions of religious membership, marital family, and gender roles are made, unmade, or reformed in diverse legal sites. Consequently, this legal sphere prevents the construction of a hegemonic normative family premised on institutionalized gender hierarchy as a repository of community identity. In addition, I demonstrate that processes of adjudication draw out interactions, negotiations, and discussions between and among Hindus and Muslims, civil society, and the state over the nature of the regulation of the family, gender roles, and the meaning of religious membership. I argue that interactions between ideologically diverse authority centers create spaces for dialogue across difference. I also highlight how women access, create, and change laws, discuss their agency, and outline the limits of agency.

Chapter 3 traces the processes of adjudication in Hindu and Muslim religious family laws in the Family Court of Mumbai. The chapter discusses inner contradictions between the state's attempts to govern the family through the centralization of law and the diffusion of law and authority in state law and in courts. Even though the rigid distinction between the construction of the family among Hindus and Muslims is seen to be pivotal to differentiate the two groups, I show that Hindu and Muslim families are formed along similar, though not identical, lines in state law and courts. The second section of the chapter studies the success of efforts made by the reformist judiciary in curbing male privilege in marriage and divorce. This section also argues that Muslim women get more economic rights in state laws than Hindu women do, and that the creative combination of Hindu and Muslim religious family laws with sections of civil and criminal laws increases the bargaining power of women litigants in accessing economic rights. The creative boundary stretching by legal professionals and litigants also opens up spaces for incremental reforms in law.

Chapter 4 analyzes adjudication processes in caste and informal groups and networks among Hindus. I compare the formation and functioning of caste-based regulatory bodies, informal networks, and actors in adjudicating marriage and divorce among Hindus across caste hierarchy, and I discuss the interactions between caste-based groups, civil society organizations, and the state in microadjudicative sites. I argue that democratically elected councils are more likely to encourage intercultural exchange by involving civic organizations and women's groups in debating law reform. I demonstrate that although the codified Hindu law is an overarching body of law, considerable variations of forms and values about marriage, divorce, and matrimonial property exist among Hindus. I argue that under certain conditions, the presence of ideologically diverse multiple forums increases the bargaining options for Hindu women litigants.

Chapter 5 analyzes the adjudication of Muslim religious family law in informal legal forums. Muslim Personal Law on the ground is an amalgamation of local, customary, religious, state, and international laws and customs, and it is made and unmade by interacting sources of lay, civic, religious, and state authority in various adjudicative sites. As a result, plural notions of the "Muslim family" and Muslim women's rights are constructed, debated, and destabilized on the ground. I highlight how individual litigant women, women's networks, and formal women's organizations challenge the patriarchal constructions of gender roles in law. I also trace the processes of reform in law as Muslim religious organizations and litigants debate the process of internal reforms in Muslim laws with secular organizations – especially women's organizations, state officials, and lawyers across religious boundaries. The final chapter synthesizes various arguments, outlines the conditions undergirding this model, and situates the Indian case in light of comparative debates and theoretical models in other multicultural and developing societies.

2 The Shared Adjudication Model
Theoretical Framework and Arguments

Introduction

In this chapter, I discuss the *shared adjudication* model; that is, the manner in which the Indian state shares adjudicative power with religious/societal bodies and actors in the regulation of marriage and divorce among Hindus and Muslims. This model produces justice that is multilocational, and each adjudicative site – formal or informal – provides a forum for interaction between state and societal laws and legal actors. I trace the nature of state-society relations at the interface of personal laws in diverse state and nonstate legal forums, and assess their impact on cultural accommodation and gender equality in Hindu and Muslim personal laws.

This chapter is divided into three sections. The first section classifies state and nonstate societal legal organizations and agents. The second section focuses on state-society relations in interpenetrative official and unofficial legal forums. I argue that state and nonstate actors engage in conflict, cooperation, negotiations, and communication over the content of laws governing marriage and divorce in multiple adjudicative locales. As a result, the statist version of the conjugal family and the notions of rights and obligations in marriage and divorce are destabilized, transformed, adapted, or unmade in a variety of legal settings. The third section discusses how postcolonial states might balance religious groups' demands for autonomy in the governance of the conjugal family and ensure gender equality. I contend that ideologically diverse overlapping and interpenetrative legal forums can potentially accommodate segments within religious communities, resist reification of group boundaries, promote dialog between communities, optimize women's legal options, and provide spaces for gender justice.

Theoretical Framework: State-Society Interactions at the Interface of Personal Laws

Given that both state and societal legal actors and bodies adjudicate in religious family laws of Hindus and Muslims, I combine the analytical frameworks of state-society relations and legal pluralism to answer the following question: What is the nature of the interaction between state law and actors and societal laws and actors within and across state-authored and informal legal forums? Theoretical discussions of the state have tended to follow Max Weber's definition of the state as an organization with claims to territorial integrity and the monopolization of force. Drawing from these basic tenets and complicating the notion of the state, literature on state autonomy defines the state not as reducible to societal forces but as a distinct actor rising above society: a structure of power that shapes social forces while remaining autonomous from them (Evans, Rueschemeyer, and Skocpol 1985; Mann 1986; Migdal 1988; Nettl 1968). States that are influenced by societal elements are characterized as "weak states" (Migdal, Kohli, and Shue 1994), lacking the capacity to instill order and to realize the agendas of the state.

Although some argue that state and societal actors can cooperate in order to maximize developmental activities and gains (Evans 1995; Nugent 1994), the notion of state and society as oppositional elements striving to control the local populace underpins the discussions of state and society relations. Societal resistance often undermines the state projects of modernization (Scott 1998). In other words, state and society are seen to be mutually exclusive and distinct; communities and societal actors are seen as resisting and undermining or adapting to state laws and agendas. However, the idea and practice of legal pluralism challenges the assumption of state autonomy that is widely prevalent in the body of literature in state-society relations. Some of the key questions that this literature debates are: How are the boundaries drawn between state and nonstate laws? What is the nature of the relationship and interaction between state and nonstate laws?

In general, the body of literature on legal pluralism focuses on the coexistence of state laws, including colonial laws, along with nonstate legal orders (Hooker 1975, 1976, 1984). This literature on legal pluralism also classifies types of laws coexisting in states and depicts the kind of interaction and relationship between state and nonstate or suprastate laws (Chiba 2002; Engel 1987; Fitzpatrick 1983, 1986; Galanter 1985; Greenhouse 1998; Griffiths 1986a, 1986b; Moore 1973, 1978; Sugarman 1983), and highlights the intertwining nature of international, national, and local legal orders (Santos 1995). Moore suggests that interactions between state laws and societal laws create a "semiautonomous field" that generates rules from within but that is also vulnerable to exogenous sources of law and authority (Moore 1973). Thus, Chiba identifies a dichotomous classification between official laws ("state laws or laws authorised by the state") and unofficial laws ("not officially authorised but valid outside the state"); between indigenous law ("which originates from indigenous culture") and transplanted law ("received ... or imposed by foreign cultures"); and between legal rules ("clearly formulated legal standards") and legal postulates ("ideas or ideology to base, orient, and revise the legal rules") (Chiba 2002, 194). He points to the coexistence of laws as well as conflict between these legal orders in plural legal systems (Chiba 1985, 1986). Thus, interactive state and nonstate laws can result in a range of legal arrangements in a given legal setting.[1] These interactions between different normative legal orders challenge the idea of state as the binary opposite of society.

In addition, whereas the old legal pluralism discussed the coexistence and interaction between customary, religious, and state law, the new legal pluralism is characterized by the interaction between local, national, and global scales of law, with their own legal norms and orderings. For Santos, legal pluralism is imagined as a cluster of interpenetrating legalities that

---

[1] For a typology of such an arrangement, see Yilmaz 2005; Tan 1997; and cited in Chiba 2002, 197.

are superimposed on one another and linked to ways of understanding and regulating the world, and is ever-changing, corresponding to shifts in our knowledge of the world. He describes three phases of legality – the colonial period, the postcolonial period in capitalist modern societies, and the postmodern period, which is characterized by three time-spaces of the legal (local, national, and transnational) (Santos 1995, 117), and is evident in the new epistemological paradigm in science and in society, which does not offer certitudes about ways of understanding the world, but provides ways of revising and making our explanatory tools. Thus, for Santos, law and society are interpenetrative and mutually constitutive (Melissaris 2004).

However, scholars argue that these accounts of law are analytically imprecise and do not explain the boundary between law, customs, norms, and morality (Tamanaha 2001), and therefore do not help us map the interaction between law and society. In a similar vein, Teubner also addresses a question: How do we capture the interwovenness and difference between law and society?[2] Modifying the general systems theory and bringing our attention to autopoiesis, Teubner argues that understanding the intertwining and separateness of law and society requires answering the question: How do we capture the openness of a system with its closure? In an autopoietic account of law, for Teubner, a system can remain open to the physical environment and also be closed "via structural coupling and perturbation" (Teubner 1992, 1446). An open system receives input, processes it internally, and releases the output in the feedback loop. An operationally closed system receives input from the outside environment as perturbations, processes information or events internally while remaining structurally coupled to its niche, and uses these to create internal order. This system also projects expectations on its physical environment. Therefore, the perturbating event is then interpreted as the success or failure of its expectation, thus the system itself

[2] Teubner argues that the general systems theory does not adequately explain legal pluralism and that the closure of legal systems seals legal discourses from other social discourses. He modified the theory and offered self-reflexivity as a way in which law becomes responsive to society (Teubner 1983).

defines its environmental constraints. In other words, the system does away with "... the internal distinction between self-reference and heteroreference" (Teubner 1992, 1446), uses the events in the physical environment as conditions of its own operations, and sees them as opportunities or constraints to bring about change. This process plays out in multiple settings in a system and produces change.

However, Teubner agrees that even with these modifications, autopoiesis cannot explain the interpenetration and the difference between the legal and the social because both work in the same field, the society, and therefore cannot be characterized as discrete autopoietic systems. Teubner demonstrates how law responds to social systems: He defines legal pluralism as "a multiplicity of diverse communicative practices that observe social action under the binary code legal/illegal" (Teubner 1992, 1451).[3] Thus, law makes its own boundaries; this definition excludes moral norms and social practice from law, and thus this definition separates the legal from the nonlegal. He modifies the idea of structural coupling and suggests replacing perturbations with "productive misreading" in the sense that legal discourse is not only perturbated by the social discourse, but the latter is "productively misread" by law as norm-creating sources; he also adds that structural coupling requires "linkage institutions" – that is, institutions that would tie law to formal organizations and networks would in turn bring about "responsiveness" as law through linkage institutions, as these are linked to social discourses (Teubner 1992, 1447). Thus, these processes change the interiors of legal organizations and networks.

---

[3] Elaborating on "communicative practises," Teubner analyzes the discourses and their structural coupling: "In ... market transactions, we have simultaneous but causal parallel processing of diverse legal and nonlegal communicative chains that are operationally closed to each other. Each chain builds up structures of its own: concrete day-to-day interactions of transacting parties, communication within formalised contracts and organisations ... and claims and counterclaims within diverse and competing legal discourses official and unofficial ... and each concrete communicative event will be processed in these different discourses which in spite of their mutual overlap ... remain closed to each other. Over time ... [t]hey do not causally influence each other ... rather, they use each other as ... perturbations to build up their own internal structures" (Teubner 1992, 1453).

Livia Holden, in her study of Hindu customary laws in Central India, uses Teubner's argument to suggest that in the Indian case, notaries, for instance, are one such "linkage institution" that interpret customary and state law (Holden 2005). Even though I agree with Holden in the sense that I also find that a number of lawyers cum notaries, lawyers cum notaries cum clergymen, and a host of other formal organizations and informal networks exercise adjudicative authority, I find that Teubner's model remains somewhat inadequate to capture the decentralized nature of law in the Indian case of shared adjudication. For instance, I have discussed "private divorces" undertaken and adjudicated by individuals. Teubner's binary code of legal/illegal is empirically unproductive because in India, for many individuals (Hindus and Muslims alike), the legal and the social remain undifferentiated – the dissolution of marriage by mutual consent of both parties, or two families, is perceived by these individuals as legal (under the binary code legal/illegal), social/customary, and moral. Similarly, whether these individual agents or even customary councils could be classified and categorized as linkage institutions remains questionable as, for Teubner, these institutions are internal constructs that are mere conduits, devoid of interdiscursivity. Thus, Teubner's otherwise persuasive account fails to capture the multitude of normative legal strategies and does not allow us to capture the breadth of the empirical canvas presented in the Indian case.

Tamanaha, drawing from Teubner, argues that law is whatever social actors discuss and construe as law. He suggests that rather than searching for the essence of law, we should accept that law is whatever label actors attach to it. For Tamanaha, the legal pluralism's failure to arrive at a definition of law, to pin down its essence, in itself suggests that there is no essence of law (Tamanaha 2001, 313). Thus, law is what people in a given social arena classify as law and therefore, legal pluralism exists when people identify with more than one kind of law in a social arena (Walby 2007).

However, the case of adjudication in marriage and divorce in India shows that while people *experience* law as a mixture of morals, social norms and practices, customary law, religious law, state law, and so forth, as law-navigating *subjects*, they distinguish between state law and nonstate law as emanating from different forums and have competing and contesting views about the hierarchy of plural laws. Turning to Migdal's modification of state-society relations offers us a new way to approach this empirical dilemma. Migdal (2004a)[4] calls for a state-in-society approach by which the state is imagined as a unified, territorially defined, and public entity, but is materialized as embodying multiple practices wherein the state and societal actors interact and engage in contestations over "systems of meaning that imply boundaries quite different from those represented in the image of the state" (Migdal 2004a, 26). Combining insights from two strands of literature; I place adjudicative forums at the analytical center, as law-producing, law-interpreting, and law-enforcing mechanisms. In other words, while I agree that people experience different types of law at once across time and space, I use the phrase "state law/formal law/official law" to capture the law generated and interpreted by official forums, and use the phrase "societal law/nonstate law/unofficial law" to capture laws generated from society-based legal formations. To clarify further, this distinction between state law and societal law does not affirm legal centralism or establish the hierarchy of state courts and law in all instances. In the Indian case, this distinction between state law and societal law is based on the imagined idea of state autonomy upheld by state and societal actors even in face of contradictory evidence and practice. I find that the analytical retention of this fiction for the purpose of this study is useful in order to understand both the interpenetration and independence of state and societal laws.

Considering that the shared adjudication model places adjudicative loci at its center, and these diverse adjudicative bodies and actors are the

---

[4] As he elaborates this model, Migdal sites examples in which the state and various societal forces are engaged in struggles over authority in a variety of *social settings*. Through her discussion of religious courts in Israel, Woods, following Migdal, demonstrates how social movements shape state laws in the judicial process and how social groups capture the state through the establishment of religious courts. Thus, she focuses on the impact of social forces on lawmaking in *formal courts* (Woods 2004).

physical environment in which state-societal laws interact, how do we capture internalities of these state and nonstate loci? For empirically, we see hybrid legal formations that include lower courts, especially state-run Family Courts, which institutionalize the presence of social workers and judges who often work with local NGOs to "resolve disputes through consensus." We also find that many society-based legal councils, which have their own "constitutions," pass laws that may change in response to changes in state law, evolve procedures for "appeal," and appoint lawyers on their societal legal committees, thus self-consciously maintaining the distinctness of societal laws and at times, adapting to state laws.[5]

We have seen that Migdal reconceptualizes the state as an entity; not unified, but with "multiple forms of institutionalization" (Migdal 2004a, 14), which can enter into "alliances with other societal actors." He distinguishes between "seeing state," presenting the state as a coherent organization, and "doing state," which involves responses and interactions between state officials and societal actors in multiple sites (Migdal 2004a, 15). The Indian variant of legal pluralism in the case of shared adjudication represents a legal landscape in which formal and informal legal actors and organizations are interpenetrative. Santos's specific discussion of interactions between various customary, religious, neighborhood courts, people's tribunals, and national courts in Mozambique is illuminating in this context (Santos 2006). For Santos, the interaction between legal orders is often conflicting, but it also makes different legal orders permeable, open to reciprocal influences. According to Santos, "[O]ut of this porosity evolves ... legal hybrids, that is, legal entities or phenomena, that mix different and often contradictory legal orders or cultures, giving rise to new forms of legal meaning or action"

---

[5] For instance, the Meghwal caste council among Hindus have established formal procedures for appealing cases in their caste council. The *Dar ul Qaza* of the Deoband seminary is one such example under the Muslim family law. The sectarian ulemas are associated with a *madrasa* founded in the town of Deoband in the United Provinces (now Uttar Pradesh) in 1867. The Deobandis emphasize the study of law and the Hadith (the traditions attributed to the Prophet Muhammad) and self-consciously seek to reform variants of folk Islam, or popular Muslim practices.

(Santos 2006, 46). In the Indian context, the boundary between state and society shifts as different actors engage in "doing state" in hybrid locales. Thus, even within organizational hybrids, state and societal laws can be perceived as distinct, even if they are porous and intertwined in reality.

Thus, I marry the framework of state-society relations to the debates on legal pluralism in order to investigate the interactions between state and societal actors and institutions, and assess their impact on cultural pluralization and women's rights in law. How do state institutions and organizations interact with one another? What is the movement of laws within and between formal and informal actors and organizations? How does the interplay between state and nonstate laws and actors impact the basis of the state? How does the model of shared adjudication illuminate debates on cultural pluralism and gender justice in matters of personal laws?

Arguments

I argue that the Indian model of legal pluralism in which the regulation of marriage and divorce is shared by the state, internally heterogeneous religio-cultural communities, and civil society (especially women's groups) provides spaces for intra- and intercultural accommodation, and it offers possibilities to bring about gender equality in law.

I contend that interacting state and societal legal organizations and agents are locked in a paradoxical movement that I term the centralization of law and decentralization of law. The Indian state seeks to consolidate its authority by infiltrating and shaping the conjugal family from above. However, in a legally plural system characterized by heterogeneous legal actors and institutions, state law and organizations are captured, appropriated, resisted to, or transformed by societal agents. This interdependence between state and societal legal orders demonstrates that the state law is, at times, shaped by societal laws, that it often determines societal laws, and that state authority is consolidated in some instances and diffused in others. The movement of the centralization of law as well as the decentralization of law show how this variant of legal pluralism serves to further the agenda of the liberal democratic state to penetrate society as well as to restrain it. Similarly, it serves to fulfill the goals of societal actors and institutions as well as limit them.

The presence of multiple legal actors in the legal sphere activates the centralization and decentralization of law in society, and results in the formation of various internally splintered and interacting normative worlds in which different images and practices of the family, the link between religion and law, and women's rights in the family are formed, discussed, negotiated, and fashioned by both state and societal agents. These interactions enable the transmission of plural ideas of the nature of the conjugal family and of gender across religious and cultural cleavages in different legal forums; they allow societal actors to appropriate and tailor their own selective images of the conjugal family and to generate meanings about religious membership. These open-ended interactions between state and society, as well as within societal groups, provide spaces to conduct and promote intra- and intercultural dialog on law reform and gender roles and rights.

Thus, in contrast to the body of literature on multicultural citizenship that maintains a critical tension between cultural autonomy and intragroup equality, I argue that in a pluralized legal field characterized by shifting centers of authority, cultural pluralism in recognition of family laws can facilitate gender equality in law. I claim that similarities rather than differences characterize the adjudication and governance of Hindu and Muslim laws. I also demonstrate that while Hindu and Muslim women are not granted equal rights in religious family laws, Muslim women do not face greater discrimination. Indeed, Muslim women are awarded greater economic rights under the religious laws governing marriage and divorce.

The Indian Model: Juristic Diversity in the Legal Landscape

Both state courts and societal bodies and actors adjudicate in matters concerning marriage and divorce among both Hindus and Muslims in

India. My study investigates heterogeneous legal forums in a metropolis and develops the typology of organizations and actors that adjudicate in societal spheres in matters of personal laws. The following sections provide the taxonomy of organizations and actors that adjudicate in matters related to personal laws of Hindus and Muslims, and discuss the interaction within and between formal and informal systems.

Formal Legal Organizations and Actors: The Lower Courts

The state-established Family Courts and district and sessions courts share jurisdiction in family matters at the lowest rungs of the formal legal system, though the Family Court has emerged as the specialized court, dealing with the bulk of matrimonial matters in recent years in Mumbai. Studies on civil litigation in India suggest that low rates of litigation in India are due to the alienation of litigants from a lengthy, expensive, cumbersome, corrupt, and inefficient formal legal system, especially within the lower courts (Baxi 1982; Chodosh 2004; Galanter 1966, 1968, 2004; Galanter and Krishnan 2003; Khare 1972; Kidder 1973, 1974; Mendelsohn 1981; Morrison 1974). However, the Family Court in Mumbai is speedy, efficient, and the corruption level is lower than in other courts. Furthermore, the formal system is accessible to women – legal aid is more easily available, litigants can fight their own cases, and women litigants are exempted from paying court fees. Even though mistrust of the courts in India drives some litigants away from the formal legal system, approaching the Family Court is the only avenue for divorce for individual litigants who wish to terminate interreligious marriages under secular laws, or who belong to castes and sects that traditionally disallow divorce. Besides, this study shows that the interpenetration of state law and forums and societal laws and forums allows the state law to act as a backdrop for negotiations within society (see also Cohn 1965, 1987; Kidder 1973, 1974); paradoxically, while this limits the use of state courts in matrimonial matters under the jurisdiction of Hindu and Muslim personal laws, it enhances the penetration of state law in the society.

Legal Organizations and Actors in Society: An Overview of Typologies, Structures, and Functions

What organizational arrangements follow legal polycentricity (Petersen and Zahle 1995)? This study examines the variation in societal organizations, associations, and agents that adjudicate in matters of marriage and divorce. Some of these legal organizations are active, some are redundant, yet others are in the process of reviving and reinventing themselves. The state's policy of shared adjudication and the decentering of law has spurred societal legal actors to create innovative participatory conditions within the legal system by setting up organizational structures and procedures, developing competencies in law and legal procedures, appropriating legal symbols and rhetoric, initiating intracommunity dialog on family matters, committing to undertake legal reforms, and, in some instances, working out conditions to limit the power of those who adjudicate in societal forums. Whereas some informal legal forums rely on coercion to enforce their dictates, others fall back on consensus. Some actors extend the limit of their authority whereas others intervene within state-circumscribed boundaries. These organizations, networks, groups, and individuals create a heterogeneous, multicentered, and culturally plural legal landscape.

The following section gives an overview of diverse societal legal organizations and agents. Three typologies encompass legal actors and institutions adjudicating in the personal laws of Hindus and Muslims.

Formal Organizations

Societal organizations adjudicating in personal laws in Mumbai include structured organizations that are registered with the state[6] and are thus subject to the supervision of the state; these organizations are further

---

[6] The caste and sect councils (*panchayat*) as well as NGOs that fall under this category are registered under Section 18 of the Bombay Public Trusts Act (XXIX of 1950) as "Charitable Trusts," and fall under the jurisdiction of the Commissioner of Charity, Mumbai. Under the Act, "public trusts" are trusts established for "a public religious or charitable purpose."

subclassified. The first subcategory includes *ethnic organizations*, such as caste councils and sect councils (*panchayats*), whose jurisdiction in the governance of family law extends to members of a specific caste, subcaste, or sect. This study demonstrates the variation in ethnic organizational structures among castes and sects of Hindus and Muslims. I investigate the interplay between caste formation, lawmaking, and adjudication in three caste councils (*panchayats*) among Hindus and one sect council among Muslims. I delineate the similarities and differences in laws and operations of the *panchayats* among Hindus and Muslims of similar caste and occupational status, and I discuss the variation in each forum in accessing women's rights in family law.

To elaborate, I demonstrate that a caste group of Hindus called Meghwal has evolved what I call a *democratic participatory justice system* to regulate family matters. The legal hybrid includes elements of a traditional justice system (the *panch* system), democratic procedures, and the formal legal system. The caste laws practiced within this group award more rights to women than do state courts. I also examine the traditional justice system of Sai Suthars, another Hindu subcaste. The caste council of this group is not active, and divorces are largely negotiated among family and caste networks. This study also discusses the caste group of Kutchi Visa Oswal (henceforth KVO), which seeks to wrest the control over family matters from the state, and envisages the creation of an arbitration system that would "technicize"[7] justice by introducing advocates, social workers, mental-health professionals, and family therapists as adjudicative committee members. This study also assesses the internal regulation among an Islamic sect, the Khoja Shia Ithna Ashari, which has maintained its traditional adjudicative system – a hybrid of Islamic laws and customary practices. These societal organizations engage in an ongoing process of dialog on the trends in marriage and divorce within their sphere, and they familiarize themselves with developments in state law. They organize internal discussions among their members, facilitate periodical review committees

---

[7] See Rosanna Langer, "The Juridification and Technicisation of Alternative Dispute Resolution Practises," *Canadian Journal of Law and Society* 13 (1998): 169.

on marriage and divorce in their respective caste or sect, and facilitate dialog with legal professionals, social workers, and, in many cases, women's organizations, as well as other state actors such as the police. They also familiarize themselves with developments in state law and discuss the necessity of reforms within the caste/sect sphere.

This typology also encompasses *interest-based* organizations such as civil society organizations,[8] charitable trusts, religious organizations,[9] political parties, and women's groups.[10] These organizations present a civic source of authority in the shared adjudication model. These organizations adjudicate in family matters, penetrate both formal and informal legal systems (indeed, some are housed within state police stations), provide their own normative discourse, act as moral watchdogs of community organizations, and help individual litigants against the community, thus offsetting the remit of societal authority over individuals in everyday processes of adjudication. They also perform another important function. Religious organizations, NGOs, and women's groups engage with other groups in the discussions of reforms in family matters at broader collective levels. Thus, they help transform individual voices, experiences of litigants, and aggregate strategies used by various legal orders to create

---

[8] These are professional organizations working on grassroots or advocacy work on a range of issues, including women's issues. They often provide legal aid to women litigants and carry out legal literacy campaigns.

[9] These organizations do not fall neatly into categories of ethnic organizations or civil society organizations. Chatterjee has argued for a conception of political society to classify organizations that employ the rhetoric of "community" and organize around issues concerning "property" (Chatterjee 2004). However, these organizations fall outside this conception as well. These are affiliated to and funded by religious or charitable trusts. Many of their activities are *civic* in nature, ranging from the organization of blood drives to interventions in slum rehabilitation. However, they also claim to represent specific religious or cultural groups and employ the rhetoric of identity politics.

[10] The groups to which I refer are organizations that work on a variety of issues, including women's issues. The latter category refers to feminist organizations that work exclusively on issues related to women, and are associated with autonomous women's movements in India. These also include women's groups that are affiliated with women's wings of leftist parties. These groups have consistently worked on the issue of reforms of personal laws since the 1970s (see for instance, Gandhi and Shah 1992).

a ground, or initiate collective processes of legal change. The formal organizations, especially civil society actors, women's organizations, and organizational offshoots of social movements, are the sources of civic authority which enhance the ideological diversity of the legal sphere under the shared adjudication model.

The Doorstep Courts – Informal Associations, Groups, and Networks

Informal associations and networks such as *jamaats* (collectives), *mohalla* (residential) committees, neighborhood associations, and unregistered and loosely bound groups, including women's groups, also adjudicate in matters of family law among Hindus and Muslims. These are not registered with the state. These groups are less likely to socialize individual litigants into normative codes of conduct. These groups perform a "gate-keeping function" (Macauley 1986, 455) by filtering the members' access to the formal justice system. They can restrict litigants' access to courts or, conversely, assist the state in implementing laws or facilitating litigants' access to legal system. Their reach is in proportion to the accessibility and legitimacy of the state courts.

Individual Legal Actors

Individual litigants, notaries, lawyers, clergy, family members, middlemen, members of political parties, and strongmen comprise the third layer of adjudicative agents of informal intermediaries. Their reach is ad hoc and, with the exception of lawyers, they do not count as lobbies in matters of law reform. Many societal actors lack training in formal law, though most of them acquire legal knowledge and competency in state law and the functioning of state courts. The legal procedure involving individual legal actors often lacks transparency and can subvert the meaning of law and the legal process. Women litigants unsupported by affinal and social networks or civil society organizations are more likely to be at a disadvantage when they are forced to deal with individual actors in legal processes.

Interactions between State and Societal Organizations and Actors

This section analyzes the interaction between state courts and informal organizations and actors, as well as the interaction among different organizations and actors in the legal landscape. I argue that state and nonstate legal actors simultaneously strengthen and constrain one another in an interpenetrative legal setting. To elaborate, I demonstrate how multiple societal organizations and actors enter into competition with the state over governance of family laws and thus pose a challenge to the authority of the state in the legal arena. However, this competition does not capture the range of interactions between the state and societal legal actors. The data show that organizations and actors also cooperate, communicate, and negotiate with the state and devise the means to curb their informal authority. In a heterogeneous legal setting characterized by many competing power centers, legal organizations and actors also counterbalance one another's power. I also suggest that informal legal organizations strengthen the state by mimicking state laws and procedures and by enforcing state laws.

The Question of Legal and Extralegal Authority and Accountability

A body of literature on legal informalism argues that the presence of other forms and agencies of justice can undermine the basis of the liberal state and violate individual liberty (Abel 1982a; Baxi 1982; Fiss 1984), although recent studies indicate a shift in this debate. A number of authors acknowledge the reach of informal systems of justice and shift the discussion to reforming and fine-tuning alternate dispute systems to overcome the pitfalls of legal informalism (see Alberstein 2006; Resnik 2003). Feminist analyses of the decentralization of laws of marriage and divorce in the West also suggest that informal systems harm the interest of women in divorce negotiations given that mediation processes are neither value-free nor gender-neutral (Bailey 1989; Bottomley 1985; Bryan 1992; Grillo 1991). The literature on women's rights in community courts in India agrees with this critique (Dhagamwar 1992; Nishat 2003).

This study suggests a more complex picture than discussed by these authors. It argues that it is not only the presence of multiple actors within the legal system, but also the ideological and organizational diversity of these legal actors, and dynamic interactions between them, that helps predict their contribution to cultural pluralism. For instance, in Chapters 4 and 5, I show how communities exceed the remit of authority granted to them by the state and subject individuals to social boycott, "persuasion," shame, reprimand, and ridicule by caste and sect authorities. Selective incentives and the rigid enforcement of caste endogamy are also used to ensure compliance. Thus, communities can coerce individuals, especially those more vulnerable to community pressure. I also show that formally organized legal bodies within segments of religious or caste groups strive to shape normative behavioral codes among its members and in handling family matters; they are more likely to offer incentives to individuals and impose sanctions. The study also contends that the state legal system is more likely to lose ground when in competition with well-organized caste and sect councils (*panchayats*). I argue that nondemocratic and well-organized caste and sect organizations are more likely to coerce individuals within the caste or sect than democratic organizations. Informal organizations mediate litigants' access to state law and formal legal procedure. Informal actors, such as lawyers, point their clients toward society-based informal justice systems. Strongmen also intimidate and harass various litigants, minimizing the authority of the state. Families and individuals often mediate in matrimonial matters, and women unsupported by affinal networks are forced to compromise their rights. The leveling of charges of corruption against all actors and bodies (except feminist groups) are commonplace, though corruption is also experienced by women and male litigants in state courts. Thus, the presence of diverse actors often undermines the state.

However, I have also found that the presence of other organizations and actors can also strengthen the state.[11] The individuals use societal actors, including strongmen, to enforce state laws. Thus state law is extended in the societal arena by informal actors. Lawyers use state law to negotiate their clients' rights in society, and lawyers as official bearers of caste, sect, or civil society organizations help the outreach of state laws. Civil society organizations use state law to bargain and negotiate women's rights in informal legal forums. Organizations at the societal level draw on the rhetoric, techniques, and procedures of state courts;[12] this brings the image of the state into informal legal locales.

In addition, in some instances, informal organizations also make themselves accountable to their constituents. For instance, I discuss the process of inner democracy within the caste council of Meghwals in Chapter 4. Regular and transparent elections are a mechanism used by the subcaste to ensure minimal internal accountability among the Meghwals. Secondly, the power of such caste- and sect-based organization is often challenged from within by individual litigants and their families. These castes and sects are not homogeneous and are governed by multiple centers of authority. These actors use inner factionalism within castes and sects to arm themselves against coercion exercised by informal bodies. A sect member belonging to the Ithna Ashri Khojas,[13] reflecting on the ongoing power struggles over the control of their sect council, said: "We have mastered the democratic game – we do not have political parties in our *jamaat*, but we have factions instead – the *jamaat* is

---

[11] A number of studies on legal informalism, which came out in the 1980s in the United States, argue this (see, for instance, Abel 1982a; Delgado 1985; Harrington 1985; Hofrichter 1982; Merry 1982a, 1982b, 1989; Tomasic 1982).

[12] For instance, parties are issued letters to come to community courts, and these are often referred by litigants and these bodies as "summons." The Meghwal Panchayat and the *Dar ul Qaza*, religious courts of the Deoband ulema, have provisions for appeal against "judgments," or decisions delivered at local levels.

[13] Interview with Shirin Maneckia, March 5, 2003, Mumbai.

not a property of one family or clan or an individual; we counterbalance one another." The threat of exit by individual sect or caste members is also a tool used to guard against informal pressure exercised by any one center of authority. For example, addressing the biannual review of caste laws,[14] a Hindu woman caste-member urged her "sisters" to go to a local Muslim women's organization, Awaz e Niswan, and ask them to assist them in realizing their legal rights if a "woman's plea fell on deaf ears of caste officials." She added: "I will go a step further – our caste is spread across Mumbai; each suburb of Mumbai now has women's organizations and our sisters know about these resources and we use them, but we call upon our caste council to publish a list of these organizations and give this information to all caste members so that we know who to approach if we want help that is denied to us by our male brethrens."[15]

Informal justice forums do not function in isolation from the state or other actors and institutions; as a result, the coercive power of informal organizations is also challenged from external factors. Plural adjudicative systems comprising state agencies, civil society organizations, religious and ethnic organizations, and state actors in the adjudication of personal laws offset the concentration of power; these diverse bodies are often used by group members as resources to resist or balance informal institutional authority. For instance, individual women litigants often use women's organizations to offset the power of caste and sect *panchayats*; these also seek assistance from the state courts. The presence of an active civil society contributes to regulatory mechanisms at the societal level as well as at the level of the state. Thus, in a heterogeneous legal sphere characterized by different organizations, including civil society organizations, these counterbalance each other's power. Such interactions between state and society, as well as among societal organizations, provide spaces for discussions and exchanges about the nature and content of family law across religious and caste boundaries.

---

[14] Biannual Review Meeting of the Meghwal Caste Council, June 18, 2003, Mumbai.
[15] Interview with Kesarben Chauhan, September 16, 2002.

An Open-Ended Conception of State-Society Relations among Heterogeneous Legal Actors

The data discussed earlier show that in a legally plural society, justice is multilocational, and each adjudicative forum – formal or informal – provides a platform for the interaction between state law and legal actors as well as societal laws and actors. This dynamic of simultaneous intervention is not captured merely by imagining state and society as locked in contests to establish hierarchical order. It has also been argued that state-society relations can be simultaneously conflicting and cooperative (Nugent 1994).

However, the interpenetration of state law and societal laws and institutions here creates a flow of legal actors, facilitators, and gatekeepers across formal and informal spheres, and the range of interactions between state and societal actors demonstrates a range that is broader than the two approaches delineated previously. Indeed, I suggest that state and societal actors are bound in the processes of communication and negotiations over the content and meaning of personal laws in mixed adjudicative sites. These dynamic processes of communication fashion and reconstitute the interiors of both state and societal legal orders. The Indian model evinces a need for an open-ended and process-oriented conception of state-society relations that encompasses not only the binary of conflict and cooperation, but also communication between state and society.

The Paradoxical Movement between State Laws and Societal Laws

The following section traces the interaction of laws within and between formal and informal legal forums. I contend that the interacting legal actors and institutions evince a paradoxical legal movement in both formal and informal legal systems. I term this tension the *centralization of law and decentralization of law* and demonstrate how state law is both

THE SHARED ADJUDICATION MODEL

Legal Systems	The Dynamic of Interaction within and between State and Societal Laws	Outcome
Formal Legal Forum	Production, Interpretation, and Execution of State Laws → Centralization of Law Fragmentation of Law Societalization of Law → Decentralization of Law	
Informal Legal Forums	Extension of State Laws Adaptation to State Laws → Centralization of Law Resistance of State Laws Transformation of State Laws Generation of Societal Laws → Decentralization of Law	

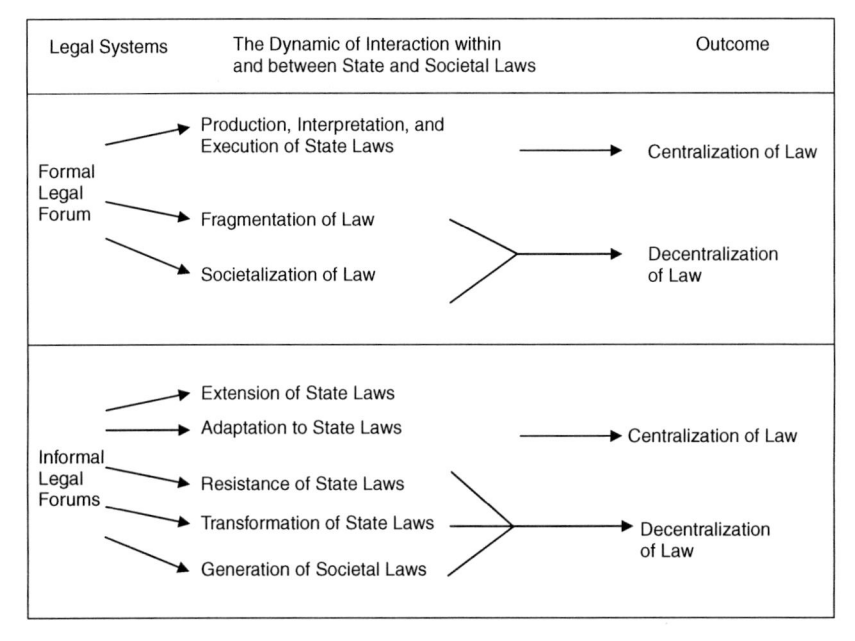

Figure 2.1. Dynamics of interaction: state laws and societal laws.

influenced by societal laws and determining of societal laws. The centralization of law refers to the state's attempts to penetrate society, shape individual subjectivities, and influence lawmaking in various legal forums. The decentralization of law suggests the fragmentation and pluralization of law within both state and societal legal forums. As a result, personal law is made and unmade in a variety of settings.

The Centralization of Law in the Formal Legal System

As shown in Figure 2.1, the centralization of law[16] is evinced in the attempts of the state to infiltrate society, secure individual liberties, and

---

[16] Werner Menski, in his discussion of Hindu law has pointed out the lack of centralized authority when it comes to Hindu law (Menski 2001). I suggest that the state project aims at both the unification as well as the decentering of law. The centralization of law is also seen in the state's roadmaps for judicial reforms to increase its legitimacy and effectiveness.

shape the subjectivities of citizens through the generation, interpretation, and execution of personal laws in state courts. Through the regulation of personal laws, the state courts define the social institutions of marriage and divorce, and ascertain the criteria of membership in caste or religious/cultural groups. The rhetoric of violence (Santos 1995) also contributes to the centralization of law. State law and courts also restrict and circumscribe juridical power of societal actors, redistribute property rights among family members, and enforce the compliance of judicial verdicts and state laws. The judges also restrict the power of societal actors to allow or derecognize customary divorces. For instance, data show that judges in the Family Court selectively recognize customary divorce among Hindus and Muslims; they disallow *faskh*, judicially arbitrated Islamic divorce by the clergy under Muslim Personal Law. Given that the codification of customs and lawmaking through judicial precedents has been the feature of the Indian legal system, the centralization of law is a part of the lawmaking function of courts in India. Standardization, systemization, and routinization of law in courts (Heydebrand and Seron 1990) lead to judicial consistency and establish the hierarchy of courts as a judicial system.

The centralization of law is also seen in the state's roadmap for judicial reforms to increase its penetration and legitimacy. For instance, the data show that the Family Court in Mumbai fast-tracks justice and disposes of cases between three and five years old to avoid congestion in the court. Workshops and conferences for Family Court judges and court officials within the state and across the region facilitate the discussion of common trends and problems, especially administrative issues,[17] and impact the centralization of law.

---

[17] These issues include dealing with delays in the disposal of cases, norms for disposal of cases in the Family Court, creation of prelitigation panels to advise litigants in the family court, and issues concerning self-representation of litigants. These conferences of Family Court judges and counselors in Maharashtra have been held from 1991 onward (see Bombay High Court circular FC/PJ/967/1992). The Family Court judges also participate in regional workshops for Family Court judges.

Fragmentation and Societalization of Law in State Courts

The decentralization of law in state courts, as described in Figure 2.1, is the result of two movements within state legal institutions. One is the fragmentation of law, which arises from factors such as the failure of lower courts to follow judicial precedents, the arbitrariness of judicial discretion, the lack of coordination between courts, and the conflict of jurisdiction among lower courts. This leads to the internal fragmentation of state law, tempers the synergy of judicial precedent as the source of law, and results in the loss of judicial authority. Thus, the tension between the centralization of law and the decentralization of law within the state arena serves at times to consolidate or diffuse state authority as well as the agenda of the state within the state legal system.

The second movement leading to the dispersal of state authority in the formal legal system is the societalization of law, which shows the diverse ways in which societal actors and institutions filter into the state judicial system. It refers to the recognition, institutionalization, and legitimation of societal forms of law and legal structures within the state legal system. The state law recognizes customary divorce, provides mandatory intervention of social workers in marital disputes, and seeks the intervention of societal actors as mediators, witnesses, and consultants on societal laws. Thus, society filters into the state legal system in various ways, leading to the societalization of law. Secondly, the judiciary relies on a wider sociocultural and religious base to accommodate cultural communities. For instance, judges in the state system have tended to base their opinions on the creative interpretation of religious texts rather than on constitutional sources.[18] The judiciary is often asked to recognize or validate societal practices and customs related to marriage and divorce among subsections of diverse religious and caste communities'.[19] In many cases, judges call on

---

[18] See, for instance, *Shamim Ara* v. *State of UP and Another*, AIR SCW 4162 (2002); *Dagdu s/o Chotu Pathan* v. *Rahimbi Dagdu Pathan and Others* (Aurangabad bench of Bombay High Court, May, 2002).

[19] For instance, while adjudicating on a case of dowry-related violence, the judge asked a delegation of caste members whether the practice of dowry was common to customs

caste or sect members as witnesses in order to seek their views regarding the prevalence of practices claimed by either party in litigation.[20] Thus, judges engage in a dialog with sections of society in matters of family law within courts; consequently, society enters into the formal, legal system in myriad ways.

Centralization of Law in Informal Legal Forums

As outlined in Figure 2.1, the centralization of law – the tendency of the state law to serve as a tool to shape societal institutions and domestic affairs of citizens – persists in the societal arena as well. I demonstrate how societal actors, especially professional lawyers, notaries, and civil society organizations, extend state law into society, as well as the values, procedures, rules, ceremony, rhetoric, and techniques of the formal legal system. The centralization of law is also reflected in the juridicisation of legal techniques, and the law forms in society as caste and sect organizations adopt procedures of state courts.

To elaborate, state laws and judicial precedents often form the backdrop of interlawyer negotiations and adjudication in caste and sect councils (*panchayats*) in Hindu and Muslim personal laws. Changes in state law affect the intragroup dialog over reforms in community law as well. The adaptation of state law refers to the manner in which societal actors and institutions adapt to state laws imposed from above.[21] Informal organizations often seek to work alongside state courts in order to bolster their power and legitimacy in their communities. The centralization of law

---

of that particular caste (interview with Esha, member of the Meghwal Caste Council, November 25, 2002, Mumbai).

[20] In one case, the judge asked caste members whether the practice of cross-cousin marriage was part of the integral custom of the caste (interview with VK, March 6, 2003, Mumbai).

[21] For instance, the data show that polygyny was outlawed or restricted by some Hindu caste *panchayats* after the codified Hindu law prohibited the practice. Similarly, state courts' nod to polygyny among Muslims has compelled some Islamic sects like Ithna Ashari Khojas to declare the practice legally valid and "Islamic," despite the fact that their customary laws disallowed the practice.

is also apparent when societal actors uphold and enforce state laws in the everyday practice of law. Lawyers, caste factions, women's committees, residential committees, sects, and women's organizations all use state law to bargain for women's rights in everyday legal negotiations. At other times, state decisions are enforced by community authority or societal actors. Community forums often mimic or draw from state law, procedures, and rhetoric to establish community mediation and adjudication forums. Informal organizations at the societal level evolve judicial organizations and procedures, drawing from state legal procedures, traditional forms of adjudication, and innovative practices.

The Decentralization of Law in Society

The decentralization of law in society occurs through the generation and execution of societal laws – at times, remaining within the circumscribed boundaries of state law, at other times, exceeding the remit of authority granted by the state. Societal legal organizations and actors resist state law by withdrawing from state courts, boycotting the use of state courts, socializing group members to internalize norms of the societal group as opposed to the state, and sanctioning and normalizing noncompliance with state law and legal procedures. Formal caste organizations and sect organizations are more likely to resist or challenge state laws and thus contribute to the process of the decentralization of law.

Some societal laws and actors transcend the parameters established by state law. The adjudication process shows societal legal actors stretching the boundaries of state law through a creative interpretation of the spirit of the law or creating new laws to fill the silences in state law. Litigants also shape their legal claims beyond the parameters of state law. The decentralization of law at the societal level also evinces how law is not only local but is imagined in spatially intersecting discourses of international human rights and cultural and folk myths and practices. Many women's organizations and religious organizations use the discourse of international human rights and cite legal developments in other countries to secure women's rights in personal laws in societal legal forums. Information about international legal trends and debates in other societies, especially in Islamic societies, also influences the manner in which law and rights are imagined and adjudicated. Different legal actors also construct different norms of conjugality and regulate these through lawmaking from below.

Characterizing the Legal Landscape: Legal Flexibility, Fragmentation, and Change

The constant tensions between the dynamic of the centralization and the decentralization of law presents a legal situation in which the content of personal laws on marriage and divorce is subject to multiple interpretations from a variety of different legal sources. As a result, the law itself is formulated and reformulated in a variety of settings, and is an outcome of negotiations between diverse actors. Similarly, the concept and meaning of the conjugal family is also an outcome of this process of negotiations. Given the situation, justice is uneven.

The following section relates how the dynamic of the centralization and the decentralization of law shapes conjugal families within the personal laws of Hindus and Muslims. Current discussions on personal laws view the formal legal system as a hermetically sealed legal entity; they do not consider the inconsistencies of law in the formal system and the interpenetration of formal and informal legal spheres and their impact on cultural pluralism and gender equality. I argue that contrary to prevailing analyses, the interdependent legal systems construct Hindu and Muslim families along similar, though not identical, lines.

Dispelling Myths about Contesting Areas in Hindu and Muslim Personal Laws: Not So Different After All?

The Indian state does not provide a norm for a standard family; it allows variation in family forms across religious and cultural groups. However, it establishes certain parameters to standardize the family according to each personal law. Drawing exclusively from the analysis of judicial precedents in state courts, many scholars point to areas of dissimilarities between the rights given to the Hindu conjugal family as opposed to those given to the Muslim family, and they point to the greater discrimination of Muslim women under Muslim Personal Law (Gangoli 2003; Jaising 2000; Narain 2001; Parashar 1992; Sunder Rajan 2003). In contrast, I argue that tensions between the centralization and the decentralization of law within formal and informal arenas has led to a particularized and fragmented legal situation in which the law itself is expanded and resisted, made and unmade, in diverse legal arenas. This process allows the presence of heterogeneous family forms in law, of which some forms may be the same in both communities. This study argues that in some instances, the dynamic of centralization and decentralization of law constructs the Hindu family along similar, though not identical, lines as the Muslim conjugal unit. To illustrate the impact of this dynamic interaction between laws and actors, let us look at the example of state and societal regulation of polygyny in Hindu and Muslim religious family laws, as its regulation has been a bone of contention between these two religious groups, the state, and feminists. The practice of polygyny is criminalized under Hindu law and sanctioned under Muslim law. Through the centralization of law, the Indian state has attempted to shape the Hindu family form, overriding societal practice that allowed polygyny among Hindus. But polygyny is difficult to prove in courts. Legal nonrecognition of second or third wives among Hindus works against the economic interests of these wives, although in some cases, the reformist judiciary has awarded them economic relief (see also Menski 2001, 139–230). Hence, the dynamic of the centralization and decentralization of law within the state legal system leads either to the acceptance or to the penalizing of polygyny on a case-by-case basis among Hindus. At the societal level, my data show that some Hindu castes that practiced polygyny have disallowed it by adapting to reforms within state law. Other castes allow conditional polygyny, and the data show that individual Hindus practice it routinely. Thus, the practice of polygyny exists among Hindus at the societal level. In the case of Muslims, the state law allows polygyny among Muslims and recognizes Muslim wives' right to maintenance (Menski 2001; Towards Equality 1975) Hence, there is regulation and acceptance but also restraint of the practice by state courts as judges enforce Muslim wives' economic rights stringently. Thus, Muslim women in polygynous marriages are offered greater protection in formal law. Similarly, although ultraorthodox segments of the Muslim community safeguard the right of Muslims to practice polygyny, and although individual Muslim men exercise their right to contract more than one marriage simultaneously, many individuals resist this practice, and my data also show that subgroups, such as the Ithna Ashari Khojas among Muslims, restrain polygyny. The data also show that village-based endogamous circles and customary authority also restrain their members from practicing polygyny.[22] Hence, the economic situation of bigamous wives among Hindus and Muslims shows more similarities than differences, and thus polygyny is accepted and restrained in various ways in state and societal forums among Hindus and Muslims.

Balancing Cultural Accommodation and Gender Justice

This section of the chapter argues how this dynamic can accommodate cultural communities and provide spaces for gender justice. I argue that a polycentered legal setting that divides the legal authority between the state, civil society actors, ethnic groups and organizations, as well as various societal actors offers multiple avenues of action to individual litigants on a case-by-case basis. A polycentered legal setting also leads to interactive opportunities between diverse state and nonstate legal actors within and across religious and sect cleavages, and thus offers avenues for cooperation, conflict, communication, and dialog within and between various religious groups, civil society, and the state. These

---

[22] For instance, I interviewed members of endogamous groups of Sunnis hailing from the Bharuch district in Gujarat, who also disallow polygyny, and the Qureshi *Jamaat*, collective, in Mumbai, who ban the practice as well.

processes generate a consensus on the nature, content, and direction of reforms within and between the state and society.

Normative Heterogeneity and Cultural Accommodation: Making and Unmaking Religious Communities, the Conjugal Family, and Gender

The Indian case of shared adjudication in personal laws evinces a legal setting characterized by dynamic interaction between various organizations, actors, and institutions. I draw from Cover's characterization of the nomos to discuss the implications of the interplay between legal actors and organizations. Cover has argued that both states and nonstates construct nomos, a normative universe wherein law and narratives are intertwined, and create, through interpretive commitment, a legal/moral world of obligation and reality from which the rest of the world is perceived. The nomos, an outcome of a collective process, is jurisgenerative. It is backed by violence and does not require a state (Cover 1983). In the Indian model, we see several heterogeneous, splintered, and internally contested normative spheres construct, maintain, and sanction identical, overlapping, or conflicting ideas about the nature of belonging in religious communities, the composition of the conjugal unit, and the construction of gender within the family. Thus, the statist understanding of family, marriage, and gender is challenged, reformulated, or adapted in different settings. This creates spaces to accommodate difference, which can be explored further.

Preventing the Ossification of the Boundaries of Religious Groups

Proponents of cultural accommodation, through the recognition of group rights for cultural communities, have grappled with the question that special group rights would lead to the ossification of community boundaries. It is argued that personal laws categorize, label, produce, and fix exclusive religious identities, establish the meaning of membership in a religious group, and distinguish the majority community from the minority community (Cohn 1987, 1996; Pandey 1990; Shodhan 2001).

The state project is partially successful. However, we also find that although each personal law establishes the criteria of group membership in a religious community, some subgroups are diverse and resilient enough to maintain certain distinct niches to define themselves in terms other than those conferred by the state. The data also show how these group members negotiate different identities in everyday legal activities and subvert state agendas in actual practice. In other words, the state confers ascriptive identities from above, but the meanings of membership in a religious group are contested, transformed, and adapted in multiple locations. Moreover, the data also show that there exist different bases of power within segments of state-fashioned religious communities. The law practiced on the ground is not interpreted or adjudicated only by religious authority as per doctrinal interpretations. Indeed, adjudication in religious law is undertaken by a number of social and secular actors, organizations, and institutions. Hence, the link between religious identity and religion-based personal laws is somewhat tenuous on the ground.

We see that group identity, in its everyday manifestations, is tied to local socioeconomic specificities and hierarchies through the intricate ties of caste and sect politics (see also Gilmartin 1988). At the same time, there are conceptions of broader, nationwide religious moral communities formed through the modality of governance by religious laws. However, locally anchored and particularistic religious identities do not always coalesce with the idea of an overarching religious, legal, and moral order. As a result, heterodox notions of local laws and what comprises "Hinduness" or "Muslimness" coexist in creative tensions with one another. This is another factor that prevents the homogenization of religious identities.

Accommodating Intragroup Difference and Facilitating Intersocietal Dialog

The heterogeneous legal setting allows factions and different societal actors to adjudicate in marriage and divorce; this policy provides smaller segments of sects and castes with autonomy in privileging and justifying their own authority. In doing so, the state accommodates dissident factions and individuals from *within* religio-cultural communities. However, this model also provides spaces for society-centered initiatives for intragroup accommodation. We see that internally differentiated religious groups also interact with other power bases within religious groups over questions of the content of laws and what constitutes legal authority. These interactions allow intracommunity differences and dialog across differential positions within religious groups.[23]

This policy also creates spaces in adjudicative processes for intercultural and intercommunity dialog *between* diverse sections of religious communities, the state, NGOs, and especially women's organizations. Hindu lawyers engage with Muslim NGOs, religious leaders, and sects in negotiating rights for the clients; similarly, Muslim lawyers discuss cases with caste and sect leaders from both Hindu and Muslim communities (see also Vatuk 2003). Likewise, religious organizations and charitable trusts work with litigants from different religious communities. Civil society organizations, especially women's organizations, engage with individual women litigants on everyday legal activities and also enter into dialog and/or confrontation with community groups, religious bodies, and caste/sect organizations and individual actors. They also run campaigns, initiate discussions with members of civil society, lobby the state for changes in the law and legal structures, and engage with all adjudicators on matters of personal laws. The clergy and caste and sect councils are more likely to be approached by members of their own religion, caste, or sect in the regulation of the family, but these legal actors and bodies engage with one another in cases involving intercaste, interreligious, and intersect marriages as well. Thus, these ongoing interactions

---

[23] For instance, I discuss the campaign around Muslim women's right to a *talaq e tafwid* that evens inequality in Islamic laws of divorce. This campaign has brought together large sections of Islamic bodies, actors, and organizations, as well as civil society organizations and women's wings of political parties, to experiment with internal reforms.

facilitate cross-community engagement in matters related to religious family laws, and allow cross-pollination and cross-fertilization of ideas about law, family, and marriage.

Making and Unmaking the Conjugal Family

The overlapping and convergent normative legal worlds aid in the creation of plural ideas about the family and gender in the legal sphere. For example, the data show that while the state law puts forth a definition of legitimate marriage and outlines conditions for divorce, societal institutions advocate a range of possible connubial unions contravening the state's definition of marriage. In such a landscape, the "conjugal family" is shaped and reshaped by the state, segments of religio-cultural communities, civil society, and especially women's organizations. Indeed, multiple forums and actors in themselves do not sufficiently challenge gender roles within the family, and many normative ideals about the nature of marriage and divorce fall short of imaging and constructing outlines of nonpatriarchal families and communities. However, under the shared adjudication model, plural images of the family offer individuals and communities a cultural "tool kit" (Swidler 1986) from which they selectively adapt aspects of the family and negotiate with other actors to validate these. Thus, the family largely continues to be imagined within patriarchal parameters, but feminists, certain castes, and sects and societal networks interject visions of a gender-just family or, minimally, alter gender-unequal beliefs and practices prevalent in notions of the family. Secondly, we also see that under certain conditions, aspects of regulation in the family among subaltern groups present images that are different from the dominant visions encoded in the state law and the laws of dominant castes. As a result, statist norming of conjugal life and the conferring of identities are negotiated, challenged, stabilized or destabilized, and reformulated in a variety of legal settings. The multicentered and interactive legal systems allow the transmission of different ideas of the family and identity across legal forums. These overlapping

THE SHARED ADJUDICATION MODEL

and fragmented normative worlds often enable litigants and members of society to imagine, fashion, discuss, choose, and dispute between diverse notions of the family, gender, and the meaning of religious affiliation within society. For instance, there are diverse opinions about *mehar*[24] under Muslim Personal Law. Some civic sources of authority are against fixing a high amount of *mehar* as the inability to repay the amount by the husband at the time of divorce harms the interests of wives who want speedy divorce.[25] Feminists have long argued that fixing a high amount of *mehar* protects women's rights in the family. A doorstep group of slum women in Mumbai, the Hamraz group,[26] has revisited this provision and argues that *mehar* should be thought of as a sum paid in two installments, concrete and speculative, in the sense that the fixed amount of *mehar*, set high, should be handed to the woman at the time of marriage, but the second part of the amount should be calculated on the basis of the woman's contribution to the family, incrementally calculated, and handed over to her at the time of divorce. Meanwhile a clergyman opined that the amount of *mehar* should be substantial and should increase tenfold at the time of divorce in cases where husbands divorce their wives "unilaterally, arbitrarily and without just cause."[27]

The argument requires further elaboration: I do not suggest that the mere presence of different adjudicative centers of authority increases pluralization and women's rights. I show instead that shared adjudication by ideologically diverse actors such as the state, civil society organizations including women's groups, religious organizations, and informal networks is a condition for the claim made here. Secondly, the presence of *civic* sources of authority needs additional emphasis, for ongoing

---

[24] *Mehar* is the sum of property that the wife is entitled to receive from her husband in consideration of marriage. It can be prompt (given to the woman at the time of marriage), or deferred (given to her upon death or divorce) (Mulla 1955, 249).

[25] Interview with Iqbal Maniar, Public Complaint Center, January 22, 2003.

[26] Interview with Khatoom Gafoor Sheikh, member, Hamraz Group, at the book release function organized by the Women's Research and Action Group, April 22, 2003, Mumbai.

[27] Interview with Maulana Qasim Ansari, Kurla (East), Mumbai, March 14, 2003.

microprocesses of adjudication can produce localized, fragmented change. However, sources of civic authority play an important role in broadening the scope of change by initiating or participating in broader discussions among and between lay, civil, religious, customary authorities, and the state, and thus, they help convert social change in localized, fragmented adjudicative processes into collective processes of change.

Hindu and Muslim Personal Laws and the Question of Gender Equality

The literature on personal laws argues that the legislature has bargained away women's rights in the personal laws of Hindus and Muslims to accommodate religious communities. Another argument is that Muslim women suffer more discrimination than do Hindu women in matters of personal laws (Narain 2001; Parashar 1992). Feminist scholars and activists have pointed out that women are denied formal and substantive equality under all personal and secular laws governing the family. Scholars working on the Uniform Civil Code debate have argued that Muslim women's economic rights are compromised by the community and the state. Many others also hold that the Muslim Women's (Protection of Rights on Divorce) Act 1986 denies equal economic rights to divorced Muslim women. Others argue that this Act is useful only when it is interpreted by pro-women judiciary (Gangoli 2003). Recent judicial developments suggest that the accommodation of the Muslim community in matters of maintenance of divorced Muslim women post–Shah Bano case is beneficial to Muslim women (Agnes 2002; Shankar 2003; Subramanian 2004). Given the interpenetration of legal forums, discussions of gender equality and justice require an understanding of the function and operation of both state and societal legal systems, and of the dynamic of centralization and decentralization of law. The data indicate that state courts at times have interpreted this law in favor of Muslim women, and that middle-class Muslim women also get relief under this provision. Indeed, I argue that the Muslim Women's (Protection of Rights on Divorce) Act 1986 grants more rights to Muslim women than Hindu women receive in the formal legal system, and the Act impacts societal negotiations for divorce as well, offering protection to women who receive compensation outside of courts. However, these reforms have not traveled into the society, as women's groups and other civil actors have been slow to realize the potential of the legal developments in the higher courts. The failure of feminist groups to widely publicize these reforms in state courts has limited the impact of legal reforms in the adjudication process in state courts. This limitation is also offset to some extent by lawyers who negotiate settlements for their clients based on this law in society. Other societal actors have sought to level gender inequality in laws of maintenance for Muslim women and bridge the gap between the rights of maintenance granted to Hindu and Muslim women. For instance, the All India Shia Personal Law Board recently approved a *nikahnama*[28] roughly modeled along the lines of maintenance given to women under Hindu law as well as under secular law, that grants a divorced Muslim woman the right to maintenance if she is incapable of supporting herself, or until she acquires the skills to maintain herself.[29] This example also shows the potential as well as the limitations of interdependent systems of law.

A fragmented legal landscape requires different ways of thinking and strategizing for gender justice in law. In the shared adjudication model, gender equality is an outcome of reform processes in state and societal legal forums. What is the nature of reforms in state law and courts? My study highlights that some legal developments, such as the enforcement of married women's right to the matrimonial home through the provision of Section 7(d) of the Family Courts Act 1984, have strengthened women's bargaining position in state law. Similarly, using criminal law of domestic violence to negotiate divorce and maintenance, to recover *stridhan* (property received by women at the time of marriage and as gifts postmarriage), and the more strict enforcement of maintenance laws has

---

[28] A Muslim marriage contract, in the context outlined here; it can also serve as a private contract that includes additional conditions on obligations of parties to marriage.
[29] Yoginder Sikand. 2010. "Tolerable Cruelty," *Tehelka* 7, no. 8 (February 27).

also helped individual women. In many instances, state law guarantees more economic rights to women since it can be legally enforced. What factors explain the state-led reforms from above? Subramanian has argued that judges in higher courts are more likely to back reforms when a legal issue is accompanied by legal mobilization and sufficient litigation, when these reforms do not contradict what judges believe to be group tradition, and when these changes match the judges' normative vision of the family (Subramanian 2008). However, the trickle-down of judicial precedent is only a partial explanation for changes at lower courts. The presence of capable, sympathetic, and proactive judges, interlinkages and interactions between legal personnel and civil society in the adjudication process in state courts, legal innovation and the use of social legislation by lawyers in lower courts, and the individual and collective agency of women explain the gradual shift toward gender equality in lower courts. The different ideas of conjugal family trickle up and percolate in court through individual cases as well as due to interactions between ethnic groups, legal personnel, and civil society, and reformist judges are able to enforce change at local levels. In the following section, I discuss the everyday efforts made by women's groups and women litigants in the adjudicative arenas, and suggest that both individually and collectively, this agency of women is an important factor that has pushed for reforms in state and societal arenas.

What factors determine change in societal laws? Competing ideas about diverse versions of conjugality and gender are prevalent in the society, and these remain available to societal actors who wish to reform the family. The diffusion and penetration of state-led reforms in society by lawyers and civil society, as well as informal and formal organizations, also drive change in society. In addition, we see that caste councils with links to political parties, unions, and social movements are more likely to support gender equality. Internal heterogeneity, competition, and fragmentation among societal legal actors and bodies remain important factors driving change. The religious organizations, seminaries, and clergy are also invited to participate in discussions around law reform by women's groups and civil society organizations, and are also subject to pressure to change from

THE SHARED ADJUDICATION MODEL

modernist and liberal sections, intellectuals, and scholars from within the community. These processes have been more pronounced among Muslims since the 1990s. Besides, barring the Hindu right and its women's wings, there is also a consensus among major political parties on the nature of minority accommodation and internal reforms of personal laws to counter the ideology and agenda of the Hindu right, and women's' wings of the left parties support these processes. Noninterference on the issue of the recognition of religious family laws is the official party strategy of the Samajwadi Party, but individual members of the Samajwadi Party are often approached by parties on the ground and they, at times, quietly support the reform processes on the ground. As a Samajwadi Party worker who is often approached to resolve disputes in cases of interreligious marriages on the ground mentioned: "I tell my friends, many of whom are clergy – hooliganism is not the only way to defeat the Shiv Sena. Another way to fight is not to play in their hands – if we are perceived to be anti-women, regressive, backward, we play into their hands. We have to be aggressive, be the first to support internal reforms, and show it to [the] whole of India how progressive we are."[30] In the shared adjudication model, individual and collective legal mobilization by women places their stories, voices, experiences, perspectives, and expectations on the agenda of various legal sources and bodies. These varied legal sources of authority, often in interaction with one another, respond creatively to legal mobilization by women, communicate with one another, and in doing so, they refashion the interiors of legal orders, and in many instances, rupture collusive patriarchies. Besides, the individual and collective agency of women, reflected in their participation in lawmaking on the ground and in everyday adjudication processes enables the shift toward gender equality from below. Drawing from Anthony Giddens' concept of agency, I recognize that agency is mediated by structure, and is subject to and constrained by the structure's limitations, but equally, structure is also reproduced or transformed by the agency (Giddens 1979); I elaborate on that process in this section.

[30] Interview with Haroun Musawalla, October 15, 2002, Mumbai.

Conceiving Agency and Its Limit

While women's groups have been mobilized around the question of law reform since the 1920s, the number of women's groups has steadily increased since the 1970s. The literature on personal laws highlights the agency of feminist groups in legislative processes (Gandhi and Shah 1992; Mukhopadhyay 1998; Parashar 1992); however, relatively little attention has been given to their participation and their vision of change in the adjudication process aside from their attempts at public-interest litigation to redress the inequality of the personal laws. I highlight neglected aspects of their agency.

The Agency of Litigant Women

The fragmented and polycentered legal sphere subjects individual litigants to pluralist influences and bargaining possibilities. The legally plural system creates a situation in which litigants and group members are law-navigating as well as lawmaking subjects (Chiba 2002). In the following section, I discuss both the individual and the collective agency of women litigants, and identify the incremental and transformative potential of the collective agency[31] of litigant women in influencing these normative legal spheres; I also outline the constraints faced by them. Secondly, the availability of multiple forums for seeking redress allows women litigants, especially those supported by family and social and affinal networks, to utilize the various permutations and combinations of different forums to maximize their rights in law. However, women litigants' choices are often hampered by structural and practical constraints such as the lack of information about law and legal options, the lack of resources to pursue legal forums, coercion from communities and the family, the lack of family and affinal networks, domestic violence, violence and threats from strongmen, and religious fundamentalism.

---

[31] I draw from Bina Agarwal's argument that the individual agency of women can bring about context-specific change. However, collective effort and organizing is required to affect structural change (Agarwal 1994; Schweickart 1995, 229–248).

Individual Women's Agency: Forum Switching and Gender Justice

The body of literature on the representation of women in law portrays them either as recipients of state laws or instrumentalist manipulators of law. Literature on personal laws positions women, especially Muslim women, as doubly oppressed: They are marginalized by fundamentalists from within their cultural group and face discrimination from majority communities in matters related to family laws (Mahajan 2005; Narain 2001). The literature suggests that women appropriate different legal constructions of gender roles in order to maximize their rights in law (Abu-Lughod 1990; Hirsch 1998; Moore 1998; Okely 1991; Tamanoi 1991). The literature on legal pluralism suggests that women litigants maximize their legal outcome by forum shopping and navigate different legal arenas simultaneously (Griffiths 1997). For instance, my data show that 121 out of 274 total respondents made use of, and thus intermixed, more than two legal forums. Given that women litigants' material rights within marriage are influenced by socio-legal representations as wives in state courts, women litigants appropriate or intermix forum-specific normative images of wifehood and use these strategically, often switching between the two normative worlds. In general, women traverse through different legal worlds, blend into the dominant ethos, and act out ideal-types without changing the dominant order.[32] This resistance and acting out an identity is meant to increase options rather than challenge or change the dominant ideal-types. Erin Moore has also persuasively argued that individual women in rural Rajasthan build strategic alliances with various actors and offer everyday forms of resistance and occasional public defiance to challenge hegemonic and collusive formal

---

[32] For instance, I discuss a case of Shilpa, a woman from the KVO caste who had successfully contested her husband's divorce petition by constructing the image of a docile, religious Hindu woman who is ready to reconcile with her husband despite severe domestic violence. The court prioritized the sacramental notion of Hindu marriage and ruled against her husband's divorce petition, even though the couple had been separated for sixteen years and had not lived together for more than three months. *SS* v. *RS*, Family Court Records, 2002, Mumbai.

and informal legal authorities (Moore 1994). Individual women's agency allows for conceptualizing fleeting moments of resistance for individual gains, but these do not allow space to visualize the transformative potential of women's agency within patriarchal legal structures. Neither does this conception of agency envisage challenging and changing patriarchal legal systems.

Structural Change through Individual Agency: Hindu and Muslim Women Litigants and Changes in Personal Laws

Lawmaking in the state-authored law takes place in two arenas: legislative and adjudicative. The state law regularizing marriage among Hindus was enacted in the 1950s,[33] and there have not been any significant changes in the law since. In a similar vein, Muslim Personal Law reforms have largely taken place in the adjudicative arena. Hence, women's contribution to lawmaking has largely been through the mobilization of law (Black 1973; Zemans 1982). In Hindu and Muslim personal laws, the agency of individual women through legal mobilization and the creative interpretation of law has yielded change incrementally through case-law developments in different state courts. Individual women litigants who approach the state court in cases of marriage and divorce bring in their experiences and versions of domestic roles within the family, and thus challenge the dominant versions in some instances.[34] State law does not grant divorce under the ground of "irretrievable breakdown of marriage," but state courts often have to rubberstamp customary divorces that take

---

[33] The law was amended in 1976, and the provision of divorce by mutual consent was introduced at that time.

[34] "Dispossession from the matrimonial home was the biggest hurdle faced by women litigants in case of marital violence or breakdown of marriage, as few women own immovable property in Indian society. Gradually, lawyers in the Family Court began to use a clause in the Family Courts Act 1984, which disallows the husband, who is in most cases the property owner, from dispossessing the wife. Women who fear being thrown out of the house can secure an injunction and thus be assured of shelter" (Interview with Veena Gowda, Lawyer, June 16, 2003, Mumbai).

THE SHARED ADJUDICATION MODEL 81

place within castes and groups that allow divorce on these grounds; these cases challenge the ideology of state law and procedures. The law on maintenance among Hindus and Muslims is based on the understanding of women as dependents, but cases of women group members who are viewed as primary earners within their customary laws throw different challenges to state law when their cases reach the courts.[35] These developments help envisage partial change in state structures.

Similarly, individual women's voices, experiences, and stories in millions of microadjudicative sites make public the nature and extent of gender injustice, and trigger change in societal laws and in the interiors of legal orders. A feminist working with the feminist group *Stree Mukti Sanghatana* shared: "As an activist I feel helpless and overwhelmed when women approach me with tales of horrific violence, injustice, and betrayal, but even if I cannot do much, I can at least listen to women, there is some solace in that.... They can come here and cry and rant and dissent; that is what feminist spaces are, even if there is no tangible outcome – always. But it is a process ... we feel helpless and then we brainstorm among ourselves, talk to lawyers, take the help of other organizations, and find solutions on [a] case-to-case basis. This process continues, and I find that we grow as we work...."[36] These opportunities of deliberation, communication, and confrontation in a heterogeneous legal field allow women to make claims that are informed by their own ideas of family, gender, and law; similarly, ideas of gender equality often form the basis of their legal expectations. Diverse legal actors and bodies, as their interlocutors, at times silence or ignore women's claims, but nevertheless, these remain

---

[35] "The court cannot recognise that we get more rights of maintenance in our caste laws.... Husbands know that the courts are easy – they approach them.... We work day and night and support the family and lose out when it comes to maintenance" (Interview with Pushpa Waghela, October 17, 2003, Mumbai). "State courts need to take cognizance of women's double labour in the family.... A woman might have supported her husband and earned and her contribution should be recognised when you calculate maintenance" (Interview with Vandana Nanaware, Social Worker, June 16, 2003, Mumbai).

[36] Interview with Kunda Kelkar, December 12, 2002, Mumbai.

under constant pressure to answer, to deliver, to compete, and also ultimately, to change. The active presence of state, certain religious sources of authority, and more importantly, civic legal orders and individuals in the pluralized legal field counter the gender-regressive steps of other legal forums. I show how different normative orders penetrate and communicate with one another and transform the interiorities of one another.

For instance, Muslim women's opposition to the male privilege of divorce and their demands for change has led to the popularization of forms of societal divorces based on Islamic laws (such as judicially arbitrated divorce, *faskh*), and delegated divorce by the clergy, various sects, and civic organizations. In addition, the difficulties faced by women, married under religious or secular laws, to recover their *stridhan* at the time of separation or divorce has led to a self-conscious effort by women's organizations to use Section 406 of the Indian Penal Code 1860,[37] mostly as a negotiating tool in police stations, to reclaim women's property.

Envisaging Legal Change through Collective Socio-Legal Processes

The legal change generated by individual interactions between litigants and legal actors is piecemeal and localized, but these reforms are carried

---

[37] Section 405 Indian Penal Code defines what is construed as criminal breach of trust: Whoever, being in any manner entrusted with property, or with any dominion over property, dishonestly misappropriates or converts to his own use that property, or dishonestly uses or disposes of that property in violation of any direction of law prescribing the mode in which such trust is to be discharged, or of any legal contract, express or implied, which he has made touching the discharge of such trust, or willfully suffers any other person so to do, commits "criminal breach of trust." Section 406 specifies punishment for criminal breach of trust: Whoever commits criminal breach of trust shall be punished with imprisonment of either description for a term which may extend to three years, or with fine, or with both. I discuss this in detail in Chapter 3. Based on the Supreme Court's judgment in *Pratibha Rani* v. *Suraj Kumar and Anr.* (1985) AIR 628, March 12, 1985, where the court held that a woman is the sole owner of *stridhan*, gifts given to her from husband or in-laws, as well as from her family and other sources, even during coverture. Women's organizations argue that husbands who do not return women's *stridhan*, or mortgage or damage it, should be charged under these laws in their negotiations with lawyers, religious or other legal bodies, and the police.

over to other locales by legal actors and bodies through public deliberation, street action, and consultations, and thus they are often collectivized. These strategies feed into ongoing collective processes of legal change among legal formations[38] and enable these legal formations to adopt, resist, challenge, or replicate these. Thus, the ongoing process challenging gender inequality and the cross-pollination of ideas through everyday processes of adjudication as well as collective processes of deliberation help construct a broad consensus around the need for reform and promote gender equality. For instance, the feminist groups, lawyers and feminist legal resource centers, and civil society organizations debated the content of gender-just family laws in Mumbai between 1993 and 1996. In 1996, the Mumbai-based Forum Against Oppression of Women organized a national meeting of women's groups, women's wings of the left political parties, cause lawyers, and academics participated in this meeting. In 1996, this issue was also debated in the Indian Association of Women's Studies Conference, and six different positions on law reform evolved during these discussions.[39] In a pluralized field, this encourages both the cross-pollination of ideas and strategies and competition between and among actors, and grants options to women.

Women's Transformative Collective Agency in Contouring the Socio-Legal Processes in Society

There are two ways in which the women's agency is exercised: (1) women participate in lawmaking exercises undertaken by their groups, and (2) women participate in the everyday practice of adjudication in society. Both of these processes allow spaces for change.

---

[38] In Chapter 5, I describe various intracaste and sect consultations among caste councils of the Meghwals, the KVOs, and the Ithna Ashari Khojas, as well as in religious bodies such as the All India Muslim Personal Law Board. I also describe street action initiated by local organizations such as the Public Complaint Centre, the clergy, and civil society organizations against corrupt clergymen who validate *muta* marriage.

[39] These are discussed and documented by Gangoli (1996) and Menon (1998).

In castes and sects that follow democratic procedures of lawmaking, collectives of women members as caste/sect members contribute to the shaping of the normative world created by caste/sect laws as they participate in the lawmaking process as litigators, adjudicators, and litigants; however, few elite women participate in lawmaking in sects or castes that are undemocratic in their manner of functioning.[40] The data show that in castes that favor democratic discussions on the issue of reform in laws, women form subcommittees to incorporate women's experiences, expectations, and concerns, and they have sought representation in the "constitutional committees" of the caste. In addition, women often play supportive roles to their women kin members by creating and sustaining a social world through their productive, reproductive, and cultural labor. However, their participation does not equal male participation in numbers, and they have less control over the final content of each draft of laws and legal decisions. In addition, the Indian Women's Movement has strategically utilized the opportunity to start a dialog with community elite at particular points in the shared adjudication model. For instance, in light of the Hindu right wing's rise in 1990s and after the demolition of Babri Masjid and the communal violence that followed, women's groups arrived at a consensus to pursue reforms through the process of dialog with various sections of Muslim community. Why have the clergy and conservative sections of the community been more open to these processes? Women's organizations have been vocal and visible in their struggles against communal violence and communalism, and their advocacy of justice for women victims of communal violence, criticism of antiterror laws targeting minorities, and their efforts at providing relief and rehabilitation to victims of communal violence in Gujarat and in Mumbai have increased their credibility with community organizations.

---

[40] For instance, among Meghwals, women members have formed special subcommittees to incorporate women's experiences, expectations, and concerns, and have sought representation in the "constitutional committees" of the caste since the 1970s. The caste forum organizes law review committees and holds biyearly meetings to discuss their legal concerns; many Meghwal women participate in these processes. In contrast, very few women have participated in these processes among Khola Shia Ithna Asharis.

And we see that networks of Muslim women and secular women's groups like Hakk e Niswaan and the Muslim Women's Rights Network engage the All India Muslim Personal Law Board as well as diverse sections of the Muslim community, such as the Jamiaat e Ulema e Maharashtra and other organizations in the law reform process.

Both secular and Muslim women's organizations establish study classes to read and interpret the Quran and the Hadith, and enter into dialog with the clergy and religious organizations. Secular and other Muslim women's organizations also discuss the issues and challenges around reforms of Muslim Personal Law with other organizations and women's groups across the country. There is also the widespread movement around encoding greater rights for Muslim women in *nikahnama*, the marriage contract specifying the rights and duties of the parties, among Muslims, and numerous women participate in such movements that have the potential to bring about structural changes in the community. These movements are supported by the broader Indian Women's Movement and some international women's organizations.

Women's Transformative Collective Agency: Everyday Processes of Adjudication and Visions of Change

The transformative potential of the women's collective agency is realized in their interaction with feminist groups and civic orders in matters of regulation of personal laws. Individual women litigants as well as informal groups of women across castes and sects at times engage feminist groups in intracaste lawmaking and adjudication processes. Individual women litigants as well as informal groups of Meghwal women engage feminist groups and activists from diverse caste and religious backgrounds as resource persons in intracaste lawmaking and adjudication processes. For instance, Lalitbhai Waghela, chair of the 1996 constitution committee of the Meghwals, a caste group in Mumbai, expressed:

> It has been the tradition of our caste to invite prominent intellectuals, social workers, and politicians to preside over discussions on

law reforms within the caste. In the past ten years, our women caste members have become more vocal and have insisted in including women's groups in these processes. Earlier, in [the] 1950s and 1960s, left-of-the-centre academicians (like the late Prof. A. R. Desai, a well known sociologist) used to hold discussions within the caste, we also had links with the Communist Party of India. Now our women members insist on inviting feminist leftists like Sugandhi Francis (an activist of the All India Democratic Women's Association, the women's wing of the Communist Party of India [M]). They want to broaden the discussion and talk about the family – marriage and divorce, bride-price, and death rites – not only class solidarity, and we have to be open to these demands.[41]

Feminist groups also function as watchdogs and check the abuse of authority by state officials as well as caste members. Feminist groups and activists from diverse religious and caste backgrounds are invited as resource persons to discuss developments on family laws. They are also asked to play facilitative tasks as mediators in family disputes within the caste. This allows an ongoing dialog between caste officials, caste members, and feminists on the structure of marriage and divorce in caste laws, and on the status of women within the family. Cover has argued that a legal/moral world functions around *alterity*, the ideal of what is other than the case, thus creating tensions between reality and the vision contained in the counterfactual possibility. The legal/moral world contains the present and the imagined alternative combined with the application of the human will (Cover 1983, 9). These feminist groups enter into discussions, bringing in their vision of the family that is egalitarian, gender-just, and free of violence and exploitation, and they add this to the normative repertoire available to group members. For instance, feminists consistently raise the issue of redefining the family and of extending rights to include lesbian, gay, and transsexual/transgender persons and families in many forums (see "Visions of Gender Just Realities," FAOW, 1996). The pluralizing of caste/sect worlds by other actors also challenges patriarchal

---

[41] Interview with Lalitbhai Waghela, December 5, 2002, Mumbai.

THE SHARED ADJUDICATION MODEL 87

trends in imagining gender roles. Even though this may not transform the patriarchal control of ethnic organizations and laws, this interaction interjects heterogeneous ideas of different values in family life and helps bring about partial change.

Secondly, groups and organizations of individual women engage with the clergy and caste and sect authority in matters of personal laws, and use a bundle of strategies. At times, they hold public demonstrations,[42] and at other times, street action using humor to register their protest. For example, a doorstep court (a women's informal group) working in a slum in Mumbai was approached by a Muslim woman who had received a notice of nonarbitrated and unilateral divorce, *talaq ul biddat*,[43] from her husband through a *qazi*, a Muslim clergyman. Unwilling to accept the husband's divorce, she came to the group. The group members collected local women of the area and a large group went to the same *qazi*. Alarmed at seeing the large contingent of women, he asked them the reason for their visit. The women replied that they had approached him to perform *nikah*, marriage. Not sighting a man among the crowd, the *qazi* asked: "Where is the man? How can I perform a marriage without a man?" They answered: "When you can give divorce, *talaq*, in absence of a woman, why can't you perform a *nikah*, marriage, in absence of a man?"[44]

---

[42] To cite just one example, the secular and Muslim women's groups in Mumbai organized a public demonstration to protests against a *fatwa* issued by a clergyman in Mumbai asking them not to indulge in immoral activities such as watching TV. Interview with Hasina Khan, Mumbai, January 17, 2003. The women's groups recently held protests-cum-celebrations in favor of the Delhi High Court's decision to decriminalize homosexuality in Indian law, and they have been marking the anniversary of this day every year as they await the decision of the Supreme Court around this issue (http://queer-azaadi.wordpress.com).

[43] *Talaq ul bidaat* consists of three pronouncements (of divorce) made during a single *tuhr* in one sentence, or a single pronouncement made during a *tuhr*, clearly indicating an intention to dissolve the marriage irrevocably (Mulla 1955, 267). Feminists have pointed out that this law harms the interests of Muslim wives.

[44] Incident narrated by Khatoom Gafoor Sheikh, member, Hamraz group, at the Annual Meeting to Discuss Law Reform in Muslim Personal Law, organized by Awaz e Niswan, July 25, 2003, Mumbai.

The Question of Gender Equality in the Shared Adjudication Model

In family law, gender equality can be defined as formal equality under the law – both men and women have equal access to family law, and equal rights under the law. However, formal equality under the law often does not produce gender equality on the ground (Okin 1989). In cases where formal equality is ratified in laws governing marriage and divorce, women are often poorer after divorce and share a disproportionate amount of burden in terms of child care. Similarly, Fineman discusses the conceptual categories underpinning the division of matrimonial property in divorce laws in the United States, and suggests that the shift from *need* to *contribution* has played into the hands of antifeminist lobbies, and that spurious equality has replaced need-based dependency. She argues that gender equality in divorce laws cannot be achieved under conditions of pervasive gender inequality in society, and that rather than asking for symbolic equality, feminists need to recognize women's role and labor in the family and take these into account while reforming divorce laws (Fineman 1991). Thus, in most cases, including in India, conceptions of gender equality in law have to take into account the prevailing inequality in social relations, and consider structural factors including the sexual division of labor within the family, sexual norms, and mores in society that give men more sexual freedom than women, gender constitution during socialization, and women's unequal access to political representation, education, employment, and property.

Within this context, how does the shared adjudication model shape gender equality in Hindu and Muslim family laws? In the Indian case, the debate has stagnated around the idea that cultural rights have constrained gender equality, but if we consider the breadth of the adjudicative terrain, we see a more complex reality in which we find that formal and substantive legal equality is often unpredictable and contingent in the sense that more often than not, gender equality is an outcome of individual and collective efforts. Gender equality here is incremental, contingent, and negotiated. Gender equality is not only visualized as a right fixed in law, but is a product of, implicated into, and invoked in a multitude of adjudicative processes. It is also uneven; whereas state laws grant more rights in some instances, in other instances, societal laws are more equal than state laws, and the foundational premises of multiple legal orders differ.

We also find that while this model disperses adjudicative power and challenges the hegemonic dominance of either the state or societal legal agents, there is also a discernible structural movement toward incremental gender equality in state and societal laws in adjudication processes. For this model allows, in millions of microadjudicative sites, the sharing of women's experiences and voices, challenging gender inequality, and imagining alternate and multiple ways of doing families. Change through individual efforts is often slow and localized, but the ground that it prepares paves the way for wider change through collective processes. These individual processes are collectivized by formal organizations, religious bodies, networks, and individuals, and gender equality is not fixed in law, but is open to recurrent revision and yet results in structural change. In this model, we also see that gender equality here is advanced when state-led reforms from above travel into societal arenas and coexist with societal reforms from below. In addition, this model allows deliberation, but also bargaining, accommodation, and alliance building, as well as confrontation between different actors and forums, and spurs legal innovation on the ground. The bundle of strategies used by individual and groups in multiple forums also make some legal forums accountable and amenable to change, and this in turn prepares the ground for structural change. These interactions between individual and collectives of women and other state and nonstate actors, forums, and courts lay the foundation for incremental changes in state and societal law, and a move, steadily, slowly, and from below, toward formal and substantive gender equality.

Conclusion

This book addresses the question of how states accommodate the demands of religio-cultural groups to regulate the family, and how they take steps to ensure gender equality within these groups. It analyzes the Indian model of legal pluralism in the governance of marriage and divorce under Hindu and Muslim personal laws. The Indian model of legal pluralism allows adjudicative power sharing between the state and various societal actors and organizations in the governance of marriage and divorce.

Using state-society relations as the analytical framework, this book examines the interaction between state and nonstate laws and adjudicative authorities in multiple sites of adjudication in the governance of marriage and divorce within the personal laws of Hindus and Muslims. Whereas the state law and courts normalize the family in different personal laws, interactions between state and nonstate legal actors in microadjudicative sites demonstrate that the statist construction of the conjugal family and of gender are affirmed, challenged, or destabilized in a variety of legal locales. I argue for an open-ended construction of state-society relations in which state and societal legal actors and organizations are engaged in conflicts and cooperation, as well as in communications and negotiations over the nature and content of laws regulating the conjugal family.

I argue that state and nonstate sources of legal authority construct internally contested and heterogeneous notions of the conjugal family, gender relations, and religious membership, and they transmit them across legal spheres. The coexistence of plural images of the family and of gender in law provides spaces for accommodation of intragroup factions, facilitates intersocietal interactions, and supports women's agency in matters of personal laws. The interactions between individual and collectives of women and other state and nonstate actors lay the foundation for incremental changes in law, and a move, eventually and from below, toward formal and substantive gender equality. Thus, I argue that the shared adjudication model creates the dynamic of centralization and decentralization of law, and this dynamic allows spaces to balance cultural accommodation and gender equality.

3 State Law and the Adjudication Process

Marriage, Divorce, and the Conjugal Family in Hindu and Muslim Personal Laws

Introduction

Whereas many academic discourses and popular debates pitt Hindu and Muslim laws as opposite and dissimilar to one another, this chapter, based on the analyses of trends in matrimonial disputes in Hindu and Muslim personal laws, demonstrates that there are many commonalities between judicial bargaining, interpretation, and treatment of cases filed under distinct provisions of Hindu or Muslim religious laws. Indeed, the Hindu and Muslim conjugal families are formed along similar, though not identical lines. In addition, whereas feminist and legal scholars have long assumed that Muslim Personal Law is detrimental to women's interests in part because of the Shah Bano case and the introduction of the Muslim Women's (Protection of Rights on Divorce) Act 1986, we find here that the data do not demonstrate a wide variation between rights accorded to Hindu and Muslim women; in fact, divorced Muslim women have more rights than divorced Hindu women in some instances.

This chapter examines the adjudication process in Hindu and Muslim personal laws in state law and courts, analyzes the substantive and procedural aspects of matrimonial provisions in Hindu and Muslim personal laws, and gives an overview of the relevant trends in matrimonial disputes. It discusses the function of the Family Court in Mumbai, traces the interaction between state and society within the formal legal system, and assesses its impact on the construction of the conjugal family and gender equality in state law.

The Functioning of the Family Court

The Family Courts Act 1984 was enacted at the federal level to facilitate expedious resolution of family disputes,[1] and at present, there are sixty-one courts in India.[2] Operational since October 1989, the Bombay Family Court, a complex housing seven courts, adjudicates in matrimonial disputes filed under different personal laws.[3] Jurisdiction of the Family Court is fragmented.[4] In specific matrimonial matters, the Family Court can exercise jurisdiction over any civil or district or metropolitan magistrates' court.[5] The court attempts to create a user-friendly environment. It is housed in a multistory complex – each floor houses a courtroom, offices of the judges and the social workers, a waiting area for litigants; other offices such as the record room, registrar's offices, the bar room, the library, and a canteen are located on different floors. To make the court more user-friendly, judges have also suggested that a daycare center[6] be set up on the premises along with a prelitigation center to orient litigants and familiarize them with court procedure,[7] though these measures have not been implemented.[8]

---

[1] The Family Courts Act 1984, Introduction.
[2] See http://www.lawmin.nic.in (accessed August 9, 2010).
[3] Family Courts Act 1984(3), s. 7. The court determines cases of divorce, annulment, restitution of conjugal rights, injunction in matrimonial property disputes, custody and access, and maintenance under Section 125 CrPC, as well as under the Hindu Adoption and Maintenance Act 1956.
[4] For instance, the Family Court adjudicates in matters related to divorce and maintenance under Section 125 CrPC, but it does not adjudicate in cases under the Muslim Women's (Protection of Rights on Divorce) Act 1986. These are heard in Metropolitan Magistrates' Courts. The Family Court determines cases of maintenance under Section 125 CrPC, but cases of domestic violence do not fall under its purview.
[5] See the Family Courts Act 1984(3), s. 7(a), (b): Jurisdiction.
[6] See Judge S. P. Shetye's correspondence with the Additional Registrar, Bombay High Court, no. A (SPI) 3215/96/2177/96.
[7] See Judge B. L. Joshi's note to the Additional Registrar, Bombay High Court, subs. 24(b), Agenda of the First Conference of the Family Court Judges and Counsellors, 1994.
[8] See Office Note submitted by B. J. Joshi, Judge, Bombay Family Court, October 2, 1994.

STATE LAW AND THE ADJUDICATION PROCESS 93

The Family Court provides speedy justice in an informal setting, "dispenses justice to the weaker sections and oppressed groups of the society at lower costs,"[9] exempts women litigants from payment of court fees,[10] and arranges legal aid. Aside from state agencies,[11] legal centers such as Majlis and Human Rights Law Network provide legal aid, and women's groups such as Stree Mukti Sanghatana and community organizations offer legal aid; in addition, cause lawyers in the Family Court often take up women's cases for nominal fees or for free. Whereas corruption is seen to be common in state courts in India, corruption levels in the Family Court are perceived to be much lower than other courts, though between 2003 and 2005, one of the judges was "recalled" after allegations of corruption.[12] Litigants also spoke of unviable financial expenditure billed by lawyers, sexual harassment, and pointed to violations of legal aid norms by some lawyers.[13] The court encourages self-representation by litigants and is readily accessible to litigants.[14] My data show that out of 120 litigants interviewed, 19 had chosen to represent themselves, 63 had represented themselves at least once, and 38 had legal representatives during the entire duration of the court process.[15]

[9] See Judge BL Joshi, Communication to the Additional Registrar, High Court. no. A (SPI) 3215/96/2177/96.
[10] See the article by Swati Deshpande, "HC Upholds Court Fee Waivers for Women in Some Types of Cases." *Times of India* (Mumbai), March 29, 2002. In a notification dated October 1, 1994, the Government of Maharashtra remitted the fees payable by women litigants in cases filed in any civil, criminal, or family courts under cases filed under categories such as maintenance, property, and domestic violence.
[11] The Maharashtra State Commission for Women (*Mahila Ayog*) provides legal advice and refers the parties to obtain legal aid from Bruhan Mumbai Legal Aid and Advice Cell.
[12] Personal Communication with Flavia Agnes, lawyer, August 21, 2005.
[13] Nita, a litigant, shared: "My (legal aid) lawyer did not ask me for a fee but asked me to buy him legal books – those are so expensive – where was I going to get the money to buy books worth 2,000 to 5,000 rupees?" (interview with DP, February 16, 2003, Mumbai). However, most litigants shared that the Family Court was "cleaner [less corrupt] than other courts." Interviews with HM, June 22, 2003; PW, November 9, 2002; PS, February 5, 2003, Mumbai.
[14] See also The Family Courts Act 1984 Statement of Objects and Reasons, Section 2(e), (g).
[15] In general, middle-class women are less likely to fight their own cases as they lack the legal expertise required to negotiate the distribution of property in contested cases.

The Family Courts Act 1984 advocates a consensus-based conciliatory approach to matrimonial disputes.[16] The legal procedure followed by the court is a combination of informal and adversarial legal procedures. Interspousal conciliation is institutionalized in the Family Court.[17] If the conciliation is ineffectual, a trial takes place before the judge to dispose of the competing claims of the parties. The court has the discretion to postpone the proceedings in order to enable the parties to reconcile. Records of the court are confidential.

Professional social workers attached to the court provide counseling as well as conciliatory and, at times, investigative services.[18] Some of them maintain close ties to schools of social work such as the Tata Institute of Social Sciences and College of Social Work at Nirmala Niketan in Mumbai, and with other social workers working with women's groups in Mumbai.[19]

> Women holding full-time jobs find it difficult to find the time to fight their own cases, and women with no education or primary-level education lack the confidence to navigate the system. However, women with high school-level education and above, and who hold part-time jobs, are more likely to represent themselves.

[16] The Family Courts Act 1984(4), s. 9(1), (2): It is the duty of the Family Court to make efforts for settlement: (1) In every suit or proceeding, endeavor shall be made by the Family Court in the first instance, where it is possible to do so consistent with the nature and circumstances of the case, to assist and persuade the parties in arriving at a settlement in respect of the subject-matter of the suit or proceeding and for this purpose a Family Court may, subject to any rules made by the High Court, follow such procedure as it may deem fit. (2) If, in any suit or proceeding, at any stage, it appears to the Family Court that there is a reasonable possibility of a settlement between the parties, the Family Court may adjourn the proceedings for such period as it thinks fit to enable attempts to be made to effect such a settlement.

[17] Parties are required to attend predivorce, individual, and couple counseling. Social workers also work out consent terms in defended divorces and other matters (interview with Madhvi Desai, Chief Counsellor, Family Court, June 17, 2003, Mumbai).

[18] Family Courts Act 1984(2), s. 6: The Family Court, in consultation with the High Court, can determine the institutionalization of social workers in the system and can also invite prominent citizens and members of social welfare organizations to assist the Court.

[19] One of the judges in the Family Court, Judge B.L. Parikh, is a trained social worker. Social workers trained at these schools share that in some cases, judges of the lower courts and social workers at the Family Court cross-check individual case details with them, and they are also called upon as key witnesses: "We often meet at training programmes or workshops organized by the Tata Institute of Social Sciences. Many of

STATE LAW AND THE ADJUDICATION PROCESS

Table 3.1. *Number of Cases Filed in the Family Court, Mumbai (1989–2001)*

Year	Matrimonial Remedies[a]	Injunctions (Property Matters)	Maintenance Suits	Custody and Access	Maintenance under Criminal Law, Section 125, CrPC	Total Cases[b] (Excluding Revision Orders)
1989	0463	NA	NA	NA	0139	–
1990	1845	NA	NA	NA	0663	–
1991	1839	105	042	059	0804	2849
1992	2035	104	024	073	1280	3516
1993	2184	081	091	053	1230	3639
1994	2051	067	047	046	1186	3397
1995	2055	072	167	056	1106	3456
1996	2153	094	229	053	0994	3523
1997	2234	086	235	045	0927	3527
1998	2285	056	250	033	0697	3321
1999	2936	108	293	073	1080	4490
2000	2888	088	303	144	909	4332
2001	3350	112	410	114	603	4589

Notes:
[a] The data is complied by the Family Court, Mumbai. Matrimonial remedies include cases filed under nullity of marriage, validity of marriage, divorce, judicial separation, and restitution of conjugal rights. This data include cases *across religious lines* as well as cases filed under the Special Marriage Act 1954.
[b] The data exclude revision orders, execution of decrees, and applications to recover arrears of maintenance.
Source: Compiled from Family Court Records, Mumbai, 2002.

Hence, the legal system and societal influences operate on one another within the formal legal system, leading to a diffusal of law within state courts.

An Overview of Cases Filed in the Family Court

Table 3.1 above indicates the number and type of cases filed in Family Court under religious personal laws as well as under the secular law, the Special Marriage Act 1954.

> these exchanges are also informal – some of these social workers have been our batch mates at the school of social work." Interview with Pratibha Jagtap, Special Cell for Women, April 13, 2003. Mumbai.

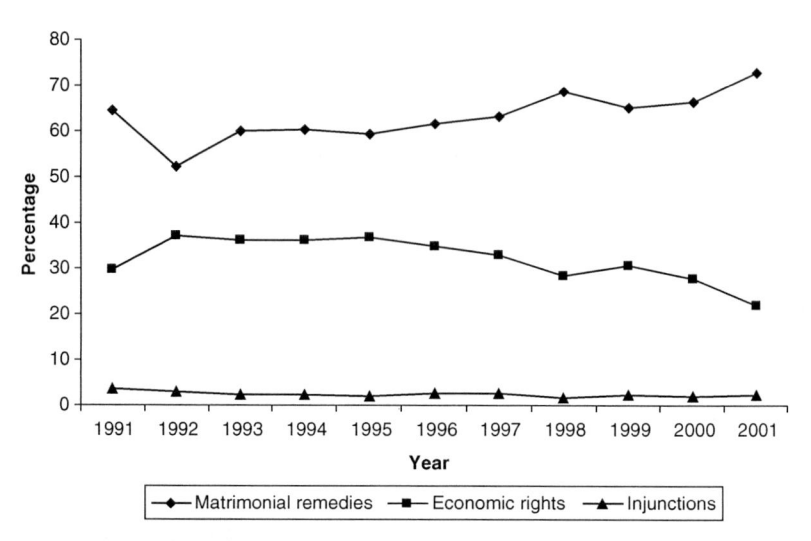

Figure 3.1. Comparison of percentages of cases filed under matrimonial remedies, cases filed under civil and criminal laws of maintenance for economic rights, and injunctions for suits.[20]

Cases from different courts were transferred to the newly functional Family Court during the period 1989–1990. The number of cases filed each year under matrimonial remedies shows a marginal increase between 1990 and 1999. The only significant increase is after 1999. However, this is due to procedural reasons, as cases previously filed in the High Court (such as cases filed under the Dissolution of Muslim Marriages Act 1939) were transferred to the Family Court in this year. The number of maintenance suits has jumped dramatically since 1995; this jump reflects a consistent trend. The favorable use of these provisions by women litigants can lead to an increased intake of these cases. The number of cases filed under Section 125 CrPC tends to fluctuate. However, it is difficult to arrive at definite conclusions because cases under this section are also filed in the Metropolitan Magistrates' Courts in Mumbai.

The data in Figure 3.1 reveal that a majority of respondents who approach the court seek help for matrimonial remedies. The number of cases filed exclusively for economic rights comprise one-third of the sample.

[20] Compiled from Family Court Records, Mumbai, 2002.

Table 3.2. *Total Number of Cases Filed and Disposed in the Family Court, Mumbai (1990–2001)*

Year	New Cases[a]	Disposed
1990	2748[b]	2227
1991	3772	4137
1992	4471	3894
1993	4143	4056
1994	3874	3972
1995	3893	5368
1996	4028	3820
1997	4085	5387
1998	3923	5403
1999	5223	5044
2000[c]	4332	3657
2001[d]	4589	3761

Notes:
[a] This includes revision orders as well as orders for execution of decrees and collection of arrears.
[b] The Family Court was established in 1989; the process of transferring cases from other trial courts had begun in 1989, but not all types of cases were transferred to the Family Court in 1990. The data exclude maintenance suits or proceedings related to property matters as well as custody and access matters.
[c] The figures showing revision orders as well as orders for execution of decrees and the collection of arrears are not available for the year 2000.
[d] Ibid.
Source: Compiled from Family Court Records, Mumbai, 2002.

The data show that limited economic rights granted to parties at the termination of marriage also account for the lower rates of legal mobilization of state courts for economic relief. These processes are elaborated in the following section.

The Disposal of Cases in the Family Court

The court follows an informal and confidential procedure and ensures the speedy disposal of cases, as evidenced by the data in Table 3.2 above.

98 ADJUDICATION IN RELIGIOUS FAMILY LAWS

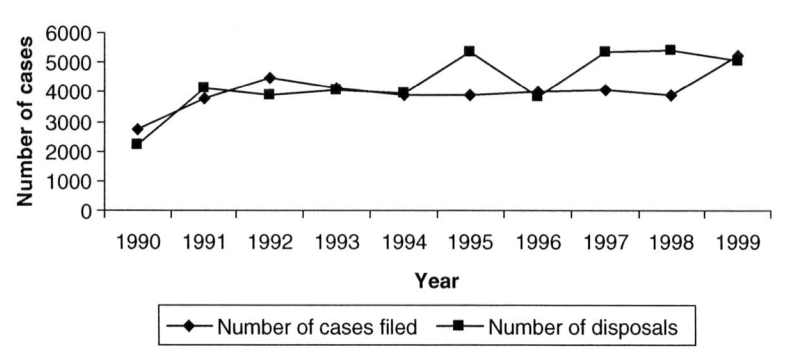

Figure 3.2. Number of cases filed and disposed (1990–1999).
Source: Compiled from Family Court Records, Mumbai, 2002.

The Bombay Family Court's efficiency is seen as positive in the Indian context where the procedure of justice is excessively lengthy, cumbersome, and inefficient; courts also grapple with an immense backlog of cases (Chodosh 2004; Galanter and Krishnan 2003).

The Bombay High Court and Family Courts in Maharashtra have evolved mechanisms to monitor the backlog of cases in order to provide speedy and effective relief; a large number of litigants find it effective and beneficial. For instance, since 1991, the Family Courts have been asked to submit quarterly reports on the disposal of cases,[21] and principal judges "are expected to offer an explanation...for inadequate disposal of cases... by their judicial officers."[22] The data in Figure 3.2 show that the number of disposals is quite high in cases filed between 1993 and 1999. The rate of disposals has been lower in cases between 1999 and 2001 due to a sudden increase of the case load in 1999, as cases under the Dissolution of Muslim Marriages Act 1939 were transferred from the High Court to the Family Court during that year in order to make the formal legal system more accessible to all sections of society.

---

[21] Judges are asked to dispose more than seventy cases per month. See communications between principal judges of Family Courts and the Additional Registrar (Inspection) Bombay High Court letter, August 19, 1991, no. FC/PJ/65/1991; May 26, 1992, no. A (SPl.) 03/10/90/1233/92; no. FC/PJ/967/1992; Circular 26/03/96. A (SPl.) 3215/96/760/96.

[22] See the correspondence between N. V. Dabholkar, Additional Registrar (Inspection), High Court (Appellate Side) and Principal Judge, Family Court, no. A. (SPl.) 3215/98/1571/96.

It is argued that the "technocratic model of justice" (Heydebrand and Seron 1990) that emphasizes informal, efficient, and speedy relief can compromise democratic values of justice such as victims' rights, judicial impartiality, and the due process of law (Fiss 1983, 1984; Heydebrand and Seron 1990; Resnik 2003). Although the model adopted by the Bombay Family Court is not always incompatible with justice, it evokes mixed responses in some litigants and judges. For instance, judges have raised the issue of evolving uniform norms to decide on cases where the civil cases are intertwined with criminal cases.[23] Meanwhile, in most cases, women litigants respond favorably to the efficient and cost-effective service of the Family Court. A few women litigants, in contrast, argue that being rushed into settlement denies them justice, as the retention of court is in itself a strategy used by clients.[24] To illustrate, a petitioner husband had filed for divorce. In response, the wife had contested the divorce, sought an injunction against the transfer or sale of the matrimonial house, and sought custody of the children. The wife was suspended from her work because of absenteeism due to domestic violence, but she had sought to challenge the suspension in the labor court; the case had been pending in the labor court for three years at the time of the interview. The judge and social worker at the Family Court, who wished to facilitate the settlement, were "advising" her to accept the partition of the matrimonial home and to forego permanent alimony. The wife was reluctant because the matrimonial home had been built from her savings, and she had supported her husband when he was in school studying for an engineering degree. The wife wished to know of the outcome of

---

[23] "Should the Family Court postpone divorce decisions until criminal proceedings in cases filed under Section 498(A) IPC, the law on domestic violence, are over?" was the question raised by Judge Sri S. M. D. Joshi. See Circular, July 19, 1996, no. A (SPl.) 3215/96/2177/96. Lawyers also concur that simultaneous legislation in civil and criminal matters can at times adversely impact women's cases: "This issue is critical since Section 498(A) allows only married women to file criminal charges of domestic violence against their husbands or members of his family. If the parties file for divorce in the Family Court and have a parallel legal case under Section 498(A) IPC going on in the Metropolitan Magistrates' Court, the criminal case against the husband can be dropped if the parties are legally divorced in the Family Court." Interview with Yasmin Sheikh, lawyer, June 22, 2003, Mumbai.

[24] Interview with SM, June 7, 2003, Mumbai.

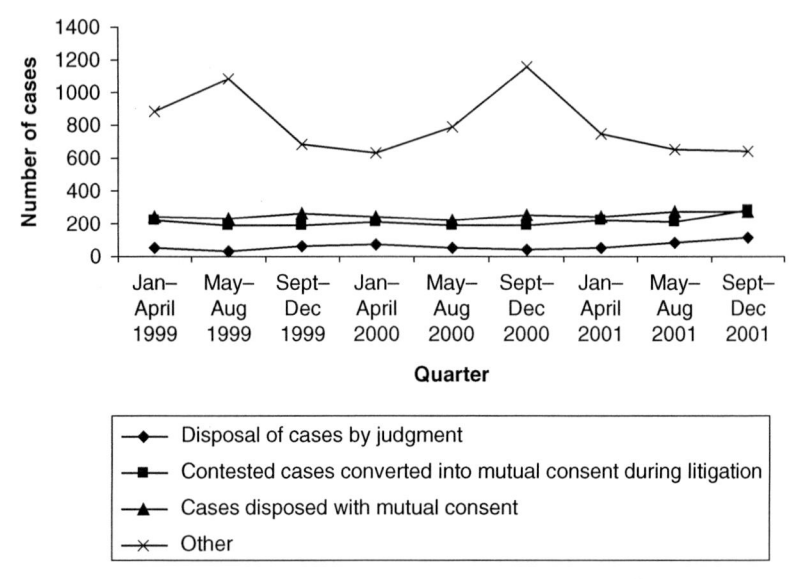

Figure 3.3. The nature of disposal of cases in Family Court.[25]

her case in the labor court before agreeing to this solution, as her employment status was a key factor in her considerations. "They [the judge and the social worker] tell me that the case has languished in court for five years ... but if I accept their deal, how will I feed my daughters?"[26]

The Nature of Justice in the Family Court: Consensual Rather than Adversarial?

Figure 3.3 indicates the degree of informalization of the court procedure in the Family Court. The procedure in the Family Court prioritizes the reconciliation and resolution of cases through consensus, and many women litigants have reacted unfavorably to these procedures.[27] There

---

[25] Compiled from Family Court Records, Mumbai, 2002.
[26] Interview with MM, May 3, 2003, Mumbai.
[27] A woman had filed for divorce after a severe episode of domestic violence. "His beatings led to my miscarriage and I went to court for divorce. In the first meeting, the social worker asked me if I wanted reconciliation! Would I want to reconcile with a murderer?" (interview with HM, June 22, 2003, Mumbai). Similar details were shared by other litigants (interview with SM, June 7, 2003, Mumbai).

STATE LAW AND THE ADJUDICATION PROCESS

is also an ongoing dialog between court personnel, social workers, and judges at the Family Court on the norms of disposal of cases. For instance, while the High Court instructs that " ... the Family Court has to see that reconciliation is brought about and that such disposals are balanced with contested disposals,"[28] the Family Court counselors follow the direction of the High Court but also discuss that " ... in a cosmopolitan city like Bombay, the spouses from various communities with different backgrounds approach the Family Court. In some couples it is very difficult to bring about reconciliation."[29]

Figure 3.3 also shows that judicial decisions through an adversarial procedure make up less than one-tenth of the total cases that are disposed. About one-fifth of the cases are disposed of through mutual consent as they are also filed under mutual consent, and the Family Court serves as an administrative body in deciding these cases. About one-fifth of cases are "converted" into mutual consent cases through the efforts of judges, lawyers, and social workers during the trial. The informalization of adversarial procedures affects more vulnerable litigants, especially women, because "the court deviates from application of substantive law and functions as an informal social work bureau."[30] Because the perceptions of social workers and judges play a large role in negotiation settlements in cases, in some cases, their biases have harmed the interests of several women litigants.[31] In one case, a husband who had defaulted on payment of maintenance complained to the social worker that his wife had come to the court accompanied by a prostitute (the social worker was persuaded because the wife was accompanied by a woman who was wearing "loud" jewelry and heavy makeup). Both the judge and the social worker reprimanded the woman litigant and not the husband, who had defaulted on his payment, despite the woman's protests. The lawyer

---

[28] See letter from the Addl. Registrar, Inspection, Bombay High Court, Dt. 04/05/90, A (SPl.) 3101/90.
[29] Circular dated July 29, 1991.
[30] Interview with NA, February 19, 2003, Mumbai.
[31] Interviews with SN, June 12, 2003, Mumbai. Interview with HM, October 15, 2002, Mumbai. Interview with Meenakshi Rushi, lawyer, Family Court, February 13, 2003, Mumbai.

of the woman in question, a feminist, mentioned that she had informally confronted this social worker about her views after this incident.[32]

The presence of feminist lawyers helps continue a dialog about women's rights, roles, and responsibilities within the family. Judges in the Family Court often view their role as facilitators and advisors. For example, a petitioner husband filed for restitution of conjugal rights while accusing his wife of cruelty and desertion. Denying the decree to the petitioner husband, the judge noted that "[t]he parties are not represented by lawyers.... I myself have tried for reconciliation but find that it is not possible" (Family Court Records, 1998).

Figure 3.3 shows that more than half of the cases are disposed of through other means. It is often argued that the Indian legal system is lengthy, expensive, cumbersome, and corrupt, and this "crisis of the Indian legal system" (Galanter and Krishnan 2003; Mendelsohn 1989) is the reason why parties withdraw from court proceedings. In addition, some cases are dismissed due to a long absence of litigants from court,[33] whereas a number of cases are transferred to other courts or dismissed due to jurisdictional conflicts. Furthermore, many scholars assume a sequential ordering in the litigants' strategy of forum shopping in formal and informal courts, indicating that litigants initially utilize informal forums, and then approach state courts either to appeal against the verdict or to seek relief in unresolved disputes (Mukhopadhyay 1998). However, this data and the subsequent follow-up of litigants who withdrew their cases also demonstrate the reverse trend. Some litigants move the court in order to settle differences at the societal level.[34] For instance, given

---

[32] Interview with IS, March 18, 2003, Mumbai.

[33] In one case, a woman was evicted from her slum and made homeless, and could not pursue the legal case. Some men litigants migrate for work, and women move back to their native villages in other parts of India. Others fail to pursue cases due to family circumstances such as death or illness of family members.

[34] For instance, given that Muslim Personal Law permits unilateral male divorce, many Muslim women file cases of maintenance in court in order to provoke their husbands into giving them a divorce (interview with Hasina Khan, feminist activist, Awaz e

STATE LAW AND THE ADJUDICATION PROCESS

that a common strategy used by male litigants is to grant divorce to wives who file for maintenance in state courts, Hindu and Muslim women who wish to initiate divorce or obtain proof of divorce from their husbands file cases for maintenance in order to provoke their husbands to grant them societal divorce. Litigants also file cases to boost their power in society and the family and to obtain leverage to settle matters within the society, or to reconcile (see also Kidder 1973, 1974). "My husband threw me out of the house with my children.... I waited for six months but did not hear from him. Then I came to the Family Court for maintenance and got temporary relief [interim order for maintenance] – my husband realised that he will have to pay for us anyway, and who will cook for him and keep his house? He sent his family members for reconciliation (*samadhan*)."[35] Some litigants approach both formal and informal forums simultaneously, and while some cases are resolved in both forums, others turn to societal forums after they file cases in state courts: "We first went to the caste-council (*panchayat*), but my husband refused to come, so we went to the Bandra court [the Family Court] and the case dragged on for five years – finally, our elders began to ask, 'What is going on?' [*he bhandan khub lhan challa*] and we worked out a settlement arrangement in the family, exchanged *stridhan* and got a divorce, *sodchithi*, and then we told the judge that we would like to settle amicably."[36] Thus, given the parallel presence of informal legal organizations and actors, cases are simultaneously adjudicated in multiple forums; this also impacts upon the nature of justice in state courts, as cases that are resolved in other

---

Niswan, January 10, 2003, Mumbai). Hindu women who have been denied divorce by husbands from their caste *panchayats* also use the courts in similar ways (interview with Vishrambhai Waghela, March 12, 2003, Mumbai).

[35] Interview with NM, September 11, 2002, Mumbai. Although many women were also duped by this ploy on behalf of their husbands: "My husband reconciled after I got the decree of maintenance, so I withdrew the case, and a month after the reconciliation, his harassment and beatings began. Imagine going through all that legal hassle all over again. I was foolish – I should never have withdrawn" (interview with JS, March 3, 2003, Mumbai).

[36] Interviews with MM and RA, June 23, 2003, Mumbai.

Table 3.3. *Number of Litigants Interviewed*

Religion of Respondents	Number of Respondents Who Sought Relief under Matrimonial Remedies	Number of Respondents Who Filed for Economic Rights	Total
Hindu	38	31	69
Muslim	15	36	51
Total	53	67	120

forums are dropped from the state courts.[37] Table 3.3 gives information on the respondents who had approached the state court.

Adjudication in Hindu and Muslim Personal Laws

State law and adjudication processes in Hindu and Muslim personal laws shape marriage, the conjugal family, and women's rights from above. In addition, the state also realizes its project of penetrating society, demarcating group boundaries, and protecting individual rights. This section discusses the construction of Hindu and Muslim marriage in religious family laws and argues that the state constructs Hindu and Muslim marriage along similar but not identical lines.

Determining "Marriage" – Outlining Boundaries of the Community, Protecting Individual Rights

Marriage ensures the reproduction of religious/ethnic groups, castes, and/ or sects; it entails entry of new members into the family and community, and perpetuates the family. The institution of marriage also perpetuates

---

[37] "I had filed a case for maintenance.... It took three years in the court and he never came even once. We had to look for other avenues – we approached our village council, they talked to his family" (interview with DY, March 23, 2003, Mumbai). "I had filed for maintenance and it looked as though the decision was going to be in my favour – then his family approached us for a reconciliation. I agreed to give it one more try. After all, I have two children" (interview with PS, June 24, 2003, Mumbai).

STATE LAW AND THE ADJUDICATION PROCESS 105

and reinforces gender relations and the sexual division of labor within the family. Under state law, the issue of the validity of marriage surfaces in decisions about the status of existing marriages, void marriages, nullity of marriage, the restitution of conjugal rights, polygyny, divorce, and maintenance. State law lays down criteria to determine valid Hindu or Muslim marriage, and shares its authority with societal actors in regulating both Hindu and Muslim marriage.

There is no uniform federal law governing the registration of marriage in India. The Hindu Marriage Act 1955[38] enables state governments to make rules regarding the registration of Hindu marriage. Different state governments have made rules for voluntary registration of marriages among Muslims.[39] In 2006, a Supreme Court bench directed all states and union territories to come up with legislation making registration of marriage compulsory and to develop sanctions for noncompliance.[40] However, states are still in the process of drafting this legislation. During adjudication, while enforcing Hindu law, the state defines what construes a valid Hindu marriage, but not with rigid precision, allowing customary variance in the solemnization of marriage. Even though in some instances the state upholds that marriage is a public affair requiring the presence of either a civic official or a religious authority, it is argued that the state often recognizes informal marriages in practice (Menski 2003, 33). There is also some evidence countering this claim (Agnes 1995b, 1999). The data in Family Court show mixed evidence[41] (see also Holden 2008), but also

---

[38] The Hindu Marriage Act 1955 does not apply to Goa and the union territories of Diu and Daman. The states of Jammu and Kashmir have their own Hindu Marriage Act 1980, and in Puducherry, the act does not apply to Renoncants (those who opted for the local Indo-Franco law at the time of assimilation of this territory into the Union of India in 1954).

[39] These states are Assam, Bihar, Meghalaya, Orissa, and West Bengal. In Maharashtra, both private *qazis* and those registered under the Qazi's Act 1880 are allowed to informally register Muslim marriages.

[40] *Seema* v. *Ashwani Kumar* 2006 (1) KLT 791 SC. See http://timesofindia.indiatimes.com, February 14, 2006.

[41] Menski's claim holds in most cases filed in the Bombay Family Court. For instance, in a case filed under nullity of marriage under Hindu law, the parties had met at a youth camp and decided to marry in a temple in a small village in Himachal Pradesh. They went

corroborates Menski's claims in the sense that the state is more likely to recognize informal marriage when it comes to protection of women's rights. For example, in one case, the husband had tied a gold chain around the bride's neck in the presence of a few family members; this was the traditional ceremony finalizing the second marriages of parties in their caste. The court held this act as valid. "There is always presumption in favour of validity of marriage when some sort of marriage ceremony is undergone by the parties."[42]

The state, in constructing Hindu marriage, privileges heterosexuality.[43] Under state law, Hindu marriage is monogamous.[44] Hindu law contains elements of a contract and a sacrament (Menski 2003). For instance, the provision of mutual-consent divorce and tacit consent to marriage[45] are contractarian characteristics of Hindu marriage. Express consent of parties is not required under Hindu law, but parties do not need to seek parental/familial approval or consent before performing marriage because the lack of consent renders a marriage invalid.[46] However, acceptance of child marriage as a valid marriage[47] and matrimonial remedies such as restitution

---

back to live with their respective parents in different cities and realized that their parents would not be agreeable to the marriage. They decided to end their marriage after many months. They met a lawyer and filed a case under Section 7 of the Family Courts Act 1984, stating nonperformance of ceremonies as grounds to nullify their marriage and obtained the decree (interview with VK, March 6, 2003, Mumbai). In another case, though, the district court in Gujarat refused to recognize the second marriage of the parties even though the petitioner wife stated that second marriages in their caste are contracted without rituals and are also not public. Interview with GW, May 23, 2003, Mumbai.

[42] See *SI* v. *MI*, Family Court Records, 2002, Mumbai.

[43] Courts have held that marriage of a male or a female with a transsexual person is considered valid under the Hindu law, as is marriage between transsexuals (Diwan 1985, 107, citation in Nijjar 1994, 110). These cases are rarely filed in state courts, but the decriminalization of homosexuality, if upheld by the Supreme Court, would change this situation.

[44] Section 5, Hindu Marriage Act 1955.

[45] Section 5(ii)(a) of the Hindu Marriage Act 1955 requires that a person be capable of giving valid consent.

[46] See the discussion on void and voidable marriages.

[47] Under Section 5(iii), child marriage is valid but punishable. The punishment for child marriage is 1,000 rupees or simple imprisonment for fifteen days, or both. The wife in

of conjugal rights negate personal autonomy and consent as grounds of Hindu marriage. There is no specific legislation criminalizing marital rape,[48] and although a woman can lodge a complaint under the law on domestic violence, Section 498(A) IPC, or more recently under the Protection of Women from Domestic Violence Act 2005, these laws have not been interpreted to include marital rape so far (Dave and Solanki 2001).

The state also privileges heterosexuality in acknowledging Muslim marriage. Muslim marriage is a contract (Section 250, Mulla[49] [1955] 230) undertaken between persons of sound mind. A Muslim marriage, *nikah*, is comprised of an offer (made by a woman or her guardians), an acceptance of the offer (by the groom), and a payment of dower (*mehar*). There are two kinds of dower: prompt and deferred. The prompt *mehar* is payable on demand (payable upon the dissolution of marriage by death or divorce) (Section 290, Mulla [1955] 251). However, the provision of matrimonial remedies such as the restitution of conjugal rights and the lack of specific legislation on marital rape conflict with the conception of marriage as a contract among Muslims.

In Maharashtra, both private- and state-appointed *qazis* (registered under the Qazi's Act 1880[50]) can register marriage. A customary Muslim marriage does not always require a ritual solemnization of marriage, nor does it require the presence of public or religious authorities to validate it, but it is validated by the signature of witnesses recorded in the marriage contract.[51] Lawyers, caste and sect councils, and residential councils

---

such a marriage can obtain a divorce under Section 13(2)(iv) of the act if her marriage was solemnized before she was fifteen years of age and she had repudiated the marriage after attaining that age but before attaining the age of eighteen years. No corresponding relief is given to a male child (Nijjar 1994, 9).

[48] Though Section 376A of the Indian Penal Code 1860 criminalizes marital rape during judicial separation.

[49] I have privileged Mulla's "Principles of Mahomedan Law" over other texts such as Fyzee (1965), because lower courts, and indeed the Bombay High Court, tend to pursue this text (interview with Niloufer Akhtar, lawyer, June 3, 2003, Mumbai).

[50] The State of Maharashtra amended this Act in 1980 and requires private and registered *qazi*s to maintain the records of marriage performed by them.

[51] Interviews with MS and RK, March 17, 2003, Mumbai.

also have their own forms for the registration of marriage.[52] Thus, informal marriages performed in the presence of witnesses are considered valid by the Family Court under Hindu and Muslim laws.

It has been argued that the Indian state's regulation of religious personal laws fixes religious identities of its subjects and creates communities (Cohn 1996; Pandey 1990; Shodhan 2001). In addition, family laws define criteria for intermingling across groups as well as within religious groups. The state allows marriages between Hindus of different castes and thus facilitates the interaction among members of different sections of Hindu society. Similarly, Muslim Personal Law allows intermarriage among members of different sects of Muslims.[53] Interreligious marriages are regulated by the state under the provision of secular law, the Special Marriage Act 1954. In many cases of interreligious marriage, one of the parties in the marriage chooses to convert to another religion and marry under religious personal laws. The discussion of void and voidable marriages under Hindu and Muslim personal laws in the following section outlines criteria established by the state to regulate marriage and to police the boundaries of the community.[54] I show that even though distinct provisions of Hindu and Muslim personal laws regulate the matter of what constitutes a valid marriage, the state courts use the Family Courts Act 1984 that subsumes these distinctive provisions and standardizes the criteria to determine a valid marriage.

---

[52] For example, in one case, the parties had married through "telephone *nikah*." The groom was a laborer in Saudi Arabia and could not come down to Mumbai for his wedding. The ceremony was performed while he was on the telephone – he gave his consent from his end, which was heard on the speaker phone by the bride, the family, and well-wishers from both sides. The uncle of the groom, who was also a lawyer, drew up the marriage contract that was signed by witnesses from either side. Interview with RK, March 17, 2003.

[53] See Section 258, Mulla [1955] 234.

[54] In many cases of interreligious marriage, one of the parties in the marriage chooses to convert to another religion and marry under religious personal laws. In such cases, the state is often called on to define the validity of the conversion. See *D* v. *YR*, Family Court Records, 2002; *RM* v. *AM*, Family Court Records, 2002.

Void and Voidable Marriages: Streamlining Family Laws and Protecting Individual Rights

The state regulates entry into marriage by prescribing the ceremony and establishing criteria for valid marriages. The Family Court can pass a decree of nullify of marriage under Sections 11 and 12 of the Hindu Marriage Act 1955 (HMA) in cases of void and voidable marriages.[55] Under Hindu law, marriages are declared invalid on the basis of violation of kinship restrictions,[56] the existence of current marriage, and the use of force to override nonconsent of the marriage partner.[57] Section 5(iv) of the Hindu Marriage Act 1955 allows for customary divergence when it comes to kinship restrictions. In a case involving marriage between fraternal cousins,[58] the parties sought advice from a lawyer, asking whether marriage between close cousins was permissible. The lawyer affirmed the validity of their marriage because such marriages, though rare, were not uncommon in their caste. The parties eloped and married in a temple. However, both families objected to the marriage, and the couple decided to end the marriage. The same lawyer filed a case to nullify the marriage as this legal strategy represented "a swift way of ending the marriage opposed by the society," and the court declared the marriage null and void as it violated the prohibitory decrees under Hindu law. In this case,

---

[55] Section 11 of the Hindu Marriage Act lays down three grounds for voidable marriages: (1) neither party should have a living spouse at the time of marriage; (2) that the parties are not within a prohibited relationship; and (3) they are not *sapindas* (blood relatives, connected by ties of consanguinity) of each other. Marriages between parties would be considered valid wherever customs applicable to parties allow the marriage among *sapindas* and the degree of prohibited relationships, but not in cases of polygyny. Section 12 of the Hindu Marriage Act 1955 lays down conditions for a voidable marriage that include nonconsummation, nonconsent due to mental condition, evidence of force, fraud, and pregnancy of the wife at the time of marriage.

[56] Section 5(iv) of the Hindu Marriage Act 1955 allows for customary divergence.

[57] In a case of intercaste marriage, the petitioner woman filed a case under this section to declare her marriage as void, claiming that she was forcibly led to enter into the marriage by her lower-caste lover. The judge opined in her favor. Interview with CN, November 8, 2002, Mumbai.

[58] Interview with AM, March 6, 2003, Mumbai; interview with HK, October 15, 2002.

the Family Court did not investigate deeply into the validity of the custom in cases filed with mutual consent. However, judges differ in their approach, and in another case, the court had asked caste members to verify whether such a custom existed in their caste.[59] Nonperformance of religious ceremonies is also grounds for nullity of marriage, and there exist diverse legal precedents discussing whether *saptapadi* (a ceremony in Hindu marriage that involves seven steps in presence of the sacred fire (*homa*)) is essential to Hindu marriage.[60]

Under Muslim Personal Law, a marriage may be valid, irregular, or void (Section 253, Mulla [1955] 231). There is a distinction between a void marriage and an irregular marriage in Muslim Personal Law: A void marriage is one that is unlawful in itself in the sense that prohibition against it is absolute and does not "create any civil rights or obligations between parties" (Mulla 1955, 236). Irregular marriage, on the other hand, is not unlawful in itself. Prohibition to this marriage is temporary or relative and can be rectified (Mulla 1955, 236). For instance, a marriage contracted in the absence of witnesses can be deemed as irregular, as this irregularity can arguably arise from an accidental circumstance (Mulla 1955, 236). An irregular marriage can be terminated by either party by the verbalization of the intention to separate (Section 267, Mulla [1955] 237); a marriage undertaken without witnesses is irregular but not void (Mulla 1955, 232).

---

[59] Interview with AM, March 6, 2003, Mumbai; interview with HK, October 15, 2002.

[60] In one case, a petitioner wife filed for nullity of marriage under Hindu law claiming that she and her husband had solemnized their marriage in a marriage bureau in the presence of the husband's mother and brother. According to the wife, the ceremony consisted of exchanging garlands in front of a Hindu deity in the presence of a Hindu priest who recited a few mantras. The marriage was also registered under Hindu law. The parties lived together for six months after marriage. The petitioner claimed that the marriage was invalid as there was no performance of *saptapadi* (a ceremony in Hindu marriage that involves walking seven steps around *homa*, the sacred fire). The Family Court held the marriage as valid because it was performed with the consent of both parties and in the presence of witnesses. There was no *saptapadi*, but the parties had failed to prove that *saptapadi* was essential to rites and customs prevalent in their communities. Interview with Meenakshi Rushi, lawyer, Family Court, January 11, 2003, Mumbai. Interview with MH, June 12, 2003, Mumbai.

STATE LAW AND THE ADJUDICATION PROCESS 111

The Muslim Personal Law prohibits marriages between agnates, and in some cases, cognates, foster children, and women undergoing *iddat*[61] (Mulla 1955, 232–235).

The Family Courts Act 1984 serves as an overarching law obscuring specific provisions of religious personal laws in cases of interreligious marriages undertaken after the conversion of one of the parties after marriage. For instance, a bulk of cases under Section 7(a), (b) of the Family Courts Act consists of interreligious marriages.[62] Parties seeking a decree of nullity in interreligious marriages after conversion of a party to another religion are processed[63] on the grounds of insufficient proof of conversion, nonperformance of ceremonies, and the use of force to override nonconsent of a party without referring to individual provisions of either Hindu or Muslim personal law. For instance, in a case of interreligious marriage, a Hindu woman who had converted to Islam (and had filed an affidavit in the court attesting to the fact) and married under Muslim Personal Law filed for nullity of marriage under Section 7 of the Family Courts Act 1984. The judge held the marriage valid but did not consider the criteria of valid marriage under Muslim Personal Law (Mulla 1955, 230); rather, he considered the issue of validity of conversion, the absence of force, and the performance of a valid ceremony as criteria on which to base the judgment.[64]

---

[61] The period of *iddat* in the case of a divorced woman is defined as three menstrual courses after the date of divorce if she is subject to menstruation; three lunar months after her divorce if she is not subject to menstruation; if she is pregnant at the time of divorce, the period between divorce and the delivery of the child or the termination of her pregnancy, whichever is earlier. *Iddat* is a period of three months and ten days.

[62] The Indian state legalizes interreligious marriages through the Special Marriage Act 1954. However, in many cases, runaway couples find it easier to opt for religious personal laws through conversion of one of the parties, usually women, because the process is swift and private.

[63] In a case of interreligious marriage, a Muslim woman who had converted to Hinduism and married under Hindu religious law filed for nullity of marriage under Section 7 of the Family Courts Act 1984. The judge held the marriage invalid for lack of sufficient proof of conversion. Interview with RN, October 13, 2002, Mumbai.

[64] This pattern was repeated in other cases as well. See, for instance, *RN* v. *AM*, Family Court Records, 2003, Mumbai.

The state, in some cases, seeks to guard individual rights against societal practice. In some instances, the state constructs marriage as a matter of choice and individual freedom, and it protects the individual rights of litigants from societal and parental pressure. Tensions between state and society appear in the foreground in cases filed under the validity of marriage under religious laws as well as under Section 7 of the Family Courts Act 1984. This is an area in which societal practices of parental approval/consent for marriage, adherence to caste endogamy, prohibition of interreligious marriages, and preference for retention of wealth within the family/caste circles conflict sharply with the notion of marriage as a matter of voluntary choice and individual right encoded in law.[65] Whereas societal forces often try to manipulate the legal system to impose their ideas of marriage,[66] the court often protects the individual rights of the parties in the face of familial attempts to override individual choices, and reestablishes the state's intent to allow interreligious marriage. In a case involving marriage between Deena, a Hindu woman, and Yusuf, a Muslim man, the wife sought to nullify the marriage under Section 7 of the Family Courts Act 1984. Deena and Yusuf had solemnized their

---

[65] In one case, a Hindu woman was forced to file a case seeking annulment of marriage to a Muslim man after being imprisoned by her family for a month. She was made to sign papers alleging that her husband had forced her into marriage. She agreed to file the case and then used the opportunity to meet her husband in the court and escape together. "If we could not escape, I was prepared to tell the judge my natal family made me lie and cheat and not my husband." The parties withdrew the case in a month's time (Interview with RN, March 16, 2003, Mumbai).

[66] Lawyers often tend to tailor the testimonies of their clients to prove nonconsent to marriage as grounds for nullity. In a case of interreligious marriage, the petitioner, a Hindu woman, and the respondent, a Muslim man, solemnized the marriage according to Muslim rites after the petitioner converted to Islam. She was pressured by her family into filing a case under Section 7 of the Family Courts Act 1984. Her petition states that "she was cheated by the respondent in a preplanned manner. The respondent 'purposefully befriended her, took her signature forcefully and fraudulently on the marriage registration form and affidavit of conversion, and he threatened her and her family with dire consequences if she failed to cohabit with him'." Case of *RN* v. *AM*, December 2002, filed under Section 7 of the Family Courts Act and filed for annulment as per the Muslim Personal Law.

STATE LAW AND THE ADJUDICATION PROCESS

marriage according to Muslim rites after Deena, a Hindu, converted to Islam. They obtained an affidavit of conversion and registered the marriage with a *qazi*, as per Muslim Personal Law. When Deena announced the marriage to her parents, her parents imprisoned her in the house. In the end, Deena was coerced into filing for nullity of marriage under Section 7 of the Family Courts Act 1984. The lawyer could have also sought a divorce, but that would have meant acceptance of both the conversion as well as the marriage by the court and society and that was not acceptable to Deena's father. Yusuf did not accept the summons of the court and did not present himself in court. The court held the marriage valid in an ex parte judgment. The judge reasoned that the marriage had fulfilled the conditions of valid Islamic marriage, and the petitioner did not claim to be forced into the marriage.[67]

The judges use considerable discretion in such cases, especially when one of the parties claim the use of force as a reason for marriage, and as a result, the outcome of such cases is not predictable.[68] For instance, a Hindu man from a privileged family who had converted to Islam had married a Muslim prostitute. He had a valid conversion certificate as well as proof of marriage, but he claimed that he was forced into marriage by a pimp and was being blackmailed with the threat of social exposure. The court granted an ex parte divorce in this case, despite the fact that he did not produce evidence of threat and blackmail. In another similar case, the court refused to grant a decree of nullity to a Hindu woman, as she had not proved threat and coercion.[69]

The following section reiterates how the state standardizes family law by resorting to provisions of the Family Courts Act 1984 and subsuming

---

[67] Interview with Deena, March 18, 2003, Mumbai.
[68] Interview with Madhvi Desai, social worker, Family Court, Bandra.
[69] Interview with HG, June 6, 2003, Mumbai. It was difficult to verify the details of this case – I could only find the husband, and he told me the version of the details presented in the court. I could not trace the address of the wife, and hence could not hear her side of the story; the social worker suggested that the judge had used "common sense" in this case.

individual personal laws under this provision. The section also argues that there are pockets of similarity in the adjudication of Hindu and Muslim personal laws in the state court.

The Provision of Restitution of Conjugal Rights and the Standardization of Hindu and Muslim Personal Laws

The Restitution of Conjugal Rights is a matrimonial remedy under Hindu and Muslim personal laws as well as under Section 7(a) of the Family Courts Act 1984. This provision contravenes consent and individual freedom as a basis of marriage. The decree calls upon the respondent to return home to the petitioner within a specified time period; however, this order of cohabitation is not legally enforceable, and failure to comply with the decree does not carry legal sanctions. In order to be awarded a decree, parties must demonstrate a sincere desire to resume cohabitation.[70] The provision is used by both male and female litigants to pave the way for divorce or judicial separation because disobedience of a decree of restitution is seen as a form of statutory desertion and is thus a ground for divorce. Thus, restitution is not seen to be a remedy in itself, but rather as a stepping stone to other remedies.

The issue of whether the Family Court has the jurisdiction to try cases of restitution of conjugal rights under Muslim Personal Law was debated when a Muslim petitioner husband had filed a case for restitution of conjugal rights against his wife. The respondent wife argued that only the High Court had the jurisdiction to entertain cases filed for the restitution of conjugal rights under Muslim Personal Law.[71] However, the

---

[70] A petitioner husband filed for restitution of conjugal rights while accusing his wife of cruelty and desertion. Denying the decree to the petitioner husband, the judge noted that " ... [h]is claim of reconciliation is not genuine but filed with a view to obtain divorce if she does not comply with the restitution order.... If he was sincere in calling her back, he would not have made serious allegations of cruelty against her" (Family Court Records, Mumbai, 1998).

[71] Mulla's "Principles of Mahomedan Law" mentions restitution of conjugal rights as a remedy under Section 281 of Muslim Personal Law (Mulla [1955] 246).

Family Court ruled that "[t]he Family Court has the jurisdiction to entertain suits of restitution of conjugal rights filed under Section 7(a) of the Family Courts Act [and given that] the Family Court is established with a view to [ensuring] speedy justice and ... for restoring peace and harmony within the family ... there was no reason why Muslims should not get any benefits of filing redressal of grievances regarding restitution of conjugal rights or any other matrimonial matter" (Family Court Records, Mumbai, 1998).

Cases filed under this section are processed using similar criteria for Hindu and Muslim litigants. For instance, this provision is often spuriously used by both parties to harass the opposite party and drag them into lengthy litigation.[72] It is often used by men to control the wife's sexuality and property and to counter maintenance claims made by the wife.[73] This section is used quite often by Hindu women in order to prove constructive desertion and to claim maintenance under Hindu law. Although it is argued that in some cases wives can claim maintenance even if they fail to abide by the decree of restitution (Sagade 1996), case law developments seem to be more diverse.[74] The provision is used by Hindu

---

[72] In another case, the petitioner husband, a lawyer, had filed a case of restitution of conjugal rights against his second wife. The wife accused the lawyer husband of "malafide intentions by involving her in lengthy litigation through his knowledge of law" and claimed that "he (had) beaten her ... and (was) shedding crocodile tears by filing this petition." She also complained of the same to the social worker, Madhvi Desai. Interview with NV, August 12, 2002, Mumbai. The judge refused to grant the decree. Case records, *MV v. NV*, Family Court Records, 2002.

[73] In a case filed under civil maintenance by the petitioner wife, the husband responded by filing for restitution of conjugal rights. The husband had deserted his wife for many years but filed for restitution as soon as she filed for maintenance (interview with MG, April 12, 2003, Mumbai). In another case, a Muslim husband filed for an injunction against the wife for the sale of property and then filed for restitution of conjugal rights (interview with MM, January 3, 2003, Mumbai).

[74] In one case, the wife had filed for maintenance under Section 125 CrPC, and the husband filed for restitution of conjugal rights. The court gave an ex parte order in this case in favor of the husband because the wife lived in another city and did not have the resources to travel. This adversely impacted her claim of maintenance (interview with SB, March 14, 2003, Mumbai).

and Muslim litigants to contest divorce petitions, or, at times, to prove divorce,[75] and the nature of adjudication makes similarities between the cases more striking.

The Regulation of Polygyny under Hindu and Muslim Personal Laws

The Indian state has not instituted a standard family form. The state forbids polygyny, polyandry, and group marriage among Hindus.[76] The state recognizes polygyny under Muslim Personal Law. This provision is seen as discriminatory and in violation of the rights of Muslim women, and has been criticized by feminists, legal scholars, sections of the media, and the public, as well as by the Hindu right.[77]

Polygyny among Hindus persists despite the state's attempts to prohibit the societal practice. Feminists have pointed to a high prevalence of polygyny among Hindus[78] and have questioned the juridical apathy in regulating and punishing polygyny among Hindus. A section of feminists and other scholars have favored more effective laws to curb polygyny among Hindus (Parashar 1992). However, many other feminist analyses have suggested a need to shift the focus of action from prosecuting men to protecting the rights of women in informal relationships (Forum Against Oppression of Women 1996; John and Nair 2000). It is also suggested that the provision

---

[75] A Muslim husband filed a case under this section in order to provoke an acknowledgment from his wife that "the petitioner had divorced her as per provisions of the Muslim Personal Law and therefore this petition should be dismissed." Interview with NSS, January 13, 2003, Mumbai.

[76] Sections 5(1) and 11 of the Hindu Marriage Act 1955 prohibit polygyny as well as polyandry among Hindus. Polygyny is also punishable under Sections 494 and 495 of the Indian Penal Code. To prove polygyny, the petitioner would have to prove that spouses are legally married, that either spouse has entered into a second marriage during the subsistence of the first marriage, and that necessary ceremonies of the first marriage have been performed. Courts require strict proof of polygyny, prioritizing the form as opposed to intent of the marriage (Singh 1993).

[77] However, the focus of the Hindu right's ire has been the privileges extended to Muslim men rather than a concern for the plight of Muslim women.

[78] See "Towards Equality," 1975.

STATE LAW AND THE ADJUDICATION PROCESS 117

and enforcement of economic rights to women in such relationships would curb male polygyny (Forum Against Oppression of Women 1996).

Menski offers an interesting insight: The Indian judiciary has taken a sophisticated approach in dealing with polygyny in the sense that it does not favor Muslim polygynists by refusing to implement the strict legal prohibition of polygyny across all religious lines (Menski 2003, 423). However, the state ensures that Hindu women who complain against polygyny are heard, and that the economic rights of women and children caught in polygynous relations are protected (Menski 2003, 425–426). However, we find that the state speaks in a polyphony of voices on the ground when it comes to this matter. For instance, the state has formed an ordinance ensuring strict compliance to monogamy among Hindus working in government service, with a note that the government of India can permit a party to enter into such a marriage if it is satisfied that such a marriage is permissible under his personal law.[79] The state disallowed religious conversion of a Hindu man to Islam allegedly undertaken to take advantage of the provision of polygyny in a widely publicized case (*Sarla Mudgal* v. *Union of India*, AIR [1995] SC 1531).

At the level of the Family Court, the data show that polygyny among Hindus is difficult to prevent, even in cases where petitioner wives have managed to furnish proof of impending second marriages of the husbands. A Hindu wife wishing to prevent a second marriage of the husband can do so under Section 9 of the Code of Civil Procedure 1908 read with Section 38 of the Special Relief Act 1963, as there is no specific provision under the HMA to grant a temporary injunction to a wife against her husband's second marriage. However, Section 4(a) of the Hindu Marriage Act 1955 is also used for this purpose: Daya, a Hindu wife who had separated from her husband for more than five years, came to know of her husband's intention to remarry without divorcing her. She managed to obtain a copy of his wedding card and filed for an injunction. She

---

[79] Ministry of Personnel, PG and Pensions, Government of India's Letter no. 2012/98-AIS (III), March 8, 1999, as cited in *Muslim India*, 196 (April 1999): 174.

managed to stop the marriage from taking place at the scheduled time and place, but the husband remarried a week after that and even registered his second marriage. Daya managed to get a copy of the registration of his second marriage under Hindu law and filed a motion in court to validate her own marriage with the respondent. The court held the first marriage as valid. Daya did not seek to file a criminal case against her husband because she wished to file for maintenance for herself and her two children; filing a criminal case would have antagonized her husband, and she was afraid that he would harm her natal family.[80]

Cases of polygyny also come to light when the second wife files for maintenance (Agnes 1995b, 1999).[81] Many instances of polygyny among Hindu men are cited in Family Court records. Ironically, the denial of divorce or lengthy divorce proceedings in courts were cited by Hindu men as reasons for contracting second "marriages."[82] In a case for maintenance, a petitioner wife cited polygyny as a reason for leaving the matrimonial home. Compelling the petitioner wife to consent to husband's second marriage was cited as cruelty in a case of maintenance filed under HAMA 1956.[83]

Even though polygyny is practiced among Hindus, lengthy and expensive court proceedings and different legal priorities prevent women from prosecuting their husbands for polygyny. For instance, in the sample, four Hindu women who had filed for maintenance for themselves and their children reported that their husbands had married again, but they did not wish to pursue a criminal case against them as they did not see any hope of reconciliation, and they did not wish to approach the court to

---

[80] Interview with DP, February 16, 2003, Mumbai.

[81] In one case, a second wife, a resident of Mumbai, was denied maintenance in a district court in Rajkot, Gujarat, because the court did not recognize her marriage performed under customary rites (Interview with PH, May 6, 2003, Mumbai).

[82] Interviews with HP, a husband who was denied divorce and has married again, April 16, 2003; DG, March 4, 2003, Mumbai.

[83] *NM* v. *RM*, filed in 1998, Family Court Records, Mumbai. In another case of maintenance, the wife alleged that her husband had deserted her and was living with his second wife. Interview with NJ, March 15, 2003, Mumbai.

STATE LAW AND THE ADJUDICATION PROCESS 119

punish their husbands.[84] In another case, a woman sought to validate her marriage as legal but did not wish to file a criminal case against her husband because she wished to retain her sons' rights to the inheritance of her husband's property.[85] In another case filed under Section 7(d) of the Family Courts Act 1984 for the right to reside in the matrimonial property, the wife and social workers of a local NGO gave evidence of a second marriage of a husband. The wife had not filed a criminal case against the husband even in this case, as it was more important for her to strategize to secure her economic rights.[86]

Muslim Personal Law allows polygyny, and as a result, more than one wife can file cases for maintenance for themselves and children under Section 125 CrPC. They can also file for compensation after divorce under the Muslim Women's (Protection of Rights on Divorce) Act 1986. The adjudication process throws up similarities in the courts' construction of polygyny committed by Hindus and Muslims. For instance, contracting a second marriage by the husband is recognized by the Family Court as grounds of cruelty and constructive desertion among both Hindus and Muslims[87] in cases filed under the Dissolution of Muslim Marriage Act 1939,[88] as well as in cases filed under Section 125 CrPC. Analyses of case judgments in cases filed under Section 125 CrPC reveal that Muslim husbands who practice polygyny tend to show a decreased ability to support first wives in light of their increased liabilities of maintaining two families. However, judges have proven to be unsympathetic to this line of argument.[89] In one case, a Muslim man, Omar, had to pay maintenance

---

[84] Interviews with IK, March 3, 2003, Ahmedabad; RM, April 5, 2003; MN, February 14, 2003; HM, May 3, 2003, Mumbai.
[85] Interview with DP, April 13, 2002, Mumbai.
[86] Interview with Irene Sequiera, lawyer, June 8, 2003, Mumbai.
[87] Interview with ZM, March 6, 2003, Mumbai, in a case filed under Dissolution of Muslim Marriage Act 1939.
[88] Interview with JN, litigant, April 6, 2003, Mumbai.
[89] In such cases, judges are not sympathetic to Muslim husbands' responses to fight maintenance claims of first wives to support the second wife and a subsequent family (interview with SM, May 7, 2003, Mumbai).

to his first wife and two children who had filed a case for maintenance, and support his second family. Omar had repeatedly petitioned the court to revise the amount of maintenance. He had taken his second wife and younger children to the court on the day I interviewed him, intending to show the judge their "*buri halat*" (disheveled, bedraggled, impoverished state) and to "beg for mercy" and reduce the amount of maintenance to his first wife, who, he claimed, " … was richer than him and ran a commercial STD phone booth from her brother's property." Both Omar and Abdul Rashid, his lawyer, were pessimistic about being heard, though, as many judges strictly ensure that Muslim husbands pay their maintenance arrears to first wives.[90] This judge did not disappoint. "Why did you marry her (the second wife) if you could not afford to look after your first wife?" he thundered inside the courtroom, declining the revision of the previous maintenance order.

Divorce in Hindu and Muslim Personal Laws

While adjudicating on cases of divorce, judges are required to balance contradictory visions about family, sexuality, and marriage instituted in the Hindu Marriage Act 1955, the Dissolution of Muslim Marriage Act 1939, as well as in the Family Courts Act 1984. Both Hindu and Muslim personal laws allow for mutual-consent divorce. However, the Family Courts Act 1984 establishes procedures for reconciliation as a necessary part of divorce.[91] This emphasis on reconciliation contrasts sharply with the societal practice of easy divorce prevalent in some societal groups.[92]

---

[90] Interview with Abdul Rashid, lawyer, June 3, 2003, Mumbai. Interview with Niloufer Akhtar, lawyer, June 20, 2003, Mumbai.

[91] For instance, see Section 2(e), Statement of Objects and Reason, Family Courts Act 1984.

[92] This vision of the state is not shared by many caste and sect groups that allow easy access to divorce. Cases from these castes, which have to be rubber-stamped by the court, are not subjected to judicial scrutiny if they are filed under Section 13(b) of the Hindu Marriage Act 1955 and if parties convince the social workers of their "caste traditions" (interview with PW, September 13, 2002, Mumbai). See also Holden (2008).

STATE LAW AND THE ADJUDICATION PROCESS 121

Hindu law is not monolithic, and, in most cases, the notion of divorce as harmful to public morality, the institution of the family, and women's status coexists rather uneasily with the notion of individual freedom. As a result, we see judges maximizing cooperative decision making through the facilitation of mutually agreeable solutions while upholding the judicial tradition of adversarial litigation.

Section 13(a) of the Hindu Marriage Act 1955 specifies the grounds for divorce under certain conditions. The guiding principle of this provision is that divorces are granted on the basis of the commission of a matrimonial offense. Hence, courts examine the nature of the respondent's conduct before granting a divorce. Divorce by mutual consent is possible under Section 13(b) of the Hindu Marriage (Amendment) Act 1976.

The most common form of divorce in the Family Court is divorce by mutual consent. Divorce by mutual consent involves the severance of relationships, the settlement of custody matters, and postdivorce financial arrangements. In cases of divorce by mutual consent of parties filed under Section 13(b) of the Hindu Marriage Act 1955, parties present themselves before the judge and answer questions with respect to the jurisdiction of the court as well as the authenticity of the terms of agreement arrived at by mutual consent. However, the court needs to be convinced of the impossibility of reconciliation between the parties. The core of the divorce procedure lies at the negotiations that take place before the social worker or between lawyers of both parties, or between the parties themselves. Decisions about mutual-consent divorce take place at the societal level through the intervention of societal level actors.[93] The analysis of cases reveal that the majority of parties who opt for mutual-consent divorce have been married for a short time, and postdivorce financial settlements are lowest in such cases, especially in cases where

---

[93] In some instances, parties file under Section 13(b) HMA to officially validate their customary divorce (interview with GM, April 8, 2003, Mumbai). In one case, the parties had approached a women's organization for counseling and decided to file for a mutual-consent divorce because reconciliation was impossible. They also agreed on settlement terms there. (interview with PP, June 8, 2003, Mumbai).

parties do not have children.[94] Women who wish to opt out of marriage often tend to forego maintenance or alimony in exchange for a speedy mutual-consent divorce during societal negotiations. Spouses tend to avoid mutual financial obligations beyond divorce, and custodial parents tend to cover child rearing and educational expenses. Maintenance from a noncustodial parent is rare.[95]

Judicial decisions in cases of divorce are given only in cases where parties have failed to arrive at a mutually acceptable settlement. Most commonly cited grounds for cases of contested divorce include desertion and cruelty. In cases of contested divorces, cruelty consists of gendered and communal representations. Whereas divorce petitions present a distorted picture of causes of breakdown of marriage, marital misconduct on the part of Hindu wives include acts such as the refusal of sexual intercourse; disrespectful behavior toward members of the marital family, relatives, and extended family members; a demonstration of unconcern toward children; the negligence of cooking and household duties; frequent visits to the natal home; being "too modern" and "fun loving"; or "acting in an uncultured manner befitting her upbringing in a village," tearing husband's clothes, threatening to commit suicide, performance of black magic, forcing the woman to take loans and dowry demands, failing to wear *mangalsutra*; and accusing a husband of adultery or polygyny. The exclusion of the wife's name in the wedding card of her brother-in-law comprises an act of cruelty because it shows disrespect toward the daughter-in-law of the Hindu family. Women often deny these charges by reasserting that "the respondent remained an obedient and docile Hindu wife and daughter-in-law,"[96] or "the wife, coming from a village, remains

---

[94] See *BD* v. *MD*; *DK* v. *KK*; *VT* v. *PT*; *SW* v. *JW*; *CR* v. *H.*; *KP* v. *JP*; Family Court Records, 2002.

[95] In my interviews, I encountered four cases in which husbands had agreed to provide limited child support. In two of these cases, the women had to move the Family Court periodically to recover maintenance in arrears (interviews with DP, January 4, 2003; PW, November 9, 2002, Mumbai). One of these litigants had stopped filing for arrears after five years due to the "hassle of litigation" (interview with PW, November 9, 2002, Mumbai).

[96] *HG* v. *HG*, Family Court Records, 2002.

STATE LAW AND THE ADJUDICATION PROCESS

steeped into Hindu culture and traditions."[97] Hindu men's acts of misconduct include alcoholism, physical violence, threatening to commit suicide, restricting the wife's mobility, threats of violence to wife and members of her natal family, mental cruelty consisting of verbal abuse, financial malpractices, gambling, emotional and sexual indifference, failure to maintain the wife and children, and disrespect to the wife. This form of ethnic and gendered representation is followed by a majority of lawyers, but we find that some petitions, including those filed by feminist lawyers, counter this trend. Relying on cultural contexts and mindful of women's interests, their petitions seek to prove cruelty by highlighting negligence and violence underlying everyday instances and episodes of marital disputes.

Adultery is often cited as grounds for divorce, but courts require stringent proof of adultery.[98] Desertion includes unjustified retreat from the company of a spouse without his or her consent and with the permanent intention of separation (Bromley 1992; Sagade 1996). The spouse who leaves the matrimonial home is not necessarily the deserting spouse. Cases revolve around the issue of whether the spouse who has left the matrimonial home has done so intentionally or whether she was driven out of the house.[99] The fact of establishing *animus deserendi*, reasonable cause for deserting another spouse, depends on the judicial discretion of proving what amounts to reasonable cause of leaving the matrimonial home. Once again, acts of cruelty and, at times, adultery are cited as reasons entitling the innocent spouse to divorce.

The Family Court adheres to the stand of the Hindu Marriage Act 1955 that no guilty party should obtain a court divorce over the

---

[97] *NJ* v. *NJ*, Family Court Records, 2002.
[98] A petitioner wife had filed for maintenance for herself and her son citing adultery as grounds for desertion. She was able to prove adultery by showing photographs of her husband with his lover and producing neighbors and relatives as witnesses (the husband had lived in the marital home with his lover). The case proceeded for five years before the final decree was given, and she did not receive a financial settlement because she had a job as a secretary in a firm (interview with MK, April 22, 2003, Mumbai).
[99] Given the prevalent practice of patrilocality, wives are often compelled to leave the matrimonial home.

objections of an innocent party of the marriage. It has been argued that courts have been unwilling to grant divorces to petitioner husbands on the grounds of cruelty in recognition of Hindu wives' difficult situations postdivorce due to the stigma attached to divorce among some Hindus (Menski 2001, 2003).[100] The data support Menski's claim and show that the Family Court repudiates contested divorce, especially divorce initiated by men, and thus pays implicit attention to nonfinancial harm to women.[101] Women litigants who contest divorce seek to validate their conduct and position in society, and the court's refusal of divorce reaffirms this.[102] However, it does not address the issue of financial impoverishment of women due to divorce. Hence, the decision of Family Court judges emanates from the desire to prevent divorces rather than awarding legal protection to women. Women who contest divorces filed by their husbands and win in court do not gain financially in most cases.[103] Women

---

[100] There exist diverse opinions among women with respect to the question of the loss of formal marital status. Women also show an unwillingness to go to court to formalize divorce. For example, a woman had left the matrimonial home with her three children after coping with years of abuse and alcoholism on the part of the husband. She moved to a different city with her children and found work there. The husband filed for divorce; the wife did not appear in court even though she had received the summons. She argued that "she had resolved to survive alone and did not wish for any help from him. She also claimed that she did not care about her marital status – he could obtain an ex parte divorce if he so wished" (interview with Jayaben, litigant's sister, January 6, 2003, Mumbai).

[101] See *SG* v. *SG*, Family Court Records. The wife proved neglect and cruelty, and the husband was denied divorce. The wife did not get any financial settlement. See also *VS* v. *HS*; *SG* v. *DG*, Family Court Records, 2002.

[102] Petitions of divorce filed or contested by wives are often eloquent on the mental agony suffered by them as a result of marital separation. They cite lowered prestige at their workplaces and facing harassment and malice from neighbors, friends, relatives, and colleagues. Reaffirmation of marital status in such circumstances is a seal of approval of their good conduct as wives (interviews with SD, May 9, 2003; HS, June 4, 2003; KP, March 2, 2003; MJ, November 3, 2002; IS, October 5, 2002, Mumbai).

[103] A woman filed for divorce on the grounds of cruelty after seven years of marriage. She received the decree after three years. No financial settlement was made. She received custody of her three-year-old son. The respondent husband got visitation rights (interview with MH, March 6, 2003, Mumbai). In another case, a deserted wife filed for divorce

litigants face financial stress as a result of litigation, and most have to rely on the support of natal families and, in some cases, extended families and relatives.[104] In a contested divorce case, the petitioner husband filed for judicial separation in 1997. The respondent filed a criminal case against her husband under Section 498(A) IPC, after which the husband converted his petition into a petition for divorce under Section 13(1)(a) on the grounds of cruelty. The wife then filed for restitution of conjugal rights and interim maintenance. The Family Court did not grant divorce to the petitioner husband.[105] Furthermore, the Family Court denied the wife maintenance under Section 25 of the Hindu Marriage Act 1955, as the court could not "grant relief of maintenance under the HAMA 1956 in proceedings under Section 25 of the Hindu Marriage Act 1955."[106]

In some instances, the Family Court takes steps to ensure that the petitioner husbands do not take advantage of ex parte divorces in cases of divorcing couples with minor children.[107] In one case, a husband had

and obtained it, as her husband had left for the United States after the marriage and had failed, for three years, to sponsor her (interview with JP, January 12, 2003, Mumbai).

[104] About fifty-eight women litigants who filed cases in the state court lived with their natal families. Five of them lived with extended family members, and only four women lived independently because their parents had provided a home for them and their children.

[105] The judge reasoned that the husband had failed to prove allegations of cruelty: he had not produced evidence to support his denial of paternity, the alleged adultery by his wife, or the proof of assault by his wife. As for his claim that the respondent was forced to marry him, the judge stated that "no parents would force marriage over unhappiness of their daughter." The court considered the claim of filing a criminal case under Section 498(A) IPC as an act of cruelty as alleged by the husband. The petitioner had cited a case (JT [2002] (1) SC, P 25 *Savitri Pandey* v. *Prem Chandra Pandey*), and the court cited from the same judgment that "the ordinary wear and tear of family life and sensitivity with respect to conduct of the spouse cannot be cited as cruelty" (see *HS* v. *VS*, Family Court Records, 2002).

[106] The Family Court seems to have replicated the view of some High Courts in India that "the grant of ancillary relief under Section 25 of the Hindu Marriage Act is dependent on the grant of the main relief" (Sagade 1996, 53).

[107] In another case, the Family Court did not grant an ex parte divorce to a husband. The petitioner husband had filed a case in 1998 for divorce on the grounds of cruelty after being separated for three years. The petitioner wife had filed her written statement contesting divorce and had remained absent since 1999. The court denied the husband an

filed for divorce on the grounds of cruelty, claiming that his wife had deserted him and taken three young children with him. The wife lived in another city and did not attend the court for fourteen months despite having received summons. The court asked him to advertise the next court date in the largest circulating vernacular daily in the wife's city asking her to appear in court to attend the matter of divorce. The wife did not appear on the appointed date, and the court postponed the matter for six more months. However, the Family Court granted an ex parte divorce to a petitioner husband when his wife, who resided in rural Maharashtra, filed her written statement but did not present herself in court despite being "contacted repeatedly."[108] The Family Court is more lenient to husbands' pleas for divorce in cases where marriage is for a short duration, where the wife is more educated, "modern," and ably supported by her natal family,[109] when parties have lived apart for many years,[110] when

  ex parte divorce three years later on the basis of the wife's written statement. The judge opined that "every wife has always cherished her home and does not wish to leave it unless she is thrown out, especially where she has the burden of children.... The testimony of the petitioner is silent on how she left the house. It is a strong circumstance to indicate that the petitioner treated her with cruelty and threw her out" (Family Court Records, 2002).

[108] The case was of intercousin marriage, and customarily, such marriages are dissolved at the familial level. The respondent wife's family was seen as "lower" in status, and the act of the petitioner husband to file a case in court was seen as a "shameful act to assert their superior status." The respondent wife's family could not go to court because they felt they could never win and did not have the money to fight a case in Mumbai (interview with MN, maternal aunt of the respondent, March 7, 2003, Mumbai).

[109] A petitioner husband had filed for divorce on the grounds of cruelty, accusing the wife of desertion, "modern behaviour," arrogance due to her higher education, and sexual issues. The respondent wife lived in the village with her family. She sent a written statement by post, counterstating that she was an obedient and docile Hindu wife and was harassed by her husband and in-laws. She denied the husband's allegations. The husband was granted an ex parte divorce in the Family Court on the grounds that the "main objection in the respondent wife's statement was technical ... she had argued that the court had no jurisdiction over this case. However, the Family Court had jurisdiction over this matter because the couple resided in Mumbai" (*HH* v. *BH*, Family Court Records, 2002, Mumbai).

[110] A husband was granted divorce after he proved a separation period of more than fifteen years.

parties do not have children, and when husbands have succeeded in proving adultery.[111] In similar cases, the Family Court is more lenient toward women petitioners who file for divorce and thus increases the bargaining power of women litigants.

Whereas a significant number of cases are filed as mutual-consent settlements in the pretrial stage as per the aims of the Family Court, the data show a high number of cases being converted into mutual-consent applications *during* the trial, which indicates the primacy given to judge–mediated/brokered negotiated settlements in adversarial judicial procedure as an institutional policy of the Family Court. Although this conversion of cases increases the productivity of the court and heightens the quality of judgments (as the outcome is acceptable to both parties) (Galanter 1986), there is mixed evidence on the ground. Some women are able to bargain for more economic rights in cases of contested divorce initiated by husbands.[112] At times, women receive higher financial compensation in cases wherein they have filed parallel criminal cases, such as cases under Section 498(A) Indian Penal Code, as financial settlements are traded for the dropping of charges.[113] Women's ability to obtain an order to prevent the sale

---

[111] The petitioner husband was granted divorce on the grounds of adultery. The wife was also denied custody of the two minor sons (interview with UP, March 8, 2003, Mumbai). In another case, a woman was denied custody of a child and the husband was granted divorce (*KG* v. *AG*, Family Court Records, 2002).

[112] Interview with HG, April 5, 2003, Mumbai. For instance, in *AP* v. *PP*, the husband initiated the divorce, and the wife contested the divorce and filed for maintenance. They agreed to divorce, and the respondent received 100,000 rupees as permanent settlement, received her *stridhan*, and waived her right to maintenance. "Earlier I did not [want] to divorce him, but how long can you live in a marriage when you are not wanted? I have started working, it is not possible for me to continue with this court case" (interview with AP, November 13, 2002, Mumbai).

[113] In one case, a woman received the settlement of 350,000 rupees after agreeing to sign the divorce petition and dropping the case registered under Section 498(A) IPC. In *MP* v. *DP*, the woman received an amount of 350,000 rupees as settlement for withdrawing a case under Section 498(A) IPC (Family Court Records, 2002). In *DP* v. *BP*, Diyya, the wife, received 150,000 rupees as settlement and 1,000 rupees per month for children's maintenance for withdrawing a case under Section 498(A) IPC, as well as a temporary injunction against the sale of the matrimonial residence.

of the matrimonial home can lead to more property rights for them, especially when the husband and his family members need to sell the property, or in cases in which the wife obtains an injunction while residing in matrimonial home[114]; I elaborate on this matter later in this chapter.

Though women are able to bargain in such cases, settlement amounts often remain modest.[115] To illustrate: Meenakshi, the petitioner wife, contested divorce initiated by her husband and had produced the proof that her husband earned 40,000 rupees a month and owned an apartment worth 4 million rupees. However, she received 170,000 rupees as permanent alimony and 150,000 rupees as settlement for the child. The court also awarded maintenance of 1,000 rupees per month to the child. She said: "... Forget the mental agony and social isolation ... after divorce, even economically, things are tough. The school fees for my daughter come to Rs. 2,000 a month. And the pressing problem is that of shelter. We live in a two-bedroom apartment – my parents, brother, my daughter, and I. Things will be so crowded and difficult once my brother marries."[116]

In some cases, women who initiate divorce proceedings tend to forego maintenance or alimony in exchange for a speedy mutual-consent divorce, for women litigants who initiate divorce are more likely to succeed in their claims, but contested cases take longer to settle. In some cases, women ask for maintenance along with divorce in order to negotiate divorce.[117] For other women, factors such as familial and external circumstances, desire to move on to the next phase of life, litigation expenses and tiredness of the litigation process, change in residence, family and

---

[114] A woman petitioner residing with her parents-in-law and children in Mumbai while her husband worked abroad filed for an injunction preventing her husband from throwing her out of the matrimonial home and obtained an order in her favor. She could also file for maintenance for herself and her children (interview with AN, May 11, 2003, Mumbai).

[115] Also, *AS* v. *JS*, 2002; again, the petitioner husband initiated divorce and the wife, after initial contestation, agreed to divorce. She received all her jewelry and 100,000 rupees as alimony. Family Court Records, 2002. In *SM* v. *PM*, the woman initiated the divorce, and the settlement amount was 170,000 rupees. She also received her *stridhan* back.

[116] Interview with DP, November 12, 2002. *DP* v. *BP*, Mumbai, Family Court Records, 2002.

[117] *KP* v. *JP*, Family Court Records, 2002.

STATE LAW AND THE ADJUDICATION PROCESS 129

caste pressures, and judicial pressure are some reasons why they opt to convert the original petition to a mutual-consent divorce, even when the conditions of settlement are not as just.[118]

Section 29, subs. (2) of the Hindu Marriage Act 1955 allows customary divorce among Hindus, and the Family Court is asked to recognize these divorces. Through the content analysis of cases of customary divorce and remarriage in the Madhya Pradesh High Court, Holden demonstrates that the courts did not recognize customary divorce and remarriage until the 1970s. However, in the 1980s and 1990s, the courts had struck a balance between dismissal of these divorce claims and contextual recognition of these divorces, and have thus safeguarded the economic rights of women and children in such marriages, though this trend is not uniform across cases (Holden 2008). The findings here suggest that litigants come to the Family Court to revalidate their customary divorces,[119] or to change terms of their customary divorce: "My husband and I got divorced through caste *panchayat*, but he refused to give me maintenance. I then came to the Court. I told the social worker that these divorces are common in our caste, but I need maintenance for myself and my daughter. She called my husband and he came with his lawyer and he finally agreed to pay Rs. 500 to me and Rs. 500 to my daughter."[120] Women who have been coerced into customary divorce also challenge the same,[121] as do women who

---

[118] For instance, in *PG* v. *HG*, the woman litigant received 3,000 rupees per month maintenance for herself and child for agreeing to divorce even when the husband earned 30,000 rupees a month. In *HG* v. *PG*, the settlement amount was 100,000 rupees, "which did not even cover the cost of wedding" (interview with HK, April 12, 2003, Mumbai).

[119] Many Hindu litigants who obtain divorce through customary laws file cases in state courts afterward to obtain official proofs of divorce. "I was divorced through the *panchayat* and remarried. I work in a corporate firm as a peon and the Human Resources department refused to enter the name of my second wife as a beneficiary in my pension plan despite the fact I presented them with the proof of *sodchithi* (customary divorce), so I had to convince my ex-wife's family and we went to the Family Court to file a case of mutual consent divorce." Interview with MJ, May 3, 2003, Mumbai.

[120] Interview with PW, November 18, 2002, Mumbai.

[121] "My husband took me to his village, gathered his family, and told everyone that this woman is quarrelsome and I want a divorce. They were all strangers – I told them that wait 'til my family comes back, but no one listened to me. I was forced to sign and then

have been forced to sign away their economic rights in marriage by their husbands' families and caste members. In one case, a woman was forced to agree to a customary divorce, was made to sign the divorce, and was forcibly evicted from her house. She said: "My neighbour heard on TV about the legal aid centre at *Mahila Ayog* (State Women's Commission) and she came with me to that office. We talked to a lawyer who said that the caste *panchayat*'s verdict is not acceptable in law. We have filed a case against my husband for maintenance and also for my right to live in the home." [122] By and large, the Family Court has been sympathetic to women in cases where customary divorce has been fraudulently obtained or when women have been denied their rights, as I discuss in the case of Kanu and Mridu in the next chapter. The social workers and judges by and large view these divorces as "practises of lower castes," and some lawyers believe that these "divorces happen in rural areas, not in urban centres" and "are not legal."

At present, a new development is in the offing – the union cabinet in June 2010 approved the introduction of Marriage Laws (Amendment) 2010 to amend the Hindu Marriage Act (1955) and to introduce the irretrievable breakdown of marriage as a ground for divorce under the Hindu law as well as under the Special Marriage Act 1954.[123] This draft of the bill allows ex parte divorce to parties who file petition for divorce by mutual consent in court and face harassment from the other party who does not come to court or wilfully avoids the court so that the matter remains inconclusive.[124] This law will be of use to Hindu women who initiate divorce and barter their material rights in return. On the other hand, this provision would harm the interests of all women who contest

---

I came to my house in Mumbai. Then my brother brought me to court" (interview with NM, February 13, 2003, Mumbai).

[122] Interview with MP, January 23, 2003, Mumbai.

[123] As I write this, the Mumbai-based feminist legal resource center, Majlis, has invited all women's groups to discuss this new initiative by the law ministry and to counter this change to protect women's interests.

[124] http://www.livemint.com, June 11, 2010.

divorce unless their economic rights are protected and until there is a significant change when it comes to social attitudes toward divorce. Besides, as the discussion in the following section highlights, just when courts are laying down criteria to protect Muslim women from unilateral and nonarbitrated divorce initiated by men, this law, if passed in its current form without modifications, will expose Hindu women to husband-initiated, nonarbitrated divorces in state law.

Divorce under Muslim Personal Law: The Debate over Triple Talaq

Muslim Personal Law recognizes three types of divorce: the first is *talaq ahsan*, which consists of a single pronouncement of divorce made during a period of menstruation followed by sexual abstinence during *iddat* (Mulla 1955, 267). The second type of divorce is *talaq hasan*, consisting of three pronouncements made during successive *tuhr*s with no sexual relations taking place during the time (Mulla 1955, 267). The third form of divorce is *talaq ul bidaat*. *Talaq ul bidaat* consists of three pronouncements made during a single *tuhr* in one sentence or a single pronouncement made during a *tuhr* clearly indicating an intention to dissolve the marriage irrevocably (Mulla 1955, 267). Historically, courts have recognized both oral and written divorce (Section 310, Mulla [1955]). *Mehar* is defined as "the sum of property which the wife is entitled to receive from her husband in consideration of marriage" (Mulla 1955, 249) and is customarily (but not always) given to the wife at the time of divorce or death in India. One of the most debated aspect contravening women's rights in Muslim laws in India has been the judicial and societal sanctions given to *talaq bidaat*, or what is known as *Triple Talaq* (divorce). The husband gives this kind of divorce and the wife has to receive it. This form of divorce could be rendered both orally and in written form. In many cases, women are reportedly notified over telephone, telegraph, or email. Many women are divorced through letters: "My husband divorced me by sending a postcard at my mother's house while I was recuperating after the birth of my second child."[125]

It is argued that men's right to this form of divorce is balanced by the woman's economic rights in Muslim family law (Rosen 1984). In Morocco, for instance, men enjoy the right to unilateral divorce but women also enjoy the right to joint property acquired after marriage, dowry, and maintenance. Besides, remarriage is fairly common, as is help of maternal families, especially with respect to child care (Rosen 1984). However, economic rights of Muslim women are yet not as well institutionalized in law in India. Therefore, in the Indian case, even though divorce can be accommodated in societal ways (which give some relief to women) – in many religious sects and groups, remarriage is frequent, divorce is not considered a moral failure, maternal/natal families often assist in child care and shoulder financial responsibility – it cannot be denied that women bear the brunt of social, financial, and emotional consequences of divorce. This form of divorce also prevents women from reporting marital abuse[126] and consolidates gender inequality within the conjugal family.[127] – "The threat of divorce casts a shadow on marital life…. Whenever he was displeased, he would say 'I shall divorce you.' I was constantly worried; where will I go if he utters those words?"[128] The issue of the validity of written and oral divorce under Muslim Personal Law remains crucial for Muslim women (as it is also with Hindu women) who wish to prosecute their husbands for domestic violence by filing a case under the provision of Section 498(a) IPC, as only married women can file under this provision.

Moreover, in courts and in society, this form of divorce causes legal confusion because it is difficult to prove its validity. In numerous cases the husband claimed divorce and the wife opposed it, and several times

---

[125] Interview with PS, March 23, 2003, Mumbai.
[126] Interview with Vandana Nanaware, social worker, June 6, 2003, Mumbai.
[127] Ibid.
[128] Interview with KB, January 11, 2003, Mumbai.

STATE LAW AND THE ADJUDICATION PROCESS 133

wives claimed that they were divorced and husbands opposed it.[129] Over the years, the standard practice has been for husbands to mail divorces through registered post requiring the recipient's (the wife's) signature to establish the validity of divorce. This method is most popular because both the sender and the recipient have proofs of divorce, but it is not foolproof and has been challenged as, for example, in many cases where wives are unaware of the husband's intentions. In many instances, women who have no inkling of their husbands' plans to divorce accept and sign the registered mail delivered by the postman, thinking that it is a money order, then read that they are divorced.[130]

The thrust toward the centralization of law is evident in the lawmaking exercise of the Supreme Court and higher courts through the establishment of precedents in key issues. This issue of validity of triple *talaq* has percolated in Indian courts, and recently, judges in higher courts, sensitive to minority sensibilities on the matter, have laid down criteria to regulate triple *talaq* and restrain its misuse (see *Shamim Ara v. State of UP and Another*, AIR SCW 4162).[131] In this case, the court

---

[129] In one case, a Muslim wife filed a case for maintenance under Section 125 CrPC in the Family Court. Her husband produced proof of divorce in the Family Court; it showed that the wife had signed for a registered letter. The court dismissed the woman's petition for maintenance under Section 125 CrPC. The woman and her family got a *fatwa*, or legal opinion, from another clergyman, who held that the divorce was invalid as it was not communicated to the wife. The man was to remarry, and the first wife and her family contacted his future bride's family to prevent the marriage, as polygyny was not widely practiced in their community. Ultimately, the parties settled the matter privately, and the husband returned the dowry, gave maintenance during the period of *iddat*, and returned the *mehar* to his ex-wife (interview with NH, January 17, 2003, Mumbai).

[130] Interview with HMA, January 12, 2003, Mumbai.

[131] " ... We are ... of the opinion that the *talaq* to be effective has to be pronounced. The term 'pronounce' means to proclaim, to utter formally, to utter rhetorically, to declare, to utter, to articulate (see Chambers 20th Century Dictionary, New Edition, p. 1030). There is no proof of ... what the High Court has upheld as *talaq* is a plea taken in the written statement.... We are very clear ... that a mere plea taken in the written statement of a divorce having been pronounced sometime in the past cannot by itself be treated as effectuating *talaq* on the date of delivery of the copy of the written statement to the wife. The respondent No. 2 ought to have adduced evidence and proved

established the precedent that the unilateral triple divorce is valid only if it is justified and is pronounced in front of witnesses. The Court also opined that oral triple *talaq* is invalid unless both the parties have a copy of the divorce.[132] The court has given a similar verdict in the Dagdu Pathan case.[133] In this case, the full bench of the Aurangabad Division of the Bombay High Court appointed two advocates and scholars of Islamic law as amici curiae to assist it in resolving the controversy over triple *talaq*. The bench, in its decision, combined the discussion of diverse judicial precedents in the Indian courts regarding this matter in light of the constitutional norms, and also drew from sources of Islamic law and legal opinions of eminent jurists on Islamic law.[134] The bench held that the mere recitation of oral divorce in front of the witnesses or the written deed of divorce, the *talaqnama*, was not enough to prove divorce.[135] In a case of disputed Islamic divorce, the husband is required to prove that the *talaq* was not given in a whimsical and arbitrary fashion, that he had a valid reason to grant divorce, that there was arbitration prior to pronouncement of divorce (the arbitrators were people nominated

---

the pronouncement of *talaq* on 11.7.1987, and if he failed improving the plea raised in the written statement, the plea ought to be treated as failed.... Neither the marriage between the parties stands dissolved ... nor does the liability of the respondent No. 2 to pay maintenance comes to an end." *Shamim Ara* v. *State of UP and Another*, 2002, AIR SCW 4162. Cited and discussed in *Muslim India* 239, November 2002.

[132] It is argued that judges in the higher courts are more likely to give such verdicts when there is sufficient mobilization and litigation around the issue, when reforms do not contradict judges' perceptions of the group tradition, and when reforms are compatible with judges' normative visions of the family (Subramanian 2008).

[133] See *Dagdu s/o Chotu Pathan* v. *Rahimbi Dagdu Pathan and Others*, May 2002, Aurangabad bench of Mumbai High Court. *All India Maharashtra Law Reporter (Criminal)* 2: 1230–1261.

[134] The judges synthesized and discussed Mulla's Principles of Mahomedan Law, a compendium of Islamic laws published by the All India Muslim Personal Law Board, Ameer Ali's treatises on Mohmeddan Law, and took into account Maulana Mohamed Ali's "Commentary on the Holy Quran," and also quoted a jurist, Abdulla Yusuf Ali's opinions on *triple talaq* (see *Dagdu Pathan* v. *Rahimbi Dagdu Pathan and Others*, 1236–1247).

[135] Indeed, the judges opined that any *talaqnama*, which is a form of registered letter that is not addressed to the wife, would be considered invalid.

STATE LAW AND THE ADJUDICATION PROCESS 135

by respective parties), that the divorce was witnessed by two male Muslims[136] (or one male and two female Muslims, as per injunctions of Islamic law), and also prove that he did not have sexual relations with his wife following the divorce. The judges also held that there should be an attempt of reconciliation made between the two parties and their arbitrators before the husband grants divorce to the wife, to establish reasonable grounds for divorce.

In both cases, for instance, the court did not abolish the right of Muslim men to give unconditional divorce to Muslim women. Instead, the court has established conditions to regulate the extent of male privilege in granting divorce. The state's response shows that the judges sensitive to minority sensibilities have attempted to accommodate the group while protecting the rights of Muslim women.

The doctrine of legal precedent holds that following the dictates of the Supreme Court is the duty of the lower courts[137] (Carminker 1994), and that lower courts are crucial to the interpretation and implementation of Supreme Court decisions (Johnson 1987, 325). However, it is unclear when a precedent is compelling enough to command judicial obedience from judges who resist it (Kelso and Kelso 1996; Lee 1999). In spite of legal precedents, the Family Court has tended to accept unilateral divorce without examining the conditions in which the divorce took place. Judges in the Family Court seek written proof of divorce (and hence do not accept oral divorce as valid),[138] but they do not investigate

---

[136] The court here has held that a Hindu witnessing an Islamic divorce is invalid, and thus has demarcated the boundaries between religious law and customary practice, and created the divide between civil and religious laws.

[137] Arguments in favor of legal precedent can be made from the standpoint of fairness ("treat like cases alike," Schauer 1987, 595), predictability (knowing that the past decision helps anticipate present and future decisions), efficiency as each case requires little scrutiny and stability (cross-case differences are suppressed and similarities of the human condition are emphasized) (Carminker 1994; Schauer 1987, 602).

[138] The issue of validity of Muslim marriages and divorce arises time and again in matrimonial legislation concerning the economic rights of Muslim women. Muslim husbands who divorce their wives must prove this divorce in court by showing proof of divorce. Standard procedure in cases of divorce has been to send a written notice of divorce

the conditions under which the divorce took place.[139] For instance, in one case, the wife contested the divorce and the husband rented advertising space in *Tarun Bharat*, a local newspaper in their hometown, proclaiming divorce, called this "*Jaher talaq*" – a public divorce – and claimed that " ... There was no way she could miss that – everyone in her town reads that newspaper." The Family Court accepted this "public divorce" as valid.[140] In another case, the Family Court accepted the evidence of a written *talaqnama* produced by the husband despite the wife's claim that her signature on the registered letter was obtained by fraud. In another case, a woman had signed a money order for 5,000 rupees an amount equivalent to her *mehar*. The husband argued that the acceptance of *mehar* by the wife was a proof that she had received divorce. The Family Court accepted this claim of the husband without investigating whether this portion of the dower was prompt or deferred.

Intricacies of Muslim Personal Law are not usually debated in judgments of the Family Court because judges and many lawyers are unfamiliar with them.[141] Anisa, a Muslim litigant, claimed that "she was forced to sign on divorce papers by her husband and his family members"[142] but failed to convince the court. Thus, Muslim women are not granted enough protection and rights in state courts at lower levels.

In general, we see here that the state-led attempts at reforms from above are diffused due to the lack of coordination between higher and lower courts in India. Communal outlook of the judges (Mukhopadhyay 1998), fear of reversal and lack of knowledge about the Muslim Personal

---

to the wife, along with the check or money order for *mehar* and maintenance during *iddat*. The wife has to sign the registered letter in order to accept the divorce. In many cases, the wife refuses to sign the letter and claims ignorance of divorce. As a result, the husband cannot provide a valid proof of divorce in court.

[139] Muslim women have used this tendency of the courts in their favor in a few cases: A Muslim husband's petition under the restitution of conjugal rights was dismissed when the respondent wife argued that he had divorced her, and therefore the court dismissed the case (interview with AM, February 16, 2003, Mumbai).

[140] See Interview with GQ, April 6, 2003, Mumbai.

[141] See *NS* v. *SK*, Family Court Records, 2002.

[142] See *RS* v. *SMS*, Family Court Records, 2002.

STATE LAW AND THE ADJUDICATION PROCESS 137

Law, and a desire to avoid controversy (especially in the matter of Muslim Personal Law) are some reasons why judges in the Family Court do not push for strict criteria to validate triple *talaq*. During fieldwork, I also found that women's organizations and a majority of lawyers were unaware of this judgment and its implications. However, a very small number of lawyers had begun to realize the potential of the Dagdu Pathan case in bargaining outside the court. As one lawyer suggested:

Until now, I had fewer tools to negotiate a written divorce if a *qazi* delivered a divorce to a woman who had signed that letter, proving divorce. But with this judgment, almost any divorce can be seen as invalid – women have been given unprecedented leverage.... Earlier, the *qazi*, while bargaining, would suggest the contesting party was a "lesser Muslim" who placed secular law above Islamic law.... And this judgment cannot be countered by the conservative elements – the learned judges have justified their decision on the basis of Islamic law and the holy *Quran* itself.[143]

Divorce under Muslim Personal Law: Issues in Statutory Divorce

The Dissolution of Muslim Marriage Act 1939 allows Muslim women to initiate judicial divorce and lays down grounds for divorce.[144] There are relatively fewer cases filed under this act in the Family Court, and most of them are withdrawn or converted into mutual-consent divorce. The grounds for divorce are similar to the grounds for divorce under the Hindu Marriage Act 1955. Here too, the judicial construction of cruelty includes polygyny.[145] Cases filed under this act are also converted into divorce by mutual consent.[146] For instance, in one case, the wife had

---

[143] Interview with Niloufer Akhtar, lawyer, June 23, 2003, Mumbai.
[144] The grounds include the husband's lengthy absence from the marital home, his failure to perform marital obligations, cruelty, impotence, insanity, and imprisonment for a long period.
[145] Interview with FS, March 3, 2003, Mumbai.
[146] Interview with YR, March 6, 2003, Mumbai. In another case, the petitioner wife had claimed 300,000 rupees and the cost of litigation. The case was settled by mutual

filed for divorce on the grounds of cruelty and desertion. The matter was decided by mutual consent wherein the wife got custody of the children and did not ask for maintenance or *mehar*, as the husband was unemployed. The husband returned her *stridhan*. In another case, a litigant withdrew a case under this act because the societal solution of divorce secured more rights than the one in the state law. A litigant had filed for divorce under this act, but her husband absconded to another city and thus did not accept the summons. She could have obtained an ex parte divorce from the Family Court, but it would not have helped her recover her *mehar* that amounted to 100,000 rupees and *stridhan* valued at 400,000 rupees. Her lawyer suggested that she use "extrajudicial means to persuade the husband." The family members withdrew the legal case, traced the husband to another city, and recovered the dowry and obtained divorce after foregoing *mehar* as part of the bargain to obtain the divorce.[147] Muslim Personal Law accepts *khula* (divorce initiated by the wife and accepted by the husband under different bargaining arrangements)[148] and *mubaraat* (divorce by mutual consent) (see Sections 307, 319, 320, Mulla [1955]). Judges in the Family Court accept the written form of unilateral divorce given by the husbands, but do not readily recognize societal divorce by women (*khula*), nor do the judges recognize legal innovations at the community level, such as *faskh*.[149] In two cases, petitioner husbands had filed for restitution of conjugal rights, and the wives challenged the suits by showing proof of *khula* and *faskh*. Judges did not factor in societal divorces while framing legal issues in their judgments and rules in the husbands' favor.[150]

---

consent, and the wife received a sum of 30,000 rupees as part of *mehar* and *iddat* (interview with SK, February 4, 2003, Mumbai. See also *Abdul Zalil Ahmed* v. *Mustt. Marina Begum*, AIR 1999 Gauhati, 28).

[147] Interview with MA, June 12, 2003, Mumbai.

[148] Under Muslim Personal Law, the wife may instigate the divorce only with the consent of the husband, and it is usually effected by the wife offering a compensation to the husband if he releases her from the marital bond (Mulla 1955, 272).

[149] *Faskh* is a judicially arbitrated divorce (Pearl 1987).

[150] Interviews with YS, January 28, 2003; HS, January 31, 2003, Mumbai.

Menski has argued that Hindu husbands can also unilaterally divorce their wives after obtaining an order for judicial separation and then later filing for divorce (Menski 2001). There are other similarities between Hindu and Muslim laws. Divorce by mutual consent is allowed under both religious laws. The Family Court's aim to prevent divorces in society is against the spirit of provisions of mutual-consent divorce under Hindu and Muslim personal laws. Both the Hindu Marriage Act 1955 and the Dissolution of Muslim Marriage Act 1939 allow divorce on similar grounds of fault, and the manner in which these grounds are construed in legal processes are similar, as shown in the previous sections. Litigants and lawyers use similar legal strategies when it comes to countering Hindu and Muslim women's claims for maintenance, divorce, and restitution of conjugal rights.

Women and Property in Marriage and Divorce Laws

Family law establishes the state's control over the intrahousehold distribution of property. The state lays down criteria for the division of matrimonial resources. Family law is also subject to the state's policy of prevention of destitution, crime reduction, and protection of vulnerable members of the family. The Indian state's inability to provide welfare to vulnerable citizens has led the state to delegate this responsibility to the family through the enactment of laws on maintenance (Menski 2003).

Legal Provisions Applicable to Hindu and Muslim Women under State Laws

The concept of matrimonial property does not exist under any personal or secular laws. However, Hindu wives are entitled to claim maintenance under the Hindu Adoption and Maintenance Act (HAMA) 1956.[151] After

---

[151] Maintenance defined under the HAMA includes the provision for food, clothing, residence, education, medical assistance, and treatment. The act also lays down the criteria to decide the quantum of maintenance. The courts are to pay due regard to the position and status of the parties, the reasonable wants of the claimant, and the value of the

divorce or annulment of marriage, Hindu women lose the right to maintenance under this Act. Hindu wives are also entitled to seek alimony or maintenance when they petition for any of the matrimonial remedies available under the Hindu Marriage Act 1955, as maintenance/alimony and custody matters are ancillary relief under this Act (Sagade 1996, 34). Divorced Muslim women can seek maintenance under the Muslim Women's (Protection of Rights on Divorce) Act 1986.

Married women of any religion can file for maintenance under Section 125 CrPC without filing for any matrimonial remedies under any personal laws. This section is popular among poorer members of society, because the recovery of arrears is easier: The law enables the Family Court to attach the property of the defaulter in case of nonpayment of maintenance. Married women across religious boundaries can file for an injunction under Section 7(d) of the Family Courts Act 1984. They also have a right to retrieve *stridhan*[152] during the subsistence of marriage or upon divorce.

In terms of matrimonial property, Muslim women are entitled to *mehar*. According to Mulla, the amount of *mehar* should not be less than ten dirhams (Section 286, Mulla [1955], 249), but the societal practice varies considerably across sect and class lines among Muslims. The amount of *mehar* can be fixed before or after marriage (Section 287, Mulla [1955], 250), and a wife is entitled to proper dower (*mahr-i-misl*) even if "the marriage was regularised under the express condition that she should not claim any *mehar*" (Section 289, Mulla [1955], 250).

There are two kinds of dower: prompt and deferred. The prompt *mehar* is payable on demand (payable upon the dissolution of marriage by death or divorce) (Section 290, Mulla [1955], 251). A wife – and after

---

claimant's property and income derived from such property, from the claimant's own earnings, or from any other source (Sagade 1996, 29).

[152] *Stridhan* is the woman's property, and the husband cannot alienate this property or mortgage it against her will. Legally, the wife retains control over this property and should receive her *stridhan* whenever she needs it.

her death, her heirs – can sue for *mehar* (Section 292, Mulla [1955], 252). However, a wife may remit her *mehar* in favor of her husband; such remission is valid if made with free consent (Section 291, Mulla [1955], 252). In state law, a Muslim husband is bound to maintain his wife and does not enjoy the right to maintenance from his wife (Fyzee 1974; Mulla 1955). Section 2(ii) of the Dissolution of Muslim Marriage Act 1939 allows a Muslim wife to seek divorce if the husband has failed to maintain her for a period of more than two years (Mulla 1955, 245).

Maintenance and Alimony under Hindu Personal Law

Maintenance and alimony is an ancillary remedy under the Hindu Marriage Act 1955. Thus, women or men can claim maintenance or permanent alimony from the other spouse in cases filed under mutual-consent divorce or contested divorce. It is an independent remedy under the Hindu Adoption and Maintenance Act (HAMA) 1956. As per Section 18 of the HAMA, a Hindu wife is entitled to claim maintenance from her husband if the husband is guilty of cruelty, conversion, desertion, adultery, polygyny, or communicable disease.[153] Failure on the part of the husband to comply with the decree passed for the restitution of conjugal rights in the wife's favor does not disentitle a wife to maintenance under the HAMA 1956.[154] A Hindu wife loses her right to maintenance if she converts to another religion or if she is proved to be "unchaste."

Even though there is no provision to grant interim maintenance under this act, the Family Court had granted the same in several cases.[155] These provisions of maintenance under the Hindu law contrast sharply with social practices of groups and families in which both parties to marriage

[153] In one case, a woman had filed for maintenance under this act. The husband challenged the validity of the marriage by proving customary divorce. The wife was granted interim maintenance of 2,000 rupees per month (interview with KS, January 2003, Mumbai).
[154] See *KK* v. *KK*, Family Court Records, 2002.
[155] Ibid. Also, interview with KS, January 16, 2003, Mumbai.

contribute almost equally to household resources; these provisions also do not benefit women who are the primary earners in the family.[156]

While awarding maintenance under the Hindu law, the court considers the income and work of the spouses, custodial responsibility of both husband and wife after the termination of marriage, and their financial responsibility toward other dependents in the family. In rare cases, the court may also heed factors such as the length of the marriage as well as the age and health of both the spouses, but it does not respect the wife's contribution to the marriage in terms of her labor and social networks that might have benefited the couple and shaped their lifestyle during marriage. Proof of the wife's employment, however menial, usually renders her ineligible for alimony or maintenance.[157] In one case, the petitioner wife had filed for divorce on the grounds of cruelty, and had asked the court for interim maintenance for herself and her minor daughter during the period. The Family Court granted 500 rupees per month for the child, but did not grant her interim maintenance because she worked as a secretary in a firm and earned 2,260 rupees per month; this, despite the fact that her salary would not support herself and her daughter, even for a week.[158]

The establishment of fault is an important criterion for awarding maintenance, but fault does not always influence calculations in terms of maintenance and alimony under the Hindu Marriage Act 1955 as well as under the HAMA 1956. In one instance, Mina,[159] a petitioner wife, filed for restitution of conjugal rights as well as maintenance for herself and her children under the HAMA 1956. The Family Court ruled in her favor,

---

[156] In one case, a woman had paid for her husband's education and contributed to buying a house postmarriage. At the time of divorce, she was not entitled to maintenance, and was also forced to partition the property and thus treat it as a joint property. Her contribution remained undervalued (interview with SH, March 23, 2003, Mumbai). I discuss this issue in greater depth in the following chapter.

[157] In another case, the Family Court refused to grant maintenance to a Hindu wife because the husband was able to prove that the wife worked as an insurance agent in an informal capacity (interview with DP, May 5, 2003, Mumbai).

[158] Interview with HM, February 23, 2003, Mumbai.

[159] Interview with MD, January 15, 2003, Mumbai. In another case, a petitioner husband had filed for divorce. The wife filed for restitution and maintenance for herself and

and the husband challenged the decision of the Family Court on the grounds that "had the petitioner been treated with cruelty, she would not have filed for restitution of conjugal rights." She filed for interim maintenance while the case was pending in the High Court. The husband was a skilled worker in a company and earned 6,000 rupees per month. The court ruled that the petitioner had proved desertion, adultery, polygyny, and cruelty on the part of the husband. The court also opined that the husband earned 10,000 rupees while the wife earned 2,600 rupees (out of which she paid 1,500 rupees for house rent) and had custody of children for the past eight years. The wife had been deserted for eight years, and the husband had not maintained her or the children. However, the court did not grant maintenance to the wife as "she was earning [money]," but granted maintenance of 2,000 rupees per month for the children.

There are no standard measures to decide the amount of maintenance granted under the HMA 1955, but usually the amounts granted are less than one-fifth of the husband's income and property.[160] Settlement amounts are lowest in cases filed under mutual-consent divorce.[161] Many of these marriages were of short duration, and couples did not have children or joint financial investments. In mutual-consent cases, only a few parents who did not have custody paid child support.

Legally, innocent women have higher chances of obtaining financial settlements in cases of contested divorce that are "converted" into mutual-consent cases.[162] Cases filed under Section 18 of HAMA 1956 are often converted into cases of mutual consent under Section 13(b) of the HMA 1955.[163] And, as discussed earlier, whereas some women are able to take

child. She claimed that she had to leave her employment because the husband made threatening calls to her office, and she had to quit her job due to his threats. The court denied interim maintenance on the grounds that the wife was capable of working (*VS v. HS*, Family Court Records, 2002).

[160] Interviews with RS, April 16, 2003; MS, March 18, 2003; JK, May 4, 2003, Mumbai.

[161] See Sagade 1996 for similar observations.

[162] Interview with JS, June 6, 2003, Mumbai.

[163] A petitioner wife who had filed for maintenance agreed to a divorce by mutual consent and received 100,000 rupees as a settlement amount and recovered her *stridhan* (interviews with PG, June 4, 2003; VT, February 16, 2003, Mumbai).

advantage of this trend, especially when they have been able to file parallel criminal cases or obtain an injunction against the sale of matrimonial residence, the cases of divorce in which the husband gains his freedom in exchange for a financial settlement favoring the legally innocent wife are often not as rewarding for women litigants. Women are often forced to compromise during the process of divorce because they come to realize their financial and social vulnerability in the litigation process.[164] Women litigants find it difficult to prove the husband's income and to produce relevant papers such as salary slips, land records, documents showing the registration of property, details of pension funds, income tax returns, and investments.[165] In many cases, husbands are able to hide financial assets when they work in family business. "Many businesses are family owned, or husbands work for their joint and extended family or caste members. In such instances, it is difficult to prove a husband's independent income.... Property prices in Bombay are high and most middle-class families are joint families. The apartments are likely to be in the name of a litigant's father-in-law or mother-in-law. They cannot count these as their husband's property even if he resides there, or would inherit it in [the] future."[166] Male litigants tend to have more financial resources than women and are able to hire better lawyers, and thus escape the payment of maintenance and property.[167] Pressure by the court and social workers

---

[164] In two cases, women won maintenance claims but opted for reconciliation "for (their) children's futures." A woman lawyer stated that "women come to me for advice about divorce, but often do not opt for it as it can potentially render them penniless after years of marriage" (personal communication with Indira Jaising, lawyer, April 2, 1999, Washington, DC). In another case of contested divorce, the wife was forced to reconcile because she realized that the financial amount awarded to her would not be enough to sustain her (interview with KS, February 5, 2003, Mumbai).

[165] Interview with Anamika Vichare, lawyer, April 6, 2003, Mumbai.

[166] Interview with Hemang Jariwala, lawyer, February 15, 2003, Mumbai.

[167] Husbands also court arrest, resign from their jobs, or transfer their jobs to the name of another family member in order to avoid payment. Husbands who work in family businesses claim lack of income as the excuse. They use lengthy court proceedings to "tire their wives" until they drop the case; they often intimidate their wives and family members on their way to court. They take loans and show deductions in their salary slips to claim low income, and make false claims about their wives' earnings (interviews with Anamika Vichare, April 6, 2003; KS, February 5, 2003; RS, March 7, 2003, Mumbai).

to arrive at a negotiated settlement can adversely affect women litigants who have made substantive contributions to their marriage.[168]

In general, postdivorce settlement amounts are meager, and often the divorced spouse must rely on oneself, the natal family, or the new spouse for material subsistence. Although permanent alimony or settlement amounts in some cases may seem high[169] to some litigants, the amounts do not enable women to buy separate property, and as a result, they remain dependent on their natal families.

Divorce among Hindus leads to different economic and social consequences for women than it does for men. The most adversely affected divorcée women are homemakers, especially those with children, who have been married for more than ten years; women in low-paying occupations;[170] women in low-income jobs who are ineligible for maintenance; and women whose lifestyle is reduced drastically as a result of divorce.

Muslim Women's (Protection of Rights on Divorce) Act 1986

Divorced Muslim women can claim maintenance under the Muslim Women's (Protection of Rights on Divorce) Act 1986. Section 3 of the act

---

[168] In one case, a wife had supported her husband for several years on her salary, and later had filed for divorce and custody of children because the husband was violent. She was ineligible for maintenance because she worked in a school as a teacher. The husband refused to pay any maintenance for the children in exchange for divorce (interview with SP, January 24, 2003, Mumbai).

[169] Settlements in these cases remained between 100,000 and 500,000 rupees. Even though these seem like large amounts, to some, other litigants indicate that these amounts are "less than the cost of the wedding we paid for" (interview with RS, March 7, 2003, Mumbai).

[170] In most cases, husbands are able to retain their lifestyle, whereas the same cannot be said of wives; an earning wife is seen to be able to "maintain herself" regardless of changes in lifestyle that divorce might induce. The lack of a home for women is also overlooked, though this renders a divorced woman dependent on her natal family. In one case, the court refused to give a divorce to the petitioner husband and granted custody of the daughter to the wife, but failed, on technical legal grounds, to give permanent alimony to the wife and the child despite evidence that the wife was unemployed. Six months after the divorce, the wife, who was employed as a stenographer, had found employment again, but her monthly salary was 2,400 rupees, and the money was not sufficient to support herself and her daughter (interview with HS and her family members, May 2, 2003, Mumbai).

specifies entitlements for divorced Muslim women.[171] In many instances, social workers, media persons, and even lawyers are unaware of the provisions and interpretations of this law.[172] Feminist and legal scholars have portrayed this act as regressive and antiwomen, and they have argued that divorced Muslim women are only entitled to maintenance during the period of *iddat* under the act (Narain 2001; Parashar 1992; Sagade 1996; Sunder Rajan 2003). Recent literature has drawn attention to precedents from the Supreme Court, especially in the Daniel Latifi case[173] and pro-women judgments of several High Courts that have interpreted the act liberally and have awarded fair settlement amounts to divorced Muslim women (Agnes 1999; Subramanian 2005). It has been argued that the act provides more rights to Muslim women than those granted under Section 125 CrPC. While the ceiling of 1,500 rupees a month is placed on maintenance amounts under Section 125 CrPC, there is no limit to the amount of maintenance awarded under this act, and the act can potentially open doors for the distribution of matrimonial property among Muslims (Subramanian 2008). In addition, before the enactment of this act, divorced Muslim women belonging to the upper and middle strata fell through the cracks, as there was no provision to address their financial vulnerability postdivorce. They could not seek recourse to Section

---

[171] The remedy as per Section 3(1)(a) of the MWA 1986 is: (i) a reasonable and fair provision and maintenance to be made and paid to her during the *iddat* period by her former husband; (ii) an amount equal to the sum of *mehar*; (iii) all the properties belonging to her before or at the time of marriage.

[172] Interview with H. Sheikh, criminal lawyer, March 15, 2003, Mumbai. He appeared for a Muslim woman who had filed a case under Section 125 CrPC. Upon being asked to explain his legal strategy, the lawyer replied that "divorced Muslim women are not entitled to maintenance beyond *iddat*."

[173] In *Daniel Latifi and Another* v. *Union of India*, the Supreme Court bench of G. B. Pattanaik, S. Babu, D. P. Mohapatra, D. Raju, and S. V. Patil held that the liability of a Muslim husband to his divorced wife arising under Section 3(1)(a) of the act to pay maintenance is not confined to the *iddat* period, but a Muslim husband is liable to make reasonable and fair provision for the future of the divorced wife, which obviously includes her maintenance as well. Such a reasonable and fair provision extending beyond the *iddat* period must be made by the husband within the *iddat* period in terms of Section 3(1)(a) of the act. See *Daniel Latifi* v. *Union of India*, (7) SC 740 [2001].

125 CrPC because the amounts granted under this section were too low for them to go through the process of litigation. The Muslim Women's (Protection of Rights on Divorce) Act 1986 bridges this gap.

It is my contention that the Muslim Women's Act 1986 (MWA) provides additional benefits to Muslim women in ways other than those previously discussed. In some respects, the MWA is more progressive than current matrimonial legislation among Hindus. The following case illuminates my claim. A female Muslim petitioner had filed a case in the Family Court for maintenance. The husband proved that he had divorced her, and the case was transferred to the Metropolitan Magistrates' Court in 1998 to be tried under the Muslim Women's Act 1986. The court delivered a judgment in 2000 asking the husband to pay a lump sum of 200,000 rupees to his wife, and he was also asked to pay *mehar* and *iddat*. The respondent defaulted, and the magistrate gave an order of arrest under the Code of Criminal Procedure 1973 (2 of 1974) and Section 3(4) of the Muslim Women's Act 1986. The respondent was jailed for forty-five days after which time he approached the petitioner to settle the case; he paid 75,000 rupees and returned her *stridhan*. The case was settled in 2003 and by then, the wife had a child from her second marriage.[174] Divorced women who remarry lose their rights to maintenance under Section 125 CrPC. In contrast, under the MWA 1986, the remarriage of a divorced Muslim woman does not nullify her claim.

This trend of some lower courts to award a settlement irrespective of the marital status of the divorced Muslim woman was challenged, as the Daniel Latifi case remained ambiguous on the issue of settlement in light of the wife's remarriage.[175] However, recent legal developments have

---

[174] The information about the date of her second marriage was vague, but it is possible that the second marriage took place before the court arrived at a decision in the case. Interviews with Nisar Ghatte, February 19, 2003; ZS, litigant, April 23, 2003, Mumbai.

[175] In the Daniel Latifi case, the Supreme Court also reiterated that a divorced Muslim woman who has not remarried and who is not able to maintain herself after the *iddat* period can proceed as provided under Section 4 of the act against her relatives, who are liable to maintain her in proportion to the properties that they inherit from such divorced woman on her death, according to Muslim law (including her children and parents). If any of the relatives are unable to pay maintenance, the magistrate may

upheld the trend outlined here. In 2004, the Kerala High Court, in *Abdul Hameed* v. *Fousiya*,[176] held that although the remarriage of the wife could be a criteria for calculating the quantum of maintenance, remarriage could only have a limited impact on the settlement claim, and that the husband will not have a right to claim return of the amount paid to his wife who has remarried. In 2007, in the case of *V Bapputty @ Muhammed* v. *Shahida, D/O Muhammed*,[177] the petitioner wife had filed the suits against her third husband. She had earlier received settlement under the MWA 1986 from her first husband, and had not filed the case against her second husband. This time around, the court considered the question: Is a wife who has got remarried and who has received reasonable and fair provision and maintenance from her former husband entitled to claim reasonable and fair provision and maintenance again under Section 3 of the Muslim Women (Protection of Rights on Divorce) Act 1986 from the next husband who remarries and divorces her? Once again, the Kerala High Court has held that each case filed under this Act has to be seen independently, and stated that the remarriage of the petitioner wife could only have a limited impact on the calculation of the amount of settlement.

In another case, a Muslim man divorced his first wife in 1994 after four years of marriage and married a second time. The ex-wife at that time met with some lawyers who told her that she could not file for maintenance, as there was no provision for maintenance beyond *iddat* for Muslim women. "Lawyers confuse you more – I received different answers – some told me that you can't file for maintenance at all, others told me that you can get maintenance only if you file for divorce during *iddat* – I did not know where to go and what to do (*mein pareshan thi*)."[178]

---

direct the State *Wakf* Board, established under the act, to pay such maintenance. Based on this, in some cases, it was held that a former husband's obligation or liability to provide a fair and reasonable settlement to his former wife after the period of *iddat* extends only until the date of her remarriage, and, if not married, until her death (see *Rasiya* v. *State of Kerala* [2002] (2) KLT 825).

[176] See *Abdul Hameed* v. *Fousiya* [2004] (3) KLT 1049.
[177] *V. Bappukutty@Muhammed* v. *Shahid D/O Muhammed* [2007] RD-KL 1497.
[178] Interview with Shaheen Sattar, March 20, 2003, Mumbai.

STATE LAW AND THE ADJUDICATION PROCESS

Through local contacts, a Hindu neighbor introduced her to another lawyer who filed a case for compensation in 1997 under the Muslim Women's Act 1986. "Some people think that the Act applies to women only if they file for maintenance during *iddat* as specified in Section 3(1)(a) of the Act, but Section 3(3)(a) settles this doubt – a divorced Muslim woman can make an application for maintenance after a lapse of some years if she is unable to maintain herself, and she is entitled to settlement based on the standard of life enjoyed during her marriage."[179] The Court gave a verdict in 2000, awarding her a lump sum settlement of 150,000 rupees, and asked the husband to pay it in monthly instalments.

Feminist scholars suggest that the potential of the MWA can be realized only if it is interpreted in a gender-just spirit by the judiciary (Narain 2001). However, in a shared adjudication model, the law is also used by lawyers to effect settlements in society. The judicial decisions in the Dagdu Pathan case, as well as judicial interpretation of the Muslim Women's Act 1986, have begun to change gender relations on the ground, and this is visible in litigation strategies used by lawyers. "A client came to me with a registered letter delivered by her husband's lawyer, giving her a triple *talaq* – I told her that this divorce is invalid, as it does not fulfil the conditions of divorce outlined in the Dagdu Pathan case. But then, I counselled her that she can file for compensation under the Muslim Women's Act 1986: this option is better – she could then move on with her life as well, rather than hoping for the marital situation to improve. I sent a notice to the husband, announcing the intention to file for maintenance under the MWA. His lawyer contacted me and we settled the matter between us, the client accepted the divorce, and got a settlement of Rs. 250,000."[180]

Under the Act, divorced Muslim women have more rights than divorced Hindu women have under the HMA. In principle, the HMA is gender-neutral, and both husbands and wives can claim alimony under the

---

[179] Interview with Nisar Ghatte, lawyer, February 19, 2003, Mumbai.
[180] Ibid.

HMA, whereas the Muslim Women's (Protection of Rights on Divorce) Act 1986 awards settlements only to the wife. Divorced Hindu women can claim alimony or maintenance only under the HMA. Under the HMA, the payment of alimony and divorce often go hand in hand. As a result, Hindu wives who wish to obtain divorce often forego their alimony to arrive at mutually acceptable solutions. Also, contested divorce among Hindus is awarded on grounds of fault, and in several cases, courts tend to deny the wife maintenance or alimony if she is found guilty.[181] Courts also tended to deny alimony to Hindu wives in cases of dismissal of petitions for divorce.[182] Section 25(3) of the HMA allows the cancellation of permanent alimony to the wife (or the husband) on the grounds of unchastity or remarriage. Although judges have tended to rule that this provision is not an absolute bar disentitling the wife to maintenance,[183] the issue is left to judicial discretion.[184] Under this section, maintenance under the HMA is subject to revision if there is some change in the financial circumstances of either of the parties. In some cases, this affects a Hindu divorcée's interests adversely. Divorced Muslim women, on the other hand, are not subject to these pressures, because the MWA encourages lump-sum settlement, and women can rebuild their lives once they receive the order even if the process of collection of dues is stretched by the opposite parties. In addition, a divorced Muslim woman is entitled to maintenance from her husband, but if he fails to maintain her, then, under this act, if she has not remarried and if she is unable to maintain herself, the magistrate can pass an order directing her relatives who are entitled to inherit her property, or her children or parents, or extended relatives, or lastly, the State *Wakf* Board (see Section 4 of the Muslim Women's [Protection of Rights on Divorce] Act 1986) to pay her maintenance. Hindu women are entitled to maintenance only from their husbands, and legal individualism undergirding this provision harms the interests of Hindu women, because in many

---

[181] For instance, see the discussion in Sagade 1996, 50–59.
[182] See the discussion in the case of *HS* v. *ZS*, Family Court Records, 2003, Mumbai.
[183] See *Jaipal Kaur* v. *Ishan Singh*, 1983 HLR 119, discussed in Sagade 1996, 59.
[184] See Diwan 1988, 591.

cases, individual property interests, stakes, and incomes of men who have stakes in joint family incomes or run business in partnerships with their family members are difficult to prove in court. It also harms the interests of women from lower classes whose husbands are employed in the informal economy earning subsistence wages.

Maintenance under Section 125 CrPC

Married and divorced women and vulnerable members of families, including legitimate and illegitimate children and parents across religions, can apply for maintenance under Section 125 CrPC. The section is popular among the vulnerable members of the family because it provides speedy relief. The quantum of maintenance under this law is increased in the sense that in the Family Court in Mumbai, it is now generally fixed at 1,500 rupees per month. However, the Court does not award the full amount in most cases. The maximum award in cases that I came across was 1,000 rupees per month.[185] Section 127 CrPC allows the enhancement of maintenance under changed circumstances.[186] For instance, a petitioner wife was granted 100 rupees per month as maintenance in a case in 1988. She filed for enhancement, arguing the increased need due to medical expenses as well as the increase in the ceiling of maintenance amount awarded to her. The Court increased her maintenance to 600 rupees per month in 2002.[187]

To claim maintenance, a woman litigant has to prove marriage and demonstrate that she is unable to maintain herself. It is argued that proof of a valid marriage is not strictly necessary, and courts have presumed marriage in cases where women have proved cohabitation (Menski 2003). This observation is true in many cases, but a few cases show otherwise. In

---

[185] See *RS* v. *VS*, Family Court Records, 2002.
[186] Interview with MM, January 12, 2003, Mumbai. In another case, a wife had filed for enhancement of maintenance under this Act – she was awarded 200 rupees per month for herself and her son in 1992. In 2002, the court increased the amount to 400 rupees per month. The quantum of maintenance calculated in each case is often arbitrary.
[187] Interview with MM, January 12, 2003, Mumbai.

one case, Mehzabee, who had represented herself in court, accepted, in the heat of the moment, that her husband had divorced her (though she had claimed otherwise in her application), and the judge refused to grant maintenance to her under this law.[188]

A wife must prove that the husband has deserted her or driven her out of the house in order to qualify for maintenance under this law. Acts of adultery, separation by mutual consent, and refusing to cohabit with the husband without sufficient cause disentitles a wife to maintenance. The general trend since the late 1990s indicates that the standard of proof required to establish cruelty and desertion is lower in these cases.[189] Social workers and lawyers report that judges have been more open to granting women immediate economic relief in recent years: "Judges cannot help but realize the new trends [that] develop in courts over time. The Family Court has been working now since [the] 1990s, and judges realize that women in such situations need help – lower-middle-class and poor women who are separated find it difficult to survive in this city. Since self-representation is allowed, judges listen to direct stories of women; they realize the problems of women over time."[190]

---

[188] *MK* v. *SMK*, Family Court Records, 2002.

[189] This case, decided in 1994, illustrates an exception, and this type of judgment was rarer in cases adjudicated from 1996 onward. In early 1990s, a petitioner wife had filed for maintenance for herself and two sons. The husband was a skilled worker employed with an automobile manufacturer. In the judgment, the judge opined that she had been unable to prove cruelty. In the judgment, the judge reasoned that "he (the husband) has filed for restitution of conjugal rights. This shows his willingness to take her back. There is no other reason for him to get displeased with her and she has born him two sons ... if she could stay with him and his family till she gave birth to the first child, I do not see any reason as to why she could not pull on further in the circumstances." The woman had argued that her parents-in-law and others in the family beat and tortured her. The judge reasoned "the husband cannot provide her with a separate residence ... besides, a person having his service as the only source of income and such liabilities (maintenance of parents and younger brothers) can hardly go for committing offences alleged against him ... the petitioner is compelling the respondent to live separately from the joint family on flimsy grounds." The judge denied maintenance to the wife and awarded 100 rupees per month each for maintenance of two sons who remained with the mother (interview and case records of DP, January 11 and March 4, 2003.).

[190] Interview with Madhvi Desai, social worker, Family Court, September 17, 2002, Mumbai.

Under Section 125 CrPC, the petitioner wife has to prove that her husband has sufficient funds to support her but neglects to do so. In many cases, women find it difficult to prove the financial earnings of husbands, especially if they work in informal sectors of economy – as tailors, garment workers, furniture makers, autorickshaw or taxi drivers, small businessmen, money lenders, and the like. Similarly, incomes of wage workers who work for unregistered firms, or subcontractors who work as wage workers without written contracts, fixed wages, or benefits, are also difficult to prove, and judges rely on litigants' accounts of their respective financial status and use their discretion to award maintenance in such cases. For instance, a woman whose husband owned a garage and who earned 10,000 rupees a month was given 500 rupees as maintenance. Similarly, Kamala's husband owned a small grocery store and, according to her, earned 8,000 rupees per month.[191] Neither of these litigants was able to prove, on paper, the income of their husbands.

The cases of maintenance filed by women against men who work as subsistence laborers working as head loaders, cart pullers, vendors, or hawkers are rare even under this law, as their incomes are smaller and even more variable. On the other hand, women whose husbands work in the public sector or belong to the category of lower-grade employees in manufacturing, trade, or services (communications, banking, insurance, etc.) find it relatively easy to obtain the proof of income, and obtain orders attaching the salary of the husbands.

Worker turnover, though, is lower in the public sector as opposed to the private sector. Occasionally, women litigants cultivate clerks, peons, and other officers in their husband's workplaces to keep a close eye on the husband's financial dealings and thus remain alert about litigant strategies. "The clerk in my husband's company is very sympathetic. I visit his company (without my husband's knowledge) whenever he does not pay maintenance. It was the clerk who alerted me that my husband had taken out a loan so that his salary could not be attached, and I told that to the

---

[191] See *KN* v. *KN*, Family Court Records, 2002.

judge as well."[192] Although Section 125 CrPC allows both legitimate and illegitimate children to claim maintenance, husbands dispute the paternity of children to counter claims of maintenance under Section 7(e) of the Family Courts Act 1984.[193]

Initially enacted as a public-interest measure to prevent destitution, prostitution, and vagrancy, the Section 125 CrPC Act enables the state to shift its responsibility to the family to protect the vulnerable members of society (Menski 2001, 2003). It cannot be denied that many women litigants find this support necessary, though inadequate. Women who work in informal occupations to supplement this amount find maintenance paid in installments useful.[194] However, amounts granted under this act at times are not enough to prevent destitution, and the assumption that families would step in to help women is often unfounded.[195] The act requires women to prove that they are not able to maintain themselves. Women find themselves in a bind – the law renders them ineligible for maintenance if they work, but the amounts granted are so meager that the women have no choice but to work. Furthermore, in cases where working women are granted maintenance for children, the quantum of maintenance is so low that the cost of litigation exceeds the benefits received under this law.

[192] Interview with AS, March 15, 2003, Mumbai. Another respondent mentioned that she knew "... from the peon at his [the husband's] office, that so far he has not changed the name of the beneficiaries under his PPF (Public Provident Fund) and my son's future is safe" (interview with MP, January 10, 2003, Mumbai).

[193] Section 7(e) of the Family Courts Act 1984 grants the court the power with respect to suits or proceedings for a declaration as to the legitimacy of any person. Case of *HS* v. *NS*, January 7, 2003, Mumbai: here, the petitioner wife filed for maintenance for herself and children, and the husband claimed that he had divorced her and that the child was illegitimate.

[194] These women worked as tutors, took up home-based work in the garment industry, and assisted in low-scale family businesses to earn their living. Interviews with PN, March 3, 2003; NH, April 16, 2003, Mumbai. Mita, a woman litigant, mentioned that although the amount awarded by the court was quite small, her husband by and large paid the amount and this money helped her over the years – initially, she used this amount to learn tailoring and now she worked in the garment industry and lived with her brother's family. Interview with MV, February 4, 2003, Mumbai.

[195] A deserted woman who sought help in a women's shelter was awarded 300 rupees per month as maintenance. The husband did not pay his dues, and she did not move the

STATE LAW AND THE ADJUDICATION PROCESS 155

Under this law, the maintenance is given from the date of the order. This impacts women litigants adversely because in many instances, women file for maintenance after attempting informal resolutions for two to three years before taking recourse to the law. There is no provision in the law entitling the wife to claim maintenance during this period, when she might be dependent on her relatives and friends.[196] Efforts to find relief for women who have endured economic hardship during separation have not been successful. In one case, a Muslim couple was separated in February 1999, and the husband divorced the wife in November 1999; the lawyer filed a suit to recover maintenance under Section 125 CrPC for these nine months, but the court dismissed the suit.[197]

A question of whether Muslims should be exempted from provisions of this secular law came up in 1973 when the Criminal Procedure Code was amended. Subsection 3(b) of Section 127 CrPC[198] was added to it, which set the stage for the exemption of divorced Muslim women from under the purview of this act. However, a number of judgments sought to encompass divorced Muslim women under this act (Parashar 1992). This question was "settled" after the Supreme Court's decision in the controversial Shah Bano case, which led to the perception that Muslim women seldom get maintenance under this act because Muslim husbands

---

court to recover arrears for such a low amount. She was forced to find work as a domestic worker. The job entailed no minimum wage, and working hours were not defined, but she was forced to work, as the work guaranteed her shelter with her employers (interview with SK, January 7, 2003, Mumbai).

[196] "I was thrown out of the house along with my three children by my husband and waited for a year, hoping that we would reconcile, hoping that he would take me back, and when he did not, I had to come to court. We had to depend on my brother during this time" (interview with ZK, March 3, 2003, Mumbai). Also, interviews with SS, June 2, 2003, Mumbai; NL, June 12, 2003, Mumbai.

[197] Interview with Mr. M. Phanse, lawyer, June 2, 2003, Mumbai.

[198] As per this section, a magistrate can rescind the maintenance order given to a woman who has received a financial settlement following a customary divorce as per the personal laws of the parties. This was cited as a reason to stop maintenance payments of Muslim women who had been given *mehar*, and maintenance during *iddat* following divorce.

unilaterally divorce their wives to counter their claims for maintenance (Narain 2001; Parashar 1992; Sunderrajan 2001). However, Agnes (1999) indicates that a large number of Muslim women were able to file cases under this act in lower courts. Similarly, my data show that married Muslim women and dependent children tend to file for maintenance under this act.[199] Husbands also use the provision of Section 127(3)(b)[200] in order to challenge the maintenance claims of petitioners.[201] Whereas this strategy is used by Muslim husbands in a number of cases, what is often overlooked is the use of this section by Muslim wives to fulfill their goals. Muslim women tend to file cases under this act in order to obtain divorce from reluctant husbands.[202] They also use this act to validate an oral divorce given by their husbands.[203] In some cases, they are able to successfully contest divorces granted by their husbands and obtain maintenance for themselves and their children.[204] In other cases, they also arrive at a settlement amount. In one case, Khadija had filed a case for

---

[199] Thirty-three Muslim litigants who had filed these cases were interviewed. Out of these cases, maintenance was not granted in two cases. Petitions were withdrawn in five cases and transferred in four. In two cases, children were granted maintenance. Three petitions were dismissed and seventeen petitions were accepted.

[200] This section states that the magistrate should cancel the order given under Section 125 CrPC if the woman had received the whole sum of settlement based on the personal laws of the parties.

[201] A petitioner wife had filed a case under this section in October 2000 and was granted an order in her favor in July 2002. The husband was asked to pay her maintenance from the date of application. The husband produced a *talaqnama* (deed of divorce from a *qazi*) and replied that he had divorced her in April 2001, and he was not obliged to pay her maintenance under the provision of Section 127(3)(b) CrPC. The judge gave an indication that he was disinclined to believe this argument based on recent precedents. The parties arrived at a settlement: The husband paid 10,000 rupees, and the wife agreed to forego future arrears (interview with TA, December 8, 2002, Mumbai).

[202] Interviews with AS, litigant, December 9, 2002; SS, litigant, April 17, 2003, Mumbai. *AZK* v. *ZK*, March 3, 2003, Mumbai.

[203] The husband had orally divorced the wife and refused to give the *talaq* in writing. The wife wished to remarry and needed the written proof of divorce. The wife finally filed a case in the Family Court, and the husband responded by sending the registered letter of divorce (interview with FB, January 5, 2003, Mumbai). See also *SSM* v. *SM*; *KSF* v. *SDH*, Family Court Records, 2002.

[204] Examples include *RN* v. *KN*, *SB* v. *AYK*, *RS* v. *SMS*, Family Court Records, 2002.

STATE LAW AND THE ADJUDICATION PROCESS 157

maintenance for herself and her daughter. Both parties approached legal aid, and told the lawyer that "we don't want to fight, we just want to settle," and they settled for a divorce. Khadija got 1,500 rupees as her *mehar*, alimony of 20,000 rupees, and her husband offered to pay 500 rupees per month in child support.[205] The Family Court has the jurisdiction to award maintenance to dependent children.[206] In many instances, women file cases for themselves and their children.[207] In such cases, if respondent husbands succeed in proving divorce in response to wives' claims for maintenance under Section 125 CrPC, the Family Court, as per the advice of the High Court, is required to transfer these cases to the Metropolitan Magistrates' Courts to be tried under the MWA.[208]

However, in several cases, divorced Muslim women drop their claims to maintenance under the Muslim Women's Act 1986 and continue to pursue cases for their children's maintenance under Section 125, CrPC.[209] For, cases of MWA are adjudicated in the Metropolitan Magistrates' Courts, whereas cases of divorce and maintenance are decided in the Family Court. Many Muslim women litigants complain of additional costs and find it difficult to manage simultaneous litigation in two courts. Women litigants find it easier to represent themselves in the Family Court, but are intimidated by the prospect of representing themselves in the Metropolitan Magistrates' Courts because the legal culture in these courts is not client-friendly.[210] Women also find it more difficult to fight their own cases in these courts.[211] As a result, they often likely to pursue cases of maintenance for children under Section 125, CrPC and drop cases filed under Muslim Women's Act 1986.

---

[205] See *KHF* v. *HDF*, Family Court Records, 2002. Interview with Khadija, January 10, 2003, Mumbai.
[206] See, for instance, *AS* v. *AS*; *TAA* v. *SAA*; *AJK* v. *SKNK*, Family Court Records, 2002.
[207] See *MAK* v. *MAK*, Family Court Records, 2002.
[208] See Letter no. D1604/2000, July 15, 2000.
[209] Interviews with LN, March 5, 2003; BN, March 5, 2003; PS, May 7, 2003, Mumbai.
[210] Interviews with PS, July 12, 2003; Anamika Vichare, lawyer, April 6, 2003, Mumbai.
[211] Interviews with M, January 11, 2003; ZS, October 2, 2002; LN, March 5, 2003; BN, March 5, 2003; PS, May 7, 2003, Mumbai.

Implementation of Maintenance Orders

A favorable order of maintenance does not guarantee the implementation of this order. In several cases, litigant women who had been granted the order of maintenance remained ignorant of the order – a woman litigant had to change her residence due to a slum eviction drive of the Municipal Corporation, and she could not follow up her case as she was living on the streets.[212]

The institutional mechanism enforcing compliance to the decree of maintenance is also weak. Maintenance amounts are difficult to collect in ex parte orders that the court has ordered in the wife's favor[213]: A woman was granted an ex parte order of maintenance of 600 rupees per month and 500 rupees in legal costs under Section 18 HAMA, as she had been deserted for three years. The husband did not remain present in court after he had filed a written statement. The woman did not pursue the matter because she had "come to know that he had fled the city and was now living in a village after contracting [a] second marriage. It was difficult to get him to court when he was in Bombay – there is no hope that he can be contacted in a village." Furthermore, the wife can approach the court for nonpayment of arrears one year at a time, from the date the amount is due. The wife has to keep appearing in court time and again to recover arrears. In many cases, husbands delay the court procedure, appear on some dates but not others, and wait to pay up until they are likely to receive the order of attachment of property or arrest. They prevent this order by paying half or one-third of the amount due.[214]

---

[212] Interview with ML, March 13, 2003, Mumbai. In another case, a woman litigant had stopped going to court for the last two court dates due to illness of her father, and remained unaware of the court order upholding her maintenance claims (interview with NJ, March 2, 2003, Mumbai). I followed up another such case and tracked the relatives with whom another litigant, who had been granted maintenance by the Family Court, had stayed in Mumbai. The woman had gone back to her village and her maternal aunt, a daily wage laborer, and could not follow up the court case (interview with her maternal aunt, Nirmala Jadhav, May 12, 2003, Mumbai).

[213] Interview with MD, December 12, 2002, Mumbai.

[214] Interviews with PW, December 8, 2002; RL, March 6, 2003; VG, April 16, 2003, Mumbai.

STATE LAW AND THE ADJUDICATION PROCESS 159

Many women litigants complain that men even refuse to accept the summons of the court, and execution orders for the attachment of property are difficult to execute because men bribe the local police to obstruct the implementation of judicial orders.[215] In many cases, respondent husbands claim sickness, debts, and loan deductions to justify the nonpayment of dues.[216] Husbands use delay tactics until they "tire their wives out," and many women drop their cases after pursuing them for a few years.[217]

This issue has been debated among the counselors and judges of the Family Court in Mumbai as well as in regional meetings of judges. For instance, in a conference of Family Court counselors and judges, Judge A. B. Palkar of the Family Court, Bombay, stated: "While executing [the] order under Section 125 CrPC, police show lethargic attitude ... the distress warrants, arrest warrants, and summons are not even sent back [delivered] ... can the Police Commissioner, Bombay, be requested to depute special staff headed by a head constable for executing Family Court orders and to ask them to attend court regularly and support the compliance of the order in the said cases?"[218]

Nonpayment of an order under the CrPC is treated as contempt of court, and the attaching of the property of the husband is one way to recover maintenance dues.[219] In many cases, the courts have stepped in to assist women in collecting their dues. To illustrate, Maya Dande had applied for maintenance under Section 125 CrPC, and was granted

---

[215] An exasperated woman told me: "The court gives us very little, but the process teaches men important lessons in how to dodge the law – my husband does not pay maintenance and then, once I file for arrears, he begins his tricks by refusing to accept the summons of the court. He'd be at home, watching TV, but he pretends he is his brother when it comes to accepting summons" (interview with SS, October 12, 2002, Mumbai). Interviews with MI, March 23, 2003; RG, April 1, 2003, Mumbai.

[216] See *KR* v. *KR*, Family Court Records, 2002.

[217] Three women litigants I interviewed had dropped cases after pursuing recovery cases for three to five years (interviews with PW, December 8, 2002; RL, March 6, 2003; VG, April 16, 2003, Mumbai).

[218] See Circular A(SPI)/3215/96/2177/96, Bombay High Court.

[219] In *SS* v. *JS*, the respondent husband lived in Delhi, and he paid arrears amounting to 46,500 rupees after the court gave an order for attachment of his property.

1,500 rupees per month as maintenance for herself and her four children. The respondent husband had not paid his installments, and she had to file a petition under the law to recover 21,600 rupees. During the process, she came to know of his plan to take voluntary retirement on a condition to turn his job over to his brother under the (unrecorded) preferential treatment agreement between the workers and the Municipal Corporation of Greater Mumbai, in order to escape maintenance payment. Maya filed an application asking the Family Court to pass an order to deduct the amount from his Voluntary Retirement Scheme dues. Her husband received 60,000 rupees from his employer and had to pay only 21,600 rupees to his wife and four children. At the time of the interview, the husband had married again, lived with his brother, and was supported by him. The husband also had a share in the house owned by his parents. On the other hand, Maya and her four children were dependent on her family, and from now on, she would not be able to claim maintenance from her husband as he was unemployed. She and her family would have to support four young children between the ages four and ten. The salary of her husband was attached only for the recovery of arrears and not for future maintenance. This often acts against women's interests.[220]

The imprisonment of judgment defaulters is another way to extract maintenance payments from reluctant husbands. Although the court has held that arrest and imprisonment do not absolve these husbands of responsibility (Sagade 1996, 91), in practice, a few husbands choose this option over the payment of maintenance.[221] For instance, in a case spanning twelve years, a deserted wife with one daughter had filed for maintenance, and her husband chose to go to the jail twice for six months each time because of his refusal to pay maintenance. The court could not rule for property attachment because he had transferred all his property to his mother's name.[222]

[220] Interview with MD, January 12, 2003, Mumbai.

[221] In *LK* v. *AK*, in 2002, the woman had pleaded to recover arrears worth 88,000 rupees, and the husband preferred arrest over payment. See also *KL* v. *RL*, Family Court Records, 2002.

[222] Interview with LK, February 4, 2003, Mumbai.

STATE LAW AND THE ADJUDICATION PROCESS 161

Still, the possibility of imprisonment works in favor of many women, because judgment defaulters are wary of criminal records, though the collection of maintenance arrears can take as long as six years, especially when higher amounts are involved.[223] Recently, judges have ensured strict implementation of this provision and have provided relief to women. In a case filed for mutual-consent divorce, the parties agreed to divorce by mutual consent, and the husband, a stockbroker, agreed to pay 9,000 rupees per month as maintenance for his wife and two children in 1995. He had paid only 24,500 rupees until February 2000 and had not remained present in court; the wife pleaded to the Family Court for the recovery of arrears in 2000. The Family Court ordered him to pay the arrears and failing which, a warrant was issued to the local police station to arrest him for nonpayment of arrears. After that, in 2000, he paid up half the amount that was due, and the wife had to appeal to the court again in 2002. This time around, once again, the husband tried to evade payment by refusing to accept the summons, moving residence, hiding business assets, remaining absent from court, and attempting to stall orders of arrest. However, the judge assigned to this case was a "proactive, sympathetic, and pro-women judge." In 2002, the judge found the respondent "husband guilty of wilfully defaulting his payment of maintenance and sentenced him to simple imprisonment of six months," and ordered the police to arrest the respondent. The husband paid up the arrears that very day.[224] This case, to many male litigants, indicated the willingness of the court to levy and enforce criminal charges against a defaulting upper-middle-class husband, and generated a buzz in the court; this story, embellished at each telling, "travelled" (Merry 2005) in society – I heard varied stories about this case from lawyers, court clerks, male litigants, and even some caste officials, some of whom maintained indignantly that "... *suna hai waha pe*

---

[223] The strategies used by husbands to evade the payment of maintenance include refusing to accept the summons, moving residence, hiding business assets, remaining absent from court, and attempting to stall orders of arrest. Interviews with Meenakshi Rushi, lawyer, June 12, 2003, Mumbai. .
[224] Interview with SI, March 3, 2003, Mumbai.

aurato ki hi sunate hai, wo korat to aurato ki korat hai (the Family Court should be renamed women's court)!"[225] and that " ... today's judges are ready to go and imprison husbands!"[226]

Injunction for Property

This provision addresses, however inadequately, one of the lacunae under all personal laws: the lack of shelter in circumstances of marital breakdown.[227] Agnes has discussed two landmark judgments of the Bombay High Court as well as the Supreme Court,[228] and has reported that the higher courts have begun to be sensitive to the question of women's right to property, and have protected women from being dispossessed upon desertion and divorce in several cases (Agnes 2008). This data show that the lower courts like the Family Court have used this provision extensively, and this legal innovation has responded to women's needs in lower courts. Section 7(d) of the Family Courts Act 1984[229] allows women and

---

[225] Interview with Kanu Sutar, litigant, June 12, 2003, Mumbai.

[226] I was in the record room, reading through a judgment, when a male litigant came in to chat with the court clerk in charge of the record room. HS was fighting his own case of divorce without a lawyer and, seeing me there, he came along to chat and discuss his case with me. He was worried about the outcome of his own case, "given the functioning of the court." He said: " ... just look at what is going on here – today's judges are ready to go and imprison husbands! Judge Dhatrak gave an order of imprisonment to this man – he is a big stockbroker and he was humiliated like this! You write it, write it in your report," he said, sternly, "how this court only listens to women" (conversation with HS, May 12, 2003, Mumbai).

[227] Many women are forced to leave the matrimonial home; the lack of property rights and the relative poverty of women make it difficult for women to build separate houses for themselves, a problem that is accentuated in urban conglomerations, such as Mumbai with its high property prices.

[228] Agnes has discussed the case of *BP Achala Anand* v. *S Appi Reddy*, AIR [2005] SC 986 (Agnes 2008, 254).

[229] Chapter 3 of the Family Courts Act 1984 states that the Family Court will have all the jurisdictional powers of district or subordinate civil courts in respect of suits and proceedings (including) (d): [in] a suit or proceeding for an order or injunction in circumstances arising out of a marital relationship; (c) a suit or proceeding between parties to a marriage with respect to the property of the parties or of either of them. This Act

male litigants across religions to seek an order of injunction in circumstances arising out of a marital relationship. Lawyers and judges have used this provision to stretch the boundaries of the law creatively to award women minimal rights within the matrimonial home.[230]

Explaining the shift toward greater secularization and gender equality in the higher courts in Israel since the 1980s, Patricia Woods has argued that cause lawyers play an important role in linking the agendas and issues of social movements to the normative world of legal community, comprising lawyers, judges, and law clerks, and that formal and informal interactions within and between these legal actors leads to legal change (Woods 2006). In India, cause lawyers in the Family Court in Mumbai are extremely successful in carrying legal developments to civil society organizations and linking the Family Court with other NGOs, thus affecting the outcome of individual cases. The following case, handled by Irene Sequeira, who worked with the civil rights group Human Rights Law Network for several years and is now an independent lawyer, and who was able to coordinate between civil society organizations, social workers attached to the Family Court, and the judge in order to secure economic rights of a woman litigant, illustrates this claim. In one case, the husband of a woman, Sheela, deserted her and threatened to evict her from their residence in a slum. Sheela approached the local NGO, the Community Outreach Program at Dharavi, which also works on issues of housing rights for slum dwellers facing eviction. The social workers of this organization referred her to a lawyer so that she could file for maintenance, and took up her cause against her husband who was threatening to throw her out of the matrimonial home, accusing her of adultery, and denying the

---

is combined with Order XXXIX of the Civil Procedure Code 1908 pertaining to temporary injunctions and interlocutory orders. Order XXXIX allows the court to grant a temporary injunction preventing wasting, damaging, alienation, sale, or disposing of a property that is under dispute.

[230] Agnes also points to the innovative use of restitution of conjugal rights and the women's right to matrimonial residence in a case handled by the women's law center Majlis (Agnes 2008).

paternity of their child. The slum was being moved to another area, and the Municipal Corporation of Greater Mumbai was giving "transit housing" to the slum residents. Sheela's dispossession from her home would have deprived her of her right to the transit house. At the legal end, the lawyer and the local NGO kept in touch about the legal strategies, and the lawyer filed a case to prevent her from being disposed from her matrimonial home under Section 7(d) of the Family Courts Act 1984. While the case was ongoing, Sheela found out that her husband had married again. She brought this matter to the lawyer's notice, who put in an application to prosecute her husband. The judge asked for proof; the social workers of the court and the local NGO visited Sheela's husband's second home to assess whether he had married again or not. The social workers spoke to the neighbors and gave evidence of the second marriage to the judge. In the end, the judge, the lawyer, and the social workers of the organization worked together to persuade the husband to transfer the matrimonial residence in Sheela's name. They also arranged a lump-sum settlement for her and her daughter.

Increasingly, women litigants have begun to use this provision to bargain for divorce and economic rights at the time of divorce.[231] The provision also highlights women's economic contribution to the matrimonial property as sole or supplementary breadwinners, and the court, at times, protects women's right in the same, even if the property is registered in the husband's name or under joint names. To illustrate, Anisbi, a petitioner wife, claimed that the couple after marriage resided with her family for

[231] *HG* v. *NG*, Family Court Records, 2003. In another case, a Sikh woman got a settlement of 150,000 rupees from her husband using this provision, although she had initiated the divorce (*JK* v. *HS*, Family Court Records, 2002). Similarly, Nirmala's husband had married her after his first wife died; his four sons were against this marriage because they feared that she would get a share in his property, a *kholi* in a slum. The sons forced her out of the house, and she filed for injunction. She got an interim stay order and believed, at the time of interview, that this will prevent her husband's sons from disposing of the property. While the settlement is still to be finalized, and she faced "criminal intimidation" from the sons, she aims that they will give her some money so that she can live in her village with her husband (interview with NJ, January 17, 2003, Mumbai).

some years while they saved money to send the husband to Saudi Arabia to work as a laborer. The couple had five children, and because he did not send money regularly, she worked in the garment industry; her daughters too worked with her while they attended school, and took a loan from the local money lender to buy a *kholi*, a room in a slum. Soon after coming back from Saudi Arabia, her husband married a second time. She feared that her husband may forcibly evict her, or compel her to sign papers transferring the room in his name, or create a third-party interest in the same. She asked for a permanent injunction against the sale or transfer of the property, and also asked for maintenance for herself and her children. The court ruled that the husband had failed to prove that he had bought the house from his earnings, and had also failed to prove that he had resided in the matrimonial home; his earnings were substantial, and the first wife was entitled to maintenance for herself and her children.[232]

The provision is useful to women who can fight cases while living in the matrimonial home, but it is often not useful once they are thrown out of the matrimonial home and if the husband does not have immediate plans to alienate the property.[233] However, the injunction is not effective in cases where women seek reconciliation and wish to use this law to bargain if they have been thrown out of the house.[234] In rare cases, this provision has been used against women. To cite an example, Rehana, a Muslim woman who worked as an air hostess, married a man who ran his own business. She invested her income and managed it over the years; he suffered losses in business deals and began to harass her for money. She had purchased a house in her name, and he claimed that he had paid

---

[232] See *MM* v. *MM*, Family Court Records, 2002.

[233] In one case, a woman who was thrown out of the matrimonial home obtained an injunction against the transfer and sale of the property, but the injunction did not provide any leverage because the husband's family did not have any such plans, and the husband did not wish to speed up the divorce process (interview with GS, March 16, 2003, Mumbai).

[234] A Muslim woman was thrown out of the matrimonial home along with her five children, but could not obtain an injunction once she was out of the house (interview with NA, June 6, 2003, Mumbai).

for the renovation. She decided to sell this house and opt out of the marriage. He filed for restitution of conjugal rights and also sought a temporary stay order against the sale of the matrimonial residence. Rehana, the respondent wife, in return maintained that she had already sold the house and that she had received *faskh*, a judicially arbitrated divorce, from a *qazi* associated with an organization named Markani Mukhamma Sharia, All India. The court did not deem her societal divorce as valid and advised her to file for divorce under the Dissolution of Muslim Marriages Act 1939, and granted her husband a temporary stay order against the sale of the house.[235]

The practice of unilateral divorce can make it difficult to restrain husbands from selling the matrimonial house, as the married status of the wife is necessary to enforce this provision. In some cases, husbands divorce their wives as soon as the latter file for injunctions, and at times, they are able to prove divorce, leading to the dismissal of these injunctions.[236] However, in several cases, wives were able to prevent dispossession by their husbands by filing for an injunction before divorce, and subsequently not accepting the divorce.[237] As mentioned previously, the injunction is generally used as a stepping stone to other remedies because it increases the bargaining power of litigants. In one case, a petitioner wife filed for an injunction against the sale of the property the husband had bought in the name of his wife and daughter; she filed for divorce under the Dissolution of Muslim Marriage Act 1939. The husband claimed that he had bought the property by taking advantage of the Benami Transaction Prohibition Act 1988. The husband can be restrained

---

[235] See *KMAK* v. *YK*, Family Court Records, 2002.

[236] A petitioner wife filed a restraining order against her husband, his first wife, and their children. The husband responded by sending her a divorce letter. The wife had filed a case in the Metropolitan Magistrates' court under the Muslim Women's Act 1986 (interview with SA, March 4, 2003, Mumbai).

[237] A petitioner woman moved the court for an injunction after learning of her husband's plans to sell the house after contracting a second marriage. She was granted the order (interview with Rukhsanabi, April 17, 2003, Mumbai). See also *MM* v. *MM*, Family Court Records, 2002.

STATE LAW AND THE ADJUDICATION PROCESS 167

from selling the property if it is in the name of the wife under Section 7(d) of the Family Courts Act 1984; however, the lawyer argued that it was fiduciary property, and the real owner was the husband. In the end, the matter was settled by mutual agreement: The property was divided equally between the husband and the wife, and the husband also made a lump-sum payment for maintenance of the children.[238] In another case, a petitioner wife who was thrown out of the matrimonial home filed for an injunction to prevent the sale of property and tried forcibly to move back into the matrimonial home. Her marital family members prevented her violently. She filed a complaint of domestic violence at the police station and used the incident as a proof of malicious desertion in order to obtain a maintenance order under Section 125 CrPC.[239] Hindu women litigants use this remedy as a stepping stone to other cases. In cases of contested divorce, women who initiate divorce use this provision to negotiate divorce by mutual consent.[240] The newly enacted law on domestic violence, The Protection of Women from Domestic Violence Act 2005, gives protective injunctions against violence, dispossession from the matrimonial home, and for alternate residence. It also enables women to ask for economic protection (including maintenance) and will substantially raise women's capacity to bargain for more rights across religions (see also Agnes 2008).

When it comes to enforcing women's economic rights, interviews with lawyers and litigants suggest that judicial discretion plays a large role in stretching the legal boundary to award economic rights to women. For instance, even though only a married woman has a claim to the husband's matrimonial home, a pro-women judge managed to stretch the claim to

---

[238] Interview with SS, February 19, 2003, Mumbai. Interview with the husband's lawyer, Nisar Ahmed Ghatte, February 19, 2003, Mumbai.

[239] Interview with YA, June 8, 2003, Mumbai.

[240] See *HG* v. *HG*. The petitioner wife filed a case for divorce and also asked the court for a permanent injunction against the sale of his property. The respondent husband filed for restitution of conjugal rights. Finally, the case was settled, and she received her *stridhan* back and 50,000 rupees for the missing gold ornaments. She did not ask for maintenance or alimony.

widowed women as well. The pro-women judge awarded a higher quantum of maintenance and assigned legal aid to women clients when he felt they needed it.[241]

Negotiating the Retrieval of Stridhan

Even though the Indian state has prohibited dowry,[242] the practice of dowry is widely prevalent in Indian society, and the retrieval of the dowry and other joint matrimonial property at the time of divorce is of interest to women litigants as well as the natal family. In cases of divorce, the return of dowry/joint assets is finalized in court, usually at the time of divorce.[243] However, the retrieval of these assets is dogged by a lack of clarity in the law and a process of difficult negotiations that impact women's rights to property. There are several issues involved here. There exist diverse opinions about what constitutes *stridhan*. Whereas sociologists define dowry as gifts given to the husband's family through the lifetime (Uberoi 1993), there are two different interpretations in the law. In some cases, *stridhan* is narrowly defined as the gifts given to the bride at the time of marriage. At other times, *stridhan* is seen to consist of gifts given to the bride from the natal family, marital family, and other relatives and friends at the time of marriage. After the Supreme Court judgment in the Pratibha Rani case,[244] where the court ruled that gifts given to women at the time of marriage, as well as subsequently comprise her *stridhan*, women's organizations have lobbied

---

[241] Interview with Veena Gowda, lawyer, June 23, 2003, Mumbai.

[242] The Dowry Prohibition Act 1961 criminalizes dowry demands and exchange. Dowry-related violence is also a crime under Section 498(A) Indian Penal Code. A dowry usually consists of clothes, furniture, and other household items ranging from utensils to cars, jewelry, and, in many cases, money.

[243] Many communities and families have developed the practice of making a list of dowry and gift items received by the couple at the time of marriage. This list serves as evidence of dowry exchange.

[244] *Pratibha Rani v. Suraj Kumar and Anr*, AIR 628 SCR (3) 191 [1985] SCC (2) 370 [1985] SCALE 1 (458).

STATE LAW AND THE ADJUDICATION PROCESS

for the societal and legal acceptance of the second definition. However, the Family Court at Mumbai has tended to favor the former definition of *stridhan* as dowry.

In most cases, women litigants need their *stridhan* at the time of separation, be it legal or informal. Women are often forced to leave the marital home, and they are unable to take their entire *stridhan* with them. When they subsequently try to collect the *stridhan*, husbands in many cases refuse to part with it. The police refuse to register complaints by wives, classifying them as civil disputes between family members to be resolved in the Family Court. The recovery of *stridhan* is often complicated by the fact that even though women legally own their *stridhan*, they often lack control over this property, and *stridhan* may be damaged, mortgaged, or diminish in value due to usage. In most cases, women have to forego the depreciation in the value of *stridhan*.

Women who file for divorce in Family Court can only hope to recover *stridhan* at the time of resolution of the case, when couples separate and exchange their mutual belongings. This period may stretch over years in cases of contested divorce; women might not be able to collect their belongings for many years, and there is no guarantee that their belongings would be replaced.[245] In some cases, divorced Muslim women who filed cases under Section 125 CrPC for maintenance of their children pleaded unsuccessfully that the husbands should pay back their *mehar* and *stridhan*.[246] However, women litigants who wish to recover their *stridhan* but

---

[245] In one case, a woman litigant had filed for divorce on the grounds of cruelty. During the process, she came to know that the husband and his family were planning to move to another town after selling their business and residence. She filed an application in the Family Court for the recovery of her *stridhan* during the process of divorce. However, the husband remained absent on two consecutive court dates. She went to the police to register a complaint under Section 406 of the IPC to recover her dowry. The police refused to register the offense. The wife also approached a women's organization, but her husband refused to hand over her dowry, stating that "the matter was subjudice." During this time, the husband and his family left town. Even if she were granted an ex parte divorce, she would not recover her *stridhan* (interview with MM, April 4, 2003, Mumbai).

[246] *SB* v. *AYK*, Family Court Records, 2002. *RN* v. *KN*, Family Court Records, 2002.

do not wish to file for divorce find few legal options to recover *stridhan*. To some extent, women's organizations have been able to fill in this gap, assisting women to recover their *stridhan* before the court process or even after the court judgment.[247]

In general, in maters related to women's rights in law, interviews with lawyers and social workers suggest that judicial discretion is an important factor especially when it comes to legal innovation and boundary stretching. The analysis of the decisions of the Family Court does not always clarify how judges sort out facts and arrive at decisions, but the most persuasive explanation in the Indian case is that put forth by judicial behavioralists. To elaborate, it is argued that the law exercises external constraints on judges and produces judicial conformity to legal rules (Eskridge 1990; Scalia 1989; Schauer 1987). Others argue that judges rely not only on subjective preferences, but also make decisions "in good faith" in order to "further public policy aims" (Baum 1993, 445; Tamanaha 1996). However, judicial behavioralists argue that analyses of legal principles, rules, and structure of judicial reasoning are insufficient to explain judicial decision making. Instead, they highlight the role of personal elements that makeup the ideologies, politics, and experiences of judges as explanatory factors guiding judicial decisions (Gillman 2001). The gender of the Family Court judges does not seem to be an important factor explaining judicial change toward greater protection of women's rights in law. In 2002–2003, three of the judges were women, one of them was also a trained social worker, and they were perceived to be fair, but it was one of the male judges who ensured greater protection for women. A lawyer said, "Some judges view the Family Court posting as a punishment – it is not very prestigious, and a stint here does not count in furthering the career of a judge – and are, therefore indifferent, but some judges are, by nature and experience, proactive, efficient, and tough. If they also happen to

---

[247] Women's organizations had assisted in the recovery of *stridhan* in five cases while the matter was subjudice or disposed of (interviews with AJ, April 4, 2003; HS, March 5, 2003; MN and KK, February 15, 2003; PW, November 9, 2002, Mumbai).

be sympathetic to the underdog, then women respondents find some relief when it comes to specific judges."[248] Additionally, interviews with lawyers, litigants, and social workers suggest that judges who are not ghettoized as Family Court judges, but are generalists, well versed in civil and criminal law, and are familiar with the functioning of different courts are more open to creative interpretation of law, and this helps women as lawyers can juggle various laws and create solutions even as they tread on unfamiliar, and at times thin, ground. However, one of the important factors influencing the legal behavior of judges is that " ... they are exposed directly to women's stories, as many women and male clients represent themselves, especially poor women. The judges have to make decisions on these testimonies (which are often untarnished by legalese), and women's stories impact judicial decision-making, especially when judges are sensitive and able."[249]

Thus, to summarize, the concept of matrimonial property does not exist in either Hindu or Muslim personal laws. A spouse retains her or his preacquired or inherited property, and assets acquired during marriage are not equitably divided; furthermore, women are at a disadvantage, because societal practice disinherits the daughter. Furthermore, divorce and matrimonial disputes harm the interests of women across religious communities, and there exist few provisions that recognize women's productive and reproductive labor within the family (Agarwal 1994; Basu 1999; Sharma 1983). However, creative combination and boundary stretching of criminal and civil laws by innovative lawyers, judicial behavior, and links between individual women, women's organizations, and civil society and legal personnel allows the shift toward greater gender equality in lower courts. Contrary to claims made by feminist scholars (Narain 2001; Parashar 1992; Sunder Rajan 2001), data do not

---

[248] Interview with Yasmin Sheikh, lawyer, June 6, 2003, Mumbai.

[249] Interview with Vandana Nanaware, discussing a case in which the judge had asked her opinion as a social worker and sought clarifications about details presented in the court in a case in which a woman litigant had approached the Special Cell for Women for intervention for domestic violence. Interview with Vandana Nanaware, Special Cell for Women, June 16, 2003, Mumbai.

suggest a wide variation in economic rights granted to Hindu and Muslim women in state courts. Judges in lower courts have tended to lean toward a more liberal interpretation of Muslim Women's (Protection of Rights on Divorce) Act 1986,[250] and as a result, divorced Muslim women have more rights than Hindu women under this law.

Conclusion

This chapter analyzes the nature of state-society relations in state courts and highlights two contradictory and simultaneous movements in the state law: the *centralization of law* and the *decentralization of law*. Given that the codification of customs and policy making through legal precedents have been sources of legal developments in India, the *centralization of law* is a component of the lawmaking function of courts in India. The *centralization of law* is also seen in the systemization, routinization, and standardization of law (Heydebrand and Seron 1990) in courts influenced by the model of justice developed in specialized courts such as the Family Court. The *centralization of law* also evinces the intention of the state to shape from above the realms of family, marriage, divorce, intimacy, and sexuality according to morality and policies of the liberal secular state. The Indian state seeks to establish its overarching authority by streamlining family law and protecting individual rights.

At the same time, another dominant trend in the adjudication of family law in the Family Court is the *decentralization of law* within the state law. The term refers to the dispersal of law in the state legal system as well as the intermeshing of law and societal elements within state law. *Decentralization of law* is an overarching term that can be further classified in two categories. The first pertains to *fragmentation of law* arising from the lack of coordination between higher and lower courts, conflict of jurisdiction among lower courts, failure of lower courts to follow precedents, and the arbitrariness of judicial discretion. The *decentralization of*

---

[250] Interview with Nisar Ahmed, advocate, February 19, 2003, Mumbai.

STATE LAW AND THE ADJUDICATION PROCESS 173

law caused by the fragmentation of law is due to factors intrinsic to the formal legal system. This leads to the decentering of law and to uncertainty about law within the state legal system. The second category of the *decentralization of law* is the *societalization of law* within state law. This chapter describes myriad ways in which society seeps into the formal legal system. The adjudication process in the Family Court encourages the informal settlement of disputes through interlawyer negotiations, intervention of social work professionals, and interlitigant bargaining in the presence of societal actors. Judges in the Family Court, too, view their roles as reconciliators and advisors. The informalization of the legal process blurs the boundaries of the inner world of courts and the outer world of society within the state legal system. Thus, the societalization of law is caused by factors extrinsic to the formal legal system. The dynamic processes of the centralization and the diffusal of law have an impact, both on the accommodation of religious groups and on women's rights within state law.

Whereas some scholars have privileged the role of the colonial state in constructing Hindu and Muslim laws as separate and mutually exclusive categories of laws (Cohn 1965, 1996; Mukhopadhyay 1998; Shodhan 2001; Washbrook 1981), others suggest that the perceived dissimilarities between Hindu and Muslim personal laws is a product of elite manipulation of community identities (Brass 1991). Newbigin has suggested that customary laws and practices and laws of Hindus and Muslims were often similar (especially in matters of inheritance and the distribution of property), but Hindu and Muslim community leaders in colonial and postcolonial India created and made visible the differences between these two laws and communities in order to achieve political gains. She also argues that these processes entrenched patriarchal interests in both laws and consolidated gender inequality (Newbigin 2009). This chapter shows the similarities underlining these two religious laws, though the causal mechanism that I identify in this instance is the standardization of law in state courts during the process outlined as the centralization of law. Hindu and Muslim lawyers and litigants pursue similar strategies in state courts, and judges extend the Family

Courts Act 1984 to all respondents; this ensures that cases filed under Hindu and Muslim laws are adjudicated under similar, though not identical, lines.

We also find that Muslim women have more legal rights than Hindu women in some instances. In addition, the links between women's groups, civil society organizations, and Family Court lawyers, and the coordination between these and the Family Court judges and social workers, impact the outcome of individual cases in women's favor and, to some extent, produce an institutional environment that allows individuals to challenge patriarchal assumptions underlining cultural contexts of marriage in law. The presence of independent, efficient, proactive, and sympathetic judges, as well as the innovative use of social legislation by skillful lawyers, protects women's rights and, at times, creates judicial solutions to address the lack of certain rights in law. The coordination between women's organizations and the Family Court judges and social workers helps advance women's rights in individual cases, and everyday interactions between lawyers and court officials help create a legal environment that is open to a dialog on gender equality in law. The incentive for legal change in lower courts also comes from below, owing to individual women's mobilization of state courts.

4 Making and Unmaking the Conjugal Family

The Administration of Hindu Law in Society

Introduction

In this chapter, I discuss the dynamic interaction between the state and substate actors such as caste *panchayats*, women's organizations, political parties, and other informal actors in adjudication processes under Hindu law. The chapter is organized into three sections. The first section establishes the sociohistorical processes and organizational contexts of the adjudicative mechanisms practiced by three castes[1] that are placed differentially in the caste hierarchy among Hindus in Mumbai and whose practices point to the considerable organizational diversity and ambiguity in the nature of justice across castes. This section also delineates the role played by laws and customs in engendering these caste spheres. The second section of the chapter focuses on the micropolitics of adjudication, draws on experiences of litigants, and examines the nature of the interactions between state law and nonstate laws. This section also compares the adjudicative processes across castes and discusses the variances

---

[1] The focus on caste identities and activities does not reduce the individual to her caste-based circles. I highlight caste as a constructed category and caste identity as only one dimension of the sociopolitical identities of individuals. I uphold that many members choose to live outside these caste-based networks and circles, and many individuals discard their caste identities in their day-to-day practices. Given the nature of the inquiry, I focus exclusively on individuals who connect themselves to castes or participate in caste-based institutions. I also recognize that cultural groups are not essentialized, homogeneous, and monolithic entities.

in the cases. The third section also discusses the role of other formal and informal authorities in the adjudication of Hindu law in society.

The body of literature suggests two forms of organizations within castes. Caste associations are seen to be voluntary, broad-based coalitions of differing castes that align for common goals in democratic participation (Bailey 1963; Hardgrave 1969; Rudolph and Rudolph 1967; Washbrook 1975). Caste *panchayats* are decision-making bodies dominated by caste elders to solve internal caste disputes (Rudner 1994; Verma 1979), and these councils often decide on cases of marriage and divorce. Recently, scholars have studied the role of political mobilization and democratization (Michelutti 2004), political economy and employment patterns (Chowdhry 1997; Parry 2001), and discourses of modernization, nationalism, and individualism (Kapila 2004) in shaping the processes of caste formation and construction of conjugality on the ground. In light of these debates, this section of the chapter explores the question: How do broad sociopolitical contexts affect the internal organization and lawmaking in varied caste groups during processes of caste formation? What factors explain the variation in construction and regulation of marriage between diverse caste groups? This chapter traces trajectories of caste making in three castes and argues that the interaction between two processes – caste formation and the diffusion of state law – has impacted the construction and regulation of marriage and divorce. Furthermore, the comparison between different paths of caste making reveals that three interacting variables, namely, the nature of intracaste organization (the degree and extent of democracy in the caste council), the presence of intercaste civic ties (the link between castes and social movements, trade unions and political parties), and the link between family, occupation, and law, establish the premise of institution of marriage within the caste and set the platform for the reception of state law from above. The penetration of state law from above triggers diverse responses from these caste groups, and the interaction between state law and caste laws and practices also accounts for the differences in these caste-based normative versions of conjugality. I argue that castes with internally democratically elected and accountable caste panchayats which have built ties with

HINDU LAW IN SOCIETY

Table 4.1. *Accessing Diverse Adjudicative Forums under Hindu Law*

Castes	Cases Resolved in State Court	Caste-Based Resolution	Family-Based Resolution	Women's Organizations/ Other Agents	Multiple Forums of Resolution	Total Cases
Meghwal	6	15	4	6	10	41
Sai Suthar	4	–	5	4	2	15
KVO	6	n.a.	3	–	–	9
Total	16	15	12	10	12	65

political parties, social movements, and unions are also more likely to ensure women's rights in law. Based on interviews with litigants and caste authorities, I have compiled sixty-five cases across castes (Table 4.1). The number of litigants who approached state courts is lower than the number of litigants who approached various societal forums.

The number of cases from the KVOs is lower because divorce is infrequent within the group. The data show that the Meghwals have access to the highest number of societal options in legal matters.

Caste Formation and Lawmaking among Meghwals

This section outlines the processes and factors leading to the formation[2] of the "caste" of Meghwals – that is, the caste building among the Meghwals. The section also suggests that from the perspective of agents, the building of caste councils and of the regulatory institutions was intertwined, and they were simultaneous projects that were integral to the founding of the caste. Privileging a view of caste formation from below, I argue that the caste constituted itself as a group that follows the rules of marriage codified through the consensus of its members and abides by the rules of its caste *panchayat*. The following section begins with the history of migration and resettlement in Mumbai.

---

[2] This section is not meant to be an exhaustive history of caste formation. I have privileged the history of lawmaking over other aspects of the social history of the castes.

Migration to Mumbai and the Statist Construction of the "Caste"

The British began to build the city of Bombay[3] as a trading center from the late sixteenth century, and invited prominent trading castes of Gujarat to the city (especially the Kapol Banias, the Bhatias, the Khojas, the Boras, and the Parsis) and offered them economic incentives (Kakatiya 1978; Mallison 1989; Shodhan 2001). As the city expanded, its infrastructure and sanitation (which until then had been privately managed) required a large labor force. Records show that this considerable supply of labor was largely chosen from poor migrants from Kathiawar, Gujarat, and Maharashtra. Migration to Mumbai during these years from Kathiawar and Gujarat also increased due to natural factors such as persistent drought and crop failure. Famines ravaged Saurashtra over the course of many years: in 1804, 1811–15, 1820, 1825–26, 1833–35, 1838–39, 1846–47, 1864, 1869, 1877, 1878, and 1900.[4] Besides drought and famine, the advance of mechanized transport, shipping, and the introduction of railways that connected Kathiawar to Mumbai in 1855 were also factors that impacted migration.

Many workers from Kathiawar and Gujarat who performed manual labor in the Bombay Municipal Corporation (the BMC, now colloquially also called Brihan–Mumbai Municipal Corporation) came from diverse castes such as Vanakars (weavers), Barots (clan genealogists and poets), Turis (shehnai[5] players), and Nats (acrobats), and they migrated as individuals, not as caste groups. However, the colonial state created caste categories for a section of these workers who performed "polluting"

---

[3] Until the sixteenth century, Bombay was an island of a cluster of sparsely populated fishing villages. The Portuguese gifted the island to Charles II of England, who handed it over to the East India Company in 1668. The British developed Bombay as a port to guard against the political ambitions of the Sultan of Gujarat, the Marathas, and the Mughals (Campbell, as cited in Mehta 1936, 6).

[4] However, 1900 saw a great famine in Saurashtra that led to the loss of life and that spurred migration (Mehta 1936, 30). The stories of this famine (called *chhappaniyo dukal*) dominated the stories of migrants who came to Mumbai in search of food and livelihood.

[5] A traditional wind instrument made of metal.

tasks for the city,[6] and classified them as "untouchables" (the workers from Kathiawar and Gujarat were registered as "Dher" alongside other groups such as "Chamhar" and "Mahar") in state records.[7] These diverse groups did not have common rites, rituals, and histories. They also did not share a religion[8]; religious identities were fluid.[9]

[6] Several factors point to this. By 1865, the BMC expanded its services and hired many workers from provinces such as the North-West Frontiers Provinces; these did not belong to the "untouchable castes" (see *Annual Report of the Bombay Municipal Commissioner*, 1866, 2; as cited by Albuquerque 1992, 187).

[7] According to the BMC records, the number of "Dhers" employed in the BMC had increased from 47,000 in 1901 to 67,360 in 1931. In the case of the Mahars, the increase was from 21,305 in 1911 to 23,449 in 1931. About 5,645 Chamars were employed in the BMC in 1911, and their numbers swelled to 7,097 in 1931 (Campbell 1896, 271.) In addition to being employed by the BMC, these workers were employed in textile mills, railways, nontextile factories, and the municipal transport system of the city as coolies or casual laborers (Morris 1965, 74, 126). Scholars who trace the social history of the Mahar community in Bombay show that the Mahars migrated to Bombay as a "community" (Gokhale-Turner 1980; Zelliot 1995). Similar claims are made by other chroniclers who record Dalit history (Prashad 2000). However, this is not true of the migrant individuals from Gujarat who did not migrate as "castes" per se.

[8] The slums, where members of the "untouchable" caste stayed, were also areas of Christian missionary activity. Today, caste members recall that the first *pucca* slums for the community were built by the Methodist Episcopal Church. These *pucca* slums were sold to a Khoja Muslim in 1904, and a number of people reverted back to their caste identity at this time.

[9] Different groups of workers worshipped different deities, which included plants, spirits, goddesses, and gods. The castes came under the influence of several churches that remained active in the residential areas. These included the Church of Holy Cross (opened in 1898) and the Society of St. John (1873; the Evangelist Jesuits) (Campbell 1896, 220); some of the Meghwals were baptized, although most of them continued to follow their language, rites, and customs. In 1887, the Khoja community in Mumbai split into two groups, and each group recruited members into their communities. Their influence on the Meghwals was also pronounced. In 1917, the Aga Khan had an interview with many Meghwals after which quite a few of the members became Khojas. After their conversion, some found employment in businesses owned by the Khojas and shifted to the Khoja-dominated locality, the *imambara*; other families still remained Khojas and worshipped in the *Jamatkhana*, but continued to live with fellow group members and follow the traditions and cultural practices of the Meghwals. However, most of these converted families refused to live in the residential areas of the Khojas and asked the Khojas to build them more *chawls* where they could continue to follow their customs. Most Meghwal women refused to change

They were not permitted to stay within the city boundaries because of their "caste status" until the early twentieth century.[10] As the number of workers grew, the BMC constructed *chawls* in areas that were away from upper-caste neighborhoods.[11] The residential arrangement threw together the previously dispersed families of cleaners classified as "Dher." The members of these groups began to share common occupations as well as residential spaces. However, these groups were not assimilated into local castes of similar status (such as Chamhars, Mahars, and Mangs) because they shared different linguistic and cultural traditions[12]; thus, they began to organize as endogamous groups.

The social organization of these groups was loose. The smallest unit was the family, a number of families comprised a *shakh* (a branch), and these in turn were organized as *gnati*, a regional subgroup structured around an occupation. The *gnati*s were largely endogamous units made

---

their traditional dress and adopt *salwars* worn by the Khoja women. After a certain period, many families decided to revert back to their former beliefs (Mehta 1936).

[10] Most of the private buildings in Bombay were owned by members of the upper castes who did not rent them to untouchables. As a result, they had to reside in thatched huts on the outskirts of the city (however, some families managed to find rental space in buildings owned by Muslims who did not practice caste rigidly). In fact, most members' memories revolve around the struggles of their forefathers to construct huts on garbage dumps without access to water. "Large pigs could sneak in and eat food any time, and rats would bite us even then. We lifted human and animal waste (*melu*), but there was no provision of toilets for us" (interview with Gangaben Bariya, September 5, 2002, Mumbai).

[11] These *chawls* were three to four stories high, structured like barracks, and had rooms the size of eight feet by eight feet. Each family was given a room, but had to share toilet facilities with others.

[12] Rivalries existed between these three castes of roughly similar status within Maharashtra. The Mahars were the first group to organize politically; they remained distinct from other Maharashtrian untouchables. Reasons for this include their enlistment in the colonial army, employment opportunities outside the village system, access to education through Christian missions and their own political struggles, and the leadership of Dr. B. R. Ambedkar (Zelliot 1995, 27–35). Similarly, caste groups classified as untouchables and who migrated from Gujarat were more pro-Congress Party and did not readily accept Dr. Ambedkar as their leader. They also did not join the temple entry movement that was intrinsic to militant Mahar politics from 1927 onward (Zelliot 1995, 35).

HINDU LAW IN SOCIETY 181

of exogamous groups of *shakhs*. Different groups had their own systems to regulate marriage. At times, families who had migrated from nearby residential areas in Gujarat and Kathiwar formed a unit that would officiate in these matters, and these were called *"tana panch"*; other families formed *"vada panch"* based on residential proximity in Mumbai. Bob Mehta, who studied this group in 1936, noted that some groups called themselves Meghwals, and there were several mythical tales about their historical past, but these group members did not share a common memory and were unwilling to talk about reasons behind migration from western India, and it was not clear how they had come to regard themselves as a "caste" (Mehta 1936).

Nationalist Movement, Naming the Community, and Attempts at Lawmaking

The "untouchability" question occupied the center of the nationalist movement in the 1920s.[13] The decade saw the emergence of key Dalit

---

[13] In 1923, the Bombay Legislative Council passed a resolution stating that all public places were to be open to untouchables. Several followers of Dr. Ambedkar conducted campaigns such as the burning of the Manusmriti, drinking water from water sources in upper-caste areas, challenging the prohibition of the Dalits on using public places and services, and other such tactics (Zelliot 1995, 40–41). Dr. Ambedkar attended the round-table conference and asked for separate electorates for the Dalits in 1930. However, Gandhi opposed this claim, and the Gujarati untouchable community supported Mahatma Gandhi's position on this (the period of 1930–39 saw the conflict between P. G. Solanki, the leader of the Gujarati Dalits, and Dr. Ambedkar, who was seen to represent only the Mahar community) (Gokhale-Turner 1980, 275). The Poona Pact of 1932 was signed against the backdrop of Dalit agitations, and as a result, a compromise was reached between Dr. Ambedkar (who had earlier bargained for separate electorates for the Dalits) and Mahatma Gandhi (who had denied this demand, insisting that untouchability was a vice within Hinduism, and Hinduism needed to reform itself). According to the Pact, the Depressed Classes would be given reserved seats on the basis of joint electorates, and would be included in the public service and local boards. In addition, an adequate sum would be reserved in all provincial grants for the education of the Depressed Classes. The Poona Pact and its inclusion into the Government of India Act 1935 was the first step in providing a constitutional guarantee of special rights for the untouchables. Mahatma Gandhi

leaders, and legal and political gains were made within this period. Many individuals from various caste clusters of the BMC workers began to be involved in the nationalist movement. This involvement was reflected in the number of organizations that were formed among BMC workers. Between 1920 and 1950, the Servants of India Society and the All India Servants of India Society founded organizations for "untouchable" youth, which resulted in a number of youth clubs, cricket clubs, and voluntary corps.[14] Although the caste clusters remained apart from the more radical programs of the Ambedkarites, they also began to organize in order to receive education.[15] The struggles for the schooling of the children of the cleaners began during that time.[16] During

established the *Harijan Sevak Sangh* in the 1930s, and Dr. Ambedkar established the Independent Labour Party in 1936, which fought the provincial elections in 1937. The Harijan Temple Entry Bill was passed soon thereafter.

[14] The youth were mainly active in challenging caste hierarchies through individual struggles. They did not display the political assertiveness that characterized the Mahar community under the leadership of Dr. Ambedkar. These caste clusters were more attracted to Mahatma Gandhi's programs for the removal of untouchability (interview with Vishrambhai Waghela, May 2, 2003, Mumbai).

[15] The first schools for children of the untouchables in Maharashtra opened at the initiative of Mahatma Jyotiba Phule in 1852 in Poona. Subsequently, the British government established separate schools for the untouchables. In 1882, there were sixteen such schools in the Bombay Presidency (Zelliot 1995, 44). However, in 1911, only 0.48 percent of Mahars, Holiyas, and Dhers were literate in Bombay Presidency. This proportion had increased to 1.5 percent in 1921 and 2.9 percent in 1931 (*Census of India, 1911*, [Bombay, 1912], Vol. III, Part 1, Table IX; *Census of India, 1921* [Bombay 1922], Vol. VIII, Table X, 85; *Census of India, 1931* [Bombay 1933], Vol. VIII, Part 1, Imperial Table XIV).

[16] The children of the caste clusters that had begun to call themselves Meghwals were not allowed to study, because the untouchables had no facilities for education in private schools. The caste clusters of the Harijans wished to start a school and could only get space from a Khoja Muslim in the red-light district of Mumbai. Eight children of varying ages, including one girl, attended that school. It had one room and was staffed with a teacher who had studied up to the fifth grade himself; later, volunteers from the Servants of India Society taught there. These students were admitted into the Sarvajanik High School by a Gandhian principal, and the All India Servants of Untouchables Society paid their fees. This section is based on interviews with Tabhjibhai Solanki, who was one of those children who studied in that school, February 10, 2003. After two years of ad hoc functioning, the caste members wrote to Mahatma Gandhi about the state of affairs, and provisions for new schools were

these years, employment opportunities of these caste clusters began to grow. Between the 1920s and the 1950s, a few of the caste members were employed as mill workers,[17] dock workers, casual laborers in factories, or cleaners in private service.

The construction of the category of "Hindu" began taking shape in the public sphere in the late colonial period (Pandey 1990). Between the late nineteenth century and the early twentieth century, many "untouchable" castes engaged in efforts to create separate institutions within Hinduism (Zelliot 1995). In 1911, diverse caste clusters began to organize around the issue of temple entry for the "untouchables" and established organizations such as the Meghwal Sudharak Sabha (the Meghwal Reform Committee) and the Meghwal Hitvardhak Mandal (Society for Welfare of the Meghwals).[18] They tried to build a separate temple for the cleaners, as cleaners were not allowed to enter upper-caste temples.[19] The formation of these organizations was the first appearance of a section of the community classified as "Dhers," who began to call themselves

> made. Mahatma Gandhi asked volunteers from the Servants of India Society to begin teaching children there. He also intervened to secure them admission to high school.

[17] Data show that untouchables tended to be concentrated in certain sectors in all employment sources. Citing a study sponsored by the Bombay Mill-Owners' Association, Morris suggests that at that time, 13.8 percent of the workforce in the mills was clustered in certain sectors of the mills: For example, about 70 percent of the male untouchables worked in ring-spinning. Of the women untouchables, 74 percent of them worked in winding and reeling departments (Gokhale-Turner 1980, 114–115; Morris 1965).

[18] This agitation and mobilization around the issue was meant to raise their self-perception as Hindus. Since the 1830s, the Christian Evangelical forces became active in the Bombay Presidency. The presence of Christian missionaries also sparked public debates over practices of widow remarriage, the exploration of the link between Hinduism and heterodox cults such as Shaktaism, the resolution of the "caste question within Hinduism," whether Brahmins can attend "polluting" Christian schools, and over issues concerning the management of Hindu temples (Tucker 1976).

[19] This *Lakshmi Narain* temple was inaugurated by Sarojini Naidu, and many Congress leaders such as Deshbandhu Chitranjan Das and Vitthalbhai Patel were also present (*Harijano matena Sri Lakshmi Narain Mandir no Ahewal* 1935, 17). A permanent board of trustees to handle the finances and related matters was announced (*Harijano matena Sri Lakshmi Narain Mandir no Ahewal* 1935, 17–18). It was funded by G.K. Birla and the firm of Desai and Bhuta.

Meghwal. There is no strict date on which group members who were classified in government records as "Dher" came together and named themselves Meghwal. However, this term coexisted with "Dher" (and later Harijan or Vanakar) until the 1950s. The use of the term Meghwal as a subcategory of the broad term Harijan began to emerge within the process of constitution building and lawmaking in the second half of the twentieth century.

Exposure to Democratic Politics, Creating Structures of Governance, Constructing Identity through Laws

For the Meghwals, the decades between the 1950s and the late 1970s were marked by their exposure to democratic politics. The BMC institutionalized the "Preferential Treatment Policy" for this category of workers.[20] Per this unwritten policy, the BMC hires family/kin members of the Scheduled Castes at the time of retirement of any fourth-class municipal worker. Given the nature of employment in the public sector, this policy ensured the steady employment of at least one member of a Meghwal family through the generations and provided security of rental housing in *chawls*, public health, pension, and other welfare benefits. In the first decades of independence, caste members were exposed to political parties, union politics,[21] and intracaste politics. These decades also saw a proliferation of civic

---

[20] This policy is also very popular, because the BMC provides its workers with housing and health care. The BMC also provides daycare services, and its welfare department provides assorted services for the workers' families. The provision of substantive citizenship rights for the BMC workers has had a great impact on the community life of the caste members. The BMC workers are housed as tenants in the BMC *chawls*. However, as members of the same family are rehired under the Preferential Treatment Policy, the 8-feet-by-8-feet room remains in the family for generations. Controlled rent for the residential space in Bombay, where property prices are inflated, makes this policy very popular among workers (interview with Harjivan Boricha and Mavjibhai Maroo, November 6, 2002, Mumbai).

[21] There were few Meghwal members in the Bombay Kamaghar Sangh (The Bombay Employees' Union) when it was established in 1935. However, their membership quickly grew. In 1949, about 15,000 members of the Bombay Kamghar Sangh went on a long strike and gained higher wages. This participation in the strike was an

organizations within the caste. Whereas the focus of civic organizations in preindependence time was the "upliftment of the caste," the newer organizations were less charity-oriented and more active in politics.[22]

The decades following independence were marked by the efforts by sections of the castes to construct a "caste." Two different constitutions, in 1953 and later in 1964, were proposed by reformist leaders who justified the need to form a *panch* system in order to forge unity among various factions and sections of the caste, to push modernist reforms, to centralize authority through democratic governance within the caste, and to find avenues to collect revenue for caste welfare. The constitution provided a framework for the construction of identity. The Constitution of 1953 defines the caste of Meghwal as a group that follows the rules of marriage codified by the group members who agree to abide by the decisions of the *panchayat*.

As the Meghwal identity began to be consolidated, the caste members were viewed as a caste constituency because the group tended to vote en masse. Thus the *panch* system became a battleground used by different political parties to capture the caste constituency. Given the history of the caste clusters' association with the nationalist movement, their leaning toward Gandhian politics, and the penetration of the Congress Party–affiliated civil organizations (such as the Harijan Sevak Sangh and the Servants of India Society), the caste members were drawn to the Congress Party in Mumbai,[23] especially in local Municipal Corporation elections.[24] The caste constituency depended

invaluable experience that served to politicize many Meghwal caste members (interview with Jeevrajbhai Koli, April 4, 2003, Mumbai).

[22] The caste youth members organized discussion groups that were facilitated by eminent left academics such as Dr. A. R. Desai (interview with Vishrambhai Waghela, January 3, 2003, Mumbai).

[23] In the early years, it was said that "even an inert object like a lamppost fielded by the Congress Party would win an election from the Meghwal-dominated residential areas" (Interview with Lalitbhai Waghela, March 8, 2003, Mumbai).

[24] The Congress won the BMC elections in 1948, 1952, and 1961 and remained a powerful presence in these elections. In 1957, a multiparty alliance, the Samyukta Maharashtra Samiti, which demanded and created a unilingual state of Maharashtra,

on the BMC to provide basic amenities (water, electricity, government schools for children, welfare centers, daycare, and so on), and they also had linkages with the BMC given their occupational status as cleaners. The Communist Party of India also tried to make inroads, but did not enjoy broad support of the caste members.

There were also conflicts between the Meghwal leaders who were in the Communist Party and the Congress workers. During the 1950s and the 1960s, this interparty struggle was played out in the *panch* systems. Both the Congress Party and the Communist Party, along with their supporters, tried to capture the office of the *panchayat*, yet neither of these political parties established the *panch* system as a neutral independent body, and because it was not perceived as a legitimate authority, the *panch* system's constitution did not gain popular support; people could violate its rules with relative impunity. During this time, many ambitious young men of the Meghwal caste were attracted to the idea of political power and tried to build networks within the Congress Party. However, instead of building intracaste organizational structures and linking them with the party organization, the Congress Party depended on local caste politicians. The caste politicians did not allow the emergence of second-rung leadership within the caste. Moreover, the Congress Party leaders insisted on dealing with these men through their caste leaders. As a result, there was a sense of frustration among the youth and the politically motivated members. By the 1970s, caste members did not feel they had gained substantially from their loyalty to the Congress Party; murmurs of disenchantment had begun, and "this energy turned inward, towards reform of the caste *panchayat*."[25]

---

won the elections. In the 1973 elections, the Congress Party suffered a setback, and even the Shiv Sena could not retain its strength. Postemergency, the Janata party came to power in 1978. The 1984 elections installed the Shiv Sena, but the 1992 elections saw the Congress Party winning the elections once again (Thakkar 1997, 251–252).

[25] Interviews with Devjibhai Jogadia, August 12, 2002, Mumbai; Sant Khodidas, May 3, 2003, Mumbai; Pravinbhai Sosa, January 12, 2003, Mumbai.

Democratizing Panchayats, Civic Awareness, and Law Reforms: From the Panch System to the Panchayat

The decade of 1970 saw efforts to form an autonomous caste *panchayat*. This process of depoliticization took two forms: One was a continued attempt to reform the laws; the second was to further democratize the *panchayat*. An election commission was formed in 1974–75, and intra-caste elections were held[26] as a step toward the institutionalization of internal governance.[27] Another round of discussions on the issue of law reform took place within the Meghwal community. All public and intra *panch* communications (letters, circulars, announcements, and public requests) reiterated the statement that "members were requested not to discuss political issues under any circumstances" (see circulars dated July 7, 1974, September 18, 1975, and August 22, 1975. See also the pamphlet dated August 16, 1975, entitled "jaher sabha nu nimantran"). An Interim Constitutional Amendment Committee was formed; it drafted several amendments to the constitution. This time, the constitution and its amendments were discussed through a decentralized participatory process. Apart from including area-based civic bodies (such as youth clubs and welfare centers), residential committees were included in the process to elicit a range of opinions. Women were actively involved in discussing these drafts, and they participated in large numbers.[28] The women's meetings prioritized the issue of women's economic rights in the context of elopement and divorce.

---

[26] See pamphlet entitled "Programme and timetable: Election of the Caste President," filed as Document 60D, undated. Signed by the Election Commission, Mulji Gigabhai Koli (Convenor), Palji Lalji Dafda, Keshav Kalabhai Wagh, Mulji Gangjee Koli, and Kishor Jaising Singh.

[27] See circulars dated July 7, 1974 and September 18, 1975.

[28] Reasons given by the Constitution committee were, first, to ensure the representation of women, because not many women participated in the process of constitution building, and their voices needed to be heard in a process that was self-consciously inclusive. Secondly, women did discuss these matters in the inner spheres of their houses and *chawls*. It was clear that they had opinions that needed expression in a united voice through the creation of "an organised women's voice." The reformers also were of the opinion that "the Meghwal women did not have access to education

The decentralization process created a three-tier system, and local groups forwarded the amendments to the *panch* and subcommittees on various provisions. Their recommendations in turn were forwarded to the central constitutional amendment committee.[29] Three meetings with the caste members at large were held between August 5, 1975, and December 30, 1975,[30] before finalizing the draft of the changes of the new constitution, which was passed on January 26, 1976. The discussion of legal changes within the caste continued even in the latter half of the 1970s.[31]

The depoliticization of the *panchayat* that took place in the 1970s created a legacy of challenging the presence of political parties in matters of internal governance of the caste; however, this does not mean that

and 'culture' (*Sanskar*)," and this had a direct impact on their capacity as mothers. This also had a negative impact on the new generations; therefore, they needed "to come out and participate in social activities." Another reason given by the committee was to organize and mobilize women to oppose traditions that were "dominated by patriarchal biases and needed change." The reformers also perceived that women would consent to change in harmful traditions because they had more to gain from modernizing the caste laws. Women discussed reforms in public meetings as well as in several group meetings facilitated by the *panchayat*. The first women's public meeting was called on August 17, 1975; prominent social workers from Bombay were invited, and P. T. Patel chaired the meeting. Circulars of the *Meghwal Hitvardhak Samaj*, March 12, 1975, April 18, 1975, and June 16, 1975.

[29] See also *Internal Communication*, paper no. 8/75, August 10, 1975. The letter asked the local *panch* whether they had called the meetings of the women's committees as well as the beggars' committees in their respective areas. The letter also invited suggestions from the *panchs* about holding a larger meeting in which all women caste members could be present. It asked them to suggest possible dates and places for holding these meetings, and to meet with these two subject committees for their individual feedback. The letter was signed by Devshi Khuman and Karsan Chauhan.

[30] For instance, the meeting on August 5 discussed the following agendas: bride-price, marriage, economic transactions during marriage, divorce and remarriage, death rites, and duties. Other public meetings were necessary, as one meeting could not do justice to all speakers (see filed as 30A). (Public Meeting (*sabha*) to discuss social reforms, June 20, 1975.)

[31] This is suggested by a cursory perusal of a memo. The letter discusses the elopement of widows as a contested issue requiring further debate (internal communication, November 30, 1976, signed by Devshi Khuman).

these contestations have ceased or will cease.[32] The process of depoliticization met with opposition from political workers and political parties. These conflicts came out in the open in 1987 at the time of renewed dialog on the caste constitution.

Attempts at Repoliticization and the Conflict over Caste Constitution

The arrival of the Dalit Panthers[33] on the political scene offered the local youth an option in politics. In fact, all caste members were exposed to the militant politics of the Dalit Panthers,[34] and initially, the caste members were not enthusiastic, but an incident generated support for them. A Shiv Sainik was murdered while gambling in the Meghwal residential hub. The Shiv Sena had a previous history of local clashes with these Dalits; there were, therefore, internal rivalries between the middle-caste Sena workers and the Dalits. The murder was not politically motivated, but the Shiv Sena decided to play it as such. The Sena communicated to all its branches that the Meghwal caste was responsible for the death of its Sainik. The Meghwal caste members feared violent retribution and backlash from the Sena. The caste members then turned to the Dalit Panthers, who

---

[32] "There emerged a general understanding that while people belonging to different parties may be active in the *panchayat*, they will not have strong voices in running the *panchayat*. They have to create their 'social credibility' in order to make voices heard in this arena (the central *panchayat*)." (Interview with Vishrambhai Waghela, February 6, 2003, Mumbai.)

[33] The Dalit Panthers is an organization of militant Maharashtrian Dalit Neo-Buddhists (formed in 1972) who adopted the political goal of a democratic socialist state. By the late 1960s, the first generation of the Dalits who reaped the benefits of a formal education joined the "Little Magazine" movement through which they challenged the literary monopoly of the upper-caste Hindus. They draw their ideology from Buddhist and Marxist philosophies, and are inspired by the Black Panthers of the United States. Their earthy, often racy, militant literary works reflect their solidarity with peasants, laborers, prostituted women, Africans, Cambodians, Vietnamese, and so on (Gokhale-Turner 1980; Murugkar 1991).

[34] However, this incident left a mark on the public memory of the caste (interview with Vishrambhai Waghela and Kishor Marwadi, February 5, 2003, Mumbai.)

responded immediately: Namdeo Dhasal, the leader of one of the factions of the Dalits, came to address a rally in the area. The Sainiks decided not to attack, and the situation remained under control.

After this event, even though not many joined the Panthers, their political discourse brought about an awakening among the caste members.[35] This relationship gathered strength during the riots of January 1975[36] during which the Dalits suffered massive repression by the state.[37] The caste *panchayat*'s project of law reform also laid the foundation for a battleground of interparty competition to capture the caste *panchayat* in the mid-1970s. Between 1975 and the early 1980s, a Constitution Rejuvenation Committee was formed with the tacit backing of the Congress Party, which invited the Dalit Panthers to join the process. Soon, however, differences between the Congress Party and the Dalit Panthers spilled over into the public sphere; the Panthers wanted to restructure the *panch* system itself.[38] Their aim was to shift the attention

---

[35] While the Mahars had used the Dalit identity since the 1930s, the Meghwals, until the 1970s, referred to themselves as Harijans. Since the 1970s, they have adopted the term "Dalit" to refer to themselves.

[36] The Dalit Panthers competed with the RPI, the Congress Party, and the Shiv Sena on the political scene of Maharashtra in the 1970s. Over the course of a Lok Sabha by-election (an election held to fill a political vacancy – the equivalent of the U.S. special election) in 1974, the Panthers engaged in numerous violent clashes with the Hindu right-wing party, the Shiv Sena. About 80,000 Dalit voters boycotted the polls. This protest was organized by the Panthers in protest of the ill treatment of the Dalits by caste Hindus (Sirsikar 1995a, 199–200).

[37] I have focused on these stories, which have become part of the caste members' repertoire of folklore, to explain crucial changes in the formation of the caste *panchayat*. "Storytelling is crucial in constructing experimental meanings of the event after the fact and thus self-understanding of those who, on either side, participated in it" (Auyero 2002, 153).

[38] They argued that the function of the caste *panchayat* should be to ensure and facilitate the process of securing the benefits of reservations for the Dalits. Their suggestions for social welfare activities included the use of caste funds to open educational institutions for Dalit students, to start literacy classes, and to provide tuition and scholarships for educationally weak students in each residential area. Other activities included providing ambulance service as well as free legal aid for caste members. They also called for a cooperative bank, a consumer society, and the building of a large public hall for caste celebrations (*Agenda of the Panch-System*, undated pamphlet).

from inner governance to social development. They identified four functions of the caste *panchayat*: social welfare, economic upliftment, maintenance of records, and social progress with the consequent broadening of the caste agendas.

The conflict between the Congress Party and the Dalit Panthers ran deeper than their struggle to capture the caste constituency. The conflict between the two parties was about control over caste ideology (over the meaning of "Meghwal-Dalit"), icons (whether to adopt Mahatma Gandhi or Dr. Ambedkar as a caste leader), religious affiliations (especially over the nature of religious affiliations of the Meghwal caste), the social sphere (the nature and functions of the caste *panchayat*), and program agendas (what should be the general direction of the reforms). The Dalit Panthers reaffirmed the centrality of political intervention in the process of constitution making and opposed any move to Hinduize the caste.[39] Caste members joined the debates through discussions, and many wrote to both factions.[40] The Congress Party managed to garner support, and despite the controversy, the third Meghwal constitution was unveiled at the Meghwal Gnati Sammelan (Meghwal Caste Meeting) that was held on January 25, 1987.[41]

[39] The Panthers stated: "We believe that any member who is part of the *panchayat* can be a member of any political party.... We also believe that members of this *panchayat* can belong to any religion and can celebrate whichever festival they wish." *Postscript*, February 25, 1987, pamphlet.
[40] Many of these letters are handwritten, and many letters are not signed. Some members have opposed the changes in the caste constitution: "Why should we change the constitution? It is a forward-looking constitution which has been introduced by leaders with higher stature than yours. Why should self-appointed leaders meddle with the constitution?" A letter entitled "The Bubble Has Burst" (unsigned letter delivered to the Committee) accused the committees of engaging in new endeavors for their own benefits.
[41] See *Beyond Tomorrow: A Prayer to Public*, January 25, 1987; see also Minutes of the Constitution Rejuvenation Committee, September 2, 1986; internal communication, circulated to all *panchs* by the Constitution committee, September 26, 1986, signed by Paljibhai Boricha, Virjeebhai Solanki, Mavjibhai Solanki, Shyamjee Koli, and Lalit Waghela. There were several reasons for which the caste constitution was passed. In general, people supported the Constitution Committee of the Congress Party over the Panthers. One of the reasons was that the parent parties of the Dalit Panthers

This political controversy brought about a heightened sense of distaste for the interference of the political parties in the social sphere of the caste. Many individuals, especially civic bodies who had supported the process, once again called for the depoliticization of the caste. And once again, the caste members attempted to revive the social sphere of the caste.[42] The idea of democratizing the *panch* system and of amending the constitution came about in this atmosphere of depoliticization; soon, efforts began in that direction.

The Decade of the 1990s: Consolidating the Caste Identity, Social Regulation, and Lawmaking

The process of constitution making in the 1990s took place in the broader political context of the twin developments in the Indian polity: economic liberalization and rising communalism in Mumbai.[43] The economic reforms of the 1990s have had a direct impact on the livelihoods of

> went through a phase of infighting between factions; its disorganization (Murugkar 1991) also affected its organizational capabilities and strength at the ground level. This infighting also affected the popular perception of the party at the caste level. Furthermore, the programmatic agendas of the Panthers did not distinguish between the civic activities and the social regulatory aspect of the caste *panchayat*. Secondly, the modernist images of the Panthers raised fears about state intervention in the community's affairs, and the Constitution committee was able to play on these fears. On the other hand, the Congress Party supported the Constitution committee and played on the differences between them and the Panthers; the party thus built on the foundations of earlier constitutions and was able to project itself as moderate. This won over the trust of a large section who did not want radical changes. However, this process also saw the victory of the orthodox/moderates and the pro-Hindu factions of the caste.

[42] The idea of depoliticizing the caste system also reflects the political developments in Maharashtra at that time. By the mid-1970s, a general perception emerged that the fruits of development were not equitably distributed and that the Indian state had failed to deliver to the poorest. A number of social movements – the Dalit movement, the people's science movement, the student movements, and women's movements – emerged during the 1970s.

[43] In the early 1990s, the Hindu right-wing party, the BJP, and its affiliate organizations staged a political campaign to build a temple at the birthplace of one of the Hindu gods, Ram, as well as to demolish the Babri Mosque on December 6, 1992; the result was nationwide riots. Bombay was one of the cities where the riots were more severe,

workers employed in public-sector companies. The reforms have also brought a general sense of employment insecurity among the Meghwals. The Municipal Corporation of Greater Mumbai has delayed the use of the preferential policy in recent years, which caused unrest within the caste. The BMC has also withdrawn the housing policy; as a result, the workers have gradually been asked to vacate government *chawls* that had been allocated to them for generations. A number of meetings on issues have been held by the Meghwals. The caste members have also been concerned about the possibility of the privatization of the BMC and the resultant loss of rights to housing, pensions, and health care; this privatization would adversely affect intracaste organizations and activities.

At present, there are more than 10,000 Meghwal households in Mumbai. Currently, the few members belonging to the upper stratum of the Meghwal caste are engaged in white-collar professions (such as doctors, lawyers, and government officials). Individuals working as clerks, teachers, and industrial workers comprise the middle layer; many Meghwals work as cleaners in the BMC and public-sector offices. Most Meghwals are menial laborers in the informal sector. Income disparity within the caste is marginal.

The decade of the 1990s saw the fragmentation of the caste as a political constituency[44]: The caste members have not come to a public

---

and the Shiv Sena played a prominent role in the riots. The Bombay riots ravaged the Muslim communities in the city and also affected the Dalits given their proximity to Muslim neighborhoods because of their historical position of untouchability. The Muslims suffered far more losses given the pogromic character of the riots, but the Dalit properties were also affected during these riots (interviews with Vishrambhai Waghela, March 6, 2003, Mumbai; Lalitbhai Waghela, November 18, 2002; J. M. Maroo and Premjibhai Mahida, March 19, 2003, Mumbai).

[44] The 1990s were also marked by coalition politics at both the state and national levels. A majority of the Meghwals tend to favor the Congress Party, but the rise of the Samajwadi Party and the Bahujan Samaj Party has provided the Meghwals with new electoral options. The RPI does not have a base among the Meghwals. However, many Meghwals support the communist parties. The Shiv Sena has tried to woo the Dalit workers through actively taking up issues concerning the Preferential Treatment Policy in the BMC. This fragmentation of loyalties to the political parties has weakened the parties' dominance in the social sphere of the caste. The caste

consensus over its religious identity. Many caste members are tolerant of other faiths, but the 1990s have seen a rupture in this caste consensus.[45] Many caste members claim to be Hindus but add, with self-conscious irony, that they are not accepted by the Hindu society at large. Many liberal factions and the Marxists scorn the recent trends of Hinduization of the caste and criticize the caste *panchayats* for holding Hindu prayers at Hindu festivals. The caste holds Ramdeo *Pir*, who is worshipped by Hindus and Muslims, as its chief figure of faith and celebrates his pirhood and miracles through various ceremonies and public processions. However, the religious arena is seen to be separate from social and cultural fields: Thus, Ramdeo *Pir*'s opinions and dictates are confined to religious matters. There is considerable religious freedom in the caste, and so the constitution does not conjoin Hinduism with Meghwal identity.

Throughout the 1990s, the participation of the Meghwal in organizations and associations remained vibrant. There are a number of civic organizations within the caste. In addition, several *panch*s organize various activities at the local level, such as cricket matches, blood donor clinics, AIDS awareness programs, intracaste microcredit groups for

---

panchayat is seen as an independent body regulating social activities of the caste, and is seen to be distinct from political parties. Very few members of political parties are elected as office-bearers of the caste *panchayat*.

[45] There exist contesting ideas and assertions of Hindu identity among a section of the community. I came across one case in which a Meghwal family had suffered residential boycott and persecution as a result of their conversion to Islam. The residents of that building justified their boycott in light of the family's renunciation of the Meghwal identity. The members of the converted family changed their pattern of dress as well as their speech, and they began to socialize with Muslims – an act that was perceived to be anti-Meghwal. A local youth who harassed the women members of the family argued: "We have nothing against Muslims.... You can go and pray in the Mosque and bow to the *qazi* ... many Meghwals do that, but these people went too far." The youth explained what he meant by "too far": "It is as though they ceased to be Meghwals, and the women started wearing Muslim dress, *burqas*, and suddenly started speaking in Hindi.... Why, don't we belong to [the] same culture? Have they forgotten that their parents were not *nawabs* [aristocrats], but night-soil lifters?" (interview with Praveen Koli, March 7, 2003, Mumbai).

women, literacy classes, and celebrations of festivals including national festivals. The community has many poets and singers who sing both devotional and revolutionary songs. There are also women poets and writers in the caste, whose plays are performed at public meetings.

The 1990s saw the rise of the first generation of educated Meghwal workers who were experienced in labor policies and familiar with trade union politics; they understood government administration, bureaucracy, and laws. These men and women took the lead in renewed calls for community reforms. Many of these leaders have participated in workers' movements as well as women's movements, but they have been disappointed by formal politics and have sought not to "depoliticize but repoliticize"[46] the caste sphere through internal reforms and progress. Some feminists who were part of the Meghwal reform process had mediated effectively in many matrimonial disputes and had also coordinated with feminist organizations and activists in several cases.[47] The functioning of the *panchayat* over the years has been further democratized. The caste holds biannual review meetings in which caste members discuss issues concerning caste laws, and they exchange information about other forums. For instance, some women in a meeting exhorted the caste women to approach women's organizations, especially a Muslim women's organization in their area, for more help in these matters.[48]

Summary of the Constitutional Provisions: Commonalities, Continuities, and Discontinuities

The caste constitutions have been scrutinized and changed six times[49] since the creation of the caste community. The assessment and evaluation of the caste constitution is an ongoing process. The caste group

---

[46] Interview with Gangaben Bariya, September 8, 2002.
[47] Interview with Gangaben Bariya, Forum Against Oppression of Women, September 13, 2004.
[48] The meeting to discuss the current caste constitution, July 26, 2003, Mumbai.
[49] The changes were formalized in 1935, 1953, 1964–65, 1974–75, 1987, and 1993, respectively.

organizes biannual meetings to discuss laws and their implementation. They invite lawyers, women's organizations, and Hindu and Muslim political leaders to discuss legal developments. The process of lawmaking has been inclusive from the first constitution.[50] The lawmaking process has also led to the consolidation of law wherein each new constitution includes both the contents of earlier laws and some alterations that cleared earlier inconsistencies in the law.

The constitution making brings to light the agency of the caste in creating a collectivity called Meghwals. Subsequently, the term has become fixed and *ascriptive* since 1987. The caste collective has expanded the area of its jurisdiction. Many caste members from different territorial areas can also become members of the Meghwal community.[51] Different constitutions have laid down extensive guidelines, rules, and regulations governing births, deaths, engagements, marriage, remarriage, breach of promise, divorce, elopement, and bride-price (the practice of bride-price is not widely prevalent anymore and has not been replaced by dowry).[52] At different times, the functions of the *panch* have included the registration of births, deaths, engagements, marriages, divorces, and elopements; the enumeration of residents in a local area and the names of Meghwal residents; the maintenance of accounts; and the creation of records of nonadherence to caste laws and rules.[53]

Each constitution is both exhortative and authoritative, seeking maximum conformity with enshrined principles while implying that it will function on the basis of voluntary compliance.[54] Each constitution

---

[50] Indeed, the process in the 1970s epitomized this process in which a large number of institutionalized groups, representatives of different factions (who were co-opted to become members of subcommittees), and diverse bodies were consulted and different meetings were held to discuss the substance of their recommendations.

[51] See the Meghwal caste constitution, 1987, 1996.

[52] Feminist debates on dowry suggest that the replacement of this custom has had adverse implications for women's property rights (Sharma 1994).

[53] See Sri Meghwal Gnati Bandharan (1953, 14–16; 1965, 1975).

[54] For instance, the constitution prohibits child marriage (marriage in cradle) (Sri Meghwal Gnati Bandharan 1953, 1). Furthermore, each constitution holds that marriages should be performed without any economic exchanges (Kanku-Kanya

has sought to remove "harmful traditions" such as child marriage (1953, 1965, 1987, 1996), the "auctioning" of women (1953), and the remarriage of older widowers to young women (1987). The constitutions have created intricate divorce laws. The process of divorce in the 1935/1953 draft was a hybrid, and the forms of divorce therein were akin to the Islamic practice of unilateral divorce. Women who had been separated for more than six months had the right to a unilateral divorce. Men did not have the reciprocal right (1953, 1964). Grounds for divorce, such as insanity, infertility, and incurable disease, were introduced in 1987. Other types of divorce include "fault-based divorce," divorce due to "mutual incompatibility," and divorce due to "mutual fault" (1964). The constitutions recognize annulment (1953, 1996), the principle of ex parte divorce (restricted only to women, 1953), and mutual incompatibility as grounds for divorce. Intercaste marriages are allowed.

The constitutions have also sought to delineate rules concerning children and their lineage. Women within many sections of the caste clusters of the collective used to write their mothers' names after their names (1953, 1964, 1975). The state's classificatory system of fixing, standardizing, and legalizing (Scott 1998) paternal names has abolished this practice (1987, 1996). Paternity is not the guiding principle in determining guardianship of children: The mother is seen to be the natural guardian of the child, and the children from the first marriage are seen to be the "natural" children of the man whom the mother married or with whom she cohabits (1953, 1964, 1975, 1987). The concept of illegitimacy does not exist in the caste (1953, 1964, 1975, 1987, 1993).

> na lagan-Sri Meghwal Gnati Bandharan 1953, 1965; Samasta Meghwal Gnati Bandharan 1987; Mumbai Meghwal/Vanakar gnati Bandharan 1996); this is the ideal type of marriage. They also recommend that marriages should be performed with as much simplicity as possible; for instance, the section on "Guidelines Regarding Arrival of the Groom's Party: '*Varghoda*'" stresses that intracaste rivalries played out in outlandish and expensive marriages should be discontinued, and the bridegroom's procession should be small and simple (Sri Meghwal Gnati Bandharan 1953, 2).

Although most caste constitutions were amended after the enactment of the Hindu Marriage Act 1955, and lawyers working in state courts often serve as *panch* and advisors of the caste *panchayat*, only some caste laws have been harmonized to fit the framework of either the Hindu laws or the Indian Penal Code. The line between marriage and nonmarriage was more fluid in the 1950s: The constitution allowed a married woman to marry a different partner who could pay a higher bride-price (1953, 1964). Each constitution sanctions cohabitation and conditional polygyny. Polygyny is permitted in cases of sterility; however, polygyny cannot take place before five years have elapsed, and even then, the first wife's consent must be obtained before polygyny is allowed (Sri Meghwal Gnati Bandharan 1953, 7; 1996).

Finally, the constitutions have formalized women's right to ownership of property (1987, 1996), and women are recognized as economic actors and not as dependents. In addition, women's right to maintenance during marriage is safeguarded in the constitutions. Similarly, women have rights to the self-earned property.

The Gendered Sphere among the Meghwals

The social sphere of the constructed caste collectivity of the Meghwals is not bisected into the dichotomies of public/private, inner/outer, home/world, or male/female. Women within the caste are seen as economic agents and act as economic agents.[55] The democratization of the caste *panchayat* has also provided a few opportunities to women to participate in intracaste governance, though their numbers are very few. Many women workers are trade unions members and participate in social movements, including women's movements. Meghwal women are part of organizations and clubs and identify themselves as workers, committee

---

[55] The data suggest an important presence of women in the Bombay Municipal Corporation in the nineteenth century. For instance, in 1911, 1,800 men and 1,100 women classified as "Dher" and "Mahar" from Kathiawar were employed in the sanitation department (Mehta 1936, 9).

members, cultural group members, writers, dramatists, and politicians. Many Meghwal women are local *panch*, and the central *panchayat* has a woman member on its committee.

The Meghwal caste laws do not construct a patrilineal, monogamous, nuclear family with a rigid sexual division of labor within the household. Patriarchal authority within the family is neither rigid nor nonnegotiable. Joint families are the norm within the caste, but these households are comprised of various kin members as well as blood relatives and children from previous marriages. Scholars have argued that on the one hand, Dalit women have enjoyed relative sexual autonomy; on the other hand, their sexuality has been exploited by men from "upper" castes (Dube 1998). However, their status as workers in the public sector has not rendered Meghwal women vulnerable to structural sexual exploitation. Within the caste, women's sexual choices are not restricted, and sexual freedom is considered legitimate even after marriage. Although heterosexuality is privileged, a few women have formed lesbian unions and they head their families.[56] Furthermore, the constitutions do not lay down criteria regarding women's dress, appearance, or behavior.

Beside their access to more inclusive family rules, the women of the caste have built vast informal networks made up of kin members, family members, and neighbors because they tend to reside in common residential areas. They also shoulder financial responsibility as primary earners at times, and enjoy autonomy in decision making in the households and offer support to other women caste members.[57] Women also enjoy

---

[56] Interview with Champaben Waghela, June 17, 2003, Mumbai. Champaben Waghela has lived with her lover, Satoshben, for the past fifteen years.

[57] In one case, a woman, Sarla, a mother of two young children, was sexually harassed by her father-in-law. Her husband worked as a subsistence laborer, and they were financially dependent on the joint family. Sarla complained to the police, and her parents-in-law threw her out on the streets. Her husband accused her of false complaints, and she was homeless. A woman caste member, her neighbor, took her to a women's shelter, a kinwoman found her a job as a domestic worker, and another distant cousin gave her a place to stay. Her cousin worked as a domestic worker for a lawyer who offered legal aid, and she filed a case for maintenance. The only woman member in the central caste *panchayat* actively followed up her case, and the caste

access to civil society organizations, especially women's groups and the services provided by public-sector employers (such as health services, daycare for children, and counseling services), and they are members of trade unions. They have also formed microcredit groups and run women-related activities. Thus, they have access to public spaces and organizations.

However, discriminatory practices do coexist with the relative freedoms enjoyed by Meghwal women. Meghwal women are not represented in the caste *panch* in large numbers, and rules in *panchayat* elections allow women to vote only if they are the head of a household. Practices such as veiling exist in the caste as a symbolic concession to sanskritization[58] (Srinivas 1962) – symbolic because it does not prohibit women from participating in the public sphere. Many customs are changing as practices become less pro-women: for instance, the custom of bride-price is eroding, and the practice of taking on the mother's name has been replaced by patrilineal practices.

Innovative Legal Process: Democratic Participatory Justice

The Meghwal *panchayat* has not recreated the old traditional *panchayat* system but has innovatively institutionalized a *democratic participatory justice* system: The *panch* are elected representatives of the caste, and adjudication is one of their many tasks. This adjudication system is voluntary, informal, public, participatory (spectators can participate by getting involved in the decision-making process), flexible (about time, place, and presentation of proof), and decentralized. Decisions are binding, though members often refuse to abide by caste authorities

---

panchayat strongly reprimanded her father-in-law and husband, and pressured her brother to also offer her economic support (interview with Sarla Parmar, January 17, 2003, Mumbai).

[58] Sanskritization is the process by which the lower castes mimic and adopt rituals and practices of upper castes to move up the cast ladder.

and challenge them in state courts. Reasons prompting the decisions evolve in the process but are not stated in writing. The *panch* lacks penal authority, but it manages to exercise its authority by public reprimands, the collection of fines (disguised as donations), and indirect threats. Rumors, gossip, shame, public humiliation, and speculation are other tools used to enforce compliance. Charges of corruption, partiality, and social coercion are often leveled against the *panch* by caste members. The coercive powers of the caste are muted in the face of internal democracy, factionalism, and the option of exit.[59] A radical and modernist Dalit poet, who is a well-known critic of the caste traditions (of the caste's "bend towards Hinduism," among other things), has "actively encouraged his daughters to marry Christians and Muslims so that the caste *panchayat* cannot exercise social boycott through the enforcement of caste endogamy."[60]

The local *panchayats* meet at many different sites. Most of them have offices in the slums/*chawls* where they are situated. They often share these spaces with local NGOs or schools. At times, meetings are held in caste members' houses. The central *panchayat* operates out of a Municipal Corporation of Greater Mumbai's school. They hear matters of appeal and thus hear fewer cases than local *panchayats*.[61] Usually, all

---

[59] For instance, the nephew of the president of the Meghwal Panchayat died of AIDS at a young age, and the twenty-two-year-old Priya, his widow, was given very little compensation – the nephew had left some property he had earned as a laborer in the Gulf, but had willed it to his family – and caste members perceived that she had been cheated by the president's family. The faction that opposed P. K. Maroo, the president, accompanied Priya to various police stations and Special Cell for Women in order to "... register a case of cheating against the president." However, the president "had exercised his prestige" and arrived at a negotiated settlement with Priya. This episode was one of the reasons why he was not reelected when elections were held in 2005 among charges of corruption against him (interview with Galji Gohil, August 23, 2007, Mumbai).

[60] Interview with Bipin Gohil, poet, January 12, 2003, Mumbai.

[61] The annual caseload in the central *panchayat* numbers approximately twenty-five to thirty cases every year (interview with Bhimbhai Khuman, March 3, 2003, Mumbai).

officials of the caste *panchayat* are present. Some unelected members of the caste gather around and act as messengers or perform odd jobs, and add their voices to various matters. Caste-related gossip is exchanged on a regular basis: Local news, politics, and other stories are told on "slack" days.

Structure and Organization of the Meghwal Caste Panchayat

The Meghwal caste *panchayats* follows a two-tier structure. Any locality constituted of more than fifty households of the Meghwal caste can form a *panchayat*. Currently, there are fifty-five functioning local *panchayats* in the city of Mumbai, and three in other parts of Maharashtra, though these local *panchayats* are not always democratically elected. Elections for the central *panch* are held every five years. Any adult member of the caste can contest a *panchayat* election. Each household is allowed to cast one vote. Usually, this is cast by the eldest male of the house. Female heads of the household are also allowed to cast votes. In general, about 5 percent of elected members of the local *panchayats* are women. Similarly, members of the caste elect the central *panchayat* (Samasta Mumbai Meghwal Panchayat) through centrally monitored elections every five years.[62] The central *panchayat* is seen as a chief governing body in the regulation of intracaste matters.

Process of Adjudication in the Meghwal Caste Panchayat and the Provision for Appeal

Any member of the caste can give an application to their local *panchayat* for a meeting to discuss her/his case. The two sets of *panch* and the two families with their extended kin discuss the matter. The *panch* from either side act as advocates (they purposefully pay special attention to the claims and interests of the family they accompany), witnesses

---

[62] The caste has an election commission, and the central *panchayat* elections are carefully monitored and fair.

(when it comes to character reports, circumstances of domestic fights, economic situation of the families, etc.), and mediators (to bring about consensus). Judges, who try moral persuasion in cases where consensus between parties remains elusive, also participate in the proceedings. Cases in which parties fail to come to an agreement are directed to the central *panchayat*. At times, the local *panchayat* members ask the central *panchayat* to intervene. However, if either party is dissatisfied with the judgment of the local *panch*, he or she can also appeal to the central *panchayat*. Many cases are not adjudicated by even the *panch*. The parties appoint individual members from the caste to mediate disputes; many divorces take place between the two families without accessing the *panchayat* or the state.

Similarities, Dissimilarities, and Hybridity in State Law and Nonstate Law

The following section discusses the areas of overlap and conflict between state laws and caste laws of Meghwals. Even though caste laws have adapted to state laws in some instances, I show that the conceptions of conjugal family are strikingly different among the Meghwals.

Who Is a Hindu, Who Is a Meghwal?

The Hindu law defines a "Hindu" as a person who is not a Muslim or a Parsi or a Christian or a Jew (Mulla 1966, 616). As per state classifications, the Meghwals are registered as belonging to the Scheduled Castes and are therefore governed by Hindu personal law in state courts. The data show that "enumerated" Scheduled Castes such as Meghwals adapt and resist state classificatory schemes and deploy their multiple identities strategically and selectively. Historically, there has never been an internal agreement among the Meghwals about their membership in a religious community. The religious affiliations of caste members are a matter of ongoing debate, dissent, and controversy within the caste collective. Over the course of the twentieth century, the caste collective has had members who have individually practiced Islam, Christianity, or Buddhism and have remained Meghwals. The caste collective has adopted Ramdeo *Pir* as their chief deity, and caste members have worshipped the *pir* while adhering to varied sects, religions, and gods and goddesses. Religious beliefs are not seen as permanent but as temporary, and can be assembled and dismantled.[63] The push to classify themselves as Hindus was strident during the 1910s and 1920s, as well as during the 1990s. And while there has been the "Hinduization" of the caste to a large extent, voices of dissent remain active.

Viswanathan has outlined how the colonial state divided the material domain from the spiritual one by accepting the converts in the adopted religion but allowing them to be governed by their old religious personal laws (Viswanathan 1998). The Meghwal caste members have adopted and refashioned this by trifurcating the domains they inhabit: the material domain, consisting of economic activity where they define themselves as Hindus to fit into the classificatory scheme of the state to access the benefits of affirmative action programs; the spiritual domain, where they practice religious rites and rituals of the adopted religion; and the cultural-legal domain, wherein they follow caste customs, practices, festivals, and rituals (some of these may also be Hindu festivals and rites). For instance, at present, many families among the Meghwals practice Islam or Christianity in their daily life, and do not see contradictions in approaching the Meghwal caste *panchayats* when it comes to matters concerning marriage or divorce. So, being a Meghwal is not equivalent to being a Hindu. For the Meghwals, the category "Hindu" is not an ascriptive category; rather, it is a category that is displayed when

---

[63] "People dabble in religions ... people are looking for solutions, influences of different sects wax and wane in our caste. In between a lot of people followed the *Baba Santhnam*, then there came a wave of following some *Nagbawa* (Serpent saint) ... people are told that this sect will alleviate their pain or that *dargah* will yield fruits, and they run there.... many people go to Haji Ali (a *dargah*) to pray. People change their beliefs all the time anyway.... Why, people began to worship *Ram* and *Krishna* after watching TV serials" (interview with Mukesh Waghela, March 5, 2003, Mumbai).

Consent

Provisions such as the restitution of conjugal rights in Hindu law act against the notion of autonomy inherent in the concept of consent. However, consent is seen to be an integral part of the rules of the Meghwals.[64] The centrality to consent has been visible in many changes – the practice of child marriage is extinct, and levirate is practiced, but only if the parties agree to it and are of similar age. Interestingly, in addition, the rules governing consent are also applicable after marriage, and lack of consent is a valid reason to end a marriage. The Meghwal caste *panchayat* often gives primacy to individual will and freedom to marry over kinship obligations. As per a Meghwal practice, young persons often run away when being pressured into marriage by their families.[65] Unmarried couples who face opposition to their marriage plans may elope and apply to the caste *panchayat* for readmittance into the caste. They are reaccepted into the caste upon payment of fines (taxes) to the *panchayat*. The *panch* in turn negotiates parental approval of the marriage. The mediation often results in the woman's family being paid compensation money for "losing" the

---

[64] The Meghwal constitution of 1953 included a section on "Marriage by Insistence" whereby young women could insist on marrying a person of their own choosing against the wishes of the natal families. Section 2 of the caste constitution on marriage stresses that "engagements should be entered into with the consent of the parties and their families" (Mumbai Meghwal/Vanakar-Gnati Bandharan 1993, 4). Similarly, the section on "Marriage by Elopement" (*kadhpanu*) also stresses that parents should not oppose marriages of two consenting adults (Mumbai Meghwal/Vanakar-Gnati Bandharan 1993, 21). The recognition of "consent" is an important legitimizing criterion for ascertaining the distinction between marriage and nonmarriage within the caste.

[65] The tradition is widely prevalent today: Ramesh, a young man, "ran away" (*bhagi gayo*), and his parents had to pay compensation decided by the *panch* to the bride's families for "losing face" (interview with Nathabhai, *panch*, September 7, 2002, Mumbai).

daughter. Anthropologists have argued that primary marriage among these caste groups is expensive, prestigious, and ceremoniously celebrated, whereas second marriages are seen to be less privileged, less expensive, and less ritualized, as the second marriage is often seen to be contracted out of individual choice rather than undertaken for and under kinship obligations (Parry 2001). However, although this distinction was practiced among the Meghwals, since the 1970s, caste laws have been modernized and reformed to place the second marriage on par with the first marriage, and caste *panchayat* routinely applauds second marriages that are also celebrated in public. Parry has also shown that among the Satnamis of Chhattisgarh, sexuality of prepuberty women is strictly policed to ensure that the young bride is a virgin before her permanent defilement through first marriage, but married women can elope with men without disgrace (Parry 2001). Holden too reports a similar trend in central India. However, among the Meghwals, we see that both unmarried and married women elope without social disgrace; once again, this points to the recognition of consent and autonomy within caste laws.

In an analysis of runaway marriages between unmarried couples in northern India, Chowdhry describes the cultural arena as inegalitarian and the state as patriarchal but a potential ally in securing women's rights; however, she also finds that the state and traditional authorities often collude in denying sexual agency to women runaways (Chowdhry 1997, 2004). Mody has pointed out the contradiction between the acceptance of a "love marriage" in law and the societal delegitimization of this form of marriage. Mody argues that the freedom of choice inherent in the notion of a "love marriage" is seen as antithetical to social notions of familial and caste obligations (Mody 2002). However, this trend is reversed among the Meghwals. When Jayesh and Bharti, a young unmarried couple, eloped to escape parental opposition to their marriage, the caste *panchayat* registered their marriage and ensured that both sets of parents accepted the union.[66]

Indeed, a consistent change over the years, noticeable since the 1970s when women became part of this public deliberation in law reform, has

---

[66] Interview with Bharti, February 15, 2003, Mumbai.

been the primacy given to the notion of autonomy within the caste laws. Anthropologists have argued that one of the purposes of sexual control of women within various castes, enforced through caste endogamy, is to retain wealth within caste groups. However, the Meghwal caste laws do not curb sexual autonomy of its members, even to retain wealth within the group. To explain, we have seen that the lower-level jobs in the public sector, especially BMC, remain highly coveted within the caste. The BMC institutionalized the Preferential Treatment Policy for this category of workers. As per this unwritten policy, the BMC hires family/kin members of the Scheduled Castes at the time of retirement of any fourth-class municipal worker. Thus, a woman or a man would be the beneficiary of her or his spouse's job in the case of his death or illness. Given the nature of employment in the public sector, this policy ensures the steady employment and welfare of at least one member of a Meghwal family through the generations. The provision of substantive citizenship rights for the BMC workers has had a great impact on the community life of the caste members. Individual families attempt to retain this job in the family for future generations.

However, the practices of frequent divorce, elopements, and intercaste marriage go against the logic of wealth retention within the caste. Indeed, this conflict between the need to retain the public-sector employment in the family and marital instability was raised as a matter of public debate by women when caste women were invited to participate in large numbers in the constitution-making process in 1975. The suggestion to form a conservative member to introduce social boycott to curb this practice was widely resisted by women. The problem was seen in finding the way to strike a balance between the two practices. As one caste member asked: "On the one hand, the women could not be prevented from walking away with the man they had accepted, but what about the economic welfare of families that they leave behind?"[67]

The process of law reform suggests that wealth retention in the family is not enforced by caste laws. Over the years, the caste has arrived at a

---

[67] See the report: "Public meeting of Meghwal Samaj in Mumbai under the auspices of Mr. PT Patel," August 17, 1975.

creative resolution of this matter, which retains the wealth but does not negate consent as the basis of legitimacy of marriage. Indeed, consent is seen as the central factor legitimizing marriage, and this is evident in a number of laws. The creative solution is that the caste laws allow elopement of men and women before or during marriage, but the party who elopes is held responsible for financial maintenance of the family. What factors explain the delinking between occupation and endogamy within the caste group? I suggest that the diffusion of various ideas within the group through ties between caste council and other social movements has shaped notions of personhood, group membership, and social progress, and the democratic lawmaking process has formalized and encoded these ideas in caste laws.

The following case illustrates this claim. Indeed, the Meghwal caste's provisions of elopement by married parties contravene state authorities' interpretation of provisions in law to deal with runaway marriages. A married Meghwal woman, Lakshmi, a mother of four, eloped with a man from outside the Meghwal collective, taking her *stridhan* and savings of 100,000 rupees, thus violating the caste law.[68] The husband went to the police to track her down, and the police and lawyers advised him to charge her and her lover with theft, adduction, and kidnapping.[69] However, the husband and the Meghwal *panch* insisted that "elopement was quite common in their caste and they did not wish to prosecute the man she had eloped with. They wanted to recover the money, which was against the caste laws."[70] In the end, Lakshmi granted her first husband a divorce, got a favorable custody arrangement, and retained half of her savings. Through the use of criminal laws in cases of elopement, the

---

[68] Married women who elope are required to leave behind their earnings. Married men who elope are obliged to maintain their previous families (Mumbai Meghwal/Vanakar-Gnati Bandharan 1996, 21).

[69] Adultery is a criminal offense according to Section 497 of the Indian Penal Code, though women cannot be charged for it. In cases such as Lakshmi's, parties are also accused of, and often charged for, committing offenses such as kidnapping (Sections 359, 361) and abduction (Section 362, Indian Penal Code 1860). See Chowdhry (2004) for more details.

[70] Interview with Nathabhai, October 3, 2002, Mumbai.

state law affirms women as objects. The caste law is more open to sexual choices made by women, but it still reaffirms familial control over the fruits of the woman's labor.

Differing Conceptions of Marriage and Divorce: Marriage as Fixed or Fluid?

Hindu law makes a distinction between marriage and nonmarriage. Among the Meghwals, the line between marriage and nonmarriage is often shifting – a line drawn in the sand. The practice of elopement can lead to different unions, especially considering that the caste laws do not make a symbolic distinction between elopement of unmarried partners and elopement of already married partners. When married couples elope with unmarried or married partners, these combinations give rise to various forms of simultaneous marriages. In one case, Nilesh,[71] a married man, had eloped with his wife's sister, and both had asked the permission of the caste for readmittance into the caste.[72] The caste *panchayat* accepted the application and called the man's family, including the marital family, to arrange a dialog. The families came to the consensus that the man and his wives would live together, because his first wife decided to wait for six months before she decided on any "final solution." However, both women would be recognized as his wives and would have equal economic rights upon divorce. This contravenes the state laws on polygyny and on maintenance.

Hindu law and caste law also disagree on matters of divorce. As per Hindu law, the act of divorce terminates a legal marriage; thus, divorce is an irreversible act. The parties must reenact the stipulated rites of the Hindu marriage if they choose to remarry. However, the caste law has a provision titled "Undoing the Deed of Divorce." Divorce, in this case, is seen as a reversible act.[73]

---

[71] Interview with Nilesh and his father, BC, January 27, 2003, Mumbai.
[72] Both married and unmarried partners who elope are required to place an application for readmittance into the caste.
[73] Section 39 of the Meghwal caste constitution discusses caste rules in matters of divorce. Titled "Undoing the Deed of Divorce," the section states that divorced

Hindu law normalizes heterosexual, monogamous marriage and disallows other forms of unions; it disallows polyandry or polygyny. The Meghwals, however, accepted polygyny, but it was not widely practiced. The first constitution regulated polygyny. Whereas state law has prohibited polygyny since 1955, the Meghwal caste constitutions allowed polygyny in special circumstances until the 1980s. Polygyny was not seen as a controversial provision in the caste, despite wider debates in society, because divorce was easy and polygyny was practiced symbolically in many cases.[74] The caste constitution has withdrawn support from polygyny only since the 1990s.[75] Recently, the option of polygyny was revisited when it was considered in a case where a wife was infertile. The case was not pursued, because the wife was unwilling to give her consent.[76] Ironically, polygyny is easy to practice in cases in which petitioner wives have approached the state court for maintenance but do not wish

partners can, by mutual consent, reverse the deed of divorce. The parties can submit an application to their local *panchayats* informing them that they wish to "undo the divorce." In such instances, the parties should exchange property dues and pay fines of 75 rupees to their respective local *panchayats* and 50 rupees to their central *panchayat*. The applicants are then formally recognized as husband and wife by their families and caste members. In one case, the parties involved (Priya and Amit) revoked their divorce after about eleven years of separation and began to cohabitate as husband and wife, without undergoing marriage ceremonies. They informed the caste *panchayat* about their decision to "undo the divorce" (interview with Priya and Amit, May 23, 2003, Mumbai).

[74] The practice of levirate was tied to polygyny and was customarily practiced until the late 1960s. Young widows were married to unmarried brothers-in-law. However, older widows (women older than fifty years) were also married to their married younger brothers-in-law. These marriages were often symbolic and were carried out to ensure security to women in their old age (interview with Shantaben Waghela, February 6, 2003, Mumbai).

[75] The issue of polygyny has been systematically taken up by the Hindu right since the Shah Bano case in 1986, and there has been much debate on this front. Public-sector employees, however, are not allowed to contract more than one marriage; these changes in policies are also some of the reasons behind changes in the caste law.

[76] A woman was "sent back" to her natal home after her husband discovered she was infertile. The woman refused the divorce conferred on her. During negotiations, her husband's family asked her if she was willing to consent to her husband's second marriage. She denied the option and was not persuaded by either family (interview with Champaben Waghela, October 5, 2002, Mumbai).

HINDU LAW IN SOCIETY 211

to grant a divorce. Men tend to challenge the validity of marriages in such cases and then tend to marry again.[77]

Validity of Marriage

The caste laws on elopement once again bring to focus the lack of a sociolegal distinction between marriage, nonmarriage, and cohabitation. Under Hindu law, the state does make a distinction between marriage and nonmarriage. For instance, cohabitation is not recognized as equivalent to marriage; therefore, the rights of nonmarried partners are not recognized under Hindu law. Conversely, cohabitation is widely practiced in the caste, and economic rights of the cohabiters are recognized by caste laws.[78]

The caste laws of the Meghwals do not explicitly discuss or regulate homosexual unions or marriages, but these are accepted by caste members without social discrimination. In one case, an unmarried Meghwal woman gave birth to a daughter and later fell in love with another woman. Both women were married by the caste priest and have been living together with their daughter for the past twenty years.[79]

---

[77] In a case of maintenance filed by the wife, Jaya, in the state court, Ramesh's lawyer argued that the marriage was invalid. The court ruled in his favor, and Ramesh remarried even when Jaya challenged the decision in the High Court. He was able to do so because his second wife belonged to "their caste but not to their *samaj* (collective)," and as a result, the issue of the legality of his marriage remained outside the purview of the caste collective of the Meghwal *panchayat* (interview with Jaya and Ramesh Chauhan, April 14, 2003, Mumbai).

[78] The Meghwal constitution describes customary laws upon elopement ("self-chosen relationships"). This section regulates and sanctifies a vast array of sexual relationships, including when a couple chooses to adopt a sexual union irrespective of their marital status. The section lays down criteria for resolving disputes in cases involving the elopement of unmarried parties, married parties, and situations in which one of the parties (either the man or the woman) is married while the other is unmarried. Marriages by elopement are quite common among caste members. Parties who elope are seen to have committed a "socially improper act" against their individual families and fellow caste members. They are symbolically cast out until the dispute is resolved. Customary laws dictate that these parties approach the caste *panchayat* and pay required taxes (fines) (Mumbai Meghwal/Vanakar-Gnati Bandharan 1996).

[79] Interview with Hiraben Chauhan, February 23, 2003, Mumbai.

In another case, Mala, a Meghwal woman, left her husband with her three children, and was supported by her neighbor and friend, Savita, a woman belonging to another caste. The two women fell in love, but Savita was married. During the next few years, Savita divorced her husband. Both women had since cohabited for the past sixteen years,[80] worked as janitors, and raised three children. In a different case, a Meghwal man maintained two families – he was married to a woman and had children, and he also had a male lover. He openly divided his time between his two families and cross-dressed in public when with his male lover.[81] These unions were socially recognized by caste members.

Procedural Aspects of Defining Valid Marriages

It has been persuasively argued by Menski that courts also recognize customary rites; Menski suggests that many forms of marriage are recognized under Hindu law (Menski 2003, 33). In actual practice, especially among lower courts, decisions vary widely.[82] In lower courts, the validity of a Hindu marriage depends on the performance of certain rituals, such as *saptapadi*, seven steps around the sacred fire, and *homa*, an invocation before the sacred fire (Section 7(1) of the Hindu Marriage Act 1955; Mulla 1966, 638). Among the Meghwals, first marriages are ritually sanctioned and celebrated in public. Despite reforms, some of the second marriages are called *ghar gharna* and may or may not be celebrated in public.[83] State courts are often arbitrary in their

---

[80] Interview with Savita Makwana, January 23, 2003, Mumbai.
[81] Interview with Gandabhai Gamit, February 13, 2003, Mumbai.
[82] In practice, most Hindu marriages are not registered, and the courts tend to accept wedding invitations and photographs of the weddings as proofs of marriage.
[83] As per custom, the women of the groom's family come to the bride's house with a set of new clothes for the bride. The bride changes into these clothes and accompanies the women to her new marital house. This exchange takes place only between women, and the groom is never present at these occasions (interview with Shantaben Waghela, February 6, 2003, Mumbai).

recognition of caste rites and laws, which adversely affects women's rights.[84]

Secondly, the recognition of a valid marriage rests with the discretion of individual judges, and it is often difficult to prove marriage when there is no ceremony involved. Levirate among the Meghwals is recognized orally. Even if the court can presume marriages due to evidentiary proofs such as common residence, levirate is difficult to prove because joint residential arrangements are the norm among the Meghwals. At times, such marriages are only recognized among small kin circles within the caste.[85]

Divorce in Caste Laws

Legalizing divorce is one of the reforms made under Hindu law in 1955. However, in the judicial sphere, divorce is often seen as a benchmark of social instability (Menski 2003) and is not granted easily, especially if one of the parties opposes it.[86]

---

[84] Interview with Rajesh Shah, Rajkot, lawyer, March 30, 2003, Mumbai. A sessions court in Gujarat refused a maintenance request under Section 125 CrPC to a Meghwal woman, Jaya, on the grounds of invalid marriage. It was the second marriage for both parties, and it was performed without any ceremony, which was not recognized by the court.

[85] The practice of levirate in present times is tied to the Preferential Treatment Policy, which enables a Meghwal widow to be designated as a recipient of her deceased husband's public-sector job, which carries benefits to sustain the entire family. The widow's remarriage outside the family would jeopardize the fine economic balance of that family; as a result, levirate is often encouraged, especially when the younger brother-in-law is unmarried. However, the families do not register the marriage with caste authorities because the remarriage of the widow renders her ineligible for the Preferential Treatment case. Besides, the applications for Preferential Treatment cases can take three to five years to process and finalize. The marriage has to be kept invisible from the gaze of the state until the "widow" gets her job (interview with Hiraben Boricha, January 14, 2003, Mumbai).

[86] Under the Family Courts Act 1984, the role of the Family Court is to "stabilise" marriage. Section 2(e) of the "Statement of Objects and Reasons," Family Courts Act 1984 makes it "obligatory on the part of the Family Court to endeavour, in the first instance, to effect a reconciliation or a settlement between the parties to a family dispute."

Divorce is and has been a widely acceptable familial practice among the Meghwals.[87] However, the 1993 constitution stresses that "the decision to divorce should be a carefully considered [option] ... divorce should not be taken lightly." This assertion has been included as a part of diffusion of state law, and with the suggestion of lawyers who are active in caste *panchayats*, to align caste laws with state laws. In her study of Hindu divorce in central India, Holden discusses a case of a Dalit woman who wished to initiate divorce, a practice quite common among the community laws. However, the matter was resolved not only by the caste *panchayat*, but by the village *panchayat*, which had a strong presence of upper castes. This inclusion of the Dalits in the processes of village *panchayat* symbolized the end of their segregation but encouraged sanskritization. Divorce was seen to be a lower-caste practice, and the woman was denied divorce (Holden 2008). Among the Meghwals, this exhortation remains on paper, and this assertion is routinely challenged within the caste in the implementation of laws. To illustrate, a nineteen-year-old woman who had been married for less than a year had approached the caste *panchayat* for divorce and cited "indifference" as grounds to terminate the marriage. The husband was ambivalent. The *panchayat* asked her if she wanted them to effect a reconciliation once before they decided on the final outcome, at which time a spectator who was in the *panchayat* office at the time spoke up: "It seems too obvious to me that the husband is uninterested. What are we wishing for? Why not grant her divorce? Since when have we become Brahmins that we have to try to prolong marriages through reconciliation?" This view was accepted by the *panch*.[88]

---

[87] Among the Meghwals, marriage is not understood as an institution providing social stability. It is also not linked to ideas of public health or private morality. The Meghwal constitution on marriage and divorce does not lay down explicit rules on grounds for divorce. The section on divorce (Mumbai Meghwal/Vanakar-Gnati Bandharan 1996, 28) states that "incompatibility between husband and wife or irreconcilable differences between spouses can be grounds for divorce. Enmity between the two families can also be seen as providing grounds for divorce" (Mumbai Meghwal/Vanakar-Gnati Bandharan 1996, 28). Given that multiple local sources officiate in matters related to divorce, the granting of divorce is flexible.

[88] Interview with Mohanbhai Baria, June 5, 2003, Mumbai.

HINDU LAW IN SOCIETY 215

The Meghwal caste constitution has approved no-fault divorce. A woman, Maya, approached the *panchayat* for divorce in order to live with her lover. The husband was against the idea of divorce, but the *panch* "persuaded" the husband to grant her divorce.[89] Had this case been heard in a state court, the outcome would have been radically different. As per the state law and procedure, adultery as grounds for divorce is based on a notion of marital obligations wherein fidelity is seen to be a moral obligation of the partners. The role of the state is to ascertain the wrong that is committed by the guilty party, and to see that only the innocent party is allowed to remarry. Besides, the concept of "fault" is not always understood in the same manner as it is framed in the court. For example, the Family Court would not have granted a divorce to Maya in the face of her husband's opposition.[90] The court's logic of ascertaining "fault" would have established Maya as an adulteress, and the ruling in her favor would have been seen as victimizing her husband. In addition, Maya's act of adultery would be construed not only as a wrong against the married spouse, but also as a step contrary to public interest and morality. In the state's eyes, the granting of divorce to Maya would be encouraging her sexual license. However, the *panch* in this case gave the judgment based on the terms of personal freedom.

Fault has not been completely abolished among the Meghwals, however. In practice, the concept of "fault" is used to decide postdivorce financial settlements. For example, a couple, separated for more than two years, approached the *panchayat* for divorce. The young man was mentally unstable and had severely beaten his wife. Both families had

---

[89] The officiating *panch* said: "The husband was unwilling to sign on the divorce papers, but I told him that if the woman does not want to stay with you, what can be done? There is no legitimacy in forcing a woman to live with you when she wishes to be elsewhere (*bai manas ne jabarjashi sathe rakhi ne shun fayado*)" (interview with Dahyabhai, March 10, 2003, Mumbai).

[90] It can be argued that Maya's husband may not have been able to prove adultery. However, the caste *panchayat*'s decision does not rest on evidentiary grounds. Maya has asked for divorce in order to live with her lover within the caste. The difference between state law and caste law lies in the legal regulation of sexuality within marriage.

tacitly decided upon divorce, and the woman's remarriage was to be arranged. The *panchayat* granted the woman alimony because of physical violence within marriage.

Economic Rights within Marriage and upon Divorce

The Meghwal women are perceived as economic actors under caste laws. For instance, gifts given to the husband by her family at the time of marriage or during marriage are seen to be her property. If parts of her property have been sold/mortgaged or damaged, she is compensated for that at the time of the divorce as per *panchayat* rules. The *panchayat* rules also state that the woman's self-earned property – be it in form of a life insurance policy, a house/dwelling, share certificates, and so forth acquired during marriage – is her own property (neither her natal family nor her marital family has a right to it). Her own earnings are not seen as joint marital property by the caste *panchayat*. In cases of the breakdown of a marriage, the woman is entitled to all of her share of self-earned property (Mumbai Meghwal/Vanakar Gnati Bandharan, 1996, 21). The constitution is silent on permanent alimony, but it states that the husband is bound to provide maintenance for his wife and children (if applicable) during the period of "separation due to differences" (*risamana no samay*). The *panch* claims that many husbands fail to pay this amount; even so, this amount is added to the final divorce settlement in most cases. However, a married woman who elopes has to leave her self-earned property as well as her joint savings behind, or hand these over to her husband's family (Samasta Meghwal Gnati Bandharan 1987; Mumbai Meghwal/Vanakar Gnati Bandharan, 1993, 1996). A man who elopes must shoulder the responsibility of his wives and children from the first as well as the second marriage, as the case may be.

Whereas Hindu law enables the parties to make claims from each other as individuals who have entered into the marriage contract, the Meghwals can lay claims for maintenance from other family members

HINDU LAW IN SOCIETY

of their partners.[91] The economic circumstances of either party are often constrained, and the sharing of family resources is considered quite common.

The Meghwals do not recognize a husband's right to demand maintenance from the wife. In contrast, contested divorce is difficult to obtain in state courts; besides, there are procedural delays in such cases.[92] Stories about this legal trend in state courts have affected the Meghwal women's ability to bargain for their rights in marriage[93]: There have been several cases in the caste in which husbands have asked working women to compensate them during the period of separation in exchange for divorce.[94] Similarly, in cases where state law and caste law become intermeshed, caste laws that can potentially grant more rights are often diluted due to the parties' exposure to state law. In a case involving claims for maintenance, Mita, a woman who had been the primary breadwinner for the family for about fifteen years, filed a case for maintenance against her husband because she was thrown out of her matrimonial home with her three school-aged children. When the hearing date drew near, her husband, Ritesh, approached her for reconciliation.[95] The terms of the compromise involved her dropping the

---

[91] I have interviewed twelve individuals who received a financial settlement upon divorce. In all these instances, families had shouldered or shared the financial responsibility.

[92] This development is used by Meghwal men to demand money in exchange for divorce. In one case, the woman was the primary earner and wanted to divorce after three years of marriage. Her husband refused to give divorce unless she gave him a lump sum (interview with Nila, September 8, 2002, Mumbai).

[93] A Meghwal woman, Padma, explained why she had never filed a case in court despite her need to get a solution: Her husband is an alcoholic and has never worked in his life. He asks her for money. He beats her if she does not give him any, and at times he steals utensils from the house to sell and pay for his liquor. She works as a peon in a school and manages the family. She said that she had talked to a lawyer who had told her that her husband could claim maintenance from her. She was even unwilling to approach the *panchayat* out of fear that her husband may file a case for maintenance in the Family Court if she tried to upset the marital arrangement. She said it was easier for her to not to take any steps against her husband.

[94] Interview with Pushpa Waghela, October 23, 2002, Mumbai.

[95] Ritesh had a job in the private sector, and his salary would have been deducted at the source had she not dropped the case.

request for maintenance. Matters did not improve, and she approached the *panch* for a dialog. The *panchayat* asked Ritesh to pay maintenance to her and the children as per caste laws. Ritesh declined, stating that under Hindu law, he was not entitled to pay Mita maintenance because she worked. He simply disregarded the *panchayat*'s decision (*faisla*); the office lacks the ability to enforce its authority.

In addition, Hindu women can also ask for maintenance under Section 125 CrPC under state law. This section is popular among Meghwal women, many of whose husbands work in the public sector and whose payments are easier to attach through court orders. Resorting to this section contravenes Meghwal caste norms in the sense that desertion or a long separation without divorce has not been the custom among the Meghwals. Caste authorities often insist on divorce as a final solution to questions of marital disagreement. However, Meghwal women who wish for economic assistance without intending to terminate the marriage often opt for this provision. State laws around maintenance enable them to maintain subsisting marriages and increase their bargaining power within marriage. Denial of paternity is accepted by courts as grounds for contestation over maintenance claims in state courts. Among the Meghwals, children from first marriages are seen as the responsibility of the second husband and are given the same status as biological children that the couple may have in the future (Mumbai Meghwal/Vanakar Gnati Bandharan 1996).

Interactions between Diverse Societal Organizations and Actors

Contestations among Informal Legal Actors

The history of constitution making shows conflict between factions who support the idea of democratic governance and factions who wish to retain individual authority. There is also a struggle over capturing caste *panchayat*. This has resulted in factionalism and the fragmentation of the caste sphere. The authority of the caste *panchayat* is often resisted by individual actors. Similarly, some marriages within the caste are dissolved through the informal consent of the parties. These divorces are not registered with the caste *panchayat*. In some cases, divorce is mutually agreed on by both the parties and does not seem to be a *public dispute* deserving intervention by the caste. A woman whose marriage was dissolved informally stated: "People go to *panchayats* when they disagree about divorce. We did not have a dispute."[96] In such cases, parties employ mediators or kinsmen to mediate and dissolve marriages. Such divorces are *understood* but unregistered. These divorces take place when the remarriage of parties occurs among their own kin members.

In other cases, approaching the caste *panchayat* might be an option that would not benefit either party, and the marriage is dissolved "on the sly."[97] Women often tend to lose rights when justice is not a public process within the caste. Respondents suggested some instances of intimidation, threats, and coercion linked to bargaining over matters related to divorce and settlements at the time of divorce.[98] Some litigants

---

[96] Interview with Rama, February 5, 2003, Mumbai.

[97] In one case of divorce, the parties failed to come to an agreement on who would pay "the taxes" (money offered to the caste council and disguised as donations) to the *panchayat*. Both parties declined to do so, and the *panchayat* refused to give a written authorization of divorce. The parties met again without the *panchayat* and agreed on an "understanding" that the marriage was dissolved. The woman was then remarried to her cousin. "We could take such a stand because we knew we were to remarry our daughter in our own family" (interview with Bhikhabhai Boricha, kin member, December 10, 2002, Mumbai).

[98] In one case, a woman was thrown out of the matrimonial house because she was infertile. The woman's family did not wish to accept the idea of divorce and tried to negotiate for three years. However, the husband's family tried to secure a divorce after a few years and approached the caste *panchayat*. The caste *panchayat* asked the husband's family to pay the maintenance amount of caste law. The husband's family refused to pay the amount, and the intracaste adjudication process proved inconclusive. The *panchayat* then tried to pressure the woman's family through close kin members who worked as intracaste intermediaries. The husband's family threatened that they would spread rumors of the woman's infertility within the caste if the

also seek help from political parties,[99] state officials such as the police, Muslim religious organizations,[100] and women's groups.

Women's Organizations as Informal Forums of Justice: Implementing State Law without Litigation

In a socio-legal field that allows for multiple legal actors, civil society organizations, especially women's groups, often expand the reach of state law. The organizations mediate among parties "within the shadow of the law" (Kornhauser and Mnookin 1979) and replicate the functions of the state. They also provide a forum for support to women who feel silenced within the caste and who lack social support within the caste. Women of the group approach both Hindu and Muslim women's organizations in order to confront the caste authority. In the following case, a woman called Hansa approached a women's organization when her husband eloped with another married woman, Leela, and she was afraid that she and her son would be thrown out of the matrimonial home. In an intervention that spanned more than four years, the women's organization helped Hansa and Bipin negotiate and notarize their divorce, ensured informally the implementation of a maintenance amount to Hansa from Bipin, and helped Hansa retain her right on the matrimonial residence – all without resorting to formal litigation in state courts.[101]

---

wife did not agree to divorce. In return, the woman's family bargained for a settlement amount of 15,000 rupees, which was less than the amount directed by the caste. Women who are well connected within the caste, however, are less vulnerable to such threats and coercion (interview with MK, October 17, 2002, Mumbai).

[99] A Meghwal woman who had links with the *Bahujan Samaj* party asked their fellow workers to be present at the time of negotiations in order to increase her bargaining position (interview with PM, October 4, 2002, Mumbai).

[100] "Upper castes do not share residential areas with us. Historically, Dalits and Muslims have lived in adjoining areas. We live in a predominantly Muslim area. We approach social organisations of this area if we need help. There is a *Mahila Mandal* in this area; they are all Muslim and they do good work" (interview with Leelaben Boricha, January 30, 2003, Mumbai).

[101] Interviews with Hansa and Bipin, May 13, 2003, Mumbai.

Women's Organization as Moral Watchdogs: Women's Organizations and Caste Authorities

Conflict between women's organizations and caste authorities rises to the fore in cases in which women use organizational support to challenge patriarchal provisions within the caste. In such an instance, a woman, Lata, filed a case in state court for divorce and was granted a divorce. However, when Lata and her extended family went to her husband Haresh's house to collect her *stridhan*, they found that Haresh and his family had called five to seven men of their community. Haresh explained that these were the members of the local *panchayat* and that they were present to finalize the divorce because "they and their caste did not recognize divorce of the court."[102] Lata and her family were forced to comply and sign the divorce papers. They were then asked to pay the dues of 2,250 rupees as per caste laws,[103] because she had initiated the divorce proceedings. Lata and her family found that the men they believed to be local *panchayat* members were not actual *panchayat* members; on the basis of this fraud, she approached a women's organization to get the money returned and to get appropriate compensation for her damaged *stridhan*.

Conflict also arises over the use of Section 498(A) of the Indian Penal Code, the law on domestic violence. A women's organization was instrumental in helping Esha register a case against her husband, Naresh, under this section,[104] alleging physical violence due to dowry demands,

---

[102] Interview with Lata, September 11, 2002, Mumbai.

[103] A woman who initiated a divorce had to pay 2,250 rupees to the caste. This included the return of bride-price paid to her family at the time of marriage and the caste penalty for the initiation of divorce. Men only pay the latter amount.

[104] In the 1980s, the Indian Women's Movement had raised the issue of dowry-based violence and asked the Indian state to enact laws to address the issue. As a result, there was a spate of legislation prohibiting dowry-related violence. However, this also led to the association of the issue of domestic violence with dowry demands (Agnes 1995a; Dave and Solanki 2001; Gandhi and Shah 1992; Katzenstein 1989). Section 498(a) IPC is a forward-looking law in the sense that it allows women to define what they consider to be violence, including verbal abuse and emotional violence faced in the marital home. Furthermore, it places the onus of proof on the perpetrator.

because a narrow interpretation of the law criminalizes dowry-related violence. As a result, Naresh, his younger brother, and his mother who resided jointly in the marital house were arrested and were not released until the commencement of the trial; the bail amounted to 20,000 rupees. However, some caste members went to the court sessions as witnesses and claimed that "dowry was not a customary practice."[105] The conflict here went on at several levels. From Esha's viewpoint, it was an issue of domestic violence and she had to fit her narratives in a predetermined framework of the law. As a result, dowry demands and violence became interrelated. From the viewpoint of the panchayat, Esha's admission went against the manner in which their social customs were recognized and ordered. The caste *panchayat* also emphasized the wider issue of police harassment of the subaltern classes and wished to "save" a fellow caste member. What they refused to address was the issue of sanctioning domestic violence through their support of Naresh.

Bargaining for Women's Rights vis-à-vis the State and the Caste

Women's organizations privilege state law and often attempt to stretch the meaning of the law to secure maximum rights for women. Both Hindu law and the caste constitution recognize a woman's right to her *stridhan*. However, access to *stridhan* is finalized at the time of divorce in the caste rules as well as in the state law, along with distribution of other property.[106] Women often demand access to their property during

> Potentially, the law also holds not only the husband but the entire marital family accountable for domestic violence in cases where the couple resides with the joint family (Mukhopadhyay 1998). However, the patriarchal biases of the police and the judiciary are evident in their conservative interpretation of this law as "dowry-related domestic violence that would lead a woman to commit suicide." This bias of the state has led to low registration and conviction rates in such cases, despite a high incidence of domestic violence (Dave and Solanki 2001).
>
> [105] Interview with Esha, November 25, 2002, Mumbai.
> [106] Similarly, the Meghwals have formalized a system for the registration of *stridhan* at the time of marriage when caste elders and caste *panchayat* members record gifts given to the bride and the groom at the marriage venue. The lists are given to

marriage, or at the time of informal separation, or during the process of litigation for maintenance.[107]

However, there is no provision in civil law that allows women control over property. In these cases, women's organizations often step in. They mediate between family members, and in cases where a husband's family is unresponsive to a woman's demands, they try to involve the police by either persuading the police to lodge cases under Section 406 IPC[108] or by attempting to persuade the husband's family members to part with the wife's *stridhan*. The meaning of *stridhan* is also disputed between the state, the caste, and women's organizations. The courts often interpret *stridhan* as dowry, as does the Meghwal caste *panchayat*. Women's groups hold *stridhan* to mean "gifts given to women by both the natal and marital families at the time of and during the marriage."[109] Hence, women's organizations attempt to stretch the interpretive scope of laws and use different legal tools and extralegal bargaining to broaden the scope of women's rights in law.

The section above highlighted the hybridity and difference between state law and caste laws, and discussed how interactions and negotiations among various societal actors impact women's rights in legal forums. The following section discusses the adjudication of Hindu law in a subcaste of Sai Suthars.

> both the parties and are returned to the woman at the time of divorce. However, caste authorities are reluctant to return *stridhan* except at the time of divorce because caste practice intertwines the return of property with the breakdown of marriage.
>
> [107] Most women need their property at this time because they attempt to rebuild their lives, and movable property such as jewelry is useful for this purpose. They also fear permanent loss of this property from the marital home. Most respondents complained of receiving damaged property, and almost all respondents claimed receiving less than what they had originally been given. The caste *panchayat* has more success in recovery because the caste registers gifts given to the woman at the time of marriage and assiduously recovers these at the time of divorce.
>
> [108] The section is used to prosecute for criminal breach of trust. It is used by women's organizations to recover dowry and women's property (see Dave and Solanki, 2001).
>
> [109] Interview with Vandana Nanawade, June 20, 2003, Mumbai.

The Caste Panchayat among the Sai Suthars

This section focuses on a subcaste group known as Sai Suthars, which is primarily organized as a regulating unit of endogamous circles. The subcaste is also part of the broader local supracaste association comprised of 108 similar subcaste groups classified by the state as "Other Backward Classes."[110]

Internal Governance of Family Matters among the Sai Suthars

As per caste folklore, individual young men of the subcaste came to Bombay in search of livelihood from Saurashtra in the early 1900s. Many of them worked as tailors and did not require access to credit, capital, or other help from other caste members to start their trade.[111] "We could rent some space under any staircase and begin tailoring. Unlike other castes, we did not live in clusters but were spread out across Mumbai, for our fellow caste members are also our competition … after all, how many tailors can a locality support?" The caste members tended to work largely in the private sector, as tailors and small-time traders, and did not form or join professional guilds or unions. Some caste members also worked as weavers, carpenters, and blacksmiths. There was insignificant contact between fellow caste members in the initial years, and there was "no demand to organise across caste lines as there was no perceived need for caste unity for upliftment of the caste."[112]

Members of this subcaste remained spectators to the sociopolitical developments in Mumbai in the first half of the nineteenth century. They

---

[110] This term refers to socially and economically backward groups. These groups do not enjoy all the benefits of affirmative action programs granted to the Scheduled castes and Tribes.

[111] Interview with Bipinbhai Parmar, January 23, 2003, Mumbai. They did not succeed financially as a group and did not participate in educational activities. Most caste members consider themselves Hindus. They do not have common religious Gurus or heads. There are no religious power centers within the caste sphere (interview with Kanubhai Galia, February 3, 2003, Mumbai).

[112] Interview with Kanubhai Galia, January 22, 2003, Mumbai.

did not participate in the nationalist movement as a group, and were not perceived as a vote bank by political parties. Their financial status during these years remained low, as did their educational status (young men entered into traditional occupations from an early age; young women married early). Young men who migrated to Mumbai in these years went back to villages to marry and left their brides behind in the villages. They visited their families in villages while earning their livelihood in Mumbai. The village remained a center of their social activities and duties. Until the late 1960s, they were governed by their *gnatis* in the village in which the *panch* (usually comprising adult male leaders of the caste in each village or a cluster of villages) ruled in family matters.

The idea of forming a *panchayat* among the Sai Suthars was mooted in 1965 as a mechanism to promote caste consciousness at a micro level and to communicate among fellow subcaste members from endogamous circles. Subsequent years have not seen significant organizational activities. The caste *panchayat*, since its inception, has been dominated by prominent members of the caste. Elections are not regular and are not called every five years.[113] A president of the *panchayat* remained in power for fifteen years and was unchallenged by other caste members. A reformist faction consisting of caste members who had succeeded economically as small traders and who worked in the public or corporate sectors as clerks and middle-level managers in small domestic firms from within the caste tried to challenge this, and managed to get one of their members elected. Elections were regularized for two terms; however, more factional infighting led to the reversal of this policy. The office bearers largely perceive caste *panchayat* as a body to yield and consolidate their social prestige. The *panchayat* celebrates Hindu religious festivals, provides marriage bureaus, subsidizes wedding ceremonies, and facilitates meetings between marriageable candidates within the subcaste. Broader participation and opinions of the caste are not highly caught in matters of

---

[113] Interview with Khushalbhai G., January 10, 2003, Mumbai.

everyday administration of the *panchayat*. Women do not officiate in the *panchayat*.[114]

An opportunity to revitalize the *panchayat* came in the 1980s when the subcaste joined a broad organization of Gujarati OBCs to reclassify themselves as "Dalits" in order to access benefits of the reservation policy. Approximately 300 subcaste groups belonging to four OBC castes formed an organization called "Society for Promotion of Vanza-Weavers" (*Samasta Vanza Vanakar Samaj*, now renamed *Samasta Vanakar Samaj*), and classified themselves as a Scheduled Caste of "weavers" for state records. The federation promoted intercaste activities, youth clubs, and cultural events, established scholarships, subsidized marriage ceremonies, and started intracaste periodicals to unite these castes.[115] It has been argued that horizontal intercaste alliances can secularize the internal spheres of the suborganizations (Kothari and Maru 1965). However, that does not seem to be the case here. Subcastes such as Sai Suthar do not support the idea of intermarriage among these allied caste groups. Indeed, the tailors who believed themselves to be superior to other OBCs pledged allegiance to another caste organization, the Association of Mumbai Tailors, in order to endorse intracaste intermarriage.[116]

Governance of internal affairs, especially the handling of legal matters, has not been the mandate of the subcaste *panchayat*, as the urban, city-based *panchayat* has not been able to replicate the authority of traditional village *panchayats*, nor has it been able to adapt to changing times and rebuild its sphere of authority. There are several

---

[114] Male members insist that they have tried to induct women into their programs, but women members of the caste deny these claims and suggested that there had been male resistance to their nonparticipation: "They are unwilling to support change in form of social practises such as veiling – on the one hand, you oppress women and then you ask them to join the council – how can these things happen simultaneously?" (interviews with Geetaben Parmar and Kanubhai Galia, January 10, 2003, Mumbai).

[115] Interview with Sushila Parmar, January 12, 2003, Mumbai.

[116] Interview with Pratapbhai Divecha, February 7, 2003, Mumbai.

reasons for this. The *panchayat* does not have sufficient resources to propose economic incentives. It does not offer any proximity to the government or political parties. It also does not promote social programs or activities. The caste has only a thin layer of the upper stratum of families who are financially better off. In general, however, there is no significant class disparity among caste members, and the nature of their professions does not require them to engage in group activities.[117] The subcaste lacks a cultural sphere and does not promote music, theatre, or literary activities. The caste *panchayat* does not have linkages with other political organizations such as unions. However, individual caste members involved in other voluntary organizations can bring in their agendas and politics into the internal caste sphere.[118]

The Gendered Sphere among the Sai Suthars

Women members of the caste identify the lack of education, financial dependence, and domestic violence as their key problems.[119] Caste practices such as veiling, which go hand in hand with restricted mobility, are other issues cited by them for their nonparticipation in the public activities of the caste *panchayat*. A bulk of women workers from this caste are employed in low-income informal work (such as teachers, nurses, piecemeal workers in garment factories, and telephone

---

[117] At present, many members of the subcaste pursue traditional occupation as tailors. A few members are also professionals. The educational levels of caste members are not high, and women are more likely to be educated than men because there is social pressure on the men to take up occupations. Income disparity among caste members is not very high (interview with Kanubhai Galia, January 10, 2003, Mumbai).

[118] Interview with Khushalbhai Galia, January 10, 2003, Mumbai.

[119] This section is based on interviews with a number of caste women of diverse class and occupational statuses and is largely based on the perceptions and experiences of women members of the caste. The respondents are Geetaben Parmar (January 10, 2003), Chandrikaben Waghela (February 13, 2002), Prabhaben Galia (April 17, 2003), Sumanben Tolia (April 23, 2003), and Deepali Mandekar and Sana Sheikh (February 13, 2002).

operators).[120] The sanskritizing ambition of the caste is apparent in the changing caste customs such as the prevalence of dowry in place of bride-price and the lowered value of women's participation in the workforce in upper-middle-class families within the caste.

Traditionally, caste customs allowed widow remarriage and divorces, and they were quite common. The subcaste practiced polygyny (though it was not widely accepted) as well as bride-price.[121] At present, divorces are readily available and remarriages are quite common. Widow remarriage has been a customary practice, and the demands of marital fidelity expressed through sexual chastity even after the death of the husband are not enforced; in fact, women have considerable sexual freedom within the caste.[122] Sexual control of young women is enforced largely through the emphasis on caste endogamy, though women find spaces to escape community policing through family support, and women with a higher education and professional status find it easier to transgress the requirements of caste endogamy.[123]

Not many women are active in civil society organizations, women's movements, or unions. Semiorganized and nonparticipatory groups

[120] Many male members pursue the traditional occupation of tailoring, and women contribute to the household economy by "assisting" in tasks related to tailoring (sewing hems, buttons, and embroidery). Cultural practices and taboos do not "allow" them to set up shop because sewing is considered to be a male activity. Nevertheless, some women, especially single women, have chosen to practice this trade.

[121] Interview with Khushalbhai Galia, December 20, 2003, Mumbai.

[122] A successful businesswoman who had struggled to work as a businesswoman and had succeeded in establishing a separate business for herself was labeled a "loose woman." Her husband distributed pamphlets to members of the caste, advertising her alleged affair with a man. However, caste *panchayat* members sided with the woman and reprimanded her husband (interview with RM, March 15, 2003, Mumbai).

[123] Gitaben Parmar, a businesswoman who is visible in the caste council, mentioned that she had actively encouraged caste exogamy for her daughters, and many other families had begun to follow their examples. "Our girls are more educated than boys – the boys begin to assist their fathers in their business from [a] young age, but these days, daughters study more.... I sent my daughters to convent schools and they work as professionals. There was no chance that they would marry men from our castes. My daughter fell in love with a Muslim and I encouraged her to marry – people talked for a while, but I knew the family, and understood that she will be

such as the Sai Suthars provide few opportunities of interchange among women caste members. The women of the group have formed loose networks through social activities – celebration of festivals, caste-sponsored dinners, and collective weddings – which have enabled them to exchange information and to help devise strategies to counter family violence and legal struggles. However, most of this support is covert and does not see women through times of legal or financial crisis. In fact, women are often forced to fall back on family and kin members to sustain them through legal processes. Unlike women belonging to the Meghwal community, Sai Suthar women, as a group, do not possess enough individual resources to support other women members. Besides, their lack of higher education and their low participation in the public sector are some reasons why these women have not been able to participate in social organizations or in supracaste horizontal networks that their caste members have formed. Some individual women, however, access both types of women's organizations. They also access Muslim women's organizations or the *mohalla* committees on an individual basis. The lack of support from women caste members also has an impact on individual women's choice of legal forums and their rights within the family.

Fragmented Caste Panchayat *and the Adjudication of the Family within the Caste*

The adjudicative process within the caste is bifurcated. Given the lack of societal mechanism of justice, the informal justice system among the Sai Suthars is decentralized and performed at the familial level. The Sai Suthar caste *panchayat* does not usually officiate in matters of marriage and divorce.[124] Marriages are dissolved informally in the presence

 happy there. My other daughter has also married a Maharashtrian, not a man of our of caste" (interview with Gitaben Parmar, January 20, 2003, Mumbai).

[124] Indeed, *panchayat* members deny the existence of the practice of customary divorce in their subcaste. There are two reasons for this denial: First, they believe customary divorce as a practice contravenes Hindu personal law, which is the state law administered by the state court; second, they believe that "such practises exist among

of family members. At times, some male caste members act as arbitrators, relying on "common sense" and notions of "appropriate social behaviour."[125] This process is called "dissolution at home" (*ghar mele patavavu*). The procedure is not public and often lacks transparency and accountability. Divorces within this subcaste are quite common, and perceived grounds of fault are cruelty, inappropriate conduct of either party or their families, infidelity, and incompatibility.

The Sai Suthars did not openly discuss homosexuality, nor was gay marriage included in any discussion of caste laws. However, caste members expressed opinions about homosexuality in the context of divorce. They also mentioned the infidelity of gay men and discussed the suffocation faced by caste women who were married to gay men. Given that marriages are dissolved in the caste, rumors about homosexuality as a cause of divorce or marital discord also figured predominantly in their accounts of homosexuality. In one case, speculation about a young man's sexual orientation was high, especially considering the fact that the marriage was dissolved within a two months and the woman received a large lump-sum settlement.[126]

There are no established legal rules and procedures within the subcaste. In general, parties who want a speedy divorce and who are able to work out matters concerning financial and custodial arrangements through mutual consent choose not to approach state courts. In most instances, bargaining for postdivorce financial arrangements depends on a person's social networks within the caste, the perception of fault (such as the neglect of spousal duty as per caste norms), information about state law, and the financial capacity of the parties.[127]

---

lower castes." They therefore seek to distance themselves socially from lower castes, especially "weavers" (interview with Bipinbhai H, March 6, 2003, Mumbai).

[125] Interview with Bipinbhai H, Caste President, March 6, 2003, Mumbai.

[126] Interview with Vajubhai Valand, January 13, 2003, Mumbai.

[127] In one case, a woman could not approach the court for economic relief because her husband's family had undergone financial losses and "there was no hope of proving his income." They chose instead to dissolve the marriage informally through caste mediators.

The Caste Is the Public Sphere and the State Private

Within the caste, parties tend to choose the option of informal dissolution in order to "salvage the honour of the wronged party."[128] Proceedings in state courts are believed to be "private" by caste members as the details of conjugal life are not "officially" heard by other caste members and mediators. The caste sphere is a "public" sphere wherein social reputations acquire meaning. In one case, a woman's husband had an extramarital relationship with his sister-in-law. Nisa, the wife, did not inform her family of this until he deserted her after ten years of marriage. Nisa's family approached her husband's family for an informal dissolution of marriage and insisted on a series of meetings involving various caste members as arbitrators in order to "bring about social pressure" on his family and to arrange a large financial settlement for her. This settlement was based on the concept of "fault," and the publicity of this case through caste networks was instrumental in resolving the settlement in Nisa's favor. Nisa shared: "I suffered in this marriage ... if I had gone to court, it would have been quiet, no one would have known. But when we have joint meetings mediated by the caste, people come to know. They know that I am not at fault. I should be compensated. We talked to a lawyer. Proving adultery is difficult in court. But in the caste, people understand you.... They know your family, they have seen you grow, they understand who is who and what is what.... That is justice."[129]

---

[128] Interview with Nisa H., January 11, 2003, Mumbai.

[129] Interview with Nisa H., January 11, 2003, Mumbai. In another instance, a woman who sought divorce a month after her marriage to the son of a prominent caste leader managed to retrieve her *stridhan*, recover the cost of marriage, and get an additional sum of money as alimony for not filing the case of annulment and agreeing to an informal settlement. The breakdown of this marriage in its very early stage led to speculation within the caste about the son's sexual impotency; this perception of "fault" on the man's side made the bargain agreeable to both parties (interview with Kanubhai G., May 5, 2003, Mumbai).

In the Shadow of State Law and Courts

Informal bargaining between families at the time of divorce often rests on the "idea of the state" (Gupta 1995; Migdal 2004b). The state is perceived as the guarantor of the economic rights of women, and this perception is used to bargain for rights on an informal level.[130] For instance, a woman who receives maintenance from her husband as part of a settlement through customary divorce stated: "It is the law. A wife can get half of her husband's salary as maintenance for her children. We have taken the divorce through informal channels, but we know the law. Everyone knows this much."[131] At the same time, perceptions of lengthy court procedures and corrupt court officials deter litigants from approaching state courts, especially in cases of mutual-consent divorces. "In case of a compromise, what does it matter whether it is done in the court or in our house? It is cheaper to do so in the house – you do not have to wait forever for justice.... Besides, we know the law. Details of settlements upon marriage are regularly reported in newspapers. A wife is entitled to half the share of her husband's property. Anyone who reads papers knows the law. We go by the state law in our negotiations."[132]

Justice through "Other Means"

The lack of a mediating forum between individuals and the state often leads people to resort to extralegal means to resolve issues as they arise. For instance, Geeta[133] had been separated from her husband for eight years; she has two children. She had filed a case for maintenance in the

---

[130] "Men in our caste know that the court gives maintenance to women and children. I and my brother told them that either you pay for us or we'll go to the court – but he (the husband) agreed to give money. He [husband] said that 'he preferred to give his money to his son rather than to lawyers and corrupt judges at the family court' but I know that I can always go to the court if he does not pay up" (interview with Neelaben Chawda, March 19, 2003, Mumbai).

[131] Interview with Nikita M., October 22, 2002, Mumbai.

[132] Interview with Kanubhai G., May 5, 2003, Mumbai.

[133] Interview with Geeta, March 7, 2003, Mumbai.

Family Court. Her husband did not attend the court dates, and the court gave her an ex parte order of maintenance. Her husband refused to come to the court or to pay maintenance. She did not pursue the matter legally. She later found work in a garment factory. She relies on her natal family for support, but when she needed extra money for a financial crisis related to her children's health, she had to rely on "other methods" to extract money. Her brothers have ties to local goons, and she often relies on them to collect informal maintenance amounts from the husband. She argues that the lack of caste organization and support systems is one of the reasons she has to opt for these methods. Women's informal intracaste networks enable some women to access women's organizations for individual cases. In one case, the local informal organization (the Mohalla Committee) headed by Yasmin Sheikh, a Muslim lawyer was instrumental in helping a woman, Pavitra, challenge the informal pressure of the caste members to sign divorce papers.[134] Other women have approached women's organizations for legal aid[135] and for filing cases of domestic violence.

Women's Experiences in State Courts

Women litigants from within the caste approach the state court when they need economic relief and when it cannot be arranged through mutual consent. Women litigants who have successfully pursued their cases see the state law as a guarantor of economic rights.[136] Some

---

[134] "I went to my husband's house with Yasmin Sheikh and she managed an amicable settlement" (interview with Pavitra H., April 2, 2003, Mumbai).

[135] A woman litigant had been receiving free legal aid from a women's organization for five years at the time of the interview (interview with Ambika Soni, March 6, 2003, Mumbai).

[136] Sai Suthar women who come from poor families, who can prove their husbands' income, and who did not wish to remarry were more likely to pursue the option of maintenance through state courts and to perceive the courts as the guarantor of minimal economic rights. In one case of maintenance, Mamata was awarded maintenance under Section 125 CrPC in 1990. Since then, she has been receiving maintenance through the court. Her husband has tried to dodge his payments. Mamata has had to

litigants have withdrawn their cases midprocedure for a variety of reasons,[137] whereas some women have successfully pursued their cases in the Family Court. As a woman litigant revealed, "Initially, I was scared of the court – I am not educated and did not know where to go, what to do ... but it has been five years and I have pursued my case regularly.... Sometimes I have a lawyer, sometimes I represent my case."[138] However, state courts do not always guarantee more rights for women, as the case below demonstrates.

Dual Patriarchies of the Family and the State

The issue of conflict between customary laws and state laws arise when the validity of customary divorce is challenged in court; state responses to customary divorce are not unified. Mridu, a woman belonging to this subcaste, was married to Kanu for twenty-two years and they had adult children. In 1991, Kanu forced her to sign papers of customary divorce and gave her 100,000 rupees and a small one-room house in their ancestral village as alimony from him; he asked her to leave the matrimonial house. Kanu was the joint owner of a house, which was worth 10 million rupees, and the sole owner of a business that was housed on a property worth 15 million rupees. Mridu went to stay with her son and daughter-in-law who lived in an apartment that Kanu had bought for them on mortgage. Mridu stayed with her son for about a year but refused to accept the divorce as it was fraudulently obtained. Besides,

---

file for "recovery of arrears" after six months of nonpayment; this has occurred three times. However, she is assured of minimum support.

[137] In one case, a woman was forced to leave the marital home with two daughters under the age of five. She sought to train as a nurse and raise her two young daughters while pursuing a case for maintenance. However, she withdrew her case because frequent court dates seriously inconvenienced her: Each court date led to the loss of a workday. In another case, a woman dropped her case because she did not trust her lawyer who was from the same caste. She suggested that her lawyer was "friendlier with her husband as a fellow caste man and she did not trust him to safeguard her interest" (interview with Ashalata, May 3, 2003, Mumbai).

[138] Interview with Naina C., October 17, 2002, Mumbai.

the settlement given to her at the time of the divorce was not enough to sustain her. During this year, Mridu came to know of procedures in the Family Court from a group of Muslim women who were members of a microcredit group in her neighborhood, along with some women of her caste. The group introduced her to a lawyer, and she filed a petition for maintenance in the Family Court.

Mridu petitioned the Family Court for maintenance under the Hindu Adoption and Maintenance Act 1956. In her petition, she proved his income and attached proofs of the actual worth of his property. In response, Kanu argued that they belonged to the Scheduled Caste and customary divorce was allowed in their caste.[139] He claimed that he had already divorced her and paid her alimony. He claimed to be excused from maintenance payment by questioning his status of marriage. He also claimed that he had suffered heavy losses and was in debt (he brought proofs of unpaid loans). He also claimed that his business property could not be liquidated and that his house belonged to his joint family and was not his own. Sidestepping the issue of the validity of customary divorce, the Family Court judge gave an order for interim maintenance of 2,000 rupees per month to Mridu after three months.

Kanu petitioned the High Court against the order of interim maintenance granted by the Family Court, arguing that his marriage was dissolved by customary divorce and that Mridu had already accepted 100,000 rupees as alimony. He was not obliged to pay any maintenance to her. The respondent, Mridu, did not accept the settlement as binding. The High Court agreed that "the woman had accepted customary divorce" and referred the case back to the lower court "to record the prima facie findings of the case and to dispose of the application only after hearing the parties again." Until then, the ad hoc maintenance of 2,000 rupees a month was continued.

---

[139] In claiming his "Scheduled Caste identity," Kanu and his lawyer relied on the common assumption among judges and lawyers that customary divorces are allowed only in Scheduled Castes and Tribes.

The case was referred back to the Family Court. However, two months later, Mridu withdrew the case for maintenance due to financial difficulties. Kanu had stopped payment of the mortgage amount for the house he had given to his son as soon as Mridu filed a case, and it became apparent that her son was supporting her. The son was not financially solvent and could not manage to pay the mortgage, legal fees, and support his family. The interim maintenance amount given to Mridu was less than the monthly dues of society fees for the house. The case seemed lengthy, and she had little hope of winning because she could not afford the legal fees. Mridu approached her immediate and extended family to work out a compromise with Kanu. After a few meetings and the persuasion of the children, Kanu and Mridu were "reconciled," and she agreed to withdraw the case for maintenance. Kanu and Mridu were not legally remarried because "they were considered married by default as caste members and others did not know about the divorce."

This case illustrates how women are coerced into signing the divorce papers. The decision of the High Court forced Mridu back into matrimony with her husband because the negligible financial amount granted to her was not enough to sustain her, even during the process of litigation. Customary divorce is not seen to be a private affair: The state invalidates contracts that contravene the provisions of Hindu law. Mridu's argument that she was coerced into signing the divorce was not upheld by the High Court, even when the evidence pointed to the loss of substantial economic rights to Mridu. In this case, however, the High Court safeguarded the validity of customary divorce, overruling the interim judgment of the Family Court that had taken a more sympathetic view of the woman's economic conditions.

As thus demonstrated, the adjudication in Hindu law among the Sai Suthars is carried out by caste authorities or state courts. In regulating divorce, the Sai Suthars rely on contemporary customs, state law, or the perceptions about state law. In the caste's unorganized and fragmented *panchayat*, women's rights in the family depend on their social and

HINDU LAW IN SOCIETY 237

family networks and support from within the caste, and still the process does not ensure accountability or transparency in adjudication.

Struggles for Legal Autonomy in Family Matters among the Kutchi Visa Oswals (KVOs)

This section explores the movement for legal autonomy in family law–related matters within a subcaste of a Jain[140] religious community in Mumbai. About 10,000 members of this caste collective in Mumbai came together in June 2003 to attend a public meeting to consider the future of the family within their subcaste in the context of two "social evils": rising divorce rates and increased caste exogamy, especially by young women.[141] Further investigations revealed that only about six cases of divorce have been resolved in the Family Court of Mumbai in last four years and a "few cases" of intercaste, hypogamous marriages have been reported among the poorer sections of the caste. What factors then explain the rising concern about the threat to the caste from intercaste marriages and divorce?

The Kutchi Visa Oswal (KVO) is a mercantile subcaste of Jains and belongs to the upper stratum in the caste hierarchy of Gujarat.[142] Historically, the caste has never practiced divorce, and as such is not eligible to rule in matters of customary divorce as per Hindu law. A

---

[140] There is considerable literature on the Jains as a socio-religious community (see, for instance, Carrithers et al. 1991; Fox 1969; Laidlaw 1995). Hindu law classifies Jains as Hindus. Whether or not the Jains consider themselves Hindus is a matter of discussion among social scientists (Carrithers and Humphrey 1991, 73). Some scholars stress the Jains' self-perception as a community that is different from Hindus, whereas Cottam Ellis (1991) stresses the Jain-Vaishnav interactions and highlights commonalities. Singhi (1991), too, prioritizes the primacy of caste over religious identities in his studies of the Jains.

[141] There exist no records of the number of divorces within the caste. Divorces are stigmatized as antisocial and alien within the caste. Desertion is seen as a common social problem (interview with Shirish Malde, July 5, 2003, Mumbai).

[142] The subcaste is further divided across religious sects and subsects as well. I have not focused on these divisions because they are not relevant to the matters discussed here (interview with Shirish Malde, July 5, 2003, Mumbai).

number of factors explain the emerging demands for caste autonomy in family matters. I argue that this mercantile caste collective has built an engendered caste order that ties family to intracaste wealth through control over family law. The caste collective seeks to reify caste boundaries through the reaffirmation of caste endogamy and to reinforce ties between family and business through the retention of dowry wealth within the caste collective. The movement for legal autonomy aims to prevent intrafamilial division of resources postdivorce.

The KVOs and the History of Migration to Mumbai

The KVO are a subcaste of Jains who practice caste and village endogamy in twenty villages in Kutch in Gujarat. They owned land and were farmers in the villages in Kutch. The KVOs began to migrate[143] to Mumbai from late the 1800s to the early 1900s; these migrants connected the "traditional activity to new enterprise"[144] by entering into the business of selling agricultural yields from villages in Kutch to Mumbai. They also worked as brokers for city dealers in grains, and captured the wholesale and retail trade in grains. By the 1970s, the subcaste members emerged as a powerful lobby within the Bombay Grain Dealers' Association and diversified into areas such as staple commodities, timber, cement, transport agencies, and real estate. As migration increased, the subcaste developed informal financial cooperation between caste members along the lines of trust; they established banking and credit networks among fellow caste members and traders.

Increased economic activity within the group improved educational opportunities through hostels and scholarships for fellow caste members. As a result, many male members availed themselves of opportunities for higher education in Mumbai. A professional class began to grow in

[143] Interview with Leeladharbhai Gadda, June 5, 2003, Mumbai. There are no precise records of this migration, and I have relied on oral records and have tried to substantiate these by documentary evidence when available.
[144] Interview with Leeladharbhai Gadda, June 5, 2003, Mumbai.

the subcaste from 1950 onward. The subcaste members are segmented into two classes: Traders and professionals comprise the upper classes, and the weaker sections of the caste tend to work as clerks, bookkeepers, and assistants in businesses owned by fellow caste members. Very few members are employed in the government service. The subcaste did not have a history of participating in the nationalist movement as a group and did not, as a group, develop a relationship with any political party. On the whole, the subcaste group's linkages to political parties as a caste-based vote bank remain negligible, although individual merchants and traders tend to cultivate bureaucrats and leaders of political parties as business contracts.

Forming a Panchayat

The members of the subcaste were governed by the *mahajan* (caste authority) in different villages. Migrants who came to Mumbai established a caste *panchayat* as a locus of caste organization. The caste *panchayat* was formed through the initiative of young professionals who had gained from other caste-based organizations formed by Velji Napu, a prominent caste elder.[145] They also started an intracaste magazine, called *The Path*, which reports on caste activities, serves as a discussion forum within the caste, and opens up avenues for internal communication within the caste. The caste *panchayat* was controlled by a faction of the caste and did not hold

---

[145] Napu, a nationalist lawyer, stressed the importance of a modern education and opened a hostel in 1915 for young caste members who wished to study in Mumbai. He identified a socially active caste member, Anup Shah, and invited him to be the warden of the hostel. The hostel became the hub of social reformist ideas and youth activities. These young members then settled in various professions in Mumbai and began working for the "upliftment of the caste and to bring about caste unity." During 1945–47, Velji Napu asked Anup Shah to visit Kutch and participate in caste activities there in order to bring about better coordination between the village *Mahajan* and caste members in Bombay. Many former students who had studied in the caste hostel also returned to Kutch and interacted with fellow caste members there. Such initiatives cemented the ties between villages and the caste group in Mumbai (interview with Leeladhar Gadda, June 23, 2003, Mumbai).

democratic elections between 1960 and 1990. There was vocal opposition to the "capturing of this institution" from within other factions of the caste. Elections were held again in 2003, and a new governing body comprised of younger caste officials came to power this time around.[146]

The caste *panchayat* from 1947 to the 1970s served the twin goals of welfare and social control. Income disparities within the group were not marked between the 1950s and the 1960s, and the goal of the caste *panchayat* was caste unity and the upliftment of members. Since the early 1970s, a section of the trading elite emerged as an economically powerful group within the caste; in fact, their "ostentatious display of wealth created jealousy and raised questions about caste unity."[147] The caste *panchayat*, dominated by the professionals, held a campaign for austerity among marriage and social occasions, and began to picket weddings and ceremonies "which exhibited vulgar display of wealth."[148] Two incidents of "social boycotting" and picketing of marriages form part of the repertoire of caste folklore. On November 29, 1970, a grain merchant invited 300 people for the engagement ceremony of his daughter, despite the advice of the caste *panchayat*. Most caste leaders and members of women's organizations within the caste stood outside the venue waving black flags. Many guests decided to boycott the function. A similar situation occurred in May 1970: a caste member called the police and launched a criminal case against members of the caste *panchayat*. An attempt was also made to codify and reform caste traditions by laying down rules for performance of rites during marriage, birth, and death. However, these efforts were not fruitful. As a leader explained: "We realized that while strategies such as picketing and boycott of caste members contained certain forces within the caste, it also brought a realization that the caste *panchayat* had neither the authority nor the power to control fellow caste members."[149]

Since the 1970s, the caste *panchayat* has been seeking to address the growing economic and social stratification within the group by

[146] Editorial page, *The Path*, June 2003.
[147] Interview with Leeladhar Gadda, June 23, 2003, Mumbai.
[148] See *The Path* 500 (June–July 1997): 23–24.
[149] Interview with Sushila Shah, July 5, 2003, Mumbai.

representing a collective organization to facilitate the cooperation between economically and professionally differentiated caste members. The caste *panchayat* began to function in the capacity of a welfare organization.[150] At present, the caste *panchayat* runs group insurance schemes for different economic strata of the caste, arranges collective health camps, provides free treatment to patients who suffer from tuberculosis, gives scholarships to needy students, provides interest-free loans for housing to approximately fifty families per year, runs a microcredit program for women of the caste, and helps provide a market for their homemade products. The caste runs a "book bank" from which about 2,400 students were given textbooks for free. The caste *panchayat* also runs free health care programs for their members in the village; about eighty-two poorer caste members were provided healthcare worth 300,000 rupees. The caste *panchayat* congratulates students for their educational achievements and holds youth camps, spirituality workshops, drawing and elocution competitions, picnics and summer camps, drama competitions, folk dances, music festivals, and mountaineering camps for the caste youth. The caste *panchayat* also runs computer classes and marriage bureaus, and it arranges collective weddings every year.

Ironically, factionalism contributed to a growth of smaller, intracaste organizations at the neighborhood levels, resulting in a rich associational sphere that encourages intracaste interaction and organization.[151] These include cricket clubs, yoga classes, hiking clubs, elocution competitions for the youth, and women's committees, which tend to organize for economic activities such as producing and marketing food and household products, as well as for social purposes such as organizing cultural festivals and folk dances. Many caste members organize charitable activities. For example, doctors from within the caste may organize camps to distribute free services to weaker members of society. There also exist temporary organizations formed in response to natural disasters that may affect the caste; for

---

[150] Interviews with Shirish Malde, July 5, 2003; Leeladhar Gadda, June 5, 2003, June 23, 2003, Mumbai; *The Path*, April 2003, May 2003, June 2003.
[151] Interview with Shirish Malde, July 5, 2003, Mumbai.

instance, many caste members organized to send relief to villages in Kutch following the earthquake in Gujarat in 2001. Participation in common religious activities, such as attending public addresses and participating in rituals in Jain temples, also form an important part of common activities drawing caste members together. Some of these activities are independently held by local committees and some are facilitated by the caste *panchayat*. The group at present has two diverse power centers in regulation of the family: One of these is the caste *panchayat*,[152] and the second center is the influential villagers who are the loci of social authority.

The village *Mahajan* yields considerable social authority. The *Mahajan* collects "taxes" at the time of marriages of any village subcaste members. The village *Mahajan* plays a role in arranging marriages, presides over social functions, mediates in property disputes, and runs charitable trusts for caste welfare within the twenty villages. Caste members seek glory within the subcaste through charitable acts such as the construction of hospitals, residences, hostels, and guest houses, as well as the establishment of charitable trusts for caste members in the villages. Families visit villages to celebrate Jain festivals with pomp. The village is a site of social competition to display wealth and to uphold social standing. These activities played an important secondary role: They also sustained caste endogamy.

Family, Capital, and Religio-Cultural Organization

It has been argued that family and business identities are intertwined among mercantile communities. Among castes that are clustered

---

[152] There is intracaste factionalism: A faction of the caste had broken away and had challenged the monopoly of the factions that controlled the caste *panchayat*. They sought to establish a parallel organization; however, this parallel organization is not recognized by fellow caste members as a *panchayat*. There is also internal power struggles over the informal control of the *panchayat*, given that there are no regular elections. The older members of the caste *panchayat* resigned en masse in 2002, ostensibly to "make way for the new blood."

around particular trades, a family's credit, signifying its business worthiness, comprises its moral standing, intracaste social reputation, and the personal conduct of all its members. Good marriages between business families increase the "credit worthiness of its members" (Fox 1969; Laidlaw 1994, 355) and increase the business confidence in that family (Laidlaw 1994; Rudner 1994). Religious activities, too, form an arena for competition over status within the caste. The caste members contribute funds for the construction of Jain religious temples, residences for Jain religious figures, and meeting halls. They sponsor religious talks and discussions, and participate actively in religious gatherings, prayers, and public addresses by Jain religious figures, as well as travel together for religious pilgrimages to Jain temples.

The moral rectitude and religiousness of "its" women are the twin grounds on which a family's honor is also assessed. The women's participation in religious activities such as fasting, as well as their attendance at and hosting of religious festivals, demonstrate the women's sexual chastity and their economic austerity, which assures the caste at large that the family's credit will not be dissipated either through sexual misconduct or by economic profligacy (Laidlaw 1995, 356). There is a sexual division of labor in the religious sphere as well: Women fast and men give donations and celebrate the breaking of the fast with great pomp. This "giving" by men in the form of donations and the "giving up" of women are complimentary tasks (Laidlaw 1995, 356).

Caste endogamy is favored in the community because it ties business families together, retains dowry wealth within the caste, and opens avenues of joint economic activities. Given the importance attached to inheritance, sexual restraint among women is prized and made public through religious rituals. Marriage ties or alliance building are closely linked to the economic activities of the caste because hypergamous marriages increase the business confidence of both parties. Divorce and the division of property postdivorce are problematized because they upset the fine balance between business and family.

Gendered Sphere within the Caste

The interlinkages between religious observance, occupational structures, and familial practices engender the caste sphere. Historically, caste and village endogamy was strictly practiced, and dowry exchange was common in the cases of marriage between families of equal economic status. Financially weaker families used to mortgage young daughters to moneylenders, as their marriages to wealthy elderly men could fetch a high bride-price. The caste laws did not allow for divorce and widow remarriage. Maintenance to a deserted wife was provided in the form of separate residence or separate quarters within a residence in the marital house. Polygyny was also practiced. Women's mobility and chastity were controlled. Women did not inherit property. Widowed women were seen to be inauspicious and were excluded from rituals and religious festivities.[153] Finally, the veiling of women was quite common.

At present, women members of the caste collective are not seen as independent economic actors despite their higher education. In practice, in many families, daughters do not have equal rights to inheritance, and sons are groomed to take over any family-owned business. Housework, childrearing, and maintenance of kin ties remain the domains of women's labor. The sexual division of labor is rigidly observed within the caste.[154] Women spend a vast amount of time in cultural labor attending to intracaste "social relations"[155] and perpetuating a sense of community. Women maintain caste boundaries through endogamous marriages and retain dowry wealth within the caste. They also socialize children, especially daughters, into religious and caste ethos and thus ensure the

---

[153] See letter to *The Path* by Harshi Sawla, *The Path*, May 7, 2003.

[154] Many women of the caste talked about the difficulties in finding educated husbands for their professional daughters. A woman trained as a gynecologist could not find a husband in the same caste because most men did not want "a working wife."

[155] These activities include attending birth and death ceremonies; visiting sick relatives and kin members; helping various kin members at the time of marriage, crisis, and on social occasions; visiting relatives and kin members in villages; participating in intracaste celebrations and festivities; helping arrange marriages; charity work with fellow caste members; and hosting feasts.

perpetuation of the community. Women's sexuality and chastity are rigidly policed, given the importance of property in maintaining the business community. Religious attendance and participation are an integral and expected aspect of women's social lives. Religious activity is another domain that segregates the worldly, male domain of commercial activity from the pure female acts of religious observance (Humphrey and Laidlaw 1994). Women caste members who oppose the traditions thus elect to exit from the social membership of the caste.

Since the late 1980s, there have been attempts to "reaffirm endogamous marriages, to prevent breakdown of marriages through resocialization of the youth, and to evolve internal means of regulation of divorces."[156] Yet the caste has moved for partial legal autonomy. The next section presents an analysis of divorce cases from within the caste to explain reasons behind the caste's movement for legal autonomy.

Protecting the Good Woman: Denial of Divorce in the Family Court

A husband, Suresh, filed for divorce on the grounds of cruelty and desertion by his wife, Shilpa. He alleged that she was "indifferent, immature, irresponsible, and aloof" toward his family members, and that she "practiced black magic." In June 1985, she "fell off the stairs and had to be admitted to the hospital." In May 1990, the parties were reconciled through the efforts of her family at a joint meeting between their respective families. She returned to his home after "assuring the

---

[156] Interview with S Malde, July 5, 2003, Mumbai. Also, U Gada, "Then and Now ...," *The Path*, May 2003; N Gala, "Analysis of the Questionnaire on Marriage," *The Path*, May 2003, 48–52. After the unsuccessful attempt to codify caste customs in the early 1980s, an attempt was made by a caste-based organization in 1989 to collect social opinions on marriage and related practices. The caste *panchayat* at that time did not respond. However, in early 2003, the caste *panchayat* designed a survey to "discuss caste practises in marriage and divorce" and distributed the questionnaire to 25,000 randomly selected caste members. The results of this survey were presented and discussed in a caste magazine. This event was a precursor to a movement for "social reform" within the caste that mobilized hundreds of thousands of caste members to come together to discuss marriage-related reforms.

assembled of her good conduct in future," but the arrangement did not work.

The respondent, Shilpa, replied that in June 1985, she was asked to bring 200,000 rupees and 50 g of gold. When she pleaded her inability to meet the demand, her husband attempted to kill her by throwing her down the stairs. She was badly injured, yet she was ready to go back to her marital home "as befitting her wifely duty," but her husband refused to accept her. She claimed to have sent eight registered letters asking her husband to take her back, and produced the proof. She also challenged his allegation of "desertion," claiming that she had stayed in her marital home in the village in 1997 and had undertaken a religious fast, which was celebrated by her family; she had not deserted him. In her testimony before the court, she claimed that she was willing to go back to her husband despite having her life threatened. The wife's lawyer has built the case around the image of a wronged, long-suffering, and religious wife who was fighting divorce.

While the court case was proceeding, Shilpa's family and other caste members attempted to "resolve" the case. In both the court and within the caste, Shilpa was proved as a good woman, religious and devout, who had been willing to reconcile despite "domestic difficulties," a euphemism for severe domestic violence. Both caste members and the court felt that the husband should be denied divorce, as he was at fault. The court in this case ruled in favor of the wife and refused the divorce to her husband.[157] This decision of the court was hailed as

---

[157] The court opined that the husband has failed to prove cruelty and desertion. The husband's case was based on the grounds that the wife had deserted him for eight years. The court accepted the husband's claim, but it held that he had failed to prove desertion due to fault in her conduct. The court also observed that the husband had not filed for "restitution of conjugal rights" despite his claim of desertion, whereas the wife had documentary evidence, in the form of letters, to show her willingness to reside with her husband "despite the wear and tear of the family life." Thus, the husband had not proved *animus deserendi*; therefore, his case was dismissed. The husband's allegation that the wife practiced black magic was cited as cruelty. According to the court, the examination of witnesses revealed that the wife practiced black magic with the intention of "helping her husband instead of harming him."

one in which the court upheld the sanctity of marriage and disallowed its breakdown.

Rubber-Stamping Informal Settlements

While the incidence of divorce is very low, and divorce is seen to harm the social sphere of the caste, it is also seen as a consequence of modernity and westernization by some caste members. As a woman lawyer in the caste opined, "While divorce is against social propriety and should be curbed, it cannot be denied if both parties are adamant."[158] But divorce is an internal matter of the family and of the caste: Caste leaders mediate in divorces, and these agreements are rubber-stamped in the court. In one instance, a wife, Neelam, filed for divorce within six months of marriage on the grounds of cruelty.[159] Two months after filing the case, the extended families of both parties asked prominent caste members to mediate in the dispute. A joint meeting was held at the woman's house, and the parties decided to terminate the marriage by mutual consent and agreed on a financial settlement. The parties then filed an application in the court to "convert" the case into one of mutual-consent divorce.

The two cases just described show that the ideology of the state and of the caste are not different when it comes to ideas about conjugality; indeed, the second case illustrates how the caste continues to be a legitimate mediating body in cases of divorce. Despite the court's agreement

[158] Interview with Sushilaben Shah, June 26, 2003, Mumbai.

[159] In one case, the parties were married in December 1999 and within a month, the wife, Neelam, had accused her husband, Ilesh, of attempting to kill her. The husband alleged her of indifference and neglect toward his parents and her household duties during the brief period they stayed together. They separated in February 2000. The wife returned to her matrimonial home in April 2000. She left the matrimonial home once again after a quarrel in July 2000. The grounds of cruelty included the quarrelsome nature of the wife, her refusal to serve her husband and her in-laws, her unsociability ("she was cold towards her husband's relatives"), neglect of household duties (failing to attend to her husband during his mealtimes, failing to be present to receive a father-in-law on his return from the hospital), her "pampered upbringing" (which renders her unfit to be a "proper wife"), her desire to visit her natal family and relatives, and her indifference toward her husband.

with caste decision, however, the KVOs have moved for legal autonomy. It is my contention that the legal developments in civil and criminal laws from the late 1980s to the early 2000s account for this movement for legal autonomy within the caste. For instance, the law on domestic violence enacted in 1986 penalizes both the husband and the in-laws for physical and mental cruelty meted out to married women, and the violence serves as a bargaining chip in some divorce cases. For example, Haresh and Meena obtained a divorce through mutual consent after a year of litigation. During the interview, Haresh admitted that his wife had not filed a case of domestic violence,[160] but the threat of the case and the possibility of arrest lowered his bargaining status. Reflecting on the process, Haresh said, "We had separated for some months and our lawyers told us that she can file a case on me and my parents for dowry related harassment. My parents are old ... how can we outlive such shame on our society? Besides, I have to travel abroad for work, and a criminal record creates problems for [getting a] visa.... My wife and her lawyer know this and are squeezing me."[161] Meena got the custody of the daughter and a settlement of 500,000 rupees. Haresh has also agreed to pay for his daughter's marriage in the future.[162] Thus, the possibility of registering a criminal case increased the wife's bargaining power in this case.

Secondly, new legal developments and the legal strategy of applying civil law on property and tenancy rights to matrimonial property (Singh 1993), especially with respect to married women's right to residence, has created the possibility of the intrafamilial division of resources in matters of divorce. To illustrate, Amisha, a woman, filed for an injunction on the matrimonial property after her husband filed for divorce. The

---

[160] Research shows that the police's perceptions of the misuse of this section by women lead to police reluctance to file cases under Section 498(A) IPC. There were only 232 cases filed under this section in 1999–2000 in the entire city of Mumbai, even though the prevalence of domestic violence is very high (Dave and Solanki 2001).

[161] Interview with Haresh Gadda, January 7, 2003, Mumbai.

[162] Meena complained that "the agreement provides for her daughter but not for her" (interview with Meena, July 5, 2003, Mumbai).

husband had to sell that apartment and give her one-third of the money as a settlement before she agreed to divorce.[163] Nisha and Ashesh's case serve as another illustration: The couple were married in 1998 and resided with the joint family for a few months before moving into a separate apartment bought by Ashesh's father in his name. After facing years of domestic violence, Nisha approached a lawyer and filed for maintenance; she made an application in the court for "nonalienation and transfer of the property while the case is pending." Ashesh worked in the family business, and his lawyer argued that "Ashesh could not pay maintenance as he was fired by his father and was unemployed." Nisha found it difficult to claim maintenance because she could not obtain proof of Ashesh's independent income. Papers showing Ashesh's ownership of the flat was the only piece of evidence that could prove Ashesh's income.[164] Finally, Nisha gave up the claim on matrimonial property and received maintenance in the amount of 5,000 rupees per month for herself and her children. Thus, women use the "civil provision on right to matrimonial residence," as a leverage with varied results, but the availability of this legal remedy questions the basis of the internal organization of the caste.

Claims of maintenance bring to the fore additional issues that intertwine business practices with family matters. A recent judgment ordered a middle-class businessman to pay a monthly maintenance amount of 10,000 rupees to his wife. He defaulted on his payments for two years, and the ex-wife had to file for arrears. Though he has defaulted on his monthly payments to his wife, he claims that "the amount of maintenance is negligible for a man of his means," but "the real discomfort lies in the state prying into my business records.[165] The

---

[163] Interview with Susheela P., July 9, 2003, Mumbai.

[164] "Her claim on [the] right of residence in the matrimonial property remained the only point on which she could bargain" (interview with Veena Gowda, Nisha's lawyer, June 7, 2003, Mumbai).

[165] Tax evasion by businessmen is very high in India under the current tax structure. Therefore, any records involving the exposure of "real" income are seen to invite the scrutiny of the tax authorities.

business is owned in partnership with a fellow caste member and a distant cousin ... it is a question of *saakh*, of social prestige, in the caste – many of my clients belong to my caste – they do not trust divorced men: 'He could not manage his (personal) life, how is he going to manage our money?' Besides, it is the nature of the business – financial liquidity is a problem in my line of work – money is good in some months, bad in others – we do not have fixed income and I am asked to pay monthly sums by the court. It inconveniences everyone here, I mean my partners – I have to ask my partners to 'fix' my income while their families are inconvenienced."[166] This case illustrates the views of caste members that divorce endangers the ties of business. Furthermore, traditional mercantile activity avoids state scrutiny in business affairs. As a caste member opined: "Once the case goes to court, everything is out in the open. Now, many professionals – lawyers, doctors, brokers – do not pay taxes.... In our caste, even if you are a professional, you still have income from the business – family income, you understand ... and it is not shown on paper. And in business – show me a single business man in India who does not maintain dummy accounts – now all of the financial transactions involving not only the husband and wife, but your entire financial history opens up in courts in these divorce cases. How can that be [permissible]?"[167] The process of divorce and the distribution of property expose business practices to the scrutiny of the state.

Thus, consensual ties between the state and the caste are weakened in cases of maintenance and the enforcement of married women's property rights. Whereas the state offers minimal succor and a small portion of men's earnings, the division of property threatens the very fabric of the social order of the caste. The increased call by women for economic rights at the time of the breakdown of marriage has led to calls for preventing divorce and for "recreating the *panch* system."[168]

[166] Interview with Nisha, litigant of the caste, January 6, 2003, Mumbai.
[167] Interview with Sanjay Shah, March 12, 2003, Mumbai.
[168] Interview with Uday G., July 10, 2003, Mumbai.

Social Movement around Marriage and Divorce – Reaction to State-Led Reforms

According to a respondent, "The 'social movement' within the caste is about three 'evils': increased divorce rates, caste exogamy, especially by young women, [and] rising aspirations about marriage."[169] The movement seeks to reorganize the caste *panchayat* ("we wish to resuscitate the *Mahajan*"[170]) by demonstrating a desire for the substitution of the current caste *panchayat*, which functions as a charitable organization, for a functioning, community-based "judicial" *panchayat*. There was no public discussion about homosexual marriages in the caste at this juncture.

There are both facilitative and controlling aspects to internal governance. One is the preventive aspect: the vigorous promotion of caste endogamy through evolving mechanisms to curb intercaste marriages.[171] The other aspect is to chalk out legal strategies to reaffirm caste control over matters related to marriage and divorce. Legally, the caste has two choices.[172] One is to "recreate a tradition" – that is, to institutionalize the practice of divorce by performing them. If challenged in court, the caste

---

[169] Interview with Susheela P., July 9, 2003, Mumbai.
[170] Interview with S. Malde, June 7, 2003, Mumbai.
[171] This includes the increased involvement of the village *Mahajan*. It is suggested that the village *Mahajan* as well as the caste *panchayat* would create lists of "suitable matches," and these would be circulated among interested caste members. Many caste members have also suggested purchasing advertising space in the caste magazine to increase "the choice of matches." Some have argued to "increase the endogamous circles to include more villages and other castes of horizontal social status." The other suggestion revolves around the resocialization of young people and negating the influence of TV and western media through premarital counseling. The caste *panchayat* sponsored large gatherings of youth of marriageable age chaperoned by their parents who encouraged more interaction between caste members. Young men and women are encouraged to look for matches within the caste, and women are exhorted to "lower their expectations." Their families are also counseled about their expectations and roles in the changing social milieu (see Special Issue on Premarriage Counselling, *The Path*, May 2003).
[172] Interviews with S. Malde, June 7, 2003; Sushila Gadda, June 9, 2003, Mumbai.

could argue that it has customarily practiced divorce, and therefore the KVO caste *panchayat* should be authorized to issue judgments in these matters. However, this is seen to be a difficult tactic to use because there might not be enough historical proof to validate the stand of the caste *panchayat*, and an adverse judgment could stall the entire process. The second option is to create a mediation body within the caste and to vest it with informal authority.[173] The caste has begun the process of designing the formal committee that would operate in different residential areas of the city. The committee would be comprised of psychologists, social workers, and prominent caste members, and it would have two women representatives. The committee members would be nominated, not elected. Any family or caste member would approach the committee members and call for a meeting. The committee would counsel the couple and their extended families for reconciliation. Couples whose cases cannot be reconciled would be advised to move to court after the couples and the caste committee "formalize" the divorce arrangements. The families would sign private contracts as per the advice of the moral authority of the caste. As per this solution, caste members can reapply private contracts between parties to authorize decisions taken during the course of mediation. The group members believe that this provision would compel the parties to abide by the decisions made during mediation. The divorce in the Family Court would be a formal stamp on the process undertaken within the caste. The movement demonstrates the caste members' aspirations to contest the disruption of intracaste social order due to state law, and to seek authoritative legal expression in order to curtail shifting values.

State-Society Encounters in Law: Comparison of Caste-Based Legal Forums

The processes of organization building and lawmaking in the three castes across caste hierarchy show the variations in adjudicative

---

[173] Interviews with S. Malde, June 7, 2003; Leeladhar Gadda, June 15, 2003, Mumbai.

processes under Hindu law. What factors explain the differences in marriage laws and practices of varied caste groups? A number of factors explain the divergence in rights granted to women across castes. The data discussed above show that internally democratic caste *panchayats* that interact with external actors – political parties, social movements, women's organizations, religious organizations, and trade unions – are more likely to evolve democratic justice systems, interact with different sections of the society, and increase women's options for justice. The data show that among various castes, historical practices play a role in determining women's rights in law. However, assessing caste formation and lawmaking within these groups also illustrates how these processes are fluid and influenced by state policies, economic activities, and the influence of informal actors, movements, and organizations. Thus, caste laws and customs are subject to revision. The study highlights that the gendering of caste spheres also shapes women's rights in society. The participation of Meghwal women in the labor force, especially in the formal sector, and their exposure to social movements as well as to party and local politics have ensured their higher status within their group. The caste laws recognize them as agents, and women, too, participate in the internal governance of the caste.

The Meghwal women have formed informal networks within their castes through which they share information and support women members. They have also consistently forged linkages with women's organizations and are therefore able to increase their rights and challenge patriarchy. The women of the Sai Suthar group participate in the labor force, but they are not seen as equal economic actors. The women of the KVO group enjoy greater economic and educational status, and they participate in intracaste activities. However, their participation is limited to social and cultural activities, such as creating income-generating programs for poorer women and supporting caste celebrations. They do not interact with other social movements, social organizations, or civic bodies, and their exposure to party politics is limited. As a result, these organizations often mimic patriarchal agendas, such as enforcing caste endogamy and restricting divorce. The women of the KVOs are not recognized as economic agents, and their challenge to the economic order within the caste is via individual acts of resistance through the pursuit of legal options under state law.

The data show that state law has penetrated into the castes' traditions and has impacted the legal developments in the various castes. In some instances, this impact has had negative consequences for women. For instance, the greater penetration of state law has led to the erosion of pro-women customary practices among the Meghwals. However, the criminalization of domestic violence, the introduction of the right to matrimonial property, and the stricter enforcement of maintenance laws in state courts have had a positive impact on gender relations across castes.

These findings reiterate the need for continued reforms in state laws and courts, though these reforms may lead to a reactionary mobilization against the liberal agenda of the state. For instance, we see that the KVOs seek to maintain differences through the assertion of caste endogamy as a principle of organization; this opposes the state's vision of interchange among various Hindu castes through the legitimization of intercaste marriages. However, such reactionary mobilization would exist in tension with changing gender relations within the caste, and would generate individual opposition, as seen in cases of litigant KVO women who have successfully been granted economic rights upon divorce. The shared adjudication model is creatively used by a number of actors to adjudicate in Hindu law in society. In the following section, I discuss other societal actors and bodies that administer Hindu law in society.

Other Societal Legal Bodies: Women's Organizations

The issue of legal reforms has been on the agenda of feminist groups in Mumbai since the 1970s, and they have successfully participated in the Indian Women's Movement's efforts to introduce social legislation around violence against women, reform of religious family laws, and legislation to ban sex determination and sex preselection (Gandhi and Shah 1992; Gangoli 2006). As a result, the Indian Women's Movement in Mumbai has strong ties to the legal community of judges, social workers, and lawyers, especially in the Family Court, as reform in family law has been an important agenda of the women's movement in Mumbai and in India. In Mumbai, feminist legal resource centers such as Majlis and legal organizations such as Human Rights Law Network and Lawyers Collective offer legal aid to women across religious, class, and caste cleavages in cases of marital disputes. These social workers and activists, lawyers, court counselors, and academics participate in conferences, street protests, workshops and seminars,[174] organize gender-sensitivity workshops for the police,[175] often work collaboratively with one another as well as with other civil society organizations on individual cases, and initiate legal campaigns[176] by sharing new legal developments with civil society and academicians. These linkages enable innovative legal developments to travel in society (Merry 2005):

> Feminist legal resource centres such as Majlis and Human Rights Law Network often organise workshops on family law and we learn of new legal developments. These help us enormously in our work because prelitigation intervention can strengthen legal cases of women. So, in a way, legal strategies sometimes start with us – and the injunction against the sale of matrimonial property and Section 498(A) IPC

---

[174] For instance, the feminist organization Women's Centre had initiated discussions on personal law reforms in 1985–86 with other women's groups in Mumbai. Interview with Sandhya Gokhale, Forum Against Oppression of Women Mumbai, October 12, 2002, Mumbai. Between 1993 and 1995, the Forum Against Oppression of Women debated law reforms in personal law with other women's groups in Mumbai, and later organized a national conference on this issue (see Gangoli 2006; Menon 1998).

[175] Interview with Kalindi Majumdar, former Vice-Principal, Nirmala Niketan College of Social Work, October 7, 2002, Mumbai.

[176] I discuss one of the campaigns for law reforms in Muslim Personal Law in the next chapter. Since the 1980s, women's organizations have protested against any move to introduce the irretrievable breakdown of marriage as a ground for divorce in Hindu law and the secular law.

are useful tools and we use these to bargain for women's rights when women approach us for help in cases of domestic abuse, and we make sure that we give this information to women who approach us even if their cases have not yet reached the Family Court. Women have many social networks and what you tell one woman travels to another....[177]

In the adjudicative arena, women's organizations are perceived to be important interlocutors who negotiate specific rights for women across religious, class, and caste boundaries. The organizations offer specific services – feminist counseling, legal aid, and arrange for shelter for women in crisis situations. Their expertise is widely recognized, and in many cases, residential committees, neighborhood associations, microcredit groups, social workers (fixers), and big-men (wealthy, influential men/community leaders) of local areas refer cases to women's organizations, especially in cases where women need help to register criminal cases, to recover *stridhan*, or to assist in legal aid.

The previous section discussed the difficulties women face in the retrieval of *stridhan* at the time of divorce or separation. Women's organizations have been able to fill in this gap, assisting women to recover their *stridhan* before the court process or even after the court judgment.[178] Women's organizations use legal developments innovatively to bargain for women's rights in law in society. For instance, given the problems in recovering *stridhan*, women's organizations use Sections 405[179] and 406 IPC 1860 to persuade the police to file cases under these laws to help women retrieve *stridhan*. Indeed, after the Supreme

---

[177] Interview with Vandna Nanaware, June 16, 2003, Mumbai.

[178] Women's organizations had assisted in the recovery of *stridhan* in five cases while the matter was subjudice or disposed of (interviews with AJ, April 4, 2003; HS, March 5, 2003; MN and KK, February 15, 2003; PW, November 9, 2002, Mumbai).

[179] Sections 405 and 406 of the IPC deal with criminal breach of trust: Whoever, being in any manner entrusted with property, or with any dominion over property, dishonestly misappropriates or converts to his own use that property, or dishonestly uses or disposes of that property in violation of any direction of law prescribing the mode in which such trust is to be discharged, or of any legal contract, express or implied, which he has made touching the discharge of such trust, or willfully suffers any other person so to do, commits "criminal breach of trust."

Court judgment in the Pratibha Rani[180] case, women's organizations, especially the Special Cell for Women and Children, succeeded in persuading the Police Commissioner of the city to send a written communication to all police stations, instructing them to register cases under Section 406 IPC to help women recover their *stridhan*.[181] In individual cases, activists of women's organizations accompany women to police stations insisting that they register these cases against husbands who refuse to return their wives' *stridhan*. In most cases, the police refuse to register the cases, but call the husband and his family; the police officials, women's activists, and the two parties exchange *stridhan* after bargaining and negotiations.[182]

The police are more open to register a case under Section 406 IPC along with Section 498(A) IPC, the law on domestic violence.[183] Women litigants often approach women's organizations for help when the police refuse to register cases under Section 498(A) Indian Penal Code 1860, the law on domestic violence:

We had accompanied a woman who was bleeding from a head wound and the police refused to register the case under Section 498(A) IPC. I had to spend a day at the police station persuading them to do so. The police think that these are small offenses, they call these *"mia bibi ka zaghda"* (trivial domestic fights). The police do not think that domestic violence is [a] crime, they think the women are misusing these laws. We also insisted on filing the case under Section 406 IPC. But once we filed

---

[180] *Pratibha Rani* v. *Suraj Kumar & Another*, AIR 628 SCR (3) 191 [1985].
[181] Interviews with Kunda Kelkar, activist, Stree Mukti Sanghatana, November 13, 2002, Mumbai; Vandana Nanaware, Special Cell for Women, June 16, 2003, Mumbai.
[182] Ibid.
[183] "The police are more reluctant to lodge cases under Section 406 IPC because they think that these are domestic civil matters and should not be resolved under criminal law. Also, filing of a criminal case requires more paperwork and the police face a huge workload. They are overworked and underpaid ... policing is a high-stress job in Mumbai ... and they are reluctant to file cases and put in more work in what they consider as civil and trivial matters. They are more open to include this section when they file a major case of domestic violence" (interview with Vandana Nanaware, social worker, Special Cell for Women, June 16, 2003, Mumbai).

the case, it was easier to recover the *stridhan* and we managed to recover all her *stridhan* that day.[184]

Police resistance in registering these cases is an issue raised again and again in conferences and workshops with the police to sensitize them with women's issues and immediate concerns in law.[185]

Women's organizations assist in cases where families of Hindu or Muslim lesbian women threaten them with forcible marriages or penalization under Section 377 of the Indian Penal Code.[186] For instance, social workers at the Special Cell also coordinate with lesbian women's groups, such as Stree Sangam,[187] and other women's groups for individual cases. Pratibha Jagtap of the Special Cell shared:

> [M]any feminist groups that run a hotline for lesbian women get calls for lesbian women who want to leave their houses to prevent their parents from forcibly marrying them off to men. These groups often coordinate with us. In one case, the couple wanted to leave their local city and go to Bangalore. We advised that they can submit an application to their local police stations stating that they are major, above eighteen years of age, and that they are leaving their families of their own will. This is a precautionary measure, so that they are not charged with kidnapping or theft at the family's instigation.... Another time, activists of a local women's group had gone to rescue a lesbian woman who was imprisoned in her own house. They began a dialogue with the family, but faced hostility and threats from the family, neighbours, and local "fixers" of that area. These people surrounded them and the atmosphere turned ugly within minutes. Sensing danger [concerned about

---

[184] Interview with Kunda Kelkar, activist, Stree Mukti Sanghatana, November 13, 2002, Mumbai.

[185] The Family and Child Welfare Department of Tata Institute of Social Sciences had hosted these conferences with the police on the specific question of police attitudes to the registration of cases under laws on domestic violence in 1999 and 2000.

[186] The Section 377 of Indian Penal Code 1860 criminalized male homosexuality. However, this legal provision was also used to threaten lesbians by their families. The members of the family could not lodge a case against lesbians under this section, but could use it as a threat to involve the police and use the coercive authority of the police as a tool to browbeat lesbian women.

[187] Since 2003, the group has been renamed LABIA (Lesbians and Bisexuals in Action).

their physical safety], they called us. We contacted the local police station and helped them [the activists] to leave that "tense locality" and avoid a potentially dangerous situation.[188]

Earlier in this chapter, I have shown the nature of women's organizations in everyday processes of adjudication in caste councils – they play the role of advocates for women, negotiate women's rights in caste councils, act as watchdogs, and pressure groups against antiwomen caste practices. The modernist and secular women's organizations in Mumbai have been sensitive to questions of communalism, and have engaged with greater self-reflexivity with religious sects, clergy, and customary groups among Muslims to reform the Muslim Personal Law, especially post Hindu–Muslim riots in Mumbai in 1992–93, following the Babri Masjid demolition. Their engagement with Hindu caste groups has been less reflexive[189] but consistent. Most groups acknowledge, however, that in everyday aspects of their work, feminists are invited by caste *panchayats*, doorstep groups, and women's networks to speak on legal reforms and domestic violence, and have been invited to help facilitate intracaste discussions on specific issues.[190]

Legal Actors in Society: Notaries, Lawyers, Middlemen

Apart from caste groups, the adjudication of Hindu law in society also involves other informal actors. Prominent members of castes, or neighborhood or even family friends, serve as middlemen in certain cases. For

---

[188] Interview with Pratibha Jagtap, social worker, Special Cell, September 17, 2002, Mumbai.
[189] The reason being: "Modernist secular feminists have always questioned caste traditions and family patriarchies in their personal lives, and in their political lives. We have been critical of caste and religious patriarchies. We are used to confronting these community practises and laws, rather than colluding with them" (conversation with Sandhya Gokhale, Forum Against Oppression of Women, October 12, 2002, Mumbai).
[190] "The Baudhha Panchayats of Mahar Dalits has often been in touch and we have been invited as speakers.... In one instance, a Jain women's 'ladies social club' who knew one of the social workers at the Special Cell invited us to address their ladies club" (interview with Vandana Nanaware, Special Cell for Women, June 16, 2003, Mumbai).

instance, Navin Mehta,[191] a businessman, helped in arriving at "consensual solutions" in three cases. He is a successful and well-respected businessman in his caste and told me that he had "solved" three cases in the last two years. His "entanglement with family law" began when his close friend shared that his daughter was unhappy in her marriage, and that he suspected that his daughter's husband was having an affair with another woman. Mehta hired a private detective to follow the man in question, and obtained proof of adultery. He then met a lawyer to understand the legal situation. After that, Mehta and his friend confronted the son-in-law and asked him for a divorce. The son-in-law denied the affair, refused to return the *stridhan*, and declined to give a divorce. Mehta then showed him the photos of him with another woman, threatened to publicize these in his family, and asked him to return the *stridhan*, working out the terms of divorce "strictly as per law." The divorce was then finalized as a divorce by mutual consent. However, after this case, Mehta has been contacted by members of his extended family and other caste members to assist in divorce, and he periodically does so. He claimed that now he knows the family law as much as any lawyer of the Family Court.

Similarly, lawyers also negotiate divorce under Hindu law in society. Cases of mutual-consent divorces are more often than not negotiated in lawyers' offices, and both lawyers and notaries work with caste associations and other organizations in finalizing societal divorces, or "converting caste laws into state law." A Muslim notary[192] shared that a group of Hindu Tamil migrants came to him and asked to notarize a "double divorce." The man had two wives and he wanted to divorce both "because they fought among themselves." The notary explained to the husband and to the group that he cannot legally issue a divorce certificate to both women at once under Hindu law, and that his first wife was his only legal wife, but no one was willing to believe him because polygyny was allowed under the caste laws, and both wives had equal status

---

[191] Interview with Navin Mehta, February 22, 2003, Mumbai.
[192] Interview with A. K. Syed, May 18, 2003, Mumbai.

under their customary laws. The notary then came up with a "legal" solution – he asked this man to give his thumb impression on the paper (he was illiterate), finalizing the customary divorce with his first wife. Then he made him give his thumb impression on a marriage certificate with his second wife, and then he finalized the second divorce. Indeed, lawyers often see their role "as counsellors who try to reconcile parties and not advocate divorce." Lawyers also carry law in society – many caste *panchayats*, voluntary organizations, have lawyers on their boards and they advise them in legal matters.[193]

Whereas some lawyers extend state law in society, others subvert the legal process. In a case of contested divorce that was renegotiated into a mutual-consent divorce, a middle-class woman was granted maintenance of 10,000 rupees a month. The husband expressed his inability to pay that amount. The lawyer called both parties after the divorce and renegotiated the amount, and the woman agreed to reduce the amount to 7,500 rupees a month.[194]

Leveraging Authority: Strongmen and Political Parties in the Adjudication of Hindu Law in Society

Hansen has argued that sovereignty in postcolonial India has been fractured, and beside law and a system of regulation, strongmen, community bodies, and other forms of informal authorities (what he calls "repertoires of authority," comprising businessmen, politicians, criminals, middlemen, and networks of fixers and strongmen belonging to or having links with political parties and social movements) exist and function, at times independently of the state, at times within the state, and at times both, and sees these institutions as limiting the state authority in India (Hansen 2005). These actors influence adjudication, and the

---

[193] "These lawyers get clients if we do not resolve matters within the caste, and we get free legal advice" (interview with Raja Jadhav, member, the Bauddh Panchayat Samiti, November 8, 2002, Mumbai).
[194] Interview with DP, April 13, 2003, Mumbai.

use of strongmen to "solve matters" was reported by many litigants. Women litigants[195] also complained of physical threats and assaults on themselves and family members. Some litigants stated that their husbands sent goons to intercept them on their way to court, used abusive language in public places, and harassed them at work by making abusive phone calls and maligning their character. Many women litigants complained of harassment by strongmen who are hired by husbands to make threatening phone calls to women litigants,[196] to beat members of their families,[197] to harass them on their way to state courts,[198] and to spy on their activities.[199] Women litigants who are granted maintenance by courts complained of this form of harassment. Many women litigants receive maintenance but have to work to sustain themselves. However, proof of employment can jeopardize the legal status of these wives, and women reported that strongmen followed them and reported their activities to the husbands who then asked for the withdrawal of maintenance. Other experiences of intimidation included the husbands using goons to evict them from their homes, knocking on their doors in the night, and instigating neighbors to throw garbage and other things inside their houses. Male litigants[200] accused their wives and their families of using threats of filing false criminal cases, sending goons to threaten them and their family members, and maligning them at their workplace. The use of strongmen to collect maintenance amounts or arrears decided by the court, and at times, to retrieve *stridhan*, was among other complaints

---

[195] Interviews with RS, March 7, 2003; SM, June 7, 2003; AJ, April 4, 2003; HS; March 5, 2003; FS; March 3, 2003, MN and KK, February 15, 2003; PW, November 9, 2002 Mumbai.

[196] Interview with NB, February 12, 2003, Mumbai. Interview with MP, March 7, 2003, Mumbai.

[197] Interview with NS, March 14, 2003, Mumbai. Interview with JM, February 12, 2003, Mumbai.

[198] Interview with GP, October 12, 2002, Mumbai. Interview with HP, October 10, 2002, Mumbai. Interview with HK, October 10, 2002, Mumbai.

[199] Interview with NS, March 14, 2003, Mumbai.

[200] Interviews with SS, February 19, 2003; YA, June 8, 2003, SA; March 4, 2003, Mumbai.

made by male litigants. Though the Meghwals lived in neighborhoods where networks of strongmen were quite common, their interference in marital disputes was not reported due to the presence of a well-organized *panchayat*.

From among the political parties, the Hindu nationalist party, the Shiv Sena's women's wing, the Mahila Aghadi intervenes in family matters related to marriage and divorce. Eckert has discussed how the Aghadi workers use feminist rhetoric but reinforce patriarchal ideas of wifehood, marriage, and gender roles within the family, and police the boundaries of the Hindu community, discouraging intercaste and interreligious marriages (Eckert 2003). The Mahila Aghadi uses sensational means to humiliate women who transgress the boundaries of "a good Hindu woman." In one case, after ten years of severe domestic violence, Anjani had filed a case under Section 498(A) IPC against her husband's family, and he and his mother were arrested. After being released on bail, the husband and his mother complained to the Mahila Aghadi, accusing Anjani of "attacking their family honour" by "filing a police case." Anjani was forcibly dragged out of her house late in the night and threatened by the Aghadi workers. She approached a women's organization and then reported to the Aghadi women that she had "gone to the court" (*mee korat keli*) to report them. The woman claimed that she was left alone after that.[201] In another case, Magshara, a woman whose husband was having an affair, approached the local Mahila Aghadi; the workers "caught him red-handed" and blackened his face in the slum. The husband, in retaliation, filed for divorce.[202] The actions taken by the Aghadi women are public, coercive, and theatrical, but they do not help women in sustained legal struggles. They also lack legal knowledge, and there are no networks between the women's wings of the right-wing parties and the lawyers, social workers, and the Family Court. Indeed, members of the Shiv Sena itself seek other avenues besides the Mahila

---

[201] Interview with Anjani Waghmare, March 23, 2003, Mumbai.
[202] Interview with Nirmala Jadhav, October 10, 2002, Mumbai.

Aghadi in several cases. To illustrate, Sumitra's brother is a Shiv Sainik, and they went to the local branch when her husband asked her for a divorce. The Mahila Aghadi women called him and coerced him into reconciliation. She went back to live with her husband, he refused to speak with her for a few days, and she returned to her brother's home and later filed a case in the Family Court.[203]

The Shiv Sena workers or criminal elements rarely intervene in cases when parties belong to organized caste *panchayat*. The Meghwals do not report the involvement of strongmen or the Shiv Sena in solving family disputes. The Shiv Sena workers also rarely intervene in family matters of Muslims. However, they are likely to intervene in interreligious marriages and harass the family members of recent converts. They are countered by the Samajwadi Party on the streets of Mumbai. In one instance, a Hindu woman eloped with a Muslim man, Ayaz, and her father approached the local Sena branch to "rescue" his daughter. However, Ayaz lived in a locality with a strong presence of the Samajwadi Party, and he had contacted them; the Shiv Sainiks in this case laid the matter to rest, "lamely consoling" the father that "they will beat up Ayaz if he ever set foot in that locality."[204]

The women's wings of the CPI (M), All India Democratic Women's Association (AIDWA), actively intervene in individual cases and participate and initiate campaigns on law reforms. They share strong ties with women's groups, women in trade unions, and other civil society organizations. Their workers are often asked to intervene in individual disputes and are invited to address intracaste gathering among the Meghwals.

---

[203] In another instance, a Shiv Sainik, an OBC, with interests in real estate in Thane, with criminal links, and influence over his fellow party workers and local strongmen, chose to approach the Special Cell for Women, a women's organization. In a bid to access social prestige, he had married his daughter to an upper-caste man who was a software engineer. When his daughter and husband separated a few months after marriage, he came to the Special Cell "... as these problems require a different approach – I can gather many men and threaten him [referring to his son-in-law] but how will that help my daughter?" (interview with Suresh Teli, December 10, 2002, Mumbai).

[204] Interview with Ramesh Chauhan, January 12, 2002, Mumbai.

Conclusion

In this chapter, I discuss the "shared adjudication" model in Hindu law, as both the state and caste groups strive to shape individual and familial subjectivities through lawmaking and adjudication. The interactions between the state and societal actors over the definition and administration of Hindu law impact the normative configuring of the conjugal family as well as the material domain of the family, because these normative world views have an impact on the intrahousehold division of property.

In the model of shared authority, the normative material world shaped by the state coexists with the normative material worlds imagined and practiced by societal actors and institutions. The normative and material worlds of the state and/or the caste are not unified, coherent entities – they are both internally contested and shaped by their interaction with one another. Certain aspects of these diverse, fragmented worlds overlap as well. For instance, both the state and caste *panchayats* privilege patriarchal, heterosexual families and retain male authority over economic resources. The Meghwals and the Sai Suthars share the idea of personal freedom inherent in divorce. The conflict between the normative and material worlds of the state and the caste is most pronounced in the case of the Meghwals. The Meghwal caste laws and practices differ from the state over the regulation of family structure, the definition of marriage, the regulation of cohabitation, the acceptance of patrilineality, the criteria for group membership, the sexual autonomy of individual members within the family, and the economic rights and obligations of family members. The KVOs share aspects of the normative ideology of the state, but they reject the notion of personal freedom inherent in the notion of divorce and intrafamilial distribution of wealth.

In addition, Hindu law in society is adjudicated by women's organizations, political parties, middlemen, notaries, and lawyers. These discrete and intertwined organizations and actors compliment one another on some occasions and conflict on other occasions. These different legal bodies produce contesting and complimentary ideas over the constitution of marriage and attach different legal meanings to the duties and rights of wives in marriage. Multiple interacting normative worlds of law both challenge and confirm state-centric norming of institutions and identities, and create possibilities of refashioning gender roles from the margins.

5 Juristic Diversity, Contestations over "Islamic Law," and Women's Rights
Regulation of Matrimonial Matters in Muslim Personal Law

Introduction

This chapter outlines the nature of adjudication in matrimonial matters under Muslim Personal Law in Mumbai. The chapter highlights the interplay between state law and nonstate law, analyzes the interaction between multiple sources of legal authority, and discusses the processes of community-initiated reforms in Muslim Personal Law. Given that multiple societal actors and bodies adjudicate and produce law, the adjudication process demonstrates how the content of Muslim Personal Law itself is a subject of contestations between law-producing and law-legitimating agents. This chapter demonstrates that multiple representations and understandings of "the Muslim family" and Muslim women's rights within the family coexist in the adjudicative arenas, and shows how these are tied to different understandings of "Muslimness." Thus, the religious identity premised upon in Muslim religious family law is fluid and subject to constant revision.

This chapter also discusses the impact of these state-society interactions on women's rights in law, describes how the decentralized legal sphere offers avenues for women's agency, and shows the limits of this agency given the asymmetrical position of women within the family, society, and the law.

The Nature of Muslim Personal Law and the Classification of Legal Actors and Institutions in Societal Arena

Muslim Personal Law in postcolonial India is based on local custom, Islamic laws[1] and precepts,[2] customary laws made by sect-based organizations, state-law enactments, and judicial precedent.[3] The state courts administer the uncodified Muslim Personal Law as well as state-enacted law. In general, state law recognizes uncodified Islamic law when it comes to marriage and divorce, but it privileges statutory law in matters of maintenance.

The state allows multiple actors and avenues in the regulation of Muslim Personal Law. The societal actors who adjudicate in Muslim Personal Law can be classified in three categories: individual actors, such as lawyers, the clergy, family members, and strongmen, comprise the first category; religious organizations, women's organizations, and sect-councils make up the second category of adjudicators in Muslim Family Law; and doorstep courts, such as residential committees and women's ad hoc groups, form the third category of adjudicators. The typology suggests

---

[1] The term "Islamic law" covers both the *Sharia* (the divine law) and *fiqh*, which is the product of human understanding that sought to interpret and implement the *Sharia* (Esposito 1982, 105). Islamic jurisprudence has developed as the science of interpretation of both the Quran (the revelation of God) and the *sunna*, which is the Prophet's statements and the tacit approval of certain deeds of which he had knowledge (Haddad and Stowasser 2004, 5). The elaboration of law depended on the Quran and the *sunna* and on the application of juridical reasoning to discover the reason behind each rule and to apply it in a specific context (Esposito 1982; Hallaq 2001; Pearl 1987). Thus, the interpretive science relied on a methodology called *ijtihad*. The resultant body of law – classical *fiqh* schools (*madhabib*) – in which the details of law are stated and recorded are Hanafi, Maliki, Shafi, and Hanbali.

[2] Most Sunni Muslims in India follow the Hanafi law, although Shafi, Maliki, and Hanabali laws are also adhered to in some pockets of the community. Many Shia communities follow the Shia law, and sects such as Bohras, Khojas, and Ismailis follow sect-based laws (An-Na'im 2002b).

[3] There is a history of state action in Islamic laws in India. The development of Anglo-Mohmeddan law in state courts during the colonial period was a combination of British legal precepts and local Islamic rules and practices (Fyzee 1965; Mukhopadhyay 1998; Parashar 1992; Pearl 1987).

that although religious factions of the Muslim community exercise some authority in matters of governance of Muslim Personal Law, they are not the sole spokespersons or adjudicators on the ground. There exist different power centers within the legal sphere, and legal activity is localized and decentralized in everyday legal practice. The following section discusses how these sources of legal authority shape the process of adjudication in laws relating to marriage, divorce, and maintenance among Muslims, and argues how law is made and unmade by legal actors in society.

Individual Legal Actors and "Private" Divorce

Under Muslim Personal Law, the right to unilateral divorce, both oral and written, lies with men. This provision in law has been widely criticized by feminists and Muslim moderates as perpetuating a gendered power asymmetry within the marital family. In many cases, divorces happen without warning, are delivered through letters, and women are often dispossessed from the matrimonial home after divorce. In some cases, Muslim women are divorced by telephone or through email.[4] In Chapter 2, we saw that the Family Court does not accept written divorce unless the woman has received it, and in most cases, divorces are mailed through registered post, which requires the recipient's signature. This method is most popular, as both the sender and the recipient have proof of divorce. However, it is not foolproof, and women are forced into acceptance of such divorce, or are handed this kind of letter by deception: "I knew all about how men divorce their wives [by] sending registered letter, so when I went to my brother's place after a fight, I did not accept any mail from him. But then, I received a mail from his uncle. He is the respected elder of the family (*ghar ke bade hai*); I opened it without suspecting anything and there it was, the *talaqnama*. I was cheated."[5] Women are also forced to accept divorce letters.[6]

---

[4] Interview with Pratibha Jagtap, social worker, November 6, 2002, Mumbai.
[5] Interview with JM, May 20, 2003, Mumbai.
[6] "My husband held a knife at my throat and divorced me." Interview with JS, March 12, 2003, Mumbai.

The issue of the validity of written and oral divorce under Muslim Personal Law remains crucial for Muslim women who wish to prosecute their husbands for domestic violence by filing a case under the provision of Section 498(a) IPC, as only married women can file under this provision. To cite an example, a Muslim litigant was forced to drop her complaint midway through proceedings because the police accepted her husband's claim that he had divorced her before the police filed a charge sheet, and dropped the case in the middle of the investigation, as "… in many instances, the police believe that Muslim men are allowed to give triple *talaq* to women without their consent, and this lack of knowledge about Muslim law coupled with communal outlook in the police as well as in society damages women's rights in law."[7]

In few cases, women use the ambiguity about oral divorce and the proof of divorce to their advantage. In one case, the husband divorced a woman through a postcard that was unregistered. The postcard divorce was received by the wife, but as the mail was not registered, she did not sign it. The husband thus could not prove divorce. The wife pretended that she did not receive the divorce, and filed a legal case for maintenance against the husband under Section 125 CrPC. The court ruled in her favor, because the husband could not prove divorce. The wife shared her strategy: "… I do get some maintenance from him and I have heard that he cannot get married again – no one in our community will give him a daughter since he is financially obliged to maintain me…. He thinks that he will have his revenge by refusing to divorce me, but I'll show his postcard to everyone the day I wish to remarry, though I am in no hurry to do so."[8]

In some cases, husbands delegate the right of divorce to their male kin members.[9] For instance, in one case, a man had migrated to the Persian Gulf as a laborer after his marriage. His *nikahnama*, the marriage

---

[7] Interview with Noorjehan Niaz, Women's Research and Action Group, August 4, 2008, Mumbai.
[8] Interview with FG, November 12, 2002, Mumbai.
[9] Interview with HK, March 6, 2003, Mumbai.

contract, specified the delegation of the right to divorce under certain conditions. His wife insisted on divorce within a few months. Because the man could not return from the Gulf due to monetary constraints, it was seen as unfair to ask the wife to wait until his return. As a result, the husband's cousin gave a delegated divorce to the woman.[10]

Women's organizations and civil society organizations differ on the delegated divorce, for feminists opine that the right of delegated divorce could be misused by the marital family if it is granted against the woman's wish.[11] In other cases, Muslim men are encouraged by civil society organizations and women's organizations to delegate the right of divorce to their wives at the time of marriage.[12] In some instances, divorces are given following community procedures in the presence of witnesses.[13] Indeed, many practitioners of Islamic law in India believe that the process of arbitration is necessary to check the arbitrary power of Muslim men.[14]

A woman may approach the court to divorce her husband by filing a case under the Dissolution of Muslim Marriage Act 1939. At the societal level, a wife may ask for *khula*, a form of divorce initiated by the wife, though the wife's legal recourse to divorce through court is not equal to the husband's legal capacity to end a marriage at will. However,

[10] Ibid.
[11] "In one case, the husband and wife liked each other, but the in-laws did not like the girl and the husband's cousin divorced her while the husband was sent away for some business. We ask that this right should be delegated only to the woman and no one else" (interview with Hasina Khan, Awaz e Niswan, June 6, 2003, Mumbai).
[12] Delegating the right of divorce to women increases the wife's bargaining power within the marriage. There is resistance to the incorporation of this right in the marriage contract. However, the practice is standardized in some families and localities. I discuss this form of divorce later in the chapter (interview with Iqbal Maniar, Public Complaint Centre, May 23, 2003, Mumbai).
[13] This is the case in more organized sects such as the Khojas, the Memons, and the Bohras (Engineer 1988). It is also used in the Qureshi *jamaat* and in small village-based endogamous circles. Interview with Noorjehan Niaz, August 4, 2008, Mumbai.
[14] "A strategy to curb this abuse of divorce is to insist on arbitration before divorce. If there were more regulatory conditions attached to divorce, the number of divorces would be reduced" (interview with Sajidbhai Lakdawala, Dar ul Qaza, June 17, 2003, Mumbai).

the woman-initiated divorce, the *khula*, is finalized only if the husband accepts the divorce. In practice, a woman who wants to opt out of the marriage may buy the repudiation from her husband. In many cases, the payment takes the form of money, goods, or foregoing the right of *mehar* during *iddat* (alimony).[15] In some cases, the *khula* can be converted into *talaq*, in the sense that a husband may choose to repudiate his wife by granting the wife's requests[16] or by opting for a mutual-consent divorce.[17] Vatuk, in her study of *khula* in *qazi*'s courts in Hyderabad, reports that husbands often obtain the form for *khula* from *qazi*'s office and coerce women to initiate *khula*, and that parties try to avoid the social stigma of having initiated the divorce (Vatuk 2008).

Individuals and extended family members can also adjudicate or negotiate divorce under Muslim Personal Law. In many cases, divorce is subject to claims and counterclaims of parties, and as such, is often sorted out among family members. To cite an example,[18] a Muslim wife filed a case for maintenance under Section 125 CrPC in the Family Court. Her husband produced proof of divorce in the Family Court in form of a registered letter. The court dismissed the woman's petition for maintenance under Section 125 CrPC. The woman and her family got a *fatwa*, or legal opinion, from a clergyman, who held that the divorce was invalid because it was not communicated to the wife. The man was

---

[15] Interviews with litigants: MA, March 5, 2003; NS, April 15, 2003; QS, February 14, 2003, Mumbai.

[16] A woman who was married to her cousin was granted a *khula* by her husband at her insistence. Her dowry was also returned to her (interview with MS, February 14, 2003, Mumbai). "Personally, I have found that cross-cousin marriages remain easier to dissolve – the families do share emotions ties, and they are more willing to listen to the woman" (interview with Vandana Nanaware, social worker, Special Cell, June 10, 2003, Mumbai).

[17] Initially, the woman had asked for *khula* and the husband denied it. The parties approached the women's organization for mediation. The parties were divorced in a women's organization through mutual consent. They divided their property, and the husband gave an assurance of maintenance for the children. The deed of divorce (*talaqnama*) was stamped by a notary (interview with NS, January 17, 2003, Mumbai).

[18] Interview with NH, January 17, 2003, Mumbai.

to remarry, and the first wife and her family contacted his future bride's family to prevent the marriage, as polygyny was not widely practiced in their community. Ultimately, the parties settled the matter privately, and the husband returned the dowry, gave maintenance during the period of *iddat*, and returned the *mehar* to his ex-wife.

Interlawyer Negotiations

Interlawyer negotiations can expand the law into an informal arena, as state law acts as a backdrop to the negotiated settlement in the societal arena (Kornhauser and Mnookin 1979). Interlawyer negotiations are often based on legal precedents, and lawyers are often instrumental in resolving the dispute without going to court.[19] Thus, developments in state law help in bargaining for rights in society at the prelitigation stage as well as during litigation. Whereas communities and families differ in their acceptance of oral divorce, lawyers tend to privilege written divorce — many lawyers draft divorce notices for their male clients. Lawyers also counter clergy-given divorces in some instances.[20]

The theory of democratic professionalism holds that professionals can play a role in extending the reach of state law in the societal arena, and can thus increase popular participation in democratic affairs (Olson and Dzur 2004, 139). However, lawyers can also limit the reach

---

[19] A female client had approached a lawyer after her husband had given her an oral divorce. She wished to contest the divorce. The lawyer convinced her and her family to accept the divorce and to file for a settlement under the Muslim Women's (Protection of Rights on Divorce) Act 1986 because this would give her more rights. The lawyer sent a notice to the husband. In less than two months, the parties and their lawyers arrived at a settlement of 100,000 rupees, and the *mehar* was returned to the woman (interview with Nisar Ahmed Ghatte, lawyer, February 19, 2003, Mumbai).

[20] Lawyers differ in their views on the validity of divorce under Muslim Personal Law. Some lawyers hold that oral divorces are legally invalid. They also opine that *talaq ul bidaat*, unilateral divorce pronounced in one sitting, was valid only if performed under certain conditions (Interview with Nisar Ahmed, February 19, 2003, Mumbai). Other lawyers opine that both oral and written divorces performed under any conditions are valid (interviews with Rashid Ahmad, lawyer, March 4, 2003; Ahmed Razaq, lawyer, March 14, 2003, Mumbai).

of state law in society and promote societal justice. For instance, some lawyers advocate private vigilante justice to speed up the legal process or to collect dues.[21] Lawyers also do not keep abreast of new legal developments. For instance, many lawyers do not advise clients to file cases under the Muslim Women's (Protection of Rights on Divorce) Act 1986, despite the fact that the law can potentially grant more economic rights to Muslim women.[22] These factors halt the positive impact of legal precedents. Lawyers of different religions acquire proficiency in Hindu as well as Islamic statutory and societal laws in order to facilitate societal negotiations.[23]

The Clergy

A wide variety of clergymen adjudicate in Muslim Personal Law. They represent the religious/moral authority of experts with specialized training and experience. Many *qazis*, Muslim clergy, are registered under the Qazi's Act 1880[24] and are allowed to perform religious rituals and marriage ceremonies.[25] Some clergy are not trained in accredited institutions. Most clergy are trained in India,[26] and very few are trained in

---

[21] A Muslim woman had filed for divorce under the Dissolution of Muslim Marriage Act 1939. Her husband fled Mumbai with her dowry worth 900,000 rupees and some jewelry. He refused to accept a summons of the Family Court and did not attend the court date. While the woman might have applied for an ex parte divorce from the Family Court, the lawyer advised the family to "seek other means." The woman's brother managed to trace the husband and "recovered" the dowry and jewelry by hiring local strongmen (interview with RA, July 11, 2003, Mumbai).

[22] The lawyer had filed a case in the Metropolitan Magistrates' court for maintenance under Section 125 CrPC for his client. He claimed that the Muslim Women's Act 1986 was not known to judges, and women did not get rights under this law (interview with A. Rashid, advocate, March 4, 2003, Mumbai).

[23] Interview with Hemang Jariwala, lawyer, March 10, 2003, Mumbai.

[24] The powers of the *qazis* to settle civil disputes were diminished after the colonial state introduced civil courts. Qazi's Act 1880 only allows the *qazis* to perform religious duties such as the solemnization of marriage.

[25] For a discussion of the provisions of the Act, see Ephroz 2003, 67–69.

[26] Interview with Mujib Musawala, social worker, September 5, 2002, Mumbai.

ISLAMIC LAW AND WOMEN'S RIGHTS 275

the seminaries in the Middle East: "There are no standard qualifications required to be a practicing *qazi* in Mumbai. Technically, any adult Muslim male can open 'shop.' Most *qazis* are not knowledgeable about various doctrines of Islamic laws."[27] Furthermore, it is difficult to arrive at an estimate of the number of clergy who officiate on matrimonial matters, especially considering that some clergymen combine their religious and professional/legal activities.[28] Apart from their legal/professional work, they perform religious duties and, as such, solemnize marriages, advise community members on matters of religious laws, and finalize mutual-consent divorces at the community level.

The clergy also maintain official records of registration of marriage, although these records are not standard. In one instance, a married forty-two-year-old man eloped with and married a nineteen-year-old woman, Mahek, and got a *qazi* to certify this marriage. Fifteen days later, the husband left her and sent her a notice of divorce, *talaq*, through the same *qazi*. The woman approached a women's organization, and the activists of the organization accompanied her to the *qazi*'s office so that she could get a copy of the marriage contract (*nikahnama*) and file a case for maintenance under Section 125 CrPC. However, the *qazi*, who had been bribed by the husband, refused to give her a copy of the *nikahnama*. The women's organizations contacted another pro-women *qazi* that they had worked with in previous cases; he prepared another *nikahnama*, and Mahek was able to file a case for maintenance.[29]

Some religious clergy are linked to networks of Islamic schools or organizations.[30] Some clergy who opine on religious matters are

---

[27] "A number of clergy are trained in Iran, Iraq, and Syria" (interview with *qazi* Ahrar Mohammed, May 19, 2003, Mumbai).

[28] For instance, some lawyers are also registered as *qazis* and function as both (interview with Syed Hussein, February 13, 2003, Mumbai).

[29] Interview with FC, February 20, 2010, Mumbai.

[30] The Sunni community organization called Imarat E Shariat, which has been active since 1921 in Bihar and Orissa, manages a network of Sharia courts ("houses of dispute settlement") across states (Mahmood 1995, 108–109). This organization has been visible in Mumbai since the mid-1990s. *Qazis* linked to this network offer legal

attached to a mosque, whereas others are independent and work from their homes or offices or in spaces attached to mosques. Some clergy are associated with religious charities and foundations.[31] The clergy are seen as sources of authority by Muslims, but in some cases, they are approached by Hindus to dissolve interreligious marriages among converts to Islam.[32] For instance, Reshma, a Hindu woman, had converted to Islam and married Abdul. After one year, she wanted a divorce and her husband refused to grant her divorce. Her father went to the local Samajwadi Party member who introduced him to a *qazi*. This *qazi* called Abdul and his family and held joint meetings with both the families and facilitated divorce.[33]

Strongmen

The use of physical violence, coercion, and threats as a strategy used against opponents in the litigation process has been mentioned frequently by various litigants seeking recourse to the formal and/or informal legal system. The underworld,[34] the militant wings of political parties,[35] and offshoots of political parties often get involved in "family

---

advice to litigants. In 1996, women's groups lobbied progressive *qazis* in Mumbai to popularise *khula*, *faskh*, and *talaq e tafwid*. "One of the *qazis* in Imarat E Shariat accepted and gave pro-women judgements. Many women's organisations sent their women clients to Maulana Israr Ahmed. The Maulana charged Rs. 3,000 per divorce. His son took over as *qazi* after his demise, and women litigants accuse him of corruption" (interview with Vandana Nanaware, June 6, 2003, Mumbai).

[31] For instance, the organization Jamaat e Ulema e Maharashtra runs religious charities that also house clergy who offer services of adjudication in matters of Muslim Personal Law (interview with Haroun Musawala, September 5, 2002, Mumbai).

[32] Interview with Haresh Panchal, January 20, 2003, Mumbai.

[33] Interview with *Qazi* Rehman Qureshi. Mumbai. 25 October, 2002, Mumbai.

[34] A Muslim husband refused to accept the *khula* his wife's family sent him. The wife's brother used the underworld contacts to "persuade" him to accept the *khula* (interview with HM, March 14, 2003, Mumbai).

[35] The militant Hindu right-wing party, the Shiv Sena, has a women's wing (Mahila Aghadi), whose members often mete out "informal justice." A Muslim man approached the local Mahila Aghadi office to seek help to divorce his wife whom he claimed was a "Hindu prostitute." The woman, Aminabi insisted hat she was a

ISLAMIC LAW AND WOMEN'S RIGHTS

matters," though their help is sought relatively infrequently by people in such matters.[36] Other private mediators include so-called social workers[37] (also called "fixers") and big-men (wealthy, influential men/community leaders) who use a mix of threat and moral persuasion to negotiate with the opposite party on behalf of litigants. These strongmen are often employed or appealed to by the families to coerce husbands to give a divorce,[38] to recover *stridhan*, and to collect maintenance.[39] They are also employed to recover *stridhan*: "I had to go to my natal family to deliver the second child, a daughter, when my husband sent me a notice of divorce. He had custody of the first child.... They also had my *stridhan*. He refused to return it unless I accepted the divorce.... We waited another year, attempting to negotiate, but he got married again. Finally, my father and some cousins went to his house to pick up the dowry and related items. They refused to give us anything. My father then went to the local strongmen and asked them to help – we are not that sort of people, but what does one do in such a situation – how many mouths can my father feed? The local *dada* was helpful: we recovered my *mehar*, *stridhan*, and arranged for maintenance."[40]

The strongmen are also used to evict women out of residential premises during the dispute. For example, a Muslim man divorced his wife

---

Muslim. The Aghadi women dragged Aminabi out of her house to be presented at the local meeting of the Mahila Aghadi of her residential area, and they compelled her to accept divorce (interview with AK, June 6, 2003, Mumbai).

[36] Interview with NS, January 5, 2003, Mumbai.

[37] Men residing in the same locality as the litigants who help female and male litigants access services and resources; they are able to help due to their networks with local political party leaders, police, local businessmen, unions leaders, and, at times, criminal elements.

[38] "My wife's brothers had some connection with the local *Bhai-log* mafia. She went home to her natal family and refused to come back. Her brothers sent goons to ask me to sign on the *talaqnama*, the deed of divorce" (interview with SK, February 15, 2003, Mumbai).

[39] "I have a court order – he is supposed to give me maintenance every month – but he did not come to court even once. I could file another case, but what is the point? Finally, we had to settle the matter informally" (interview with PS, March 13, 2003, Mumbai).

[40] Interview with PS, September 13, 2002, Mumbai.

after eight years of marriage – she refused to accept his divorce and continued to stay in the one-room house where they were the tenants of the Municipal Corporation of Greater Mumbai. The husband tried to evict her from the premises, and sought the help of the local goons to persuade her to accept the divorce and to throw her out of the house with their three children. The woman filed many complaints against him at the local police station.[41] The intimidation of litigants and their families,[42] their interception on their way to the police station or to an organization,[43] making threatening phone calls, hurling abuses within the neighborhood and work spaces,[44] and beating male family members[45] are all common tactics used by musclemen mediators.

Organized Legal Bodies, Doorstep Courts, and Processes of Adjudication

This subsection discusses the diverse laws and processes of adjudication in organized societal legal bodies, and it highlights divergent ideological positions regarding the content of the law.

The Administration of Muslim Personal Law in the Dar ul Qaza

Historically, the Deobandis[46] has sought to mobilize and unify the Muslim community using the symbol of Muslim Personal Law as an

---

[41] Interview with Ishrat Noor Ahmed, June 13, 2003, Mumbai. See records of complaints filed as noncognizable offenses against the husband: 1544/89, dt. 23/6/89, 2451/90, on 16/12/1990; 2514/90 dt. 18/12/90; 758 dt. 14/4/91; 7327 dt. 13/06/91; 33/91 dt. 7/6/91; 1072/92 on 25/04/92; 1332/92 on 17/05/92.

[42] Interview with PS, March 13, 2003, Mumbai.

[43] Interview with HK, January 10, 2003, Mumbai.

[44] Interview with JK, 12 April 2003, Mumbai.

[45] Interview with Vandana Nanaware, social worker, Special Cell for Women and Children, June 7, 2003, Mumbai.

[46] The Ulemas of the Deoband doctrinal orientation have established *Dar ul Qazas*, or courts of justice. The sectarian ulemas are associated with a madrasa founded in the town of Deoband in the United Provinces (now Uttar Pradesh) in 1867. The

ISLAMIC LAW AND WOMEN'S RIGHTS

element binding the religio-legal Muslim community (Metcalf 1982). The Deobandis have also been active in influencing the All India Muslim Personal Law Board. Since the late 1990s, the Deobandis have established *Dar ul Qazas* (place of justice), or community courts, as a mechanism to converge diverse interpretations of Sharia.

One of the *Dar ul Qazas* in Mumbai is located in a predominantly Muslim area in central Mumbai, and is housed in a building leased by the Jamiat Ulema E Maharashtra. The office is staffed by a *Mufti*, juriconsultant, and a secretary who maintains records. In the two years since its establishment, thirty-five of sixty cases of divorce have been "resolved" by the *Dar ul Qaza*. The procedure adopted by the body is standardized, informal, consensual, and inexpensive.[47] The body seeks to standardize the divorce procedure. A party seeking their help informs them of the problem and specifies the kind of help required, then signs the consent form as the first step. The *Dar ul Qaza* officials then send a registered letter to the second party asking them to meet the officials on a specified date. This notice is sent four times to accommodate counterresponses. The woman receives an ex parte judgment if the husband fails to come to the *Dar ul Qaza* despite all efforts. Parties who come to the *Dar ul Qaza* sign a consent form verifying that they have approached the *Dar ul Qaza* of their own accord, and have agreed to abide by its decisions. The consent form is signed by the parties before two witnesses. The parties

---

Deobandis emphasize the study of law and the Hadith (the traditions attributed to the Prophet Muhammad) and self-consciously seek to reform variants of folk Islam, or popular Muslim practices. They distinguish their teachings not only from their Shia rivals but also from the teachings of the Barelvis who affirm the authority of not just the Prophet, but also of the saints and the holy people, as religious guides and mediators between Gods and human beings. The Ahl i Hadith insist on the Quran and the Hadith as the only sources of religious guidance, and deny the classical schools of law as well as the practices that are not backed by the scriptures (Zaman 2002, 11). However, many madrasas claim to represent Deobandi Islam, though they are not formally affiliated with the parent body.

[47] Parties are charged 250 rupees for their case. However, this seems to be a variable practice, as some parties are charged 500 rupees to register a case in other *Dar ul Qaza* in Mumbai (interview with Wahabuddin Khan, September 7, 2002, Mumbai).

also demonstrate their faith in *Dar ul Qaza* by agreeing not to approach the state courts in appeal. The proceedings at *Dar ul Qaza* are discontinued in cases where parties approach the state court despite signing the agreement form.

The cases in this organization range from reconciliation[48] to divorce,[49] *khula*, and *faskh*.[50] The *Dar ul Qaza* officials report that the *khula* is not often encouraged, as women tend to lose their rights to *mehar*. According to them, *khula* may be granted to a woman if she is not at fault and if the husband accepts the divorce. If the woman is not at fault, she receives her *mehar* but has to forego maintenance during *iddat*. If she is at fault, then she has to forego *mehar*, maintenance during *iddat*, and her *stridhan*. In one case, a woman and her young son, aged two-and-a-half years, were deserted by the husband. The woman had come seeking *khula*. The husband refused to grant her a divorce and declined the paternity of the child. The *Dar ul Qaza* officials held that there is a presumption of legitimacy on the child born in marriage, and that should be exercised in favor of the woman unless the husband proves otherwise. The husband finally agreed to give a divorce and returned the *mehar*, *stridhan*, and maintenance during *iddat*, while the woman signed away her right to file for additional maintenance. "We try to convert the *khula* cases into *talaq* cases, as women receive more economic rights."[51]

[48] In one case, a man had divorced his wife Nagma, and she had approached the *Dar ul Qaza* for assistance in the recovery of *mehar*. She complained of severe mental and physical violence. The couple had three children who were in the custody of their father. The *mufti* stated that he spoke to the children, who wished for reconciliation. After several meetings, the man revoked the divorce (there was some confusion here – the mufti claimed that the man had just threatened to divorce, Nagma claimed that the husband had given the divorce). The mufti said that they were aware of the risks involved and that they periodically followed up on the case after the reconciliation (interview with Mufti Wahabuddin Khan, September 7, 2002, Mumbai).
[49] The body validates both written and oral divorce, and recognizes three types of divorce as Islamic: *talaq ahsan*, *talaq hasan*, and *talaq ul bidaat*.
[50] *Faskh* is judicial dissolution of marriage for causes stipulated in Islamic law (Pearl 1987).
[51] Interview with Fahimuddin Khan, the *Dar ul Qaza*, Jamiat e Ulema e Hind office, south-central Mumbai, September 7, 2002, Mumbai.

The organization also grants *faskh*, judicial dissolution of marriage for causes stipulated in Islamic law (Pearl 1987). However, the *mufti* associated with this particular *Dar ul Qaza* opined that it is essential that the woman prove her case in order to obtain *faskh*. The woman can claim *faskh* on many grounds: the inability of the husband to maintain her; cruelty and harassment by the husband or in-laws; dowry demands; sexually transmitted disease, especially HIV; and alcoholism on the part of the husband. Given the uncertainty attached to oral divorce, women often approach *Dar ul Qaza* in order to obtain proof of divorce.[52] At *Dar ul Qaza*, women litigants are not granted permanent alimony beyond the period of *iddat*. As the *Dar ul Qaza* officials can only persuade male litigants by their moral authority, they have limited success in recovering women's *stridhan* in cases of *khula* and *faskh*.[53]

Residential Committees

Some areas in Mumbai have a residential committee usually comprising of socially prominent male residents who have connections with political parties, the police, and the Municipal Corporator of the area. The committee takes up civic issues related to the efficacy of public utility services in their area, and it celebrates public festivals. Some residential committees are more cohesive, whereas others are more disorganized and function in an ad hoc manner. Many residential committees take up issues concerning Muslim Personal Law, and evolve internal

---

[52] A man had given an oral divorce to his wife four years earlier. The woman did not have proof of divorce, and she wished to remarry. She had come to the *Dar ul Qaza* to obtain the proof of divorce because she feared that her second marriage would be considered illegal. The *Dar ul Qaza* granted her the judicial divorce *faskh* after the first husband refused to respond (interview with Fahimuddin Khan, September 7, 2002, Mumbai).

[53] "Husbands are reluctant to give away the *stridhan* at the time of divorce, especially when husbands do not accept women-initiated divorce. We try to go as a delegation of religious persons and persuade them to respect our decisions on the basis of our moral and religious authority" (interview with Fahimuddin Khan, September 7, 2002, Mumbai).

mechanisms for reform. For instance, a residential committee banned the practice of triple *talaq* after many deliberations. "We sought the opinions from many sources – we called the clergy, religious leaders, lawyers ... and heard their views ... and we had a meeting and decided that we do not wish to go against the religion, but this form of divorce is un-Islamic."[54]

At times, residential committees can also extend the outreach of state law by monitoring cases in their areas and helping families gain access to legal aid and courts.[55] For example,[56] a husband beat his wife regularly and was abusive to neighbors who wished to protect her. The residential committee referred her to the court for maintenance. The woman in question got a favorable judgment and had been receiving maintenance for two years at the time of the interview. She approaches the residential committee when her ex-husband fails to pay maintenance for several months. The man is reprimanded and asked to pay the arrears; he abides by the residential committee because he has a criminal record and can be picked up by the local police whenever there is communal disturbance in the city. The "good word" of the residential *chawl* committee saves him from police harassment.

---

[54] Interview with members of the Melibai Chawl Committee, Andheri East, February 2, 2003, Mumbai.

[55] The residential committee interviewed here is from Andheri East, Mumbai. Most residential members are Sunni Muslims hailing from Gujarat. About forty Muslim families live in the neighborhood *chawls* and work as small traders. The committee members meet every Friday. In one case, the residential committee members ensured that the man provide maintenance to his ex-wife and monitored the payment granted to her under state law. "Men in our *chawl* are persuaded against quick divorces without sufficient cause.... Our job is to act as mediators in cases wherein parties are thinking about divorce.... Sometimes we talk to the couple directly – at other times, we talk to their families.... We discourage hasty action in such matters" (interview with Bilas Qazi, member, Residential Committee, March 17, 2003, Mumbai).

[56] This interview is based on the meeting with residential committee members of a *chawl* in Bandra West (interview with Hussain N., member, Residential Committee, March 17, 2003, Mumbai).

In other cases, residential committees can reinforce conservative interpretations of texts and thus limit women's legal options and curtail their rights. Women litigants can avoid their intervention more easily in cases where the committees are not very powerful or when their natal families can shield them against the dictates of the committees.[57] In some cases, they also accept help from women's organizations in the negotiations with residential committee members: "In a case, the members of the neighbourhood had come to give evidence against the woman who had approached us. The neighbours who were members of a residential *jamaat* were bribed and bought by the husband as witnesses against the wife, whom he accused of infidelity. The residential committees favoured the husband. We confronted the residential committee members – where were you when he was beating her 'til she fainted in the street of your *chawl?*"[58]

Followers of Islamic religious movements also influence the legal sphere. Activists of movements such as the Tabligh i Jamaat,[59] which work in specific residential areas of Mumbai, often intervene in cases of domestic disputes. In some cases, they work through residential or other local committees to intervene and influence the sphere of the family: "The Tabligh i Jamaat networks through familial/religious work and has control over madrassas in some areas. Their influences very strong, and it is difficult for feminist organizations to make inroads into areas

---

[57] "The members of the residential committee in our area had come to ask if they could be of help to me when my husband divorced me, but I was determined to go to the court and did not see how they might help.... I prefer to be distant with these 'social workers' who force their help on people" (interview with PS, February 13, 2003, Mumbai).

[58] Interview with Naseem Sheikh, member, Awaz e Niswan, January 17, 2003, Mumbai.

[59] The Tabligh i Jamaat is a religious movement founded by Maulana Muhamed Ilyas (1885–1944), a Sufi *aalim* who preached conformity to Sharia and advocated a spirit of tolerance and compromise. His teachings sought to revive the puritanical character of Islam, not through direct criticism of folk Islam and customs, but through the inculcation of religious obligations onto people. The movement is popular in northern and western India (Farouqi 1981).

controlled by the Tabligh i Jamaat. The Tabligh i Jamaat coerces women who seek help from outside sources."[60] The activists of this movement are able to influence the parties when both families have joined the movement.[61]

Civil Society and the Administration of Muslim Personal Law

There is a broad spectrum of civil society organizations[62] involved in campaigning on the issue of reforms in religious family laws, but I have limited my investigation to include organizations that privilege everyday intervention through their direct work with Muslim litigants, and that support campaigns concerning this issue.

An organization called the Public Complaint Centre was established as an interface between the Congress Party and the local populace in the Muslim-dominated part of central Mumbai, but it later switched its focus to work on the issue of personal law: "The founders realised that they were overwhelmed by Hindu and Muslim women coming to them for help regarding matrimonial matters, and they decided to shift the focus of their work to dealing with issues concerning personal laws."[63] The organization has formed a core committee comprised of local Muslim leaders, social workers, and Hindu and Muslim lawyers. They are also assisted by a few clergymen. The committee members represent different sects that make up the populace in that area. There are no women members on the core committee. The committee meets late at night, as most of the core members are volunteers. The Public Complaint Centre works on cases[64] of Hindu and Muslim women: "We ask the clients as to

---

[60] Interview with Sophia Khan, activist, July 4, 2003, Mumbai.
[61] Interview with HQ, February 4, 2003, Mumbai.
[62] These include religious organizations and charitable trusts, social welfare organizations, crisis centers, feminist organizations, women's shelters, women's wings of political parties, NGOs, and so forth.
[63] Interview with Iqbal Maniar, June 15, 2003, Mumbai.
[64] Ibid.

which law they would prefer – if they are Deobandis, we go by their laws; if they are Ahl i Hadith, we ask their clergy's opinion; and we also keep in mind the state law and our lawyers help us with Hindu law." The organization holds campaigns against the performance of *muta* marriages[65] and organizes public discussions around issues such as the validation of oral divorce. The committee also publicly confronts clerics on individual cases.[66] In one case, a husband had divorced his wife by issuing a *fatwa*. The core committee held the divorce as invalid because it was carried out in the absence of the wife. The committee reprimanded the cleric and the husband, and declared the divorce invalid. The organization has links with liberal clerics who would issue pro-women *fatwas* in favor of some women litigants.

Historically as well as presently, autonomous women's groups have been vocal, active, and dynamic actors who have consistently engaged with the issue of reforms in personal law.[67]

The broad-based Indian Women's Movement has consistently taken up the issue of law reforms in Muslim Personal Law and built alliances with Muslim feminists and Muslim women's organizations. For instance, in June 2003, secular and Muslim women's organizations came together in a three-day seminar to discuss Muslim women's legal rights. They also discussed their position vis-à-vis the All India Muslim Personal

---

[65] *Muta* marriages are temporary marriages undertaken by parties under Shia laws. The period of cohabitation under *muta* marriage is fixed, along with the amount of dower at the time of solemnization of marriage. A *muta* marriage does not create the right of inheritance between the husband and the wife, but the children are considered legitimate and could inherit from both parents (Fyzee 1965; Mulla 1955). For instance, the group had carried out a campaign against *muta* marriages performed by some local clergy for wealthy Arab men who visited Mumbai for business purposes.

[66] Interview with NS, January 5, 2003, Mumbai.

[67] I have focused on the work of women's organizations rather than on more generic NGOs who work on a broad range of issues concerning the rights of vulnerable members of society and who may take up issues of reform in personal laws. However, NGOs have often been important supporters of initiatives taken up by women's organizations.

Law Board (AIMPLB). At the end of the workshop, secular and Muslim women's organizations prepared a memorandum to present to the AIMPLB, alerting them to feminist opinions from within the community and from outside.[68]

Women's rights activists across religions use the human rights discourse in order to campaign for more rights for Muslim women under religious law. Awaz e Niswan is a feminist organization that began as a consciousness-raising group comprised of Muslim women residing in central Mumbai who came together to discuss their legal experiences and organize around the Shah Bano case. Since then, Awaz e Niswan has organized street protests,[69] hosted seminars, participated in the right to livelihood campaigns, organized relief and rehabilitation work in communal riots,[70] and organized public meetings on issues of reforms in personal law,[71] minority rights and communalism. Along with other secular and Muslim feminist group, the organization has been actively involved in taking up issues of sexual violence against minority women during communal violence, and worked actively in rehabilitation and relief work after communal violence in Mumbai in 1992–93 and in Gujarat in 2002. As Hasina Khan stated:

At first, the conservative elements in our community were against us, but at [the] time of Bombay riots in 1992–1993 and then during the

---

[68] Interview with Hasina Khan, Awaz e Niswan, July 14, 2003, Mumbai.

[69] It has spearheaded public protests and campaigns against dowry. In 1991, the group organized a public demonstration against a dowry death; Muslim women participated in the protest in large numbers. More recently, in April 2005, the organization also initiated a public protest against the religious clergy's injunctions to Muslim women, asking them to wear a veil.

[70] The organization coordinated a sustained rehabilitation process after the violence against Muslims in Gujarat in 2002, which was orchestrated by the Hindu right with the complicity of the state of Gujarat (interview with Hasina Khan, January 10, 2003, Mumbai).

[71] Awaz e Niswan has been an active participant in the process of debating reforms in personal law initiated by the Indian Women's Movement in 1996. The organization has also kept the process alive since then (interview with Hasina Khan, January 10, 2003, Mumbai).

violence in Gujarat, they realised our efforts and ability to generate resources for rehabilitation ... we also campaigned for sexual violence against Muslim women...all these efforts improved our credibility with them and we find the difference. We still disagree on some issues, but they are more willing to listen to us and do not dismiss our views as opinions of these *baal kati auratein*, modernist Westernised women. Since mid-1990s, we have been able to engage them in a consistent dialog on issues related to women's rights in law.[72]

At the grassroots level, the organization runs a counseling center and literacy classes, and it organizes computer training for young women. It has also established the first feminist shelter for women in Mumbai. The organization adjudicates in matters concerning Hindu and Muslim personal law, and is one of the few organizations within the community that advocates the recognition of same-sex marriage and the rights of bisexual, homosexual, and transgender persons. The organization reaches out to Muslim lesbian and bisexual women. As Hasina Khan shared:

> In one case, a Muslim woman whose husband was working as a laborer in Saudi Arabia came to us for help. She had fallen in love with another woman and wished to divorce her husband. We had begun to work on this case, and the husband came back from the Gulf. The woman refused to have sex with him and faced severe sexual violence for some time. But finally she provoked him into giving her unilateral divorce. After which both women came to us for help and support, and now they have slowly started to rebuild their lives. We believe in legalising same-sex marriage, and face criticism from community organizations and the clergy who believe that we are un-Islamic.[73]

Awaz e Niswan has also been instrumental in initiating the Muslim Women's Rights Network, a network of more than twenty-five women's organizations, NGOs, and women's wings of political parties; the

---

[72] Ibid.
[73] Interview with Hasina Khan, January 10, 2003, Mumbai.

network works exclusively on reforming Muslim Personal Law. The network aims to engage with the community while remaining critical of community patriarchy. The counseling at Awaz e Niswan takes the form of prelitigation work through mediation, arbitration, and negotiations, as well as adjudication.

The Women's Research and Action Group, another feminist organization, was established by a group of feminist activists in the aftermath of the Babri Masjid demolition in 1993.[74] Since then, the group works on issues related to Muslim women's livelihood, education, law reform, communalism and communal violence, human rights, and police atrocities against minorities. The group has close ties with the international Women Living under Muslim Laws Network, and holds dialog with activists from the Middle East, Africa, and South and Southeast Asia; they have been involved in lobbying for international laws to prevent crimes against humanity. They have conducted a nationwide survey of Muslim women to know their views on issues of law reform, and found that 47 percent of women wanted reform within the religious framework. Since then, the group has advocated this position and has held local-, regional-, and national-level meetings of a federation of secular and religious women's groups, *hakk e niswan* (organizing for women's rights), the clergy, scholars of Islamic law, and lawyers and legal scholars. It also organizes workshops and seminars on legal education and provides legal aid.

Organizations like Awaz e Niswan and WRAG also exchange information and build alliances with international feminist organizations:

> We bring in the international dimension in all our discussions with the clergy and to the AIMPLB. It is a fact that Muslim women living in Muslim-majority countries have more rights. For instance, Syrian women get compensation if they are arbitrarily divorced, and Tunisia has banned polygyny. However, the clergy are not open to reform experiences which are pro-women. Muslim women in Pakistan enjoy more legal protection than Indian Muslim women. While the

---

[74] Interview with Noorjehan Niaz, August 4, 2008, Mumbai.

religious factions turn a deaf ear to positive international experiences, women at the grassroots level always ask why these reforms cannot be replicated in our context.[75]

Both of these organizations negotiate for Muslim women's rights vis-à-vis the state and the community:

We have always been critical of the regressive and patriarchal sections of Muslims. We have had many public demonstrations against clergy who issue *fatwa*s, against religious organizations, and they used to view us with suspicion ... but our work during communal violence during [the] riots in 1992–93 and especially the Gujarat genocide has changed their perceptions about us. They saw our ability to mobilise, take up the issue of sexual violence against Muslim women, help with relief and rehabilitation. I now sense a change in their perceptions, a glimmer of recognition, that we can be productive as allies, and we get a more positive response, *jyada sammaan milta hai*.[76]

As discussed earlier, the linkages between women's groups and feminist lawyers and legal resource centers ensure that women get some amount of protection against the threat or eventualities of dispossession from their marital property. For instance, Mumtazbi, a Muslim woman residing in a slum, was married to Altaf, who had converted to Islam; they were married for twelve years during which they bought a *kholi*, a room in a slum that was registered in his name. He then reconverted to Christianity and for Mumtaz, a deeply religious woman, his act of conversion meant that the marriage was "automatically dissolved" and divorce was "understood" between the two parties. He started living separately and she heard a rumor that he was planning to sell the *kholi*, and indeed, he had taken to showing it to prospective buyers in her absence. Perturbed that she would lose her home, she approached a women's group. The social worker advised Mumtaz "not to reveal the

---

[75] Interview with Hasina Khan, January 22, 2003. Mumbai.
[76] Interview with Noorjehan Niaz, August 4, 2008. Mumbai.

'truth' about 'the divorce that was understood' to anyone." She immediately contacted a feminist lawyer who filed a case under Section 7(d) of the Family Courts Act 1984 and obtained a stay against the sale of the property. This provided her with immediate relief, and her husband dropped his plans to sell the "matrimonial home."[77]

The Doorstep Courts

Several informal (unregistered) organizations work on domestic violence and matrimonial issues among women, especially Muslim women. One such initiative is an offshoot of peace committees (the Mohalla Committees) established by the Mumbai Police in the aftermath of communal riots in Mumbai. These committees aim to bring together the police and the public to create communal harmony and to foster trust within the Muslim minority in riot-affected areas. A lawyer, Yasmin Sheikh, was active in one such police station located in central Mumbai, a predominantly Muslim locality. During that time, she realized that many cases required intervention in matters of Hindu and Muslim personal law. As a result, she asked for and got space to function several days per week from one of the disused police beat offices (*chowkis*).[78] She received 688 complaints in three years, and reported that about 40 percent of these cases have been "settled" in the sense that parties have arrived at accepted, mutually satisfactory solutions based on state-law provisions.

About thirty Muslim women's groups associated with the Women's Research and Action Group work on issues of Hindu and Muslim law and domestic violence. Noorjehan Niaz of Women's Action and Research group stated:

[77] Interview with Mumtazbi, February 15, 2003, Mumbai. Interview with Vandana Nanaware, June 16, 2003, Mumbai.

[78] "The cases range from contestations over oral divorce, the abuse of unilateral divorce, the provision of shelter to divorced women and their children, domestic violence, and the retrieval of *stridhan*. We intervene in cases of Hindu and Muslim Personal Law" (interview with Yasmin Sheikh, January 22, 2003, Mumbai).

Many NGOs and women's groups have nurtured slum women's activism, and there are many loose networks working on legal issues in the slums. These groups [associated with WRAG] emerged as groups of divorced Muslim women and found that many other Hindu and Muslim women came to them for help. We then organized workshops to give training in Hindu and Muslim Personal Law and on the Domestic Violence Act 2005, and these women are very effective in their everyday legal interventions. They routinely coordinate with the police, *mohalla* committees (communal harmony committees), local youth groups, the police, and *ekta* committees (groups who work for community unity in face of communalism) in individual cases, and also take up public issues – accessibility of water, electricity in slums, and communal harmony. In fact, some women have been approached by political parties to contest local elections.[79]

At the grassroots level, the organization has formed thirty women's groups of slum women, the doorstep groups who specialize in Muslim law.

One of these groups, the Hamraz Group, comprised of former litigants working in a slum in Mumbai, has worked with litigant Muslim women over the past ten years. The female members of the committee assist women in matters of domestic violence, arbitrate in cases of marital disputes and custody matters, and assist with legal aid. They challenge the clergy in their orthodox interpretation of Islam and help women obtain *faskh* or *khula* through *qazis* who are known to hand down women-friendly judgments.[80] The committee also participates in various campaigns to work toward legal reforms through promoting intracommunity debates.[81] These groups draw on their own ideas of

---

[79] Interview with Noorjehan Niaz, August 4, 2008, Mumbai.
[80] "We prefer societal solutions in cases where both the parties are very poor.... People in our locality are very poor, most of them squat on some land.... Most of the time, neither of [the] parties has money or property. What use is a court to them? But if women need financial help and if the husband's family is capable of giving money, we ensure that financial assistance is given – such cases can go to court" (interview with Khatoom Gafoor Sheikh, April 22, 2003, Mumbai).
[81] They argue that *mehar* should be made incremental in recognition of women's labor in the family, and should be handed over to the woman at the time of marriage.

law. For instance, another community-based informal women's group, Samjhauta Mahila Mandal, believes that divorce should be given only in the presence of two credible witnesses from either side. They have also asked that divorced Muslim women should get *mehar*, maintenance during *iddat*, a lump-sum maintenance, and provision for shelter. They also argue for the abolition of the tradition in which the husband has a right to forego *mehar*. They argue for more maintenance for divorced women.[82]

Dispute Resolution among Organized Sects: The Khojas

The Khojas, practicing Ismailism[83] in Gujarat and in Bombay, until the 1840s, were a self-governing community that followed a version of Islam that drew from heterodox religious and cultural sources.[84] For instance, during the latter half of the nineteenth century, Khojas drew from Shia

---

They also argue for the abolition of the tradition in which the husband has a right to forego *mehar*. Finally, they argue for more maintenance (interview, Khatoom Gafoor Sheikh, member, Hamraz Committee, April 22, 2003, Mumbai).

[82] Interview with Noorjehan Niaz, facilitator of the Samjhauta Mahila Mandal, April 22, 2003, Mumbai.

[83] Ismailism is a form of Shia Islam that emerged due to a schism among Shias in 765 CE over the authority of the seventh Imam, Ismail. The followers of the seventh Imam were called the Ismailis, and they developed their own religious thought and established political power through the foundation of the Fatimide dynasty in Egypt (910–1171 CE). Their power waned in 1094 CE when the followers of Nizar, the eldest son of Imam al Mustanasir, opposed his younger brother, Mustal. The Nizaris took refuge in Persia, and later in India. The Nizari chief, called the Aga Khan, sent missionaries (*dais*) to India from the thirteenth to the sixteenth century. The Indian Nizaris who were converted by these envoys came to be called Khojas, or *Satpanthis*, and fled to India when the Aga Khan was defeated by the Shah of Iran (Daftary 1990; Ivanow 1948; Mallison 1989; Nanji 1978; Shodhan 2001).

[84] Scholars of Khoja history read the heterodoxy in different ways. For instance, Ivanow and classical Islamic scholars see the Khoja religiosity as a sign of incomplete conversion (Devji 1987), whereas other scholars view religious heterogeneity as the syncretism of Hinduism and Islam (Engineer 1989). However, other scholars suggest Khoja practices as localized versions of Islam wherein principles of Islam are decontextualized from Arab culture and grafted onto local Indian culture (Mallison 1989; Shodhan 2001).

Islam, but their practices were Sunni.[85] Their religious practices were also drawn from Hinduism[86] and Islam, and they preferred a distinct identity as Khojas.[87] The community self-identified itself as Muslim, but this "Muslimness" was fluid and not limited merely to an identity based on doctrinal essences of Islam (Shodhan 2001). This heterodoxy was challenged by their religious leader, the Aga Khan, in Mumbai. The Aga Khan attempted to control the property of the community, and advocated "a patently 'Shia' identity" over the more heterodox "Khoja" identity (Masselos 1973, 106). The Aga Khan's religious authority was legally challenged by a section of the Khoja mercantile elites who wished to retain their unique identity as Khojas. However, the colonial court ruled in favor of the Aga Khan and classified the Khojas as Shia Muslims,[88]

---

[85] For instance, until the 1860s, the mosques in the Khoja burial grounds were presided over by a Sunni *mulla*, and a portion of the funeral ceremony was as per Shia rites. Prayers and worship were also along Shia lines (Masselos 1973, 102–103). Their marriage ceremonies were performed by Sunni *qazis* (Shodhan 2001).

[86] They worshipped a *pir* (miracle man) and use *Dashavatar*, the story of the ten reincarnations of the Hindu God Vishnu, as one of their texts. They differed from the Hindu story in the sense that they held that the last reincarnation of Vishnu was Ali (Mallison 1989; Masselos 1973).

[87] "Some say we are Soones, some, Sheas. Our religion is a separate religion" (Evidence of Habib Ibrahim, KC, T, and C, June 24, 1847, cited in Masselos 1973, 104).

[88] In effect, the push to adopt a sectarian identity became pronounced after the arrival of the first Aga Khan in Mumbai. The Aga Khan was trying to raise resources to challenge the Shah of Iran even at that time, and he had joined forces with the British to that end. The Aga Khan began to establish more control over the internal affairs of the Khojas and demanded increased financial compensation. He also advocated a Shia identity (Masselos 1973, 106) and encountered opposition from Khoja elites, which lead to violence and legal conflicts. In 1861, a group of reformist Khoja mercantile elite tried to break away from the Aga Khan and claimed partition of the property held collectively by the Khoja *jamaat*. They argued that they, as Khojas, were a unique community that drew from both Shia and Sunni traditions as well as local religio-cultural practices while retaining a unique identity. The case, widely known as the Aga Khan case, was heard in 1866. The judge opined in favor of the Aga Khan: He defined the Khojas as a Shia sect and validated the leadership of the Aga Khan. The opponents henceforth came to be known as Sunni Khojas, and the Khojas thus split into two sects. Whereas Masselos attributes the growth of sectarian identity to societal actors, Shodhan argues that the involvement of the colonial state in the adjudication process superimposed the sectarian identity over Khoja identity.

and fixed hitherto loose boundaries of "Khoja Muslimness" into predetermined criteria of an essentialized Islamic sectarian identity (Shodhan 2001).

The Ithna Ashri Khoja community interviewed for this project was formed following a schism among Ismaili Shias in Mumbai in the 1860s. Since the 1860s, a group of prominent Khoja members began to meet in a space other than the Khoja *jamatkhana* (prayer hall, council office, and community hall) to offer Friday prayers. This new group identified themselves as Ithna Ashariyas, a sect of Shias. Opposition to Aga Khan's supremacy was the main agenda of the dissident group. This group claimed allegiance to essentialized religious identity – that of Shias – and claimed an undiluted Shia past free from influence of the Aga Khan. This group argued that it believed there were twelve Imams rather than the seven adopted by the Imami Ismailis. They sought to reorganize themselves in a manner that would not centralize the hold of religious figures into the Khoja sphere. Devjibhai Jamal, a member of the sect, went to Karabala and invited first Mulla Qadir Husain, a clergyman from Madras, and later Ayatollah Abdul Qasim Najifi to Mumbai to teach them the teachings of Shia Islam.[89]

As a result, since 1876, several individual and families were excommunicated from the Ismaili *jamaat*.[90] This "outcasted" group claimed that the Khojas were Shias *before* the Aga Khan and that they were "Ithna Ashari Khojas."[91] Their numbers grew after the excommunication

---

[89] See the letter by Hajee Abdallhbhoy Haji Mowjee to the Commissioner of Police, Bombay, November 10, 1900.

[90] See the letter by Hajee Abdallhbhoy Haji Mowjee to the Commissioner of Police, Bombay, November 10, 1900.

[91] In 1876–77, several persons and families were excommunicated from the Khoja Shia *jamaat* for following Athna Asari doctrines. The domain of intrasect politics and commerce were two arenas wherein the battle of identity was fought in the name of religion. They held that Khojas were Shias before the Aga Khan, and conducted their organizing and religious dissent secretively for ten years (see Janab Haji Roshan Alibhai Haji Dawood Haji Naser, a centenary presentation of Khoja Ishashari *jamaat*, AH 1319–1419). Two other persons were cast out in 1878–79, and by 1884,

ISLAMIC LAW AND WOMEN'S RIGHTS 295

of more members in 1899, and there were many instances of violence between the Ismailis and the breakaway group. The new group also continued to recruit and was open to Julehas, Moghuls, and other Muslims as members of their sect. Many Ithna Ashari dissenters were leading merchants and professionals of the sect, and the group, through its trading networks, prospered in the early half of the nineteenth century and established a social welfare system for their group. Many of the group members migrated to Pakistan upon partition because they had business interests in Karachi. Some of those left behind vast estates for the benefit of the community.

Sociopolitical Changes in the Community between the 1950s and the 1990s

The fragmented Ithna Ashari Khoja community has reconstituted itself through political alliances, provisions of welfare activities, and the administration of family laws. The Ithna Ashariyas had been vocal supporters of the Muslim League before partition, but some of its members have turned to the Congress Party since the 1960s. Their business interests, especially in shipping and real estate, have led them to cultivate politicians of a different hue.[92] Wealthy industrialists and traders[93] make

---

twenty-five such families joined the dissenters. In 1899, their numbers grew, and they came out openly against the Aga Khan, and sought to build a mosque and obtain land for their separate graveyard. See the letter by Hajee Abdallhbhoy Haji Mowjee to the Commissioner of Police, Bombay, November 10, 1900. The breakaway group did not seek any changes in the family law.

[92] For instance, many local businessmen also cultivate local Shiv Sena leaders and invite the Bhartiya Janata Party leaders to their centenary celebrations. However, most of the community members lean toward the Congress Party. The report of their centenary celebration, "A Centenary presentation of the Khoja Shia Isnaashari Jamaat" includes messages from then Prime Minister A. B. Vajpayee; leader of the Shiv Sena, Manohar Joshi; Governor of Maharashtra, P. C. Alexander; and many Congress leaders, including Murli Deora, 1998.

[93] Many of these own shipping and steel industries, whereas some are in real estate (interview with HM, January 23, 2003, Mumbai).

up the elite class within the sect, professionals and merchants fall into the middle level, and small shop owners and hawkers occupy the lower level. The *khum* (one-fifth of the savings of each individual) is given away to the *jamaat* by the wealthy members and is offered to poorer members as interest-free loans, which helps them initiate entrepreneurial activities. The Ithna Ashari Khojas run a number of welfare trusts for their community members[94] and exercise considerable hold over them. The community has sought to retain its unique identity, but the social sphere within the Ithana Asharis has changed since the late 1980s. The communal riots of Mumbai in 1992–93 and the religious violence in Gujarat in 2002 have also had an impact on the community,[95] and have led to greater Islamization of the sect.[96]

Family Laws among the Ithana Ashari Khojas
Although the Ithna Ashari Khojas gave preference to sectarian identities in the initial phases of group formation, they adhere to customary laws in regulating marriage and divorce. The sect members codified the sect laws and procedures in 1955 and amended some provisions in 1959. There have not been major changes in the family laws of the Khojas since the 1960s. The Khoja *jamaat* (assembly of adult male members)[97]

---

[94] The *jamaat* runs a number of charitable trusts as well. The Habib Trust and the Dawoodbhai Fazalbhoy Muslim Education Trust were established in 1923 to encourage education among sect members. The trusts also started giving scholarship to sect students for education in India and elsewhere. They started the Habib Hospital to give free medical aid to the poorer members of the sect and offered interest-free loans to sect members of weaker financial positions (Engineer 1989, 253–254).

[95] Many poorer members of the community were left without employment and residence during riots; they moved to a largely Muslim ghetto on the outskirts of Mumbai. The *jamaat* raised funds to provide housing for 300 such families.

[96] For instance, they have begun to adopt lifestyles and customs of the Syeds, the Shias from Uttar Pradesh. Hindi has begun to replace Gujarati as the language of communication. They have sought to make changes in family law along the lines befitting the wider Shia laws. For instance, social limitations on polygyny have begun to be eased on "Islamic grounds" (interview with HB, March 14, 2003, Mumbai).

[97] The *jamaat* in Mumbai dated back to the 1740s and was presided over by a *mukhi* (the treasurer) and the *kamadiya* (accountant) – these were not elected positions.

ISLAMIC LAW AND WOMEN'S RIGHTS

and the *jamatkhana* are two important collective institutions that discuss and rule on matters internal to the group.[98] The *jamaat* of the Khojas is divided into subcommittees, and the *gharsansar* committee (the committee for resolution of domestic matters) arbitrates in matters of marriage and divorce. At present, the *gharsansar* committee has sixteen male and two female members, and is not democratically elected. The *jamaat* follows a consensus model and does not issue edicts. Decisions of the committee are seen as binding, and there are no provisions for appeal. Failure to follow the decision of the sect can lead to social boycott by the other members of the sect.[99]

Membership in the community at present is considered to be ascriptive, and the *jamaat* maintains records of birth, death, engagements, and marriage; it also privileges sect endogamy. Members of the Khoja *jamaat* receive substantial welfare benefits. For instance, the *jamaat* is committed to the provision of housing, employment, education, medical aid, and interest-free loans to its community members. Secondly, the identity and distinctive cultural and legal practices are guarded and held sacred by the *jamaat* members; the continuation of these practices is another reason for maintaining group boundaries. As a result, sect endogamy is rigidly enforced and periodically revised in order to ensure further reinforcement. The parties seeking engagement and marriage must secure permission from the officials and give prior notice of engagement or marriage. The *mehar* is fixed,[100] and the gifts and dowry

> The *jamaat* was led by wealthy, old, and influential men of the group. The *jamaat* controlled property that ranged from cooking utensils for group dinners to burial grounds and other charitable trusts (Masselos 1973).

[98] The Ithna Ashariyas sought to reaffirm their administrative hold once again by tightening the implementation aspect of family law in 1959. An amendment to the 1955 Constitution states that the parties who received "judgement" by the council were obliged to adhere to it.

[99] This can take the form of denying burial space at the time of death or disallowing the performance of marriage in the *jamaatkhana*.

[100] At present, the earlier practices continue. The amount of *mehar* is standardized by the sect. Usually, the *mehar* is fixed at 500 or 1,000 rupees and can reach to 50,000 rupees when the groom hails from the Khoja Diaspora in Europe, North America, or South Africa.

received at the time of marriage are registered in the *jamatkhana*. Gifts received by women are considered as her *stridhan*. Women do not have ownership over gifts received and given from the groom's side.

The Ithna Asharis permit polygyny in certain circumstances, and permission of the first wife is necessary in order to remarry; permission is granted in cases of infertility, sexual impotence, or prolonged illness.[101] The maintenance of the wife and children is fixed by the arbitration committee. Divorce by mutual consent is allowed,[102] although divorce is infrequent and is given only under extreme circumstances.[103] The party who wishes to file for divorce has to file an application in the *jamaatkhana* and accept the adjudicative procedure. Parties who wish to file for mutual-consent divorce can hand in an application but must wait six months before finalizing the divorce. Fault is grounds for divorce, but committee members can still desist from granting divorce. The grounds for divorce include conversion, desertion, cruelty, and any other grounds that council may consider sufficient. Upon divorce, the wife is awarded *mehar*, maintenance during *iddat*, postdivorce maintenance for both the wife and children, and any other immovable or movable property deemed fit by the council.

Interaction with Other Forums

The Ithna Ashari Khoja community seeks to maintain social control in matters of family law and remains wary of religious influences in the

---

[101] Interviews with women members of the community suggest that first wives can be coerced into consent if they lack support from their natal families (interview with SM, February 5, 2003, Mumbai).

[102] *Khula* is also not frequently granted by the caste constitution. *Faskh* is also not a part of sect laws.

[103] In one case, a young woman of about twenty-five years, a mother of two children, had a relationship with a young male neighbor. The husband found out and approached the council for divorce. The woman wished for reconciliation. The council asked the couple to wait for some time, and many members of the committee met individually with the husband to persuade him to reconcile. Finally, the husband agreed and withdrew his application (interview with Shirinben Maneckia, member, Ghar Sansar Committee, September 7, 2002, Mumbai).

ISLAMIC LAW AND WOMEN'S RIGHTS

administration of family law. The sect is spread across the world, yet the Ithna Ashari members of the Diaspora remain in touch through sect organizations. Given the tradition and practice of endogamy, sect organizations across borders get involved in cases of domestic disputes.[104] For instance, a woman was married to a Khoja man residing in South Africa. After marriage, the husband did not send for his wife and ceased all communication with her. A woman member of the Ghar Sansar Committee was of the opinion that the woman in question should be granted a *khula*. However, there are no explicit rules on the matter in the constitution, and as a result, male members were opposed to the idea. They adopted the usual method of adjudication in such a case. They approached the South African chapter of the Khoja *jamaat* and asked them to get in touch with the man about the issue. The divorce would be finalized as per the rules of the constitution.

There are also conflicts with other forums, especially between the clergy and the Khoja *jamaat*. In one case, a male litigant divorced his wife after less than a year of marriage. He went to a *qazi*, got a letter of divorce, and handed it to his wife. The woman complained in the community forum (*jamatkhana*), because unilateral divorce is unacceptable per sect laws. The committee held the divorce as invalid and held the man and his family accountable to the sect for violating sect laws.[105] Thus, women members of the Khoja *jamaat* gain more rights through sect laws in matters related to divorce, but in some instances, they choose to seek out state courts to gain economic rights.[106]

---

[104] Interview with Shirinben Maneckia, member, Ghar Sansar Committee, September 7, 2002, Mumbai.

[105] Interview with MH, October 18, 2002, Mumbai.

[106] "A woman from our community wanted a divorce and she had three children. The husband refused to divorce her and pay maintenance, despite our mediation. She approached the state court for maintenance. We as women do not see any harm in these measures. However, state courts have yet not granted her 'justice,' as the process is lengthy and cumbersome" (interview with Shirinben Maneckia, member, Ghar Sansar Committee, September 7, 2002, Mumbai).

The Question of Representation: Who Represents the Community?

The previous section illustrates that multiple interacting sources of legal authorities adjudicate in Muslim Personal Law, and that the question of who represents the community in matters of Muslim Personal Law has not been resolved within the community. Among societal actors, the All India Muslim Personal Law Board[107] (AIMPLB) attempts to project itself as a representative organization on the question of Muslim Personal Law. Scholars have argued that the state has isolated Muslim orthodoxy and the AIMPLB as interlocutors and representatives of the Muslim community, as seen in the developments since the Shah Bano case (Hasan 1994). However, at the societal level, the issue of representation is one of ongoing debate and contestation. The AIMPLB is not a democratically elected body, although its body represents many Islamic sects and subsects.[108] However, despite these claims, the AIMPLB is seen to favor Sunnis over Shias, and is seen to propagate the views held by the Deobandis. In recent years, the Shias have established the All India Shia Personal Law Board, and the Barelvis have organized to form the All India Muslim Personal Law Board Jabid. The AIMPLB also holds discussions on Muslim Personal Law with non-Muslim and

---

[107] The AIMPLB, in its incipient stage, was a loose group of Muslim religious and community leaders who aimed to retain the Sharia in India. A group of Muslim leaders sought to safeguard the autonomy of Muslims in 1972 when the Law Minister of India sought to introduce a Uniform Adoption Bill as a preliminary move toward establishing a uniform civil code. The bill was dropped after protests. Similar contestations arose when the Criminal Procedure Code was amended in 1973. Muslim leaders sought exemption from Section 125 CrPC and lobbied to add Section 127 CrPC, which granted exemption to parties from provision of Section 125 CrPC if the law conflicted with provisions of personal laws of parties. However, the AIMPBL rose to prominence in 1986 when it organized protests against the judgment in the Shah Bano case. Since 1992, after the demolition of the Babri Mosque, the Board has involved itself in seeking a political and legal approach to the solution of the dispute involving the Ram Mandir-Babri Masjid dispute (see also Jones 2010).

[108] See "Four Law Boards: Will Muslim Women Find a Messiah?" in *South Asian Women's Forum*, Internet edition, February 7, 2005.

ISLAMIC LAW AND WOMEN'S RIGHTS 301

secular women's organizations and individuals. The AIMPLB is partially successful at establishing itself as a representative in the issue of Muslim Personal Law, but its claim is questioned and challenged by rival theological schools such as the Barelvis,[109] liberal Muslims, intellectuals, and religious organizations. The AIMPLB has, in recent years, been mired in controversy over its campaigns to exempt Muslims from the uniform Child Marriage Restraint Act 1929, claiming that the Sharia allows marriage of girls postpuberty. Some members of the Board have also issued statements against the use of contraceptives by Muslims, and have sought to implicitly extend the jurisdiction of Islamic law to criminal law.

Despite disagreements and tensions, the Board also exchanges views with women's organizations. The Muslim Women's Rights network, consisting of twenty-five organizations that have been working on the issue of Muslim Personal Law, arrived at "minimum common understanding" on issues of critical importance to Muslim women. The network proposed reforms in four areas: the regulation/banning of triple *talaq* and oral divorce, compulsory registration of marriage, the compulsory registration of divorce, and women's right to matrimonial property. In 2000, the network held discussions with members of the AIMPLB, religious organizations such as Jamaat e Islami and Tamir e Millat, and independent clergymen. The network expressed the need to revive rights given to women within the framework of Islam and human rights.[110] This is evident in the discussions concerning the AIMPLB's efforts to establish religious courts to streamline adjudication under Muslim Personal Law in society.

---

[109] The Barelvis follow the teachings of Pir Anwar Raza Khan Sufi preceptor (*pir*) who supported custom-laden but conservative folk Islam as opposed to the more sanitized and puritanical form of Islam followed by the Deobandis. Ahmad Raza Khan also formed the theological school Manzar ul Islam and endorsed the Hanafi doctrine (Jamaluddin 1981; Sanyal 1995).

[110] See the report of the Hyderabad Meeting, Muslim Women's Rights Network, June 16–17, 2001.

Divergent Opinions on the Establishment of Religious "Courts"

In an effort to determine authoritative interpretations among societal sources, the AIMPLB has sought to streamline the judicial process at the societal level by opening *Dar ul Qazas*, religious courts, wherein trained *Muftis*, largely from Deoband seminary, officiate in matters of Muslim Personal Law. This is also an attempt to sanitize Islamic practices and delink them from local custom and influences. However, the capacity to evolve a judicial process is doubtful given the localized nature of justice. Political developments suggest that the Indian state would not accept a move to centralize the societal judicial system.[111] Different opinions exist among societal actors with respect to the establishment of parallel religious courts such as *Dar ul Qazas*. Some lawyers also disagree with the establishment of the *Dar ul Qazas* and call these illegal, as these are not supported by any legislative acts: "Each local informal institution (such as the Lok Adalats and the Panchayati Raj institutions) is supported by

---

[111] Recently, a Muslim woman, a mother of four, was allegedly raped by her father-in-law. When she complained about the rape, a local cleric issued a *fatwa* dissolving her marriage. The case received wide publicity, and public-interest litigation was filed in the Supreme Court to do away with the parallel legal system among Muslims in India. The then–Law Minister Hansraj Bhardwaj also stated that no parallel judicial system would be allowed to function in India. The Supreme Court issued a notice to the center, the *Dar ul Uloom*, the seminary of Deoband, and several states where Sharia courts function. The AIMPLB plans to hand the Supreme Court a detailed report on the functioning of *Dar ul Qaza*, which they say is complimentary to the judicial system and not parallel to it. The Board argued that it is one of the forums for the redressal of grievances and that it complements the judicial system. (Joshi, Poornima, "Minority Cell Mulls Political Lobbying," *The Telegraph*, August 28, 2005). The AIMPLB also plans to lobby political parties in this matter. Other proposals to establish religious courts deliberated by the AIMPLB include a proposal to incorporate Sharia experts in the system of the Family Court. However, this plan has been shelved after the outcry in the aftermath of the alleged rape case. The AIMPLB think-tank had also deliberated over a proposal to appoint experts in Sharia law to officiate in the Family Court in India. They had also sought to reintroduce the powers of the *qazis* to settle civil disputes that were diminished after the colonial state introduced civil courts. See Subodh Ghildiyal, "Muslim Law Board Tones Down Stand," *Times News Network* (New Delhi), August 22, 2005.

ISLAMIC LAW AND WOMEN'S RIGHTS

a legislative enactment. These *Dar ul Qazas* are not supported by any such measures – they have no legal validity."[112] Sects and groups that are organized and have regulatory bodies have not adopted a confrontational stand on this issue, but would seek to retain their own system of regulation,[113] implicitly opposing the imposition of religious courts. Many women's organizations also oppose these courts and proclaim their verdicts as antiwomen. Many Barelvis do not access these religious courts, nor do many Shias or the communities, individuals, and families who abide by their local rules. The clergy, too, see these religious courts as opposing their interests.[114]

To summarize, adjudication in Muslim Personal Law in society involves diverse legal procedures, and results in conflict, cooperation, or communication between different legal actors and bodies. The following section discusses the interaction between state-law enactments and societal laws.

Conflict and Convergence between Statutory Muslim Personal Law and Societal Laws

The difference between a section of women's organizations, the state, and other legal actors is over the very definition of the family. Some women's organizations, including Muslim women's organizations, working on identity issues demand that the state redefine the notion of the family to include gay, lesbian, and transsexual families.[115] However, many other societal actors from within the Muslim community are against the redefinition of the family because it is considered un-Islamic.

Both state law and societal law as well as practices in the regulation of family law demarcate the boundaries of religious groups. The Shariat

---

[112] Interview with Nisar Ahmed Ghatte, February 19, 2003, Mumbai.
[113] Interview with MM, March 5, 2003, Mumbai.
[114] Indeed, tensions between local clergy and the *Dar ul Qazas* are rife in Muslim-dominated areas (interview with Haroun Musawala, September 7, 2002, Mumbai).
[115] Interview with Hasina Khan, Awaz e Niswan, March 6, 2003, Mumbai. See also the discussion in Gangoli (1996) and Menon (1998).

Act 1937 was enacted as a tool to construct a unified Muslim community as a step toward a conception of Muslim as a nation/political/religious community (Gilmartin 1988). As a result, the act allows inter- and intrasect marriages. However, different sects, clans, and groups practice endogamy to preserve the boundaries of their group.[116]

The Indian courts accept three types of divorce under Muslim Personal Law.[117] Historically, Indian courts have accepted both written and oral divorce in some cases (Fyzee 1965; Mahmood 1997, 2002; Mulla 1955), but in recent years, the Family Court has demanded written proof of divorce.[118] Recent developments in Muslim Personal Law in state courts suggest that the higher courts accept *talaq ul bidaat*, or triple *talaq*, as a valid form of divorce only if it is carried out in the presence of witnesses and only after attempts at mediation.[119] However, as I have argued in Chapter 3, data show that lower courts have generally not followed this judicial precedent.

The judges in these courts balance minority rights and gender justice by splitting their "hard" decisions – they do not employ rigorous measures to restrict unilateral divorce, but enforce maintenance claims. In the case of the validation of triple *talaq*, they do not express opinions about unilateral divorce or enforce judicial precedents of higher courts with respect to unilateral divorce. Nor do they supervise the provision of *mehar* upon divorce, but they provide economic rights through the strict enforcement of maintenance claims, and they treat judicial cases under Muslim law at par with cases filed under Hindu law or the secular law.

---

[116] See Engineer (1989) for sect endogamy practiced among some Shia and Sunni groups. Many other organized groups among Muslims practice both sect and caste endogamy (interview with Dr. Asghar Ali Engineer and HK, January 10, 2003, Mumbai).

[117] These include *talaq a hasan*, *talaq hasan*, and *talaq ul bidaat*.

[118] See the arguments in Chapter 2.

[119] For instance, see *Dagdu s/o Chotu Pathan* v. *Rahimbi Dagdu Pathan and Others*, May 2002, Aurangabad Bench of Mumbai High Court; All India Maharashtra Law Reporter (Criminal) Vol. 2, 1230–1261.

ISLAMIC LAW AND WOMEN'S RIGHTS

In contrast to the lower courts, *talaq ul bidaat* (or triple *talaq*) is considered illegal and un-Islamic by some societal actors.[120] Several Shia communities, and sects such as the Bohras, Khojas, and Memons do not practice or sanction this form of divorce (Engineer 1989) although they might accept it as Islamic. Other communities disagree; as one litigant said: "Islam prohibits *talaq ul biddat* – anyone who gives *talaq* like that isn't considered a Muslim in our community."[121]

Some women's organizations call to ban triple *talaq*[122] at the societal level. Other organizations, including women's groups, support triple *talaq* but seek to impose conditions to regulate it. The doorstep courts such as the Samjhauta Mahila Mandal and Hamraz Mahila Mandal popularize the verdicts and judicial precedents in cases such as the Dagdu Pathan case, and demand that divorce should be invalid unless conditions of arbitration are met.[123]

Religious seminaries disagree over the question of the validity of triple *talaq*.[124] For instance, both the Deobandis and Barelvis consider *talaq ul bidaat* as a valid form of divorce, whereas the Ahl i Hadith sect views this form of divorce as un-Islamic. Among Sunnis, scholars belonging to Deobandi and Barelvi schools agree on the validity of triple *talaq*, though they opine that this type of *talaq* is condemned by the Prophet. A Deobandi clergy,[125] who issues verdicts in cases of personal

---

[120] For instance, the Ahl i Hadith faction does not consider triple *talaq* in one sitting as a valid form of divorce (interview with Maulana Israr Ahmad, March 26, 2003, Mumbai).

[121] Interview with AS, Sunni litigant from South Gujarat, March 5, 2003, Mumbai.

[122] See the minutes of the discussion between the Muslim Women's Rights Network, comprised of twenty-five organizations, and the All India Muslim Personal Law Board.

[123] See the presentation of women's opinions on triple *talaq*, presentations by the Samjhauta Mahila Mandal and the Hamraz Mahila Mandal in a meeting hosted by Women's Research and Action Group, March 6, 2003, Mumbai.

[124] Among Sunnis, scholars belonging to Deobandi and Barelvi schools agree on the validity of triple *talaq*, though they opine that this type of *talaq* is condemned by the Prophet (interview with Mufti Wahabuddin Khan, September 7, 2002, Mumbai).

[125] Interview with Mufti Wahabuddin Khan, September 7, 2002, Mumbai.

law, said: "The Prophet even condemned murder but, once committed, a murder is a murder. The murderer's punishment in this world or by the God does not wipe out the finality of his act. We hold that *talaq* pronounced by an intoxicated or insane husband as valid." Followers of the sect Ahl i Hadith, on the other hand, disagree on the issue of validity of triple *talaq*. The clergy attached to the Ahl i Hadith Mosque in Mumbai argued[126] that "the practice of triple *talaq* is not enshrined in the Quran or the Hadith but is based on the legal precedents and as such cannot be considered valid."

Whereas religious laws may permit divorce, customary laws prohibit this type of divorce for some groups.[127] "Many sects have arrived at uneasy compromise between religious laws and custom – groups which did not practice polygyny and triple *talaq* do not validate them, and attempt to limit them. However, they do not denounce them as un-Islamic." However, many societal actors also advocate for the acceptance of oral divorce.[128] As a result, there are mixed views concerning triple *talaq*.

Many societal actors promote *talaq e tafwid*, a form of delegated divorce. This form of divorce is promoted because it "delegates the right of divorce to the wife or the husband's family members."[129] The wife is entitled to *mehar* under this form of divorce. The Islamic judicial divorce, *faskh*, is also widely practiced; however, neither of these types of divorces is accepted by the state courts.[130] Similarly, diverse and

---

[126] Interview with Maulana Israr Ahmad, March 26, 2003, Mumbai.

[127] Interview with Mohamed Habibali, member, Khoja Jamaat, April 27, 2003, Mumbai.

[128] Interviews reveal that theological schools such as the Deobandis, the Barelvis, and the Ahl i Hadith view oral divorce as reprehensible but valid (interview with Wahabuddin Khan, *Dar ul Qaza*, April 13, 2003, Mumbai). Religious organizations also accept oral divorce as valid. Some residential committees, the clergy, and lay Muslims also hold this form of divorce as valid (interviews with GS, January 19, 2003; Maulana Akhtar Mehmood, member, Bandra West Residential Committee, January 2, 2003; PS, March 5, 2003, Mumbai).

[129] Interviews with Wahabuddin Khan, *Dar ul Qaza*, April 13, 2003; Iqbal Maniar, March 17, 2003, Mumbai.

[130] For instance, a Muslim woman obtained a divorce by *faskh* after her husband filed a case against her for restitution against conjugal rights. The Family Court refused to

ISLAMIC LAW AND WOMEN'S RIGHTS

conflicting opinions exist over the regulation of *muta* marriages.[131] For instance, the Public Complaint Centre ran a campaign against clergymen who solemnize *muta* marriages and held public meetings in central Mumbai to discuss the ban of this practice.[132]

Ascertaining an ideal amount of *mehar* to provide a safety net for women in case of divorce is another point of dispute. Women's organizations argue for higher monetary value of *mehar* because it provides financial security to divorced women in the case of unilateral divorce. A higher amount of *mehar* can also act as a deterrent to divorce. The Public Complaint Centre opposes the demand for high *mehar* because it limits women's ability to ask for *khula*. However, as an activist from Awaz e Niswan, a Muslim women's organization, suggests, returning of *mehar* upon *khula* is an issue only if women opt for community divorce and not when the matter is decided by the court.[133] At times, state and societal actors may disagree on the issue of the validity of divorce, thus placing a question mark on the marital status of parties. For instance,[134] a husband divorced his wife through a *fatwa* acquired from a clergy. The woman went to a grassroots-level NGO working on the issue of divorce, and the organization declared the divorce invalid because the conditions of the divorce (the presence of witnesses and arbitration prior to divorce) were not met. The woman then filed a case for maintenance for herself and her children in the Family Court. The man argued that he had divorced his wife and produced the *fatwa*, but could not prove divorce as there was no written proof of acceptance by the wife. In the meantime, the woman continued to occupy the apartment her husband had

---

accept societally given *faskh* as a valid divorce (interview with NM, March 18, 2003, Mumbai).

[131] Interview with Iqbal Maniar, June 8, 2003, Mumbai. For instance, acceptance of *muta* marriages has been debated by the Ithna Ashari Khojas. One suggestion is that *muta* marriages should be performed after engagement and before marriage (interview with MH, April 21, 2003, Mumbai).

[132] Interview with Iqbal Maniar, June 8, 2003, Mumbai.

[133] Interview with Hasina Khan, January 10, 2003, Mumbai.

[134] Interview with NS, January 17, 2003, Mumbai.

leased from the Municipal Corporation of Greater Mumbai. He asked the corporation to evict his wife because he had divorced her, but the woman challenged his claim, and the corporation accepted her claim as valid because she could prove that she was living in the apartment. This dispute unravelled over the course of five years, and the couple's marital status remained contested during this entire period. The issue of the validity of written and oral divorce under Muslim Personal Law remains crucial for Muslim women who wish to prosecute their husbands for domestic violence by filing a case under the provision of Section 498(a) IPC, as only married women can file under this provision.

In an effort to widen women's access to divorce, the state allows Muslim women to terminate their marriage through the Dissolution of Muslim Women's Act 1939. While the Indian court largely follows the Hanafi law, it has cobbled together provisions from Hanafi, Maliki, and Shafi schools to provide grounds of divorce to the Muslim wife.[135] Both state law and Islamic law include fault as grounds for divorce. There are areas of similarities in the manner in which cruelty is construed in courts as well as in societal legal forums. For instance, the Family Court at Mumbai denied maintenance to a Muslim woman because she was unable to prove harassment. Her claim of not wanting to stay in the joint family was seen by the court as a demand of a modern, western wife who watched too much TV.[136] In many cases, the clergy's interpretation of fault rests on the wife's failure to obey the husband. Women's organizations do not accept these as grounds of fault, as they find both the court and the *qazis*' interpretation of marital fault as often "dominated by patriarchal interpretations of women's roles and obligations within the family ... that sanctions domestic violence and cruelty and silences women."[137]

---

[135] Grounds for divorce under the Hanafi law are very restricted, and as a result, the Dissolution of Muslim Marriages Act 1939 has incorporated provisions from Maliki and Shafi schools. See the discussion in Pearl (1987, 130).

[136] See *MS* v. *AS*, Family Court Records, 2002, Mumbai.

[137] Interviews with Hasina Khan, March 13, 2003; NS, Awaz e Niswan, January 10, 2003, Mumbai.

Muslim women can also dissolve their marriage at the societal level through *khula*. The difference between state law and the societal form of divorce is that *khula*, as practiced at the societal level, requires the husband's consent, whereas consent is not necessary for divorce under state law. Judicial processes at both levels can often result in the conversion of *khula* into a mutual-consent divorce.[138] Women are at a disadvantage in societal divorce; they are forced to renege on their economic rights in exchange for divorce.[139] A woman's right to divorce is often hampered by the husband's refusal to accept divorce. There are several cases in which husbands refuse to grant divorce and agree only after a large sum is paid to them.[140] In very rare cases, women wishing to initiate *khula* have been able to provoke their husbands into giving them *talaq ul bidaat*.[141] Commonly, women wishing to initiate *khula* with reluctant husbands imitate the male strategy of divorcing reluctant wives[142]; that is, Muslim women find clergymen or organizations willing to issue *khula* and send the notice of divorce to husbands by registered post. The proof of signed registered receipt by the husband (or his family members) is produced as a proof of valid *khula*.[143] However, nonacceptance by husbands has often led to confusion about the validity of the divorce.[144]

---

[138] Cases filed under the Dissolution of Muslim Marriage Act 1939 are often converted into mutual-consent divorce cases in the state law as a result of societalization of divorce as argued in Chapter 2. At the societal level, cases of *khula* are often converted into *talaq* by the clergy in order to protect the rights of Muslim women (interview with Mufti Wahabuddin Khan, October 17, 2002, Mumbai).

[139] Women who ask for *khula* often have to forego *mehar* and maintenance (interview with Mufti Wahabuddin Khan, *Dar ul Qaza*, September 7, 2002, Mumbai). Women who initiate divorce in state courts are often forced into compromising their economic rights in order to obtain divorce if they are unable to prove fault.

[140] Interview with NB, February 14, 2003, Mumbai.

[141] Interview with Vandana Nanaware, feminist social worker, the Special Cell for Women and Children, June 16, 2003, Mumbai.

[142] Women's organizations also identify women-friendly *qazis* who would be willing to issue *khula*, and refer women litigants in need of divorce to them (interview with Vandana Nanaware, June 16, 2003, Mumbai).

[143] Interviews with ZS, June 14, 2003; HK, March 5, 2003; NS, March 6, 2003, Mumbai.

[144] In one case, a Muslim woman had obtained *khula* through a clergyman. The clergyman had issued three notices to the husband asking him to appear and present his side

State law permits polygyny among Muslims but also seeks to contain it.[145] Similarly, societal actors accept polygyny because it is valid under the Sharia law, but many actors seek to restrain the practice. Some clerics agree that polygyny is permissible in Islam; they also argue that "a man should not remarry unless he can treat his wives equally well."[146] Others argue that in Islam, polygyny is a right granted to men under Islamic law, and a husband cannot bind himself so as not to exercise the right given to him in Islamic law.[147] In one case, a husband's polygyny was seen as cruelty by a cleric who issued a *khula* on those grounds. The husband went to another cleric who contested the *khula*, as he argued that polygyny cannot be considered grounds for divorce under Muslim Personal Law because it is sanctioned by the Prophet.[148] Polygyny without the consent of the first wife is not permitted among many Muslim sects (Engineer 1989). There exist other societal limitations on polygyny: "A man who wishes to remarry cannot find a bride in the Qureshi *jamaat* until he produces proof of divorce. He finds it even more difficult to find another bride if he has incurred postdivorce financial liabilities."[149]

It has often been argued that the Muslim minority in India has pushed its religious agenda in the state through legislative means, undermining the power of the state and harming the rights of Muslim women in the process (Parashar 1992; Narain 2001; Sunder Rajan 2003). However,

---

of the case. The husband had refused to come but had accepted the notices posted by registered post. The wife was granted *khula* on these grounds, and her remarriage was fixed. The husband intercepted her before her remarriage and claimed that she was still his legal wife. The woman's father had to pay him a sum to agree to divorce (interview with PS, March 4, 2003, Mumbai).

[145] Courts construe polygyny as a form of cruelty and award divorce to the wife on these grounds under the Dissolution of Muslim Marriage Act 1939. Muslim wives can argue constructive desertion to counter polygamous husbands' claims in cases of restitution of conjugal rights. For a more in-depth discussion on this point, see the arguments in Chapter 2.

[146] Interview with Wahabuddin Khan, *Dar ul Qaza*, September 7, 2002, Mumbai.

[147] Interview with Maulana Faisal Ahmad, March 23, 2003, Mumbai.

[148] Interview with BS, the woman litigant, March 26, 2003, Mumbai.

[149] Interview with AS, litigant, March 7, 2003, Mumbai.

courts in India have sought to change, modify, and reinterpret religious laws, and have, to some extent, safeguarded women's rights in the process. For instance, judicial developments on the interpretation of the Muslim Women's (Protection of Rights on Divorce) Act 1986 evince that divorced Muslim women have more rights than divorced Hindu women have. This law travels in society (Merry 2005) and results in out-of-court settlements in some cases.[150] However, religious seminaries, the clergy, and a section of religious organizations declare these developments un-Islamic and illegitimate, thereby limiting the scope of reforms.[151] The reach of this law is further limited because the women's movement, intellectuals, and moderate Muslims have been against the enactment of the law in the post–Shah Bano era, and have not grasped subsequent legal changes in this law.[152]

The issue of the recovery of dowry, or *stridhan*, brings to light the conflict between local practice, state laws, and Islamic precepts. The practice of dowry has been considered a Hindu practice, and is against Islamic laws (Uberoi 1993). Societal actors such as the AIMPLB and some clergy forbid the practice.[153] However, the practice is widely prevalent on the ground. In general, husbands return their wives' *stridhan* at the time of divorce, both in state courts as well as in the societal arena.

---

[150] "I have settled two cases on the basis of this law" (interview with Nisar Ahmed Ghatte, March 23, 2003, Mumbai).

[151] "Divorced Muslim women are allowed maintenance only during *iddat* per Hanafi laws" (interview with Mufti, *Dar ul Qaza*, September 7, 2002, Mumbai).

[152] For instance, scholars of theology and women activists actively engaged in the process of reform in Muslim Personal Law also argue that the Muslim Women's (Protection of Rights on Divorce) Act 1986 denies maintenance to divorced Muslim women. See Yoginder Sikand, "Listen to the Women," available from http://outlookindia.com (accessed May 5, 2005). Sikand has interviewed Noorjehan Niaz of the Women's Research and Action Group. Niaz argues that the denial of the right of maintenance to a divorced woman is to deny her compensation for domestic work. In this light, Niaz critiques the Muslim Women's (Protection of Rights on Divorce) Act 1986 for having taken away the rights to maintenance that divorced Muslim women enjoyed.

[153] See a declaration adopted at a conference on "Genuine Problems of Women and their Solution in the Light of Shariah," organized by the All India Muslim Personal Law Board at Jamia Milia Islamia, April 8, 2001.

Recovery of the dowry becomes more difficult in cases in which the wife refuses to accept *talaq*,[154] when the husband refuses to accept *khula*,[155] or when either refuses to accept *faskh*. Women's organizations are crucial to these negotiations concerning marital status and the retrieval of the dowry. Women's organizations advocate that the dowry is a woman's property that should be controlled by women, and that it should be retrievable at any time, regardless of the marital status of the parties.[156]

To summarize, this section demonstrates that there are multiple views on Islamic laws within the society, and heterogeneous ideas about the Muslim conjugal family, marriage, and divorce coexist in the legal sphere. The following section discusses how individual litigants and legal actors provide spaces for women's rights in law.

Agency and Its Constraints: Muslim Women's Rights in the Legally Plural Sphere

The previous sections suggest that the terrain of Muslim Personal Law is an arena for expressing and constructing alternate visions of the family, marriage, community, law, and Islam. Sugarman (1983) discusses facilitative law: law that functions not by imposing obligations but by conferring legal power to them. So, law permits private lawmaking and

---

[154] A Muslim husband divorced his wife by registered letter, which the wife refused to accept. The parties were separated for a year, and the woman heard that her husband was about to mortgage her jewelry. She went with her extended family to his house to obtain her *stridhan*, but he refused to part with it until she accepted divorce (interview with ZI, May 23, 2003, Mumbai).

[155] In one case, a woman was thrown out of the marital house following a violent incident. The woman decided to seek *khula* after that, and obtained the divorce through a *qazi*. Her husband refused to accept the *khula* or to return her *stridhan*. He claimed that custom dictated that she could retrieve *stridhan* only if he divorced her. The woman received her *stridhan* after the intervention of a women's organization. The organization argued that the *stridhan* was the woman's property, and she could claim it regardless of her marital status (interview with Vandana Nanaware, social worker, Special Cell for Women and Children, June 16, 2003, Mumbai).

[156] Interviews with Vandana Nanaware, June 16, 2003; Yasmin Sheikh, December 11, 2002, Mumbai.

interpretation and enables the individual to expand or contract her autonomy and thus promote, qualify, or subvert state policy. Within a pluralized legal sphere, legal actors "become not only law-abiding citizens, but law-inventing" (Kleinhans and Macdonald 1997, 2) and navigating subjects. The section points out that the difference between statutory and nonstatutory laws leads to the notion that marital status is a negotiated status, subject to claims and counterclaims of rival parties. As a result, at times, parties determine their own status and justify it in light of "authentic Islamic law."

The availability of multiple legal avenues enables Muslim women to engage in forum-shopping. In some cases, heterogeneous options increase the choices for litigants[157]; however, the data also show that the mere existence of multiple legal avenues may not be enough to safeguard women's rights in law. The legal arena also enables parties to "exit"[158] from one sect and enter into another without exiting a community. For instance, a man divorced his wife and then changed his mind. He converted to the sect Ahl i Hadith (and said that the conversion meant "that he prayed at the Ahl i Hadith mosque sometimes"[159]) and thus managed to proclaim his divorce as invalid because this sect does not recognize *talaq ul bidaat*.[160] The literature on the informalization of law suggests that corruption and arbitrariness on the part of society-based legal sources can consolidate the position of the powerful and violate the rights of oppressed groups (Abel 1982a; Harrington 1982; Merry 1982, 1989; Tomasic 1982). However, this case seems more opaque. The data

---

[157] For instance, a woman was denied *khula* when she asked for a divorce after her husband contracted a second marriage. The *qazi* argued that polygyny was legal in Islam, and as a result, she could not ask for *khula* on these grounds. However, she went to a women's organization that referred her to another *qazi* who argued that "Islam asks a man to remarry only if he is able to treat all his wives equally, and that is not the case here" (interview with MS, March 19, 2003, Mumbai).

[158] The term "exit" is defined as the group member's decision to opt out of a cultural group.

[159] Interview with RS, January 23, 2003, Mumbai.

[160] Ibid.

suggest that whereas some litigants are harmed by the lopsided nature of laws and the process of justice, others find ways to tweak the system in their favor by taking advantage of new developments in state law or by accessing societal power centers.

The data show that everyday legal ability is based on the knowledge, ability, initiative, awareness, and resources of a family or of individual women. Hence, education on marriage law is seen as one of the key strategies of the women's movement. Women's groups and networks circulate information about the content of laws and legal sources; thus, the organizational and institutional actors among women[161] demonstrate to women that accessing certain legal actors may precipitate certain results. Women's organizations keep a list of the clergy who give *faskh* and refer to them the cases of Muslim women seeking divorce.[162] Women's organizations refer cases to these clergymen and act as watchdogs. Women often filter back information about their dealings with various clergy and organizations to the women's organizations.[163] However, many individual women who do not have access to information might be sidelined.[164] In general, marital status then is indeterminate and subject to personal/familial negotiations. Religio-legal considerations often do not enter into the struggles over marriage and divorce.[165]

---

[161] Interviews with HK, January 12, 2003; NS, March 5, 2003; PS, March 18, 2003, Mumbai.

[162] Interview with Vandana Nanaware, social worker, June 16, 2003, Mumbai.

[163] Women's organizations confront and boycott corrupt clergy who charge women for divorce. They also hold discussions with different clergy, lawyers, and religious organizations either on the basis of individual cases or over matters of common concern (interview with Vandana Nanaware, social worker, June 16, 2003, Mumbai).

[164] A woman litigant waited three years before approaching the *Dar ul Qaza* despite being deserted for three years, as her natal family understood that they had to wait for her husband to pronounce the divorce. The husband refused to accept the *khula* but signed for the registered letter sent by the Imarat e Sharia, and this was accepted as a proof of *khula* (interview with KB, April 15, 2003, Mumbai).

[165] A woman litigant got the *khula* certified by a *qazi*. Her remarriage was arranged when her husband and some members of his family challenged the *khula* showing another *fatwa* from another source that did not validate the *khula*. The husband and his family had to be paid off by the woman's family (interviews with GS, March 6, 2003; NS, January 22, 2003, Mumbai).

ISLAMIC LAW AND WOMEN'S RIGHTS

The interactions between multiple actors enable women to act as individual litigants as well as collective groups in their challenge of patriarchy.[166] Activists working in feminist groups, too, confront multiple structures of patriarchy in their everyday activities as well as in public protests. As a social activist of Awaz e Niswan stated: "We not only had to struggle against those who seem like our 'own' within our families and communities, but also against the communal 'others' outside the community."[167] They use innovative confrontational methods to drive home their viewpoints, and engage in debates over the interpretation of law with legal actors in their area.

Many Muslims agree with the idea of being governed by Islamic laws in family affairs, but there is no consensus over which law should prevail, or what is Islamic about any law and how it is different from local practice. Indeed, individual families, clans, neighborhoods, and sect *panchayats* classify any law or practice that is commonly practiced or ratified by (generally) male authority as Islamic. In such cases, cleavages between "Islamic laws" and local laws and practices are not often seen to be repugnant to religious practice or to individual conscience. A woman litigant argued that it was considered Islamic not to practice polygyny in her community, and that customary laws dictated this. "We are Muslims ... and we believe in Muslim Personal Law. Any departure from Islamic laws is repugnant to us."[168] Such a decentralized legal sphere can, at times, give agency to some women's groups to debate, discuss, and implement their own version of Islamic law: "Women tell us time and again that they want to be governed by Muslim Law that the Mahila Mandal advocate."[169]

---

[166] I draw on Bina Agarwal's distinction between covert resistance initiated by individual women and overt action by women's groups and collectives in their resistance to patriarchy (Agarwal 1994).

[167] Interviews with Yasmin Sheikh, Hasina Khan, and Naseem Sheikh, January 10, 2003, Mumbai.

[168] Interview with NS, January 17, 2003, Mumbai.

[169] Interview with Hasina Khan, January 12, 2003, Mumbai.

The Campaign around *Nikahnama*: Reforms from Within

Given the multiple loci of law within India, there are ongoing discussions about the need for reform within Muslim Personal Law. There are three broad positions taken by different sections of the community. The conservatives oppose state intervention in the community's affairs and also oppose calls for reforms within the scope of a religious framework. They argue that the Sharia is divine and immutable, and therefore there cannot be any human intervention in its rules. The other lobby is the reformists who are divided on the issue of the need for state intervention in the matter of personal law reform, but who initiate and participate in moves toward reforms from within the community. The third, the AIMPLB, represents the accommodationist lobby who tries to balance between the two lobbies. The following section discusses one such campaign for reform within Muslim Personal Law that was initiated from below, and it assesses the interplay between these three lobbies.

The campaign to revive the custom of preset conditions protecting women's rights within marriage as a part of the *nikahnama*,[170] Muslim marriage contract, as a strategy to facilitate women's rights within the framework of Islamic laws has gained momentum in the mid-1990s when women's groups initiated the discussion of reforms in personal law. The *nikahnama* is a Muslim marriage contract that includes the names and signatures of the parties and their addresses, details about their parents, and signatures of witnesses; the *nikahnama* also specifies the amount of *mehar* and mentions whether it is deferred or paid promptly. There is no standard form in India, but these are the basic details contained in most forms. Muslim law also recognizes the right of the bride to add

---

[170] Such agreements recorded in marriage contracts were deemed valid in Indian case law. See Section 314, Muslim Personal Law; Mulla (1955, 269). In some cases, these were invalidated as is seen in a judgment of the Bombay High Court in *Bai Fatima* v. *Alimahomed*, [1913] 37 Bom. 280, 17 IC 946. This type of private agreement recorded in the marriage contract is prohibited under Hanafi, Maliki, and Shafi schools, but is allowed under Hanabali law and is incorporated in the state law of Jordan, Morocco, and Syria (Anderson 1959, 50–51).

ISLAMIC LAW AND WOMEN'S RIGHTS 317

conditions to the *nikahnama*. One of the conditions that women reformers have been trying to persuade women to attach to their marriage contract is the right of delegated divorce, *talaqi tafwid*. If the husband breaches conditions that he has agreed to in the *nikahnama*, the wife also has the right to impose sanctions – for instance, a wife may choose to live separately and be maintained by the husband (Carroll 1982). The reformers at present have included additional conditions. For instance, these new additions include obligations on the husband to provide maintenance post-*iddat*, as well as arrangements regarding guardianship and custody of future children.[171]

Since the mid-1990s, many women's groups and networks arranged seminars and meetings to discuss the details of *nikahnamas*, circulated drafts, and sought legal advice.[172] They then recirculated the amended versions among various pockets of Muslim communities. These *nikahnamas* were prepared by activists,[173] individuals,[174] lawyers,[175] organizations,[176]

---

[171] For a detailed discussion on the potential of this law in the Indian context, see Carrol (1982).

[172] Legal experts such as Prof. Satyaranjan Sathe, Vaijayanta Joshi, Lakshmi Paranjpe, and others offered their advice. See the minutes of a meeting organized by the All India Progressive Muslims Conference, June 26, 1999.

[173] See the 1996 draft of *nikahnama* prepared by a group of women's rights activists, including Prof. Ramla Baxamusa, Nahida Sheikh, Vahida Nainar, Nasreen Fazhalbhoy, and others.

[174] See, for instance, the model *nikahnama* prepared by Dr. Zeenat Saukat Ali.

[175] See, for instance, the *nikahnama* presented by Zakir Maniar, at a meeting on *nikahnama* organized by the All India Progressive Muslims Conference, June 26, 1999. See also the *nikahnama* prepared by advocate Niloufar Akhtar; Bhattacharya Chandrima, "Rights for Women in Model Nikahnama," *The Telegraph*, July 26, 2004.

[176] See *Zeenat ka Nikahnama*, prepared by Prof. Shamsuddin Tamboli, June 26, 1999, meeting on *nikahnama* organized by the All India Progressive Muslims Conference. See also the *nikahnama* prepared by The Islamic Research Foundation, prepared by Dr. Asghar Ali Engineer. Many ideas about the *nikahnama* were discussed in various meetings. See suggestions made by Khatoom Gafoor Sheikh, member, *Hamraz* Group, Mumbai. The grassroots women's organization working in a slum in Mumbai asks for a ban on triple *talaq* and its replacement with arbitrated divorce handed down by the court or women's groups. The group argues that *mehar* should be made incremental in recognition of women's labor in the family and should be handed over to the woman at the time of marriage (interview, Khatoom Gafoor Sheikh, member, the

and networks such as Muslim Women's Rights Network,[177] which prepared a summary of suggestions on reforms in personal law that could be incorporated in the *nikahnama*. Individual men and women voluntarily signed these contracts to popularize the practice during their own or their relatives' marriages.[178] However, a vexing question here was the enforcement of *nikahnama* at the time of marriage, because the *nikahnama* faced opposition from a section of the clergy[179] and also from society at large because the contract required voluntary abdication of male privilege. After many years of campaigns on the issue, several groups asked the AIMPLB to take the lead to discuss the concept of *nikahnama* throughout the country, to standardize the contract, and to work out mechanisms to ensure its enforcement. Bowing to intense pressure from various groups, the AIMPLB also took up the task of preparing its own version of the *nikahnama*[180] and placed it on the agenda in its meeting in February 2005 at Bhopal.

However, the process of internal reform in the community depends on balancing the power of the conservative and moderate forces from within the community. Before the AIMPLB meeting, eighty *ulemas*, many of them from the Barelvi sect, issued a statement intending to

Hamraz Committee, at the Book Release Function organized by Women's Research and Action Group, April 22, 2003, Mumbai).

[177] The network represents twenty-five feminist organizations across India.

[178] For instance, a woman leader of a local women's group prepared a *nikahnama* for her son's wedding that specified a condition against polygyny and granted a lump-sum maintenance to his wife in case of divorce (interview with NM, February 22, 2003, Mumbai). A Muslim activist, Syedbhai, presented his own *nikahnama* at a meeting on *nikahnama* organized by the All India Progressive Muslims Conference, June 26, 1999.

[179] Some religious clergy argued that even though this may help curb polygyny, it is not permissible in Islam because polygyny is a right granted to men under Islamic law, and a husband cannot bind himself so as not to exercise the right given to him in Islamic law (interview with Maulana Faisal Ahmad, March 23, 2003, Mumbai).

[180] For instance, Uzma Naheed, a woman member of the AIMPLB, had worked with the *ulema* and the Board members to push forth women's rights through *nikahnama* since 1994. See Bhattacharya Chandrima, "Rights for Women in Model *Nikahnama*," *The Telegraph*, July 26, 2004.

ISLAMIC LAW AND WOMEN'S RIGHTS 319

pressure the AIMPLB not to carry out wide-ranging reforms, especially those concerning triple *talaq*.[181] However, the possible move by the Board was closely watched by different sections of the community and diverse lobbies,[182] and was seen as an opportunity to portray the tolerant, outward-looking character of the Indian Muslim community.[183]

Bowing down to pressure from the conservatives, the Board declared a standard *nikahnama*, which fell short of feminist ideals. The Board recommended that triple *talaq* should be seen as reprehensible, and it made a statement that the *mehar* should be paid and that women should not be asked to forego the *mehar* payment. They did not include *khula* or *talaq e tafwid* as women's right to divorce, but they did call the practice Islamic.[184] The Board prepared a standard *nikahnama* that did not fall far short of reformist demands. Some feminist organizations and women's wings of the political parties acknowledged the internal reform process as a step in the right direction.[185] Feminist organizations, including Muslim women's organizations, however, held demonstrations against the proposal[186]; moderates and intellectuals condemned the AIMPLB's

---

[181] See "No Compromise on Triple *Talaq* System: *Ulemas*," available from http://www.outlookindia.com (accessed August 14, 2004).

[182] See Rasheed Kidwai, "Curtain to Drop on Triple *Talaq*," *The Telegraph*, April 30, 2005.

[183] "The Board [intends to] ... focus on improvement in personal conduct, reforms in marriage and divorce, and a complete ban on dowry and extravagance ... a model *nikahnama* hopes to reduce gender-based discrimination, particularly in divorce maintenance cases." See Rasheed Kidwai, "Muslim Board to Open New Chapter," *The Telegraph*, October 7, 2004.

[184] See Suchandana Gupta, "*Talaq*: Once Is Enough," *The Times of India*, May 2, 2005.

[185] See interview with Veena Gowda, lawyer with the feminist organization *Majlis* Mumbai, in "We Will Make Our Own *Nikahnama*," *The Hindu*, May 7, 2005. See also the press release prepared by the All Indian Democratic Women's Organisation, signed by Suhasini Ali (President), Brinda Karat (Vice President), S. Sudha (General Secretary), and Anwara (Member), May 5, 2005.

[186] Muslim women tore the copies of the AIMPLB's *nikahnama* in a public meeting in Mumbai called by the Muslim Women's Rights Network, Awaz e Niswan, and the Forum Against Oppression of Women. See "We Will Make Our Own *Nikahnama*," *The Hindu*, May 7, 2005. See also the interview of Nusrat Bano Ruhi in "India Muslim Divorce Code Set Out," available from http://www.bbc.co.uk/news (accessed May 2, 2005).

inability to push for pro-women reforms.[187] The process brought into the open the limitations of the AIMPLB in the implementation of legal changes. The campaign for regulation of *nikahnama* succeeded in generating public dialog and discussion on the nature of reforms in Muslim Personal Law,[188] but it failed, in a sense, because the success of the reforms depended on individual volition, which proved the limitations of the moral authority of the AIMPLB.

Competing Ideologies and Interests among Socio-Legal Actors and Institutions

The Muslim community is not monolithic; therefore, parties that debate on religious family laws face two tasks: one is to bring about changes within the community while keeping in mind the diverse interests and positions of factions; the other is to recontextualize the debate of law reform while countering religious intolerance and attacks by Hindu fundamentalists.

There is a loose consensus in favor of reforms within the framework of Islamic law among various sections, but there is no blueprint for the nature of the reforms. Neither is there an agreement within the community on the nature and degree of state intervention in the sphere of the community. For instance, religious seminaries and a section of the clergy argue for decreased state intervention. Some of their demands include the withdrawal of litigants from the state judiciary, the streamlining of Muslim Personal Law through the establishment of religious courts, the

---

[187] The Prince of Arcot, a well-known reformist, asked the AIMPLB to ban triple *talaq*. See "*Talaq* Woes Worry Prince," *The Statesman* (accessed May 5, 2005). See also Arshad Alam, "The Board of No Shame," available from http://outlookindia.com (accessed May 4, 2005).

[188] For instance, pro reform sections have used a variety of means to push forth reform. Some residential committees enforce it, as do civil society organizations. Some *ulemas* exhort Muslim men to sign the *nikahnama* in Friday sermons. See Geeta Pandey, "Muslim Women Fight Instant Divorce," available from http://www.bbc.co.uk/news (accessed August 4, 2004).

development of Islamic law in India, the expansion of Muslim law in the criminal justice system, and the increased control over the family and women. Their vision also seeks to give representation to diverse sects, seminaries, and ethnic Muslim communities. However, there exist differences between the various theological schools in India, and various theological schools have sought to establish their own Personal Law Boards.

Each party has an interest in how personal law is practiced. Lawyers tend to favor the extension of state law and oppose the establishment of societal-level religious courts, as these developments are against their professional interest. The clergy wish to retain the private, individualistic nature of justice within Islam and to retain the current system of plural legal sources. Muslim intellectuals, moderates, and a number of civil society organizations advocate more state intervention; they appeal for reforms within state laws and within the formal legal system. Among political parties, the BJP and its affiliates have renewed cries for the establishment of a uniform civil code, whereas most other parties (especially the left parties, the Congress Party, and the Samajwadi Party) are against the enactment of a uniform civil code. However, most political parties disagree with the proposal of establishing separate religious courts. A very small number of Muslims argue for a uniform civil code because it is one of the core demands of the BJP.

The issue of law reform is tied to the broader processes of struggles against communalism. At the other end, women's groups and other civic organizations are divided into two streams. One group of women's organizations pushed for reforms within the community within the framework of the Sharia. These organizations call for pro-women or feminist interpretations of Islamic law, and argue for equal rights between the sexes. The other faction of Muslim feminist organizations disagrees with the basic premise of religious personal law because they see religion as inherently patriarchal.[189] Both groups agree, however, in their vision of

---

[189] These differences are mirrored by lay Muslim women. A Mumbai-based women's organization, Women's Research and Action Group, carried out a survey of 14,624

the family that is gender-just. They argue for more procedural and substantive equality for women within state laws.[190] They also argue that the societalization of divorce creates a vested interest for the religious clergy, as it increases their power over sections of the community, including women, and influences gender relations within the family. At the same time, the clergy support internal reforms within the community and contribute to societal initiatives for reform.

The women's movement is further divided on the issue of the rights of homosexuals within the family. A section of women activists and organizations, including Muslim women activists and organizations that advocate for the rights of gay, lesbian, and transsexual persons, prefer to argue their case in the language of human rights. They opt out of the debate on reforms from within the circumscribed boundaries of religious discourse because they cannot make a case for the rights of homosexuals within the religious framework. However, they stress the importance of dialog on the definitions of family within the Muslim community.[191] In general, women's organizations are alert to the unification agenda of the Hindu right, and therefore advocate internal reform within the community; they are reluctant to demand a uniform civil code. Both factions engage in internal reform through the feminist reading of scriptures, and they engage in dialog with religious organizations, the clergy, religious seminaries, and the media. Muslim women's organizations take a more nuanced stand on this debate, as they are caught between the partisan state and the inward-looking sections of the community: "On the one hand, after the genocide in Gujarat, feminist organizations acting on

---

Muslim women across India to ascertain their views on personal law reform. About 47 percent of women wished for changes within the framework of religion, whereas 11 percent wished for secular and gender-just law, and 25 percent denied wanting changes in the law. About 7.5 percent did not know anything about the issue, and 6.1 percent did not wish to comment (Nainar 2000, 40).

[190] In Tamil Nadu, some Madurai-based Muslim women's organizations launched a campaign stating that *talaq* issued by an authority other than the state would not be acceptable. Presentation by Nazneen Barkat, ASAG, Minutes of MWRN Meeting, July 6, 2003, Mumbai.

[191] Interviews with SK, HK, January 15, 2003, Mumbai.

minority issues cannot trust the state as a saviour of individual rights. On the other hand, riots and genocides intensify the hold of patriarchal elements – after the riots in Mumbai in 1993, the clerics told women that 'the riots happened because you do not veil.' As Muslim women, we are caught between these patriarchies. But we have to negotiate both."[192] Women's groups also acknowledge that religious organizations vary in their engagement with women's groups: "The AIMPLB is more open to dialog with secular feminist groups which advocate a position of law reform through the internal consensus of the community. The AIMPLB is more reluctant to talk to Muslim women's groups which push for secular laws to govern the family."[193]

Conclusion

In this chapter, I study adjudication in Muslim Personal Law in multiple legal locales, and outline the processes of confrontation, cooperation, and communication between litigants and legal actors and bodies. I suggest that while litigants and adjudicators legitimate their legal choices and decisions as Islamic, perceptions of what is Islamic vary. The centrality given to religious laws as the defining markers of community identity is also resisted, both in everyday practice and in the national sphere, by sections of civil society, Muslim intelligentsia, social organizations, and sections of the women's movement. The language of resistance is different: It does not consent to a homogenized Indian nation, nor does it validate the Muslim identity imagined by the orthodoxy. It is also evident that the mere existence of multiple arenas may not be enough to equalize gender relations in law. However, women's individual and collective agency find expression in everyday negotiations under the law and permit the leveling of some forms of gender hierarchy.

---

[192] Presentation by Hasina Khan, member, Awaz e Niswan, July 4, 2003, Mumbai.
[193] Interview with Naseem Sheikh, Awaz e Niswan, January 20, 2003, Mumbai.

6 Conclusion

This book poses the following questions: How do accommodative arrangements advocating cogovernance by state and society in legally plural societies impact on the interactions between and within religious groups and other societal bodies? How do they shape gender equality in the family? What is the nature of state-society interactions in the adjudication of religious laws in legally plural societies? The study aims to describe, understand, and, in the end, explain the functioning of the Indian policy of legal pluralism as an accommodative measure in the governance of marriage and divorce among Hindus and Muslims. The Indian state has adopted what I call a shared adjudication model in which the state and a broad range of societal bodies share adjudicative authority. In other words, the Indian state, in the governance of religious family law, adopts the strategy of "regulated autonomy" by which it incorporates religious groups into the governance of the family and circumscribes their sphere of autonomy. This strategy is an outcome of the Indian state's desire to shape the family and gender from above while balancing the plural demands of groups.[1] The model has been crafted

---

[1] Rudolph and Rudolph (2001) suggest that the uniform civil code debate presents an ongoing tension between the idea of legal centralism and the practice of legal pluralism through the recognition of religious personal laws. Even though they do not make this point with regard to legal informalism, I have retained this analytical lens because it captures the working of legal pluralism on the ground. The Indian state has, time and again, regulated marriage and divorce in religious communities through legislative amendments, enactments, and judicial precedents. For instance, the

from above but it been creatively interpreted, shaped, and used by societal actors and bodies, its boundaries challenged, changed, and stretched on the ground.

Given that the Indian state recognizes state and nonstate laws and allows adjudication in formal and informal arenas, how do we distinguish between state and societal laws and characterize interactions between official and unofficial legal arenas? Some scholars working on law and society in India argue that the interacting state and societal legalities are autonomous but linked (Holden 2004), whereas others posit that legal pluralism reframes our understanding of boundaries between state and society and fragments state sovereignty (Hansen 2005); still others argue that legal pluralism blurs the boundaries of state and society, and, counterintuitively, homogenizes the legal sphere (Eckert 2006). I suggest instead, to retain the fiction of the analytical distinction between state and society. I show that in the shared adjudication model, the state is imagined as an autonomous entity, but "doing state" in the interstitial spaces of legal hybrids involves the making and unmaking of meaning of these boundaries. Following Tamanaha's nonessentialist conception of law (Tamanaha 2001), I posit that rather than looking for the essence of law, we should classify law emanating from the state institutions as state law, and from societal bodies as societal laws. The state-society interactions in varied legal arenas homogenize and fragment the law, and state authority is strengthened in some instances and weakened in other instances.

This book focuses on adjudication processes in formal and informal legal forums in Hindu and Muslim religious family laws. Each religious group is internally heterogeneous; ethnic and religious organizations, doorstep courts, social and family networks, political parties, NGOs,

Supreme Court has opposed any move to establish "parallel courts" and has opposed any move by religious clergy to intervene in cases related to criminal laws, especially in cases of rape. See *Fatwas* not Binding: Muslim Personal Board," available from http://outlookindia.com (accessed March 22, 2006). There has been the move by the Supreme Court toward compulsory registration of marriages. See "Supreme Court Makes Marriage Registration Compulsory," *The Times of India*, February 14, 2006; "Make Registration of Marriage Compulsory," *Outlook*, February 14, 2006.

women's groups, and individuals (including lawyers, strongmen, and the clergy) constitute different sources of adjudicative authority. State-society interactions in law demonstrate the paradoxical movement of law, which I call the centralization and decentralization of law. I show that as the state attempts to extend its authority, state law is received, resisted, appropriated, adapted, transcended, or integrated in societal laws. Thus, the movement of law creates different normative universes in which ideas about family, gender roles, and religious membership are aired and exchanged between and within religio-cultural groups in different legal settings.

Existing debates in the Indian context overlook similarities in the accommodation of Hindus and Muslims in the adjudication of religious family laws. In the state-run Family Court in Mumbai, judges use the Family Courts Act 1984 to override specific sections of Hindu and Muslim religious laws while regulating void and invalid marriages; they also extend matrimonial remedies such as the restitution of conjugal rights and the right to reside in the matrimonial home to both Hindu and Muslim litigants. There are other similarities between Hindu and Muslim laws. Unilateral divorce is allowed among Muslims, and my data also reconfirms Menski's account that Hindu husbands can also unilaterally divorce their wives after obtaining an order for judicial separation and later filing for divorce (Menski 2001). Divorce by mutual consent is also allowed under both religious laws. The Family Court's aim to prevent divorces in society is against the spirit of the provisions of mutual-consent divorce under Hindu and Muslim personal laws. Both the Hindu Marriage Act 1955 and the Dissolution of Muslim Marriage Act 1939 allow divorce on similar grounds of fault, and the manner in which these grounds are construed in legal processes are similar, as illustrated in the previous sections. Similarly, while polygyny is permitted under Muslim Personal Law, the courts protect Muslim women's rights by enforcing maintenance claims. Muslim societal actors also restrain polygyny. Similarly, polygyny is criminalized in Hindu law, it is often difficult to prosecute men under this law and it is practiced in societal laws.

Although state law does not grant equal rights to women, analyses of judicial cases and processes in state courts reveal a shift toward gender equality. For instance, in the case of Hindu law, the Family Court repudiates contested divorces initiated by men and pays attention to nonfinancial harm caused to Hindu women. The Court is more lenient to Hindu women who initiate divorce. In the context of Muslim Personal Law, with regard to women's economic rights post divorce, I argue that the Muslim Women's (Protection of Rights on Divorce) Act 1986 offers Muslim women more rights to claim maintenance under state laws than Hindu women receive. And although women across religious cleavages do not have equal rights to matrimonial property, the creative stretching of the law boundaries by combining provisions of civil, religious, and criminal laws, the stricter enforcement of maintenance claims, and the inclusion of civil society organizations in adjudicative processes in state courts all have played a role in increasing women's bargaining capacity in state law. The courts also tend to balance cultural accommodation and women's rights by relying on different provisions of Islamic laws and harmonizing these with constitutional provisions.

What factors explain reforms in lower state courts? Legal innovation and the creative use of social legislation by lawyers, interlinkages between judicial authority, lawyers, and civil society, and the interventions of reformist judges, as well as individual and collective agencies of women in moving courts, placing their stories and demands on the agenda of the court, negotiating legal system in order to maximize legal gains, and representing different versions of conjugal life influence change in state courts.

In a shared adjudication model, reforms take place in multiple state and societal legal sites. In the societal arena, we see that many competing societal laws and adjudicative forums provide more rights to women than do state law and courts. I discuss the "democratic participatory justice" system developed by the Meghwals and demonstrate that caste laws do not control women's sexuality; they recognize the economic contribution

CONCLUSION 329

of women and, in the end, offer more protection to women than state laws do. Similarly, societal laws also offer Muslim women protection from polygyny and unilateral divorce. We see that following the Shah Bano controversy, the rise of the Hindu right since the 1990s the Muslim religious organizations and religious seminaries came under pressure from feminists, civil society, and liberal sections from within the Muslim community to push for reforms. Faced with religious violence after the destruction of the Babri Mosque in 1992–1993 and in Gujarat in 2002, the presence of the Hindu right in the electoral arena and the global politics of the war on terror following 9/11, the Muslim religious leaders and bodies have responded to calls for reform in Muslim Personal Law and are engaged in ongoing dialog with women's organizations on the ground. The civil society and women's groups have taken up issues of communal violence and minority discrimination, and have been critical of the Hindu right; as a result, minority religious bodies have been more open to engagements with these groups on the matter of law reform.

We also see that competitive party politics, democratization, and political economy have also impacted the lawmaking and reform processes in caste councils as well as in residential and doorstep courts – some of them have sought reform of group practices through dialog with religious and civic authority. Besides, even though these informal organizations can violate individual rights, these can also develop processes and mechanisms that can play a role in checking abuses of power within societal legal forums and show the deployment of two types of mechanisms. I demonstrate that although informal legal organizations use tactics like social boycott, ridicule, shame, and intimidation to enforce their laws, intragroup factionalism and competition between external sources of authority at times prevent violations of individual rights. Furthermore, organizations also evolve self-regulatory measures from below to check the abuse of authority. In addition, individual and collective women's agency in negotiating and moving societal legal forums enable reforms from below.

Women's groups and others intervene in everyday adjudicative processes as well as the collective processes of reforms. In addition, women's groups have been able to provide services and support to women through their networks and linkages within the police, the courts, and other welfare organizations in Mumbai; community organizations have had to adapt in order to retain their influence in the community. With regard to the Muslim Personal Law, we see that from 1990 onward, the women's organizations also arrived at a consensus among them on the need to pursue reforms within the Muslim community and became involved in these processes. Their secular outlook, work during communal violence, and resistance to Hindu fundamentalism increased their credibility vis-à-vis religious seminaries and groups; their willingness to drop the demand for a uniform civil code created a possibility of ongoing dialog between conservative and moderate sections of Muslims on law reforms and impacted change.

Given that multiple sources of authority cogovern the conjugal family, I argue that the intertwined and interacting state agencies and professionals challenge, compete, cooperate, and communicate with one another across legal sites. Legal professionals, state officials, women's organizations, community leaders, and members of political parties intervene and negotiate with one another while adjudicating in individual cases; thus, they all participate in community-initiated processes of law reform. For instance, women from a Hindu caste encourage other women to approach Muslim women's organizations in order to access rights. Negotiations in such cases involve dialog between Muslim women's organizations, Hindu litigants, and the caste authorities. I discuss the public campaign against Muslim religious clergy who promote *muta* (temporary) marriages. The campaign was organized by the Muslim religious organization led by a group of social workers, clergy, lawyers, and businessmen that helps both Hindu and Muslim residents of a locality in central Mumbai.

A pluralized legal sphere balanced by civic, religious, and lay sources of authority facilitates cultural accommodation and allows spaces from which to negotiate women's rights. The data on adjudication in microlegal sites show that individual actors maintain and negotiate religio-cultural hybridity in practice and switch between religious identities. At the level of groups, we find that each religious group has several regulative and justificatory authority centers, none of which represents the internal consensus among the group. Intragroup heterogeneity questions the rhetoric around "authentic religious laws" and prevents an essentialized understanding of religious communities, because religious laws do not symbolize the unity of religious groups. In fact, a range of actors and organizations decide the content of religious family laws and encode different notions of family forms, values, and meanings into these laws. Indeed, conjugality itself is fluid, differently imagined, fashioned, and negotiated by varied actors. Thus, the notion of a particularistic religious identity grounded in the institution of the family and premised on rigid and hierarchical gender roles is challenged from within religious communities. In other words, diverse and contested notions of the idealized Hindu family and Muslim family exist in both communities and are linked to different understandings of religious identities, as subunits within religious groups hold diverse ideas about what comprises "Muslimness" and/or "Hinduness." These processes of imagining, constructing, and communicating the conjugal family prevents the homogenization of religious identities.

I submit that state-society interactions in adjudicative processes reveal fissures that prevent the cementing of group boundaries. First, codified Hindu laws and uncodified Muslim laws are reasonably fluid, and ideas about normative Hindu or Muslim families are contested in state courts and informal forums. As a result, the idea of a normative conjugal family as a repository of community identity is challenged in legal sites. In addition, litigants and organizations also cross over religious and caste boundaries. Individual litigants "exit" their caste, sect, and religious groups through tactical maneuvers across religious and intrareligious boundaries. Furthermore, both Hindu and Muslim litigants approach a variety of secular and religious charitable organizations for legal assistance during adjudicative processes; this forum shopping by litigants necessitates dialog, confrontations, and compromise between and among litigants and organizations. Once again, the study does not claim that heterogeneity of legal forums in itself allows for more bargaining possibilities. The option of ideologically diverse legal forums, especially the presence of sources of civic authority, especially women's groups, civil society organizations, and social movements, ensures the effectiveness of this model. The process of internal reforms in laws of different sects, castes, and communities necessitates both deliberation and interaction between state officials, religious organizations, women's groups, lawyers, and state officials such as the police.

The body of academic work on family law reforms in multicultural societies maintains a critical tension between group rights for minorities and women's rights in the community. This body of work fails to capture the dynamics of the Indian model of accommodation through shared adjudication because it facilitates more cultural diversity and gender equality than one might expect, given extant theory and research. The modalities of interactions between state and societal actors create spaces for individual and collective agency of women. The shared adjudication model allows litigants to switch forums to access their rights. I describe individual women's agency in increasing their bargaining power through combining legal alternatives. I also discuss women's collective agency in transforming laws and legal structures through their participation in lawmaking processes, especially in societal forums. Economic contexts, cultural ethos, political affiliations, and internal democracy within caste groups shape gender relations within organized caste groups and provide structural conditions for women's agency. Women's agency is constrained by poverty, domestic and religious violence, the lack of affinal and social networks, and the sexual division of labor within the family. Gender equality is an outcome of small processes and setbacks, localized efforts and a bundle of strategies, interventions in everyday processes of adjudication and collectivization of agendas, concerns and solutions through broader sociopolitical processes of law reform. It is a negotiated, uneven, and ongoing process; slow but holding forth a promise of structural change from below.

What Factors Would Bring About a Change in This Model?

Adopted in the 1950s, this model was an outcome of a bargain between the modernist and conservative postcolonial elite among the Hindus and Muslims and the Indian state. However, as we have seen, many more stakeholders are now involved in debating personal law reforms. Altered circumstances undergirding this arrangement would account for change in this model. For instance, the rise of Hindu religious fundamentalism and its access to the Indian state would severely constrain this model, as the Hindu right would prefer unification of laws and wish for assimilation of minorities in law; the reason being that central to the construction of a Hindu nation is the idea of a Hinduized uniform law,[2] a homogenizing and civilizing force that would turn religious minorities into unmarked citizenry. Control over the conjugal family is central to this image of a uniform civil code as a disciplinary project of the Hindu nation. The elements in the Hindu nationalist vision of the family include the prevention of intercaste and interreligious marriages through the control over women's sexuality, mobility, and reproduction. The BJP's accession to power in 1999–2004 did not bring about this outcome, as the party led a coalition government, but their ability to tamper with the model increases if the party gains a complete majority.

Similarly, a modernist consensus about the unification of all laws would also change the model.[3] At present, many more stakeholders have entered this debate. The left parties in the 1990s dropped their demand for a uniform civil code and built a consensus to engage with the community for internal reforms. The increased fragmentation of politics

---

[2] It is argued that the BJP has never clarified the content of a uniform civil code, and it is questionable whether they would wish to universalize the Hindu law to govern all Indians. However, the Rashtriya Swayamsevan Sangh, the "cultural affiliate" of the BJP, has made its agenda more explicit: It believes that the Hindu Code, which governs Sikhs, Jains, and Buddhists, should also be applicable to Muslims and Christians. See "Sikhs Belong to Hindu Samaj," *The Indian Express*, May 2, 2007.

[3] Such attempts have been made by the modernist elite in 1950s and 1970s, but have not succeeded (see Parashar 1992).

and competitive party politics would not push this issue on the agenda of other parties. In addition, another significant change on the ground has been the increased strength and organizing capacity of civil society, especially the women's movement. The women's movement has grown in numbers since the late 1970s, and the number of NGOs and community organizations in India has increased substantially since India adopted economic liberalization in the 1990s. These bodies have also sought the dual-pronged approach to balance cultural accommodation and gender equality. The ethno-religious organizations among Hindus and Muslims also wish to retain their authority to govern the family; given the situation, the enforcement of a uniform civil code seems unlikely.

Furthermore, the model is also an outcome of negotiations between and within the Congress Party and religious groups. The conflict between modernists and conservatives within the Congress Party in the 1950s over the nature and degree of reform in Hindu law led to a pragmatic concession that resulted in what I call the shared adjudication model. This arrangement accommodated the conservatives who believed that this would separate the marital practices of upper castes that disallowed divorce from those of lower castes that customarily practiced divorce (Derret 1963). A change in this balance (in other words, a modernist consensus among sections of Hindu religious group and the state about the creation of a unified, centralized authority in Hindu law) would also change the meaning of this model. However, although there are many criticisms of the misuse of power by caste councils on the ground, especially in north India, there are no such concrete proposals on the ground. Besides, there is also a possibility that such a change would not prevent the misuse of authority by caste councils, but would drive these processes underground.

What conditions undergird this model? Necessary conditions include resolution of bargaining and accommodation as state craft to resolve cultural conflicts, the presence of civic organizations and social and women's movements with broad agendas, a shared consensus among major political parties and actors on cultural accommodation around personal laws, the leadership flexibility within internally diverse ethno-religious groups, and independent and reformist judiciary. On the other hand, rising religious fundamentalism and ethno-religious violence, demobilization of social movements, including women's movements, and political instability would compromise the celebratory aspects of this model. Furthermore, the shared adjudication model is not specific to urban areas, as overlapping jurisdictions exist in rural areas. The absence of ideologically diverse actors would undermine the optimal functioning of this model regardless of the geographical setting.

An additional question requires a mention here. The ethnography of adjudication reveals that the ideas and constructions of the conjugal family prevailing among Hindus and Muslims counter the Hindu nationalist project of enforcing a uniform civil code that would homogenize the Indian family along the lines imagined by the Hindu right. Furthermore, interactions and communication between women's organizations, religious organizations, ethnic organizations, and members of religious communities structure the formation of key institutions in society, create spaces for intercultural interactions, and oppose the Hindu right's agenda. This evidence also unveils a puzzle: Spaces for intercultural mingling and dialog exist concomitantly with episodes of religious violence in the same sites in India. However, dominant explanations of ethno-religious violence in India suggest that riots are manufactured from above, by political parties, by "institutionalised riot systems," for political and electoral gains (Brass 2003; Wilkinson 2004). Another explanation is that Hindu Muslim riots happen in the absence of interethnic associational linkages in civil society organizations (Varshney 2001). In light of these explanations, the above trend no longer appears as contradictory and anomalous as suggested.

The Shared Adjudication Model Compared to Other Proposals for Accommodating Communities and Ensuring Gender Equality

How do the findings pertaining to the Indian case travel to other contexts, debates, and models? In this section, I place this argument in light of some recent arguments. In Chapter 1, we began the discussion with state-centered approaches and society-centered solutions to the resolution of the question of facilitating cultural pluralism and gender equality. We find that the proponents of uniform laws guarantee neither gender equality nor cultural accommodation. They sidestep the issue that the emphasis on uniform civil code can potentially generate forms of exclusion in ways that would marginalize minority religious groups, including Muslims as well as *adivasi* and lower-caste groups in India. In particular, they do not consider the centrality of the uniform civil code in the ideology of the Hindu right as a tool to build a homogenized nation-state. They also assume that uniform laws would be gender-just without considering the possibility that religious law can be shaped in ways that is both culturally sensitive and gender-just. Besides, the examples from Turkey and Europe show that enacting uniform laws does not ensure legal centralism – unofficial laws and customs prevail in Turkey and England (Yilmaz 2005).

The shared adjudication model is less in tension with the society-centered approach, though proponents of the society-centered approach like Chatterjee overlook the similarities in the nature of accommodation between the majority and minority groups in the Indian case. Chatterjee's solution for an inner democratic forum that is accountable and transparent need not be gender-just. Besides, we see that individuals and groups constantly mould and shape the meaning of law and marriage and gender in context of heterogeneous moral and legal reference points, and it is unclear whether this boundary crossing is possible in groups that would be moored to their group identities. I am also sympathetic to Scott's suggestion about a societal solution to resolve ethnic divide, though pursuing legal reforms exclusively in the domain of society would entail privatization of justice and would not be feasible in the context of family law reform. However, his suggestion for a dialog between ethno-religious groups over the meaning of their traditions is persuasive. Scott has not identified institutional and other means that would make this possible, and I find that the shared adjudication model contains some elements from Scott's proposal: It broadens the range of actors who would participate in this process and provides institutional avenues for this dialog to take place.

Other scholars have taken a different route to explain the balancing of group accommodation and gender equality without slipping into essentializing groups. Shachar argues for an institutional design that would allow the *nomoi* groups, that is, religio-cultural groups, autonomy to regulate the family while protecting rights of vulnerable individuals within these groups. She calls for a "joint governance" model that allows *nomoi* groups and the states to govern jointly over the family. She argues for the bifurcation of power between the group and the state in the sense that the *nomoi* groups would have the right to govern issues concerning group boundaries (who can marry whom and how) and determine the conditions of marriage (what constitutes a valid marriage) (Shachar 2001). The state, on the other hand, should govern the distribution of resources within the institution of the family. She suggests that this prevents the ossification of group boundaries, and protects women's rights in the family. However, this proposal allows cultural groups the power to control the boundaries of the community, and this would cement group identity and fail to protect the more vulnerable members of the group. Furthermore, Shachar does not visualize a connection between demarcating and distributive functions of family law. For instance, an ethnic group that normatively imagines marriage as a sacrament between two complimentary but unequal individuals would have a different scheme for distribution of property than a group that sees marriage as a contract between equals. The dissonance between the image and reality of the family form and its economic organization would lead the state to justify and choose one version over another. The state's privileging of one family form and economic rights over another would not fulfill conditions of equality; furthermore, it would provide an incentive for these groups to change the shape of their family and move toward the state-preferred version. Secondly, giving cultural groups exclusive authority to regulate the boundary of the family could possibly still cement group boundaries.

In contrast, in the shared adjudication model, some Hindu women are given legal advice by groups of Muslim women, Hindu and Muslim lawyers, and secular and religious women's groups; other civil society organizations acquire knowledge of religious laws of the state as well as of Islamic and/or customary laws, and in some cases, individuals juggle multiple religious identities – a caste Hindu can also profess to be a Muslim or a Christian. The group members convert from one sect to another, or from one religion to another. Hindus approach Muslim clergy to help dissolve their interreligious marriages, and broader campaigns for legal change necessitate alliance building and dialog across groups and religious boundaries. As the empirical examples in Chapters 4 and 5 demonstrate, these interactions allow the making and remaking of the meaning of religious identity, law, and the family. Even though these interactions do not prevent the cementing of boundaries completely, they allow pluralization within each religious-ethnic group as well as ongoing intergroup exchange. The shared adjudication model also grants the state the sole authority to regulate the distribution of property. However, in a system of bifurcated authority, the dissolution of marriage is linked to the distribution of property, and a neat separation is not maintained in practice.

In *Multiculturalism without Culture*, Anne Phillips argues that multicultural policies, if premised on a thick and notion of culture, reify group boundaries, and strengthen the authority of elite group members. Even though Phillips agrees that group members can believe in and live through a strong notion of group identity and make claims based on these beliefs, she argues for a multiculturalism grounded in the concept of individual rights that will ensure the protection of gender equality within the group. To elaborate, she argues that the state should continue to provide institutional support to minority groups, but she also asks that the state design multicultural policies that meet the needs of vulnerable groups, but do not privilege and reinforce the authority of dominant group members within the group (Phillips 2007).

Phillips discusses the policy of adjudication under the Sharia law in Britain and agrees that religious councils based on the four schools of Sharia should be allowed, and that more progressive readings of law should be publicized so that women can approach such forums. However, this would still ossify religious identity, abolish customary laws that may or may not allow more spaces for gender equality, and give preference to the theological/textual readings of law and consolidate the authority of the jurists. Secondly, this would not allow the involvement of other forms of authority that can also intervene legally – women, civil society organizations, the majority of the community, and other cultural groups – and thus would not foster intercultural engagement.

The shared adjudication model questions several aspects of Phillips's claim. For instance, the Indian case shows that minority groups in India have made contextual claim to the recognition of religious laws and have professed a strong belief in a strong notion of culture. Facilitating the claims to recognize religious laws has not cemented group identities to the extent that Phillips premises. I show here how the shared adjudication model has allowed multiple, ever-shifting, and intermingling notions, ideas, practices, and beliefs of Hinduness and Muslimness to flourish. Secondly, the model has fragmented religious authority on the ground. In Chapter 4, I highlight the debate, within the Muslim community and in society at large, over the question of whether the state should recognize parallel religious courts established by the Deoband school. We see the internal diversity of views and opinions and power centers within the Muslim community, and find that the claims of multiple spokesmen to speak on behalf of the group are contested by many other power centers from within the group. Thus, the promotion of internal diversity within a group can indeed counter the ossification of group boundaries.

Phillips envisages a version of multiculturalism grounded in the concept of individual rights that will ensure the protection of gender equality within the group. Whereas Phillips suggests a state-centered approach of crafting multicultural policies from above, Sarah Song has turned to deliberative democracy over multiculturalism as a preferred instrument of cultural accommodation. She argues that deliberative democracy is an important process, as it helps clarify the nature of conflict between different groups, brings to light the varied interests at stake in cultural conflict, allows minority groups to challenge cultural stereotypes held by the dominant groups, and points out double standards of the state and majority groups. She suggests that free and equal status of participants and respect for the basic rights of citizens (freedom of expression, conscience, and association) are minimal conditions for starting the process of deliberation. Song also explores the question of how culturally diverse states ensure justice for religio-cultural groups and secure justice for women within these groups. Song advances "a right-respecting accommodationism" (Song 2007, 9) that ensures the recognition of minority groups' demands for cultural rights on grounds of present discrimination, historical injustice, and state establishment of culture. In addition, she argues for inter- and intracultural deliberation as the means to address and resolve the varied context-specific demands for recognition made by cultural groups.

The limit to accommodation in this case is provided by the protection of the basic rights of individual members of minority groups. Song recognizes that gender equality is an incomplete achievement in all societies and cultures. However, she argues that minority groups that undermine the equal rights of women or practice gender discrimination should not ask to be accommodated. Her preconditions are stringent and would hamper the process of initiating public deliberation in divided societies. Also, her assertion that the majority and minority cultural groups should disallow their particular interests in the public domain limits the terms and modes of communication between the participants. Indeed, shared adjudication allows women to make claims for gender equality as well as to retain their modes of communication ranging from storytelling, humor, gossip, sarcasm, and street demonstrations and confrontation. Secondly, the shared adjudication model points to multiple routes of interactions between communities, allows intermingling between varied groups and actors, and facilitates the cross-pollination of ideas, beliefs, and practices in more forums than those allowed in a structured dialog proposed by Song.

Deveaux also turns to democratic theory to balance cultural claims with gender equality. She suggests that in many instances, cultural conflicts are about power, material resources, and interests, not about moral values (Deveaux 2006). Song criticizes Deveaux for subsuming questions of moral values, such as gender equality, under the idea that cultural conflicts around recognition of customary laws and practices are purely about material interests; I agree with this criticism. Nevertheless, borrowing from democratic theory, Deveaux makes a compelling case, arguing that strategically focused deliberation (Deveaux 2006, 6), in formal and informal arenas, between members of cultural groups, coupled with strategies of bargaining and accommodation, is a way to solve cultural conflicts through political negotiations and compromise. She stresses the political inclusion of women and vulnerable intragroup members by pursuing strategies that empower women to speak, as well as to check powerful community members who might silence women (Deveaux 2006). Discussing the contestations around constitutional reforms in South Africa and the debate around the conflict between customary law and women's rights in South Africa, Deveaux argues that deliberation, negotiations, and compromise can produce fair and equitable outcomes, which may also be nonliberal, although revisable (Deveaux 2006, 209). Even though I agree with Deveaux about using public deliberation in formal and informal spaces to bargain and arrive at political, revisable solutions to the question at hand, I find that deliberative democracy, in itself, is a necessary but insufficient condition to effect change in the shared adjudication model. Apart from deliberation, change is a product of a bundle of strategies including street action, political confrontation, everyday bargaining and negotiations, alliance formation, and organizational innovations.

Both Song and Phillips would agree that religious groups' claims should not be accommodated should they violate individual rights in family law. I agree with the normative concerns of these authors concerning minority rights and gender equality. However, my work points to a different route toward achieving it. The Indian case suggests that cultural pluralism has enhanced pluralization in society and carved spaces to push for gender equality from above and below. I suggest that gender equality as a starting point to ask for cultural rights is too stringent a condition to resolve cultural conflicts. Rather than including gender equality as a precondition, or a limit to cultural accommodation, state and societal actors (especially feminists) could craft state policies in ways that facilitate greater pluralization within these groups, promote the ongoing interactions between diverse stakeholders, and create enabling conditions so that both majority and minority groups (which seek recognition to or are granted cultural accommodation) work toward realizing – and later maintaining – gender equality.

The task of gender equality is not only through introducing state policies from above, and I reiterate the role of women's groups and civic sources of authority in creatively interpreting and shaping the meaning of state policies on the ground. In order to counter the collusive power of multiple patriarchies, the state, liberals, and moderates within majority and minority groups and civil society could devise strategies to enforce measures to check abuse of authority by elite group members and prevent the consolidation of power among a few members of these groups. These actors also should identify strategies to work for gender equality and facilitate, create, promote, and fund various bodies to bring about gender equality in majority and minority cultural communities on an ongoing basis. This is possible because in the shared adjudication model, the ongoing communications between different legal orders create a ground for keeping alive discussions on equality (or the lack thereof), as well as create conditions for legal innovation and transmission of ideas regarding best practices between actors, and generate a consensus for legal reforms. Gender equality under this model is understood not only as a right fixed in law, but a product of and a part of ongoing adjudicative processes. In the Indian case, so far, this process has been localized, fragmented, and ad hoc, and while in some cases, state and societal reforms have coincided and resulted in leveling of certain inequalities, complete gender equality remains elusive. Indeed, feminists could demand more accountability from the state and cultural groups to make – together with them – efforts toward this end.

Discussing Law Reform in Personal Laws

Feminists and scholars debating family law reform in the Middle East, South and Southeast Asia, and Africa point to the conflict between group autonomy demanded by ethno-religious groups and its implications for gender justice in law (Ahmad 2003; Hatem 1986; Joseph 1997; Moosa 2002; Phillips 1995, 2003). The broad discussions by feminists and modernists on law reforms in multicultural societies in the Middle East, Africa, and South and Southeast Asia posit that states should provide formal and substantive equality for women and should deepen citizenship rights in society, as the improvement of women's status in general increases their overall ability to confront patriarchal laws (Joseph 1997; Cook 1994; Moghadam 1994).[4] In a similar vein, feminists who oppose multiculturalism prefer deepening of universal citizenship for women; they believe that multicultural policies trump the right of cultures to self-govern at the cost of gender equality, because these policies consolidate male authority within these cultures (Nussbaum 1997; Okin 1999, 2002, 2005). The feminist opponents of multiculturalism overlook the role of the state in constructing ethno-religious or majority and minority communities through state policies. Secondly, they do not capture the internal differentiation and diversity of views within these groups, and view these in essentialized, monolithic terms. These scholars agree that the state is patriarchal, but suggest that feminist interventions can

---

[4] For instance, in India, the feminist group Forum Against Oppression of Women recommends that the state attempt wide-ranging reforms of the formal legal system and make it more accessible to women (Visions of Gender Just Realities, FAOW, 1996). Additionally, as the Mumbai-based feminist legal center Majlis suggests, the state should enact new laws regarding matrimonial property that can be applied to women litigants across religions (Gangoli 1996).

fracture, challenge, and change state patriarchy. However, religio-cultural communities, or cultures in their accounts, are often seen as intransigent, regressive, and resistant to change. We find though that in many contexts, feminists have developed strategies to work with and challenge cultural authority. Islamic feminists, for instance, have reinterpreted religious and textual traditions in order to argue for gender equality within the religious framework in Muslim majority and minority nations (Wadud 1999); in Indonesia and Malaysia, women have, at times, successfully mobilized Islamic courts to increase their economic rights and social status (Bowen 1988; Peletz 2002). States such as Tunisia, Egypt, Syria, Morocco, and Algeria have codified and reformed Islamic laws to redress glaring inequalities in inheritance laws of Muslims (Charrad 2001; Tucker 2008; Welchman 2007). The Indian case has implications for feminist debates on law reforms, as we find that it is not only necessary to ask for more legal rights from the state (both formal and substantive), but also call for secular, modernist, and religious feminisms' ongoing collective engagements, as well as everyday forms of engagement with religio-cultural communities.

The Indian case also demonstrates that negotiating gender equality within majority or minority communities is a task, not limited to women belonging to these communities, but for all sections of women's movements without slippage into paternalism. The study argues for feminist politics that engages meaningfully with ethnic groups and sees this engagement as an enabling rather than a defensive one. Globally, women's movements that pursue a broader reforms agenda, align with other social movements, self-consciously work with minority groups against state-led or majority-led discrimination and violence, support minority women's organizing, and build alliances with various sections in minority groups are more likely to be effective in intervening with minority communities.

A variant of the statist approach suggests that states should provide conditions for legal reforms (Bilgrami 1994). Hallaq offers that the development of classical Islamic laws was stunted during colonial and postcolonial state formation, and that states wishing to introduce the Sharia law in modern legal systems should provide conditions to facilitate the development of classical Islamic law (Hallaq 2001, 2004). In addition, states can bring various factions within a cultural group together in a bid to arrive at consensus. This data also show that ongoing dialog within society, between majority and minority, between the state and communities, and especially between differing factions within the cultural groups with differing interests, can also result in incremental reforms in personal laws and help increase intercultural dialog in society.

I do not advocate uncritical cultural pluralism, nor do I argue that the state surrender its regulatory autonomy to society. The discussion around adjudication in the formal legal forums reveals that the Indian state penetrates society, retains its authority to check rule violations and aberrations, curtails the powers of formal and informal legal organizations, and remains an authority for appeal and protection against the violation of individual rights within society. Given that the formal and informal forums are intertwined, this study shows that reforms in the content of state laws and court procedures would have both a symbolic and a material impact on informal legal forums as well.

I do not suggest that the mere presence of different adjudicative centers of authority increases pluralization and women's rights. I show instead that shared adjudication by "ideologically diverse actors" such as the state and civil society organizations (including women's groups, religious organizations, and informal networks) is a structural condition for the claim made here. In addition, the Indian situation does not represent an example of "best practices" in the governance of religious family law; rather, the case points toward devising reforms in legally plural situations by combining multiple reform strategies from state courts and societal legal bodies.

Whereas the state is an agent of change, spaces for interreligious interactions and gender equality also exist in domains autonomous from the state. Drawing from the data, I also propose another step toward concrete reforms in laws from below by focusing on informal spaces. I turn to

Teubner's concept of self-reflexive law and decentralized self-regulatory institutions for concrete proposals for change. The interpenetration of state law and societal laws and institutions creates a flow of legal actors, facilitators, and gatekeepers across formal and informal spheres. In his views on autopoietic systems, Teubner argues for the decentralization of the legal system so that state law and the legal system can structure and reform societal-level institutions from outside and can thus regulate them (Teubner 1983). Teubner identifies a legal structure, or "reflexive law," which "restricts itself to installation, correction, and redefinition of democratic self-regulating mechanisms" of societal legal orders (Teubner 1983, 239). The state should "decide about decisions, regulate regulations, and establish structural processes for future decisions in terms of organisations, procedures, and competencies" (Teubner 1983, 275). This study describes how castes and sects evolve democratic measures, create self-regulatory mechanisms, and build innovative organizational models to regulate the family. I suggest that engaging with informal agents in imaginative ways can herald social change. For instance, designing societal legal institutions by simultaneously drawing inspirations from traditional dispute resolution systems, democratic institutions, and state courts is a step toward ensuring accountability and justice. I also suggest that building informal society-based organizations that are inclusive, open, democratic, accountable, and that also incorporate feminist visions of gender justice is one of the strategies of law reform from below.

Conclusion

This book shows that the Indian model of "shared adjudication" in which ideologically diverse actors and institutions – that is, the internally heterogeneous religio-cultural groups, civil society, women's groups, and the state – share adjudicative authority, are more likely to enhance interreligious accommodation and provide gender equality.

This model creates the paradoxical movement of centralization and decentralization of law, extending state authority as well as limiting

CONCLUSION

it; engendering in official and unofficial legal forums the negotiations and debates over the nature and content of religious family law. Individual and collective legal mobilization by women influences and shapes legal processes and outcomes; the interactions between the state, women's groups, ethno-religious groups and sources of civic authority ensure the destabilization of gender inequality in state and societal laws and legal forums. In the shared adjudication model, varied legal actors dialog and dispute over meanings of faith, tradition, law, conjugality, and gender; arriving at localized internal consensus in some instances, continuing with their contestations in others. State-society interactions in interpenetrative legal sphere ensure the transmission, communication, and cross fertilization of these ideas, disputes, resolutions, and processes both within and among heterogeneous religious groups, civil society, and the state. These processes prevent the cementing of group boundaries, and enhance cultural pluralization in society.

Appendix

Cases Cited

Abdul Hameed v. *Fousiya* [2004] (3) KLT 1049.
Abdul Zalil Ahmed v. *Mustt. Marina Begum*, AIR [1999] Gauhati, 28.
Bai Fatima v. *Alimahomed*, 37 Bom. 280 [1913] 17 I.C. 946.
Bai Tahira v. *Ali Hussain Fisalli Chothia*, AIR [1979] SC 362.
BP Achala Anand v. *S Appi Reddy*, AIR [2005] SC 986.
Dagdu s/o Chotu Pathan v. *Rahimbi Dagdu Pathan and Others*, Aurangabad Bench of Mumbai High Court (May 2002).
Daniel Latifi v. *Union of India*, (7) SC [2001] 740.
Jaipal Kaur v. *Ishan Singh*, 1983 HLR 119,
Mohammad Ahmed Khan v. *Shah Bano Begum*, AIR [1985] SC 945.
Narasu Appa Mali v. *State of Bombay*, AIR [1952] Bombay.
Naz Foundation (India) Trust v Government of NCT, Delhi and Others. WP (C) [2001]. No. 7455
Pratibha Rani v. *Suraj Kumar & Anr*, AIR [1985] 628 SCR (3) 191.
Rasiya v. *State of Kerala*, (2) KLT [2002] 825.
Sarla Mudgal v. *Union of India*, AIR [1995] SC 1531.
Savitri Pandey v. *Prem Chandra Pandey* JT [2002] (1) SC, P 25.
Seema v. *Ashwani Kumar*, (1) KLT [2006] 791 SC.
Shamim Ara v. *State of UP and Another*, AIR [2002] SCW 4162.
Srinivas Aiyar v. *Saraswathi Ammal*, AIR [1952] Madras 193.
State of Bombay v. *Appa*, AIR [1952] Bombay 84.
V Bappukutty@Muhammed v. *Shahid D/O Muhammed*, RD- KL [2007] 1497.

Bibliography

An-Na'im, Abdullahi. 2002a. *Cultural transformations and human rights in Africa*. New York: Zed Books.

An-Na'im, Abdullahi. 2002b. *Islamic family law in a changing world: A global resource book*. New York: Zed Books.

Abel, Richard. 1982a. The contradictions of informal justice. In *The politics of informal justice, Vol.1: The American experience*, ed. Richard Abel, 267–310. New York: Academic Press.

Abel, Richard. 1982b. Introduction to *The politics of informal justice, Vol.1: The American experience*, ed. Richard Abel, 1–13. New York: Academic Press.

Abu-Lughod, Lila. 1990. The romance of resistance: Tracing transformations of power through Bedouin Women. *American Ethnologist* 17, no. 1 (February): 41–55.

Afifi, Mohamed. 1996. Reflections on the personal laws of Egyptian Copts. In *Women, the family, and divorce laws in Islamic history*, ed. Amira Sonbol, 202–215. Syracuse: Syracuse University Press.

Agarwal, Bina. 1994. *A field of one's own: Gender and land rights in South Asia*. New York: Cambridge University Press.

Agnes, Flavia. 1995a. Hindu men, monogamy and uniform civil code. *Economic and Political Weekly* 30, no. 50 (December 16): 3238–3244.

Agnes, Flavia. 1995b. *State, gender and the rhetoric of law reform*. Bombay: SNDT University.

Agnes, Flavia. 1997. Protecting women against violence?: Review of a decade of legislation, 1980–1990. In *State and politics in India*, ed. Partha Chatterjee, 521–560. Delhi: Oxford University Press.

Agnes, Flavia. 1999. *Law, gender and inequality: The politics of women's rights in India*. Delhi: Oxford University Press.

Agnes, Flavia. 2002. Transgressing boundaries of gender and identity. *Economic and Political Weekly* no. 36 (September 7): 3695–3698.

Agnes, Flavia. 2008. Hindu conjugality: Transition from sacrament to contractual obligations. In *Redefining family law in India: Essays in honour of B. Sivaramayya*, 236–257. New Delhi: Routledge.

Ahmad, Imtiaz, ed. 2003. *Divorce and remarriage among Muslims in India*. Delhi: Manohar.

Alam, Arshad. The board of no shame. *Outlook India*, Web edition. Available from http://www.outlookindia.com (accessed May 4, 2005).

Alavi, Hamza. 1972. The state in postcolonial societies: Pakistan and Bangladesh. *New Left Review* 74 (July–August): 59–81.

Alberstein, Michael. 2006. Mediating paradoxically: Complimenting the paradox of "relational autonomy" with the "paradox of rights" in thinking mediation. In *Paradoxes and inconsistencies in the law*, ed. Oren Perez and Gunther Teubner, 225–246. Portland: Hart Publishing.

Albuquerque, Teresa. 1992. *Bombay, a history*. New Delhi: Rashna/Promilla.

Allot, Anthony. 1970. *New essays in African law*. London: Butterworths.

Allot, Anthony and Gordon R. Woodman, ed. 1995. *People's law and state law: The Bellagio papers*. Dordrecht: Foris Publications.

Amar, Akhil. 1985. A neo-federalist view of Article III: Separating the two tiers of federal jurisdiction. *Boston University Law Review* 65 (March): 205–272.

Amien, Wahida. 2006. Overcoming the conflict between the right to freedom of religion and women's right to equality: A South African case study of Muslim marriages. *Human Rights Quarterly* 28, no. 3 (August): 729–754.

Anderson, J. N. D. 1959. *Islamic law in the modern world*. New York: New York University Press.

Anveshi Law Committee. 1997. Is gender justice only a legal issue?: Political stakes in the uniform civil code debate. *Economic and Political Weekly* 32, nos. 9–10: 453–458.

Arthurs, H. W. 1985. *Without the law: Administrative justice and legal pluralism in nineteenth-century England*. Toronto: University of Toronto Press.

Auyero, Javier. 2002. The judge, the cop and the queen of carnival: Ethnography, storytelling and the (contested) meanings of protest. *Theory and Society* 31, no. 2 (April): 151–187.

BIBLIOGRAPHY

Bailey, Frederick G. 1963. *Politics and social change: Orissa in 1959*. Berkeley: University of California Press.
Bailey, Martha. 1989. Unpacking the "rational alternative": A critical review of family mediation movement claims. In *Canadian Journal of Family Law* 8, no. 1: 61–94.
Bainham, Andrew. 2003. Men and women behaving badly: Is fault dead in English family law? In *Family law: Processes, practices and pressures*, ed. J. Dewar and S. Parker, 523–542. Portland: Hart Publishing.
Baird, Robert. 1993. On defining Hinduism as a religious and legal category. In *Religion and law in independent India*, ed. Robert Baird, 24–40. Delhi: Manohar.
Baird, Robert. 2001. Gender implications for a uniform civil code. In *Religion and personal law in secular India: A call to judgment*, ed. Gerald Larson, 145–162. Bloomington: Indiana University Press.
Baird, Robert, ed. 1993. *Religion and law in independent India*. Delhi: Manohar.
Barkey, Karen. 1994. *Bandits and bureaucrats: The Ottoman route to state centralization*. Ithaca: Cornell University Press.
Basu, Amrita. 1995. Feminism inverted: The gendered imagery and real women of Hindu nationalism. In *Women and the Hindu right: A collection of essays*, ed. Tanika Sarkar and Urvashi Butalia, 158–180. New Delhi: Kali for Women.
Basu, Monmayee. 2001. *Hindu women and marriage law: From sacrament to contract*. New Delhi: Oxford University Press.
Basu, Srimati. 1999. *She comes to take her rights: Indian women, property and propriety*. Albany: State University of New York Press.
Basu, Srimati. 2001. The personal and the political: Indian women and inheritance law. In *Religion and personal law in secular India*, ed. Gerald Larson, 163–183. Bloomington: Indiana University Press.
Baum, Lawrence. 1993. Case selection and decision-making in the United States Supreme Court. *Law and Society Review* 27: 443–459.
Baumann, Gerd. 1999. *The multicultural riddle: Rethinking national, ethnic and religious identities*. New York: Routledge.
Baxi, Upendra. 1982. *The crisis of the Indian legal system*. New Delhi: Vikas.
Baxi, Upendra. 1985. Popular justice, participatory development and power politics: The Lok Adalat in turmoil. In *People's law and state law: The*

Bellagio papers, ed. Anthony Allott and Gordon R. Woodman, 171–186. Dordrecht: Foris Publications.

Baxi, Upendra and Marc Galanter. 1979. *Panchayat* justice: An Indian experiment in legal access. In *Access to justice, Vol. 3: Emerging issues and perspectives*, ed. M. Cappelletti and B. Garth, 341–386. Milan: Giuffre.

Baum, Lawrence. 1993. Case selection and decision-making in the United States Supreme Court. *Law and Society Review* 27, no. 2: 443–459.

Beck, Lois and Nikki Keddie, ed. 1978. *Women in the Muslim world*. Cambridge: Harvard University Press.

Belley, Jean-Guy. 1997. Law as *terra incognita*: Constructing legal pluralism. *Canadian Journal of Law and Society* 12, no. 17 (Fall): 17–24.

Bhargava, Rajeev. 1998. *Secularism and its critics*. New York: Oxford University Press.

Bhatnagar, R. On triple talaq. *The Times of India*, August 24, 1998.

Bhattacharya, Chandrima. Rights for women in model *nikahnama*. *The Telegraph*, July 26, 2004.

Bilgrami, Akeel. 1994. Two conceptions of secularism: Reason, modernity and Archimedean ideal. *Economic and Political Weekly* 29, no. 28 (July 4): 1749–1761.

Bilgrami, Akeel. 1997. Secular liberalism and moral psychology of identity. *Economic and Political Weekly* 32, no. 40 (October 4–10): 2527–2540.

Black, Donald J. 1973. The mobilization of law. *The Journal of Legal Studies* 2, no. 1 (January): 125–149.

Bottomley, Anne. 1985. What is happening to family law? A feminist critique of conciliation. In *Women in law: Explorations in law, family and sexuality*, ed. J. Brophy and C. Smart, 162–187. London: Routledge and Kegan Paul.

Bowen, John R. 1988. The transformation of an Indonesian property system: "Adat," Islam and social change in the Gayo highlands. *American Ethnologist* 15, no. 2 (May): 274–293.

Bowen, John R. 2003. *Islam, law, and equality in Indonesia: An anthropology of public reason*. New York: Cambridge University Press.

Brass, Paul. 1991. *Ethnicity and nationalism: Theory and comparison*. New Delhi: Sage Publications.

Brass, Paul. 1994. *The politics of India since independence*. Cambridge: Cambridge University Press.

Brass, Paul. 2003. *The production of Hindu-Muslim violence in contemporary India*. Seattle: University of Washington Press.

BIBLIOGRAPHY

Bright, Charles and Susan Harding, ed. 1984. *Statemaking and social movements: Essays in history and theory.* Ann Arbor: University of Michigan Press.

Bromley, Peter M. 1992. *Family law.* London: Butterworths.

Bryan, P. E. 1992. Killing us softly: Divorce mediation and the politics of power. *Buffalo Law Review* 40, no. 2: 441–523.

Bunsha, Dione. 2006. A serial kidnapper and his mission. *The Hindu* 23, no. 25 (December).

Butt, Simon. 1999. Polygamy and mixed marriage in Indonesia: The application of the marriage law in courts. In *Indonesia: Law and society*, ed. Timothy Lindsey, 122–144. Sydney: The Federation Press.

Cain, Maureen. 1988. Beyond informal justice. In *Informal justice?* ed. Roger Matthews, 51–86. London: Sage Publications.

Campbell, James. 1896. *Gazetteer of Bombay* 3: 1.

Carminkar, Evan H. 1994. Why must inferior courts obey Supreme Court precedents? *Stanford Law Review* 46, no. 4 (April): 817–873.

Carrithers, Michael. 1988. Passions of nation and community in the Bahubali affair. *Modern Asian Studies* 22, no. 4: 815–844.

Carrithers, Michael and Caroline Humphrey. 1991. *The assembly of listeners: Jains in society.* Cambridge: Cambridge University Press.

Carroll, Lucy. 1978. Colonial perceptions of Indian society and the emergence of caste associations. *Journal of Asian Studies* XXXVII, no. 2 (February): 233–250.

Carroll, Lucy. 1982. Talaq e tafwid and stipulation in a Muslim marriage contract: Important means of protecting the position of South Asian Muslim wife. *Modern Asian Studies* 16, no. 2: 277–309.

Carroll, Lucy. 1983. Muslim family law in India: Law, custom and empirical research. *Contributions to Indian sociology* 17, no. 2 (July–December): 205–222.

Census of India, 1911 (Bombay, 1912).

Census of India, 1921 (Bombay, 1922).

Census of India, 1931 (Bombay, 1933).

Chanock, Martin. 2001. *The making of South African legal culture, 1902–1936: Fear, favour and prejudice.* Cambridge: Cambridge University Press.

Chaplin, Susan. 2002. Scavengers: Still marginalised. In *Dalits and the State*, ed. Ghanshyam Shah, 205–240. New Delhi: Centre for Rural Studies, Concept Publications.

Charrad, Mounira. 2001. *States and women's rights: The making of postcolonial Tunisia, Algeria, and Morocco.* Berkeley: University of California Press.
Chatterjee, Partha. 1993. *The nation and its fragments: Colonial and postcolonial histories.* Princeton: Princeton University Press.
Chatterjee, Partha. 1994. Secularism and toleration. *The Economic and Political Weekly* 29, no. 28 (July 9): 1768–1777.
Chatterjee, Partha. 2004. *The politics of the governed: Reflections on popular politics in most of the world.* New York: Columbia University Press.
Chatterjee, Partha, ed. 1997. *State and politics in India.* Delhi: Oxford University Press.
Chen, Marty and Jean Dreze. 1992. Widows and health in rural North India. *Economic and Political Weekly* 27, nos. 43–44 (October 24–31): 81–92.
Chiba, Masaji. 1985. The channel of official law to unofficial law in Japan. In *People's law and state law: The Bellagio papers,* ed. Anthony Allott and Gordon R. Woodman, 207–216. Dordrecht: Foris Publications.
Chiba, Masaji. 1986. The identity postulates of indigenous law, and its function in legal transplantation. In *Legal pluralism: Proceedings of Canberra law workshop VII,* ed. Peter Sack and Elizabeth Minchin, 33–50. Canberra: Research School of Social Sciences, Australian National University.
Chiba, Masaji. 2002. *Legal cultures in human society.* Tokyo: Shinzansha International.
Chiba, Masaji, ed. 1985. *Asian indigenous law in interaction with received law.* New York: Kegan Paul International.
Chodosh, Hiram. 2004. *Global justice reform: A comparative methodology.* New York: New York University Press.
Chowdhry, Prem. 1994. *The veiled women: Shifting gender equations in rural Haryana, 1880–1990.* Delhi: Oxford University Press.
Chowdhry, Prem. 1997. Enforcing cultural codes: Gender and violence in North India. *Economic and Political Weekly* 32, no. 19 (May 10–16): 1019–1028.
Chowdhry, Prem. 2004. Private lives, state intervention: Cases of runaway marriages in rural North India. *Modern Asian Studies* 38, no. 1 (February): 55–84.
Cohn, Bernard. 1965. Anthropological notes on dispute and law in India. *American Anthropologist* 67, no. 6 (December): 82–122.

Cohn, Bernard. 1987. *An anthropologist among historians and other essays.* Delhi: Oxford University Press.

Cohn, Bernard. 1996. *Colonialism and its forms of knowledge: The British in India.* Princeton: Princeton University Press.

Comaroff, John and Simon Roberts. 1981. *Rules and processes: The cultural logic of disputes in an African context.* Chicago: University of Chicago Press.

Cook, Rebecca J., ed. 1994. *Human rights of women: National and international perspectives.* Philadelphia: University of Pennsylvania Press.

Corrigan, Philip and Derek Sayer. 1985. *The great arch: English state formation as cultural revolution.* New York: Basil Blackwell.

Cott, Nancy. 2000. *Public vows: A history of the marriage and the nation.* Cambridge: Harvard University Press.

Cottam Ellis, Christine. 1991. The Jain merchant castes of Rajasthan: Some aspects of the management of social identity in a market town. In *The assembly of listeners: Jains in society*, ed. Michael Carrithers and Caroline Humphrey, 75–107. Cambridge: Cambridge University Press.

Cover, Robert. 1983. Foreword: Nomos and narrative. *Harvard Law Review* 97, no. 1: 4–68.

Daftary, Farhad. 1990. *The Ismai'lis, their history and doctrines.* Cambridge: Cambridge University Press.

Das, Rathin. Gujarat marriage fiat tied in knots. *Hindustan Times*, July 21, 2006.

Dave, Anjali and Gopika Solanki. 2001. *Journey from violence to crime: A study of domestic violence in the city of Mumbai.* Mumbai: Tata Institute of Social Sciences.

Delgado, Richard, et al. 1985. Fairness and formality: Minimizing the risk of prejudice in alternative dispute resolution. *Wisconsin Law Review* 6: 1359–1404.

Derret J. D. M. 1963. *Introduction to modern Hindu law.* Bombay: Oxford University Press.

Derret J. D. M. 1968. *Religion, law and the state in India.* London: Faber.

Derret J. D. M. 1976. *Essays in classical and modern Hindu law, Vols. 1–4.* Leiden: Brill.

Derret J. D. M. 1999. *Religion, law and the state in India.* New York: Oxford University Press.

Deshpande, Swati. HC upholds court fee waivers for women in some types of cases. *Times of India*, March 29, 2002.

Deveaux, Monique. 2000. *Cultural pluralism and dilemmas of justice.* Ithaca: Cornell University Press.
Deveaux, Monique. 2005. A deliberative approach to conflicts of culture. In *Minorities within minorities*, ed. Avigail Eisenberg and Jeff Spinner-Halev, 340–362. Cambridge: Cambridge University Press.
Deveaux, Monique. 2006. *Gender and justice in multicultural liberal states.* Oxford: Oxford University Press.
Devji, Faisal. 1987. Conversion to Islam: The Khojas. M.A. diss., Department of History, University of Chicago.
Dhagamwar, Vasudha. 1974. *Law, power and justice: Protection of personal rights under the Indian Penal Code.* Bombay: M. N. Tripathy.
Dhagamwar, Vasudha. 1992. *Law, power and justice.* New Delhi: Sage.
Dirks, Nicholas. 1992. *Colonialism and culture.* Ann Arbor: University of Michigan Press.
Dirks, Nicholas. 2001. *Colonialism and the making of modern India.* Princeton: Princeton University Press.
Diwan, Paras. 1985. *Modern Hindu law.* 6th ed. Allahabad: Modern Book House.
Dobbin, Christine. 1970. Competing elites in the Bombay city politics in the mid-nineteenth century, 1852–1853. In *Elites in South Asia*, ed. E. Leach and S. N. Mukherjee, 79–94. Cambridge: Cambridge University Press.
Dobbin, Christine. 1972. *Urban leadership in western India: Politics and communities in Bombay City 1840–1885.* Delhi: Oxford University Press.
Dube, Saurabh. 1998. *Untouchable pasts: Religion, identity and power among a central Indian community 1780–1950.* Albany: State University of New York Press.
Dzur, Albert and Susan Olson. 2004. Revisiting informal justice: Restorative justice and democratic professionalism. *Law and Society Review* 38, no. 1 (March): 139–176.
Eckert, Julia. 2003. *The charisma of direct action: Power, politics and the Shiv Sena.* New Delhi: Oxford University Press.
Eckert, Julia. 2004. Urban government and emerging forms of legal pluralism in Mumbai. *Journal of Legal Pluralism and Unofficial Law* 50: 29–60.
Eckert, Julia. 2005. Whose state is it?: Hindu-nationalist violence and populism in India. In *The dynamics of states: The formation and crises of state domination*, ed. Klaus Schlichte, 41–70. Aldershot: Ashgate.

Eckert, Julia. 2006. From subjects to citizens: Legalism from below and the homogenisation of the legal sphere. *Journal of Legal Pluralism and Unofficial Law* 53, no. 54: 45–75.

Eisenberg, Avigail. 2005. Identity and liberal politics: The problem of minorities within minorities. In *Minorities within minorities*, ed. Avigail Eisenberg and Jeff Spinner-Halev, 249–270. Cambridge: Cambridge University Press.

Eisenberg, Avigail and Jeff Spinner-Halev. 2005. *Minorities within minorities*. Cambridge: Cambridge University Press.

Engel, David M. 1987. Law, time and community. *Law and Society Review* 21, no. 4: 605–637.

Engineer, Ashghar Ali. 1989. *The Muslim communities of Gujarat: An exploratory study of bohras, Khojas, and Memons*. Delhi: Ajanta Publications.

Ephroz, Khan Noor. 2003. *Women and law: Muslim personal law perspective*. Jaipur: Rawat Publications.

Eskridge Jr., William N. 1990. The new textualism. *UCLA Law Review* 37: 621–691.

Esposito, John L. 1982. *Women in Muslim family law*. Syracuse: Syracuse University Press.

Evans, Peter B. 1995. *Embedded autonomy: States and industrial transformation*. Princeton: Princeton University Press.

Evans, Peter, Dietrich Rueschemeyer, and Theda Skocpol, ed. 1985. *Bringing the state back in*. New York: Cambridge University Press.

Everett, Jana. 2001. All the women were Hindu and all the Muslims were men: State, identity politics and gender, 1917–1951. *Economic and Political Weekly* 36, no. 23 (June 9–15): 2071–2080.

Farouqi, Ziya ul Hasan. 1981. Orthodoxy and heterodoxy in India. In *Communal and pan-Islamic trends in colonial India*, ed. Hasan Mushirul, 326–343. Delhi: Manohar.

"Fatwas not binding: Muslim Personal Board." *Outlook India*, Web edition. Available from http://www.outlookindia.com (accessed May 22, 2006).

Fineman, Martha Albertson. 1991. *The illusion of equality: The rhetoric and reality of divorce reform*. Chicago: University of Chicago Press.

Fiss, Owen M. 1983. The bureaucratization of the judiciary. *Yale Law Journal* 92, no. 8 (July): 1442–1468.

Fiss, Owen M. 1984. Against settlement. *Yale Law Journal* 93, no. 6 (May): 1073–1090.

Fitzpatrick, Peter. 1983. Marxism and legal pluralism. *Osgood Hall Law Journal* 22, no. 1: 115–138.

Fitzpatrick, Peter. 1986. Custom, law and resistance. In *Legal pluralism: Proceedings of Canberra law workshop VII*, ed. Peter Sack and Elizabeth Minchin, 63–82. Canberra: Research School of Social Sciences, Australian National University.

Forum Against Oppression of Women. 1996. *Visions of gender just realities*. Unpublished Draft. Mumbai.

"Four Law Boards: Will Muslim Women find a Messiah?" In *South Asian Women's Forum*, Web edition. Available from http://www.sawf.org (accessed February 7, 2005).

Fox, R. G. 1969. *From Zamindar to ballotbox: Community change in a North Indian market town*. Ithaca: Cornell University Press.

Freitag, Sandria B. 1989. *Collective action and community: Public arenas and the emergence of communalism in colonial North India*. Berkeley: University of California Press.

Fyzee, Asaf Ali Asghar. 1974. *Outlines of Mohamaddan law*. 3rd ed. London: Oxford University Press.

Fyzee, Asaf Ali Asghar. 1965. *Cases in the Muhammadan law of India and Pakistan*. Oxford: Clarendon Press.

Galanter, Marc. 1966. The modernization of law. In *Modernization: The dynamics of growth*, ed. Myron Weiner, 153–165. New York: Basic Books.

Galanter, Marc. 1968. The displacement of traditional law in modern India. *Journal of Social Issues* 24, no. 4 (October): 65–91.

Galanter, Marc. 1981. Justice in many rooms: Courts, private orderings and indigenous law. *Journal of Legal Pluralism and Unofficial Law* 19: 1–47.

Galanter, Marc. 1985. Indigenous law and official law in the contemporary United States. In *People's law and state law: The Bellagio papers*, ed. Anthony Allott and Gordon R. Woodman, 67–70. Dordrecht: Foris Publications.

Galanter, Marc. 1988. A settlement judge, not a trial judge. Judicial mediations in the United States. In *The role of courts in society*, ed. Shimon Shetreet, 295–318. Dordrecht: Martin Nijhoff.

Galanter, Marc. 1989. *Law and society in modern India*. New York: Oxford University Press.

Galanter, Marc. 2000. Fifty years on. In *Supreme but not infallible: Essays in honour of the Supreme Court of India*, ed. B. N. Kirpal et al., 57–65. New Delhi: Oxford University Press.

Galanter, Marc and Jayanth Krishnan. 2000. Personal laws and human rights. *Israel Law Review* 34: 98–130.

Galanter, Marc and Jayanth Krishnan. 2003. Debased informalism: *Lok Adalats* and legal rights in modern India. In *Beyond common knowledge: Empirical approaches to the rule of law*, ed. Erik G. Jensen and Thomas C. Heller, 96–141. Stanford: Stanford University Press.

Gandhi, Nandita and Nandita Shah. 1992. *The Issues at stake: Theory and practice in the contemporary women's movement in India.* New Delhi: Kali for Women.

Gangoli, Geetanjali. 1996. *Law on Trial.* Mumbai: Akshara.

Gangoli, Geetanjali. 2003. Muslim divorce and the discourse around Muslim Personal Law. In *Divorce and remarriage among Muslims in India*, ed. Imtiaz Ahmad, 367–396. Delhi: Manohar.

Gangoli, Geetanjali. 2006. *Indian feminisms: Law, patriarchies and violence in India.* Aldershot: Ashgate.

Gazetteer of the Bombay Presidency. 1913–1914. Bombay: Government Central Press.

Ghildiyal, Subodh. 2005. Muslim law board tones down stand. *Times News Network* (New Delhi), August 22.

Giddens, Anthony. 1979. *Central problems in social theory: Action, structure and contradiction in social analysis.* Berkeley: University of California Press.

Giddens, Anthony. 1984. *The constitution of society: Outline of the theory of structuration.* Berkeley: University of California Press.

Gillman, Howard. 2001. What's law got to do with it? Judicial behavioralists test the "legal model" of judicial decision making. *Law and Social Inquiry* 26, no. 2 (April): 465–504.

Gilmartin, David. 1988. Customary law and *Shariat* in British Punjab. In *Shari'at and ambiguity in South Asian Islam*, ed. Katherine Ewing, 43–62. Berkeley: University of California Press.

Glendon, Mary Ann. 1981. *The new family and the new property.* Toronto: Butterworths.

Glendon, Mary Ann. 1989. *The transformation of family law: State, law and family in the United States and Western Europe.* Chicago: University of Chicago Press.

Gokhale-Turner, Jayashree. 1980. From concessions to confrontation: The politics of the Mahar community in Maharashtra. Ph.D. diss., Department of Political Science, McGill University.

Goldfarb, Sally S. 1988–1989. Marital partnership and the case for permanent alimony. *The Journal of Family Law* 27, no. 2: 351–372.

Gray, John. 1995. *Enlightenment's wake: Politics and culture at the close of the modern age.* London; New York: Routledge.

Greenhouse, Carol J. 1998. Legal pluralism and cultural difference: What is the difference? A response to Professor Woodman. *Journal of Legal Pluralism and Unofficial Law* 42: 61–72.

Griffiths, Anne. 1997. *In the shadow of marriage: Gender and justice in an African community.* Chicago: University of Chicago Press.

Griffiths, John. 1986a. Recent anthropology of law in the Netherlands and its historical background. In *Anthropology of law in Netherlands: Essays on legal pluralism*, ed. Keebet Von Benda-Beckmann and Fons Strijbosch, 11–66. Dordrecht: Foris Publications.

Griffiths, John. 1986b. What is legal pluralism? *Journal of Legal Pluralism and Unofficial Law* 24: 1–56.

Grillo, Trina. 1991. The mediation alternative: Process dangers for women. *Yale Law Journal* 100, no. 6 (April): 1545–1610.

Guha, Phulrenu; Committee on the Status of Women in India.1975. Towards Equality: Report of the Committee on the Status of Women in India. New Delhi: Government of India, Ministry of Education and Social Welfare, Department of Social Welfare.

Gupta, Akhil. 1995. Blurred boundaries: The discourse of corruption, the culture of politics and the imagined state. *American Ethnologist* 22, no. 2 (May): 375–402.

Gupta, Suchandana. *Talaq*: Once is enough. *The Times of India*, May 2, 2005.

Haddad, Yvonne Yazbeck and Barbara Freyer Stowasser, ed. 2004. *Islamic law and the challenges of modernity.* Walnut Creek: Altamira Press.

Hallaq, Wael B. 2001. *Authority, continuity, and change in Islamic law.* New York: Cambridge University Press.

Hallaq, Wael B. 2004. Can the *Shari'a* be restored? In *Islamic law and the challenges of modernity*, ed. Yvonne Yazbeck Haddad and Barbara Freyer Stowasser, 21–54. Walnut Creek: Altamira Press.

Hallaq, Wael B. 2005. *The origins and evolution of Islamic law.* New York: Cambridge University Press.

Hamayotsu, Kikue. 2003. Politics of Syariah reform: The making of the state religio-legal apparatus. In *Malaysia: Islam, society and politics*, ed. Virginia Hooker and Norani Othman, 55–79. Singapore: Institute of Southeast Asian Studies.

Hanley, Sarah. 1989. Engendering the state: Family formation and state building in early modern France. *French Historical Studies* 16, no. 1 (Spring): 4–27.
Hansen, Thomas Blom. 2001a. Governance and state mythologies in Mumbai. In *States of imagination: Ethnographic explorations of the postcolonial state*, ed. Thomas Blom Hansen and Finn Stepputat, 221–256. Durham: Duke University Press.
Hansen, Thomas Blom. 2001b. *Wages of violence: Naming and identity in postcolonial Bombay*. Princeton: Princeton University Press.
Hansen, Thomas Blom. 2005. Sovereigns beyond the state: On legality and authority in urban India. In *Sovereign bodies: Citizens, migrants and states in the postcolonial world*, ed. Thomas Blom Hansen and Finn Stepputat, 169–191. Princeton: Princeton University Press.
Hansen, Thomas Blom and Christophe Jaffrelot, ed. 2001. *The BJP and the compulsion of politics in India*. 2nd ed. New York: Oxford University Press.
Hansen, Thomas Blom and Finn Stepputat, ed. 2001. *States of imagination: Ethnographic explorations of the postcolonial state*. Durham: Duke University Press.
Hardgrave Jr., Robert L. 1969. *The Nadars of Tamilnad: The political culture of a community in charge*. Berkeley: University of California Press.
Harijano matena Sri Lakshmi Narain Mandir no Ahewal. 1935. Unpublished report. Mumbai.
Harrington, Christine B. 1982. Delegalization reform movements: A historical analysis. In *The politics of informal justice, Vol.1: The American experience*, ed. Richard L. Abel, 35–71. New York: Academic Press.
Harrington, Christine B. 1985. *Shadow justice: The ideology and institutionalization of alternatives to court*. Westport: Greenwood Press.
Hart, H. L. A. 1961. *The concept of law*. Oxford: Clarendon Press.
Hasan, Zoya. 1994. *Forging identities: Gender, communities and the state*. New Delhi: Kali for Women.
Hatem, Mervat. 1986. The enduring alliance of nationalism and patriarchy in Muslim personal status laws: The case of modern Egypt. *Feminist Review* 6, no. 1: 19–43.
Hayden, Robert. 1983. Excommunication as everyday event and ultimate sanction: The nature of suspension from an Indian caste. *Journal of Asian Studies* 42, no. 2 (February): 291–307.
Hayden, Robert. 1999. *Dispute and arguments amongst nomads: A caste-council in India*. New Delhi: Oxford University Press.

Herbst, Jeffrey. 2000. *States and power in Africa: Comparative lessons in authority and control*. Princeton: Princeton University Press.

Heuer, Jennifer. 2005. *The family and the nation: Gender and citizenship in revolutionary France 1789–1830*. Ithaca: Cornell University Press.

Heydebrand, Wolf and Carroll Seron. 1990. *Rationalizing justice: The political economy of federal courts*. Albany: State University of New York Press.

Hirsch, Susan F. 1998. *Pronouncing and persevering: Gender and the discourses of disputing in an African Islamic court*. Chicago: University of Chicago Press.

Hofrichter, Richard. 1982. Neighborhood justice and the social control problems of American capitalism: A perspective. In *The politics of informal justice. Vol. 1. The American experience*, ed. Richard Abel, 207–244. New York: Academic Press.

Holden, Livia. 2004. Official policies for (Un)Official customs: Hegemonic treatment of Hindu divorce customs by dominant legal discourses. *The Journal of Legal pluralism and (Un)Official Law* 49: 47–74.

Holden, Livia. 2005. Divorcing by custom: women's agencies and lawyers' praxis in (un)official Hindu law. In *Indian Socio-Legal Journal* XXXI (Special Issue on legal pluralism in India, edited by Eberhard, Christoph and Nidhi Gupta): 60–72.

Holden, Livia. 2008. *Hindu divorce: A legal anthropology*. Aldershot: Ashgate.

Hollister, John Norman. 1988. *Islam and Shia's faith in India*. Delhi: Kanishka.

Hooker, M. B. 1975. *Legal pluralism: An introduction to colonial and neo-colonial laws*. Oxford: Clarendon Press.

Hooker, M. B. 1976. *The personal laws of Malaysia: An introduction*. New York: Oxford University Press.

Hooker, M. B. 1984. *Islamic law in South-East Asia*. Singapore: Oxford University Press.

Howland, Courtney W., ed. 1999. *Religious fundamentalisms and the human rights of women*. New York: St. Martin's Press.

Humphrey, Caroline and James Laidlaw. 1994. *The archetypal actions of ritual: A theory of ritual illustrated by the Jain rite of worship*. Oxford: Clarendon Press.

Ibrahim, Ahmad Mohamed. 2000. *The administration of Islamic law*. Kuala Lumpur: Institute of Islamic Understanding (IKIM).

BIBLIOGRAPHY

Ilaiah, Kancha. 1996. *Why I am not a Hindu: A Suddra critique of Hindutva philosophy, culture and political economy.* Calcutta: Samya.
Imtiaz, Ahmad, ed. 2003. *Divorce and remarriage among Muslims in India.* Delhi: Manohar.
"India Muslim divorce code set out." BBC Web edition. Available from http://news.bbc.co.uk (accessed May 2, 2005).
Ivanow, W. 1948. Satpanth. In *Collectanea*, ed. W. Ivanow, 1–54. Leiden: E. I. Brill.
Jacob, Alice. 1999. Uniform civil code: Reforms in Christian family law. In *Engendering law: Essays in honour of Lotika Sarkar*, ed. Amita Dhanda and Archana Parashar, 375–386. Lucknow: Eastern Book Company.
Jacobsohn, Gary J. 2003. *The wheel of law: India's secularism in comparative constitutional context.* Princeton: Princeton University Press.
Jaffrelot, Christophe. 1998. The Sangh Parivar between Sanskritization and social engineering. In *The BJP and the compulsion of politics in India*, ed. Thomas Blom Hansen and Christophe Jaffrelot, 22–71. New York: Oxford University Press.
Jain, Sonu. Women didn't receive rights without struggle. *Indian Express*. September 13, 2005.
Jaising, Indira. 2000. Gender justice and the Supreme Court. In *Supreme but not infallible: Essays in honour of the Supreme Court of India*, ed. B. N. Kirpal et al., 288–320. New Delhi: Oxford University Press.
Jamaluddin, Syed. 1981. The Barelvis and the Khilafat movement. In *Communal and pan-Islamic trends in colonial India*, ed. Mushirul Hasan, 344–357. Delhi: Manohar.
Jayal, Niraja Gopal. 2001. *Democracy and the state: Welfare, secularism and development in contemporary India.* New Delhi: Oxford University Press.
Jenkins, Laura Dudley. 2001. Personal laws and reservations: Volition and religion in contemporary India. In *Religion and personal law in secular India: A call to judgement*, ed. Gerald James Larson, 104–123. Bloomington: Indiana University Press.
Jenkins, Rob. 1998. Rajput Hindutva, caste politics, regional identity and the Hindu nationalism in contemporary Rajasthan. In *The BJP and the compulsion of politics in India*, ed. Thomas Blom Hansen and Christophe Jaffrelot, 101–120. New York: Oxford University Press.
Johnson, Charles A. 1987. Law, politics, and judicial decision-making: Lower federal court uses of Supreme Court decisions. *Law and Society Review* 21, no. 2: 325–340.

Jones, Justin. 2010. Signs of churning: Muslim Personal Law and public contestation in twenty-first century India. *Modern Asian Studies* 44, no. 1: 175–200.
Joseph, Suad. 1997. The public/private: The imagined boundary in the imagined nation/state/community: The Lebanese case. *Feminist Review* 57, no. 1: 73–92.
Joseph, Suad. 2005. Gender and citizenship in Middle Eastern States. In *Women and Islam: Critical concepts in sociology*, ed. Haideh Moghissi, 47–57. New York: Routledge.
Joseph, Suad and Susan Slyomovics, ed. 2001. *Women and power in the Middle East*. Philadelphia: University of Pennsylvania Press.
Joshi, Poornima. Minority cell mulls political lobbying. *The Telegraph*, August 28, 2005.
Kakatiya, Manjula. 1978. Bruhad Mumbaina kapol vaishya jnati ek samajshastriya anveshan. Ph.D. diss., SNDT University.
Kamali, Mohammad Hashim. 2000. *Islamic law in Malaysia: Issues and developments*. Kuala Lumpur: Ilmiah Publishers.
Kandiyoti, Dennis. 1996. *Gendering the Middle East: Emerging perspectives*. Syracuse: Syracuse University Press.
Kapila, Kriti. 2004. Conjugating marriage: State legislation and Gaddi kinship. *Contributions to Indian Sociology* 38, no. 3: 379–409.
Kapur, Ratna and Brenda Cossman. 1996. *Subversive sites: Feminist engagements with law in India*. New Delhi: Sage Publications.
Katzenstein, Mary Fainsod. 1989. Organizing against violence: Strategies of the Indian women's movement. *Pacific Affairs* 62, no. 1 (Spring): 53–71.
Katzenstein, Mary, Uday Mehta, and Usha Thakkar. 1997. The rebirth of the Shiv Sena: The symbiosis of discursive and organizational power. *Journal of Asian Studies* 56, no. 2 (May): 371–390.
Kelso, R. Randall and Charles D. Kelso. 1996. How the Supreme Court is dealing with precedents in constitutional cases. *Brooklyn Law Review* 62 (Fall): 973–1037.
Khan, Dominique-Sila. 2003. The Ismaili origin of the Hindu cult of Ramdeo Pir. In *On becoming an Indian Muslim: French essays on aspects of syncretism*, ed. M. Waseem, 264–278. New Delhi: Oxford University Press.
Khare, R. S. 1970. *The changing Brahmans: Associations and elites among the Kanya-kubjas of North India*. Chicago: University of Chicago Press.

BIBLIOGRAPHY

Khare, R. S. 1972. Indigenous culture and lawyer's law in India. *Comparative Studies in Society and History* 14, no. 1 (January): 71–96.

Kidder, Robert L. 1973. Courts and conflict in an Indian city: A study in legal impact. *Journal of Commonwealth Political Studies* 11, no. 2 (July): 121–139.

Kidder, Robert L. 1974. Litigation as a strategy for personal mobility: The case of urban caste association leaders. *Journal of Asian Studies* 33, no. 2 (February): 177–191.

Kidwai, Rasheed. Curtain to drop on triple talaq. *The Telegraph*, April 30, 2005.

Kidwai, Rasheed. Muslim board to open new chapter. *The Telegraph*, October 7, 2004.

Kikani, L. T. 1912. *Caste in courts or rights and powers of caste in social and religious matters as recognized by Indian courts*. Rajkot: Ganatra Printing Works.

Kirpal, B. N., ed. 2000. *Supreme but not infallible: Essays in honour of the Supreme Court of India*. New Delhi: Oxford University Press.

Kishwar, Madhu. 1994. Codified Hindu law: Myth and reality. *The Economic and Political Weekly* 29, no. 33 (August 13): 2145–2161.

Klein, David E. and Robert J. Hume. 2003. Fear of reprisal as an explanation of lower court compliance. *Law and Society Review* 37, no. 3 (September): 579–606.

Kleinhans, Martha and Roderick A. Macdonald. 1997. What is a *critical* legal pluralism? *Canadian Journal of Law and Society* 12, no. 1 (Fall): 25–46.

Kolenda, Pauline. 2003. *Caste, marriage and inequality: Essays on North and South India*. Jaipur: Rawat Publications.

Kornhauser, Lewis A. 1995. Adjudication by a resource constrained team: Hierarchy and precedent in a judicial system. *Southern California Law Review* 68: 1605–1629.

Kornhauser, Lewis and Robert Mnookin. 1979. Bargaining in the shadow of the law: The case of divorce. *Yale Law Journal* 88, no. 5 (April): 950–997.

Kothari, Rajani. 1988. *State against democracy: In search of humane governance*. Delhi: Ajanta Publishers.

Kothari, Rajani and Rushikesh Maru. 1965. Caste and secularism in India: Case study of a caste federation. *Journal of Asian Studies* 25, no. 1:33–50.

Krishna, Anirudh. 2003. What is happening to caste? A view from some North Indian villages. *The Journal of Asian Studies* 62, no. 4 (November): 1171–1193.

Kukathas, Chandran. 1992. Are there any cultural rights? *Political Theory* 20, no. 1 (February): 105–139.

Kumar, Ravinder. 1968. *Western India in the nineteenth century: A study in the social history of Maharashtra.* London: Routledge and Kegan Paul.

Kymlicka, Will. 1989. *Liberalism, community and culture.* Oxford: Clarendon Press.

Kymlicka, Will. 1995. *Multicultural citizenship: A liberal theory of minority rights.* Oxford: Clarendon Press.

Laidlaw, James. 1995. *Riches and renunciation: Religion, economy, and society among Jains.* Oxford: Clarendon Press.

Langer, Rosanna. 1998. The juridification and technicisation of alternative dispute resolution practices. *Canadian Journal of Law and Society* 13, no. 1: 169–186.

Lariviere, Richard. 1989. Justices and *panditas*: Some ironies in contemporary readings of the Hindu legal past. *Journal of Asian Studies* 48, no. 4 (November): 757–769.

Larson, Gerald James, ed. 2001. *Religion and personal law in secular India: A call to judgement.* Bloomington: University of Indiana Press.

Lata Mani. 1990. Contentious traditions: The debate on *Sati* in colonial India. In *Recasting women: Essays in Indian Colonial History*, ed. Kumkum Sangari and Sudesh Vaid, 88–126. New Brunswick: Rutgers University Press.

Lateef, Shahida. 1983. Modernization in India and the status of Muslim women. In *Modernization and social change among Muslims in India*, ed. I. Ahmad, 153–184. Delhi: Manohar.

Lateef, Shahida. 1998. Muslim women in India: A minority within a minority. In *Women in Muslim societies: Diversity within unity*, ed. Herbert L. Bodman and Nayereh Tohidi, 251–276. Boulder: Lynne Rienner.

Lazarus-Black, Mindie and Susan Hirsch, ed. 1994. *Contested states: Law, hegemony and resistance.* New York: Routledge.

Lee, Thomas R. 1999. Stare Decisis in historical perspective: From the founding era to the Rehnquist court. *Vanderbilt Law Review* 52, no. 3: 647–735.

Lev, Daniel S. 1972. *Islamic courts in Indonesia: A study in the political bases of legal institutions.* Berkeley: University of California Press.

Lindsey, Timothy, ed. 1999. *Indonesia: Law and society*. Sydney: The Federation Press.
Loos, Tamara Lynn. 2006. *Subject Siam: Family, law and colonial modernity in Thailand*. Ithaca: Cornell University Press.
Macaulay, Stewart. 1986. Private government. In *Law and the social sciences*, ed. Leon Lipson and Stanton Wheeler, 445–518. New York: Russell Sage Foundation.
Mahajan, Gurpreet. 2005. Can intra-group equality co-exist with cultural diversity? Re-examining multicultural frameworks of accommodation. In *Minorities within minorities: Equality, rights and diversity*, ed. Avigail Eisenberg and Jeff Spinner-Halev, 90–113. Cambridge: Cambridge University Press.
Mahmood, Tahir. 1993. *Human rights in Islamic law*. New Delhi: Genuine Publications Private Ltd.
Mahmood, Tahir. 1995. *Statute-law relating to Muslims in India: A study in constitutional and Islamic perspectives*. New Delhi: Institute of Objective Studies.
Mahmood, Tahir. 1997. *Islamic law in Indian courts since independence: Fifty years of judicial interpretation*. New Delhi: Institute of Objective Studies.
Mahmood, Tahir. 2002. *The Muslim law of India*. New Delhi: Lexisnexis Butterworths.
Mahmood, Tahir, ed. 1991. *Minorities and state at the Indian law: An anthology*. New Delhi: Institute of Objective Studies, Genuine Publications.
Mallison, Françoise. 1989. Hinduism as seen by the Nizari Ismaili missionaries of Western India: The evidence of the Ginans. In *Hinduism Reconsidered*, ed. Gunther-Dietz Sontheimer and Hermann Kulke, 93–113. Delhi: Manohar.
Mallison, Françoise. 2003. Pir Shams and his Garabi songs. In *On becoming an Indian Muslim: French essays on aspects of syncretism*, ed. M. Waseem, 180–207. New Delhi: Oxford University Press.
Mann, Michael. 1986. *The sources of social power*. Cambridge: Cambridge University Press.
Mansfield, John. 1993. The personal laws or a uniform civil code? In *Religion and law in independent India*, ed. Robert D. Baird, 139–178. Delhi: Manohar.
Mansfield, John. 2001. Religious and charitable endowments and a uniform civil code. In *Religion and personal law in secular India: A call to judgment*, ed. Gerald Larson, 69–103. Bloomington: Indiana University Press.

Matthews, Roger. 1983. Reassessing informal justice. In *Informal justice?* ed. Roger Matthews, 1–24. London: Sage Publications.

Matthews, Roger, ed. 1988. *Informal justice?* London: Sage.

Masselos, J. C. 1973. The Khojas of Bombay: The defining of formal membership criteria during the nineteenth century. In *Caste and social stratification among the Muslims*, ed. Imtiaz Ahmad, 1–20. Delhi: Manohar.

Mayer, Ann Elizabeth. 2004. Internationalizing the Conversation on women's rights: Arab countries face the CEDAW committee. In *Islamic law and the challenges of modernity*, ed. Yvonne Yazbeck Haddad and Barbara Stowasser, 133–160. Walnut Creek: Altamira Press.

Mehta, B. H. 1936. The social and economic conditions of the Meghwal untouchables of Bombay City (with special reference to the community centre at Valpakhadi) Parts I (vols. i and ii), II and III. Unpublished M.A. Thesis submitted to School of Economics and Sociology. University of Bombay.

Melissaris, Emmanuel. 2004. The more the merrier? A new take on legal pluralism. *Social and Legal Studies* 13, no. 1 (March): 57–79.

Mendelsohn, Oliver. 1981. The pathology of the Indian legal system. *Modern Asian Studies* 15, no. 4: 823–863.

Menon, Nivedita. 1998. Women and citizenship. In *Wages of freedom: Fifty years of the Indian nation-State*, ed. Partha Chatterjee, 241–266. Delhi: Oxford University Press.

Menski, Werner. 2001. *Modern Indian family law*. Richmond: Curzon.

Menski, Werner. 2003. *Hindu law: Beyond tradition and modernity*. New Delhi: Oxford University Press.

Menski, Werner. 2006. *Comparative law in a global context: The legal systems of Asia and Africa*. Cambridge: Cambridge University Press.

Merry, Sally Engel. 1982a. Defining "success" in the neighborhood justice movement. In *Neighborhood justice: Assessment of an emerging idea*, ed. R. Tomasic and M. Feeley, 172–193. New York: Longman.

Merry, Sally Engel. 1982b. The social organisation of mediation in non-industrial societies: Implications for informal community justice in America. In *The Politics of Informal Justice. Vol. 2*, ed. Richard L. Abel, 17–42. New York: Academic Press.

Merry, Sally Engel. 1989. Myth and practice in mediation process. In *Mediation and criminal justice: Victims, offenders and community*, ed. M. Wright and B. Galaway, 239–250. London: Sage Publications.

Merry, Sally Engel. 2005. *Human rights and gender violence: Translating international law into local justice.* Chicago: University of Chicago Press.

Metcalf, Barbara. 1982. *Islamic revival in British India: Deoband, 1860–1900.* Princeton: Princeton University Press.

Michelutti, Lucia. 2004. "We (Yadavs) are a caste of politicians": Caste and politics in a North Indian town. *Contributions to Indian Sociology* 38, no. 1–2 (February): 43–71.

Migdal, Joel S. 1988. *Strong societies and weak states: State-society relations and state capabilities in the Third World.* Princeton: Princeton University Press.

Migdal, Joel S. 1996. Integration and Disintegration: An Approach to Society Formation. In *Between development and destruction: An enquiry into the causes of conflict in post-colonial states,* ed. Luc van de Goor, Kumar Rupesinghe, and Paul Sciarone, 91–106. London: Macmillan.

Migdal, Joel S. 2004a. Mental Maps and Virtual Checkpoints: Struggles to Construct and Maintain State and Social Boundaries. In *Boundaries and belonging: States and societies in the struggle to shape identities and local practices,* ed. Joel Migdal, 3–26. Cambridge: Cambridge University Press.

Migdal, Joel S., ed. 2004b. *Boundaries and belonging: States and societies in the struggle to shape identities and local practices.* New York: Cambridge University Press.

Migdal, Joel and Klaus Schlichte. 2005. Rethinking the state. In *The dynamics of states: The formation and crises of state domination,* ed. Klaus Schlichte, 1–40. Aldershot: Ashgate.

Migdal, Joel S., Atul Kohli, and Vivienne Shue, ed. 1994. *State power and social forces: Domination and transformation in the Third World.* Cambridge: Cambridge University Press.

Mines, Mattison. 1994. *Public faces, private voices: Community and individualism in South India.* Berkeley: University of California Press.

Minow, Martha, Michael Ryan, and Austin Sarat, ed. 1993. *Narrative, violence and the law: The essays of Robert Cover.* Ann Arbor: University of Michigan Press.

Mir-Hosseini, Zeba. 1993. *Marriage on Trial: A study of Islamic family law.* London: I. B. Tauris.

Mody, Perveez. 2002. Love and the Law: Love-Marriage in Delhi. *Modern Asian Studies* 36, no. 1 (February): 223–256.

Moghadam, Valentine M. ed. 1994. *Identity politics and women: Cultural reassertions and feminisms in international perspective.* Boulder: Westview Press.

Moog, Robert S. 1991. Conflict and compromise: The politics of *Llok Adalats* in Varanasi District. *Law and Society Review* 25, no. 3: 545–570.

Moore, Erin P. 1994. Law's patriarchy in India. In *Contested states: Law, hegemony and resistance,* ed. Mindie Lazarus-Black and Susan F. Hirsch, 89–117. New York: Routledge.

Moore, Erin P. 1998. *Gender, law and resistance in India.* Tucson: University of Arizona Press.

Moore, Sally Folk. 1973. Law and social change: The semi-autonomous social field as an appropriate subject of study. *Law and Society Review* 7, no. 4: 719–746.

Moore, Sally Folk. 1978. *Law as process: An anthropological approach.* London: Routledge and Kegan Paul.

Moors, Annelies. 1996. Gender relations and inheritance: Person, power and property in Palestine. In *Gendering the Middle East: Emerging perspectives,* ed. Deniz Kandiyoti, 69–84. Syracuse: Syracuse University Press.

Moors, Annelies. 2003. Introduction: Public debates on family law reform: Participants, positions and styles of argumentation in the 1990s. In *Islamic Law and Society, Special Volume* 10, no. 1: 1–11.

Moosa, Najma. 2002. The role that lay Muslim judges play in state courts and religious tribunals in South Africa: A historical, contemporary and gender perspective. In *Access to justice: The role of court administrators and law adjudicators in the African and Islamic contexts,* ed. Christina Jones-Pauly and Stefanie Elbern, 99–136. The Hague: Kluwer Law International.

Morab, S. G. 1965. The Bhandari caste council. *Man in India* 45: 152–158.

Morris, Morris D. 1965. *The emergence of an industrial labor force in India.* Berkeley: University of California Press.

Morris, Henry Francis and James S. Read. 1972. *Indirect rule and the search for justice: Essays in East African legal history.* Oxford: Clarendon Press.

Morrison, Charles. 1974. Clerks and clients: Paraprofessional roles and cultural identities in Indian litigation. *Law and Society Review* 9, no. 1 (Autumn): 39–62.

Mumbai Meghwal/Vanakar Gnati Bandharan. 1993. Mumbai: Mumbai Meghwal Panchayat (Registered).

Mumbai Meghwal/Vanakar Gnati Bandharan. 1996. Third Edition. Mumbai: Mumbai Meghwal Panchayat (Registered).

Mukhopadhyay, Maitreyee. 1998. *Legally dispossessed: Gender, identity, and the process of law.* Calcutta: Stree.

Mulla, Dinshah Fardunji. 1955. *Principles of Mahomedan law.* Calcutta: Eastern Law House.

Mulla, Dinshah Fardunji. 1966. *Principles of Hindu law.* 13th ed. Bombay: N. M. Tripathy.

Murugkar, Lata. 1991. *Dalit Panther movement in Maharashtra: A sociological appraisal.* Bombay: Popular Prakashan.

Nader, Laura and Harry F. Todd, Jr., ed. 1978. *The disputing process: Law in ten societies.* New York: Columbia University Press.

Nainar, Vahida. 2000. *Muslim women's views on personal laws: The influence of socio-economic factors.* In Report compiled by Women's Research and Action Group, Mumbai.

Nair, Janaki. 1996. *Women and law in colonial India: A social history.* New Delhi: Kali for Women with the National Law School of India University.

Nanji, Azim. 1978. *The Nizari Ismai'li tradition in the Indo-Pakistan subcontinent.* Delmar: Caravan Books.

Nanji, Azim. 1988. Shariat and Haqiqat: Continuity and synthesis in the Nizari Ismaili Muslim tradition. In *Shariat and ambiguity in South Asian Islam*, ed. Katherine P. Ewing, 63–76. Berkeley: University of California Press.

Narain, Vrinda. 2001. *Gender and community: Muslim women's rights in India.* Toronto: University of Toronto Press.

Narain, Vrinda. 2005. *Anxiety and amnesia: Muslim women's equality in postcolonial India.* Ph.D. diss., Faculty of Law, McGill University.

Nettl, J. P. 1968. The state as a conceptual variable. *World Politics* 20, no. 4 (July): 559–592.

Newbigin, Eleanor. 2009. The codification of personal law and secular citizenship: Revisiting the history of law reform in late colonial India. *The Indian Economic and Social History Review* 46, no. 1 (January/March): 83–104.

Nijjar, Manjit Singh. 1994. *Nullity of marriage under Hindu law.* New Delhi: Deep and Deep.

Nishat, Jameela. 2003. A long way to go: Divorce practices among Muslim families of Hyderabad city. In *Divorce and remarriage among Muslims in India*, ed. Imtiaz Ahmad, 303–316. Delhi: Manohar.

Nishimura, Yuko. 1998. *Gender, kinship and property rights: Nagarattar womanhood in South India.* Delhi: Oxford University Press.

"No compromise on triple talaq system: Ulemas." *Outlook India*, Web edition. Available from http://www.outlookindia.com (accessed August 14, 2004).

Nugent, David. 1994. Building the state, making the Nation: The bases and limits of state centralization in "Modern Peru." *American Anthropologist* 96, no. 2 (June): 333–369.

Nussbaum, Martha C. 1997. Religion and women's human rights. In *Religion and contemporary liberalism*, ed. Paul J. Weithman, 93–137. Notre Dame: University of Notre Dame Press.

Nussbaum, Martha C. 1999. *Sex and social justice*. Oxford: Oxford University Press.

Nussbaum, Martha C. 2000. Religion and women's equality: The case of India. In *Obligations of citizenship and demands of faith: Religious accommodation in pluralist democracies*, ed. Nancy L. Rosenblum, 335–402. Princeton: Princeton University Press.

Nussbaum, Martha and Jonathan Glover, ed. 1995. *Women, culture, and development: A study of human capabilities*. Oxford: Clarendon Press.

O'Donovan, Katherine. 1999. Marriage: A sacred or profane love machine? In *Family, state and the law, Vol.1*, ed. Michael Freeman, 244–258. Dartmouth: Aldershot.

Offe, Claus. 1996. *Modernity and the state: East, West*. Cambridge: MIT Press.

O'Hanlon, Rosalind. 1985. *Caste, conflict, and ideology: Mahatma Jotirao Phule and low caste protest in nineteenth century Western India*. Cambridge: Cambridge University Press.

Okely, Judith. 1991. Defiant moments: Gender, resistance and individuals. *Man* 26, no. 1 (March): 3–22.

Okin, Susan. 1989. *Justice, gender and the family*. New York: Basic Books.

Okin, Susan. 1997. Is multiculturalism bad for women? *Boston Review* 22, no. 5: 25–28.

Okin, Susan. 1999. Is multiculturalism bad for women? In *Is multiculturalism bad for women?*, ed. Joshua Cohen, Matthew Howard, and Martha C. Nussbaum, 7–26. Princeton: Princeton University Press.

Okin, Susan. 2002. Mistresses of their own destiny: Group rights, gender, and realistic rights of exit. *Ethics* 112, no. 2 (January): 205–230.

Okin, Susan. 2005. Multiculturalism and feminism: No simple questions, no simple answers. In *Minorities within minorities: equality, rights and diversity*, ed. Avigail Eisenberg and Jeff Spinner-Halev, 67–89. Cambridge: Cambridge University Press.

Olson, Susan and Albert Dzur. 2004. Revisiting informal justice: Restorative justice and democratic professionalism. *Law and Society Review* 38, no. 1 (March): 139–176.

Pandey, Geeta. "Muslim women fight instant divorce." BBC web edition. Available from http://news.bbc.co.uk (accessed August 4, 2004).

Pandey, Gyanendra. 1990. *The construction of communalism in colonial North India*. Delhi: Oxford University Press.

Papanek, Hana. 1962. Leadership and social change in the Khoja Ismaili community. Ph.D. diss., Harvard University.

Parashar, Archana. 1992. *Women and family law reform in India: Uniform civil code and gender equality*. Delhi: Sage Publications.

Parashar, Archana and Amita Dhanda, eds. 2008. *Redefining family law in India: Essays in honour of B. Sivaramayya*. New Delhi: Routledge.

Parry, Jonathan P. 2001. Ankalu's errant wife: Sex, marriage and industry in contemporary Chhattisgarh. *Modern Asian Studies* 35, no. 4: 783–820.

Patwardhan, Sunanda. 1973. *Change among India's harijans: Maharashtra: A case study*. New Delhi: Orient Longman.

Pavlich, George. 1996. The power of community mediation: Government and formation of self-identity. *Law and Society Review* 30, no. 4: 707–734.

Pearl, David. 1987. *A textbook on Muslim personal law*. 2nd ed. London: Crom Helm.

Pearl, David. 2000. *Islamic family law and its reception by the courts in England*. Cambridge: Islamic Legal Studies Program.

Peletz, Michael G. 2002. *Islamic modern: Religious courts and cultural politics in Malaysia*. Princeton: Princeton University Press.

Perez, Oren and Gunther Teubner, ed. 2006. *Paradoxes and inconsistencies in the law*. Portland: Hart Publishing.

Petersen, Hanne and Henrik Zahle, ed. 1995. *Legal polycentricity: Consequences of pluralism in law*. Dartmouth: Aldershot.

Phillips, Anne. 1995. Democracy and difference: Some problems for feminist theory. In *The rights of minority cultures*, ed. Will Kymlicka, 288–302. Oxford: Oxford University Press.

Phillips, Anne. 2003. When culture means gender: Issues of cultural defence in the English courts. *Modern Law Review* 66, issue 4 (July): 510–531.

Phillips, Anne. 2007. *Multiculturalism without culture*. Princeton and Oxford: Princeton University Press.

Phillips, Anne and Moira Dustin. 2004. UK initiatives on forced marriage: Regulation, dialogue and exit. *Political Studies* 52, no. 3: 531–551.

Prashad, Vijay. 2000. *Untouchable freedom: A social history of a Dalit community*. New Delhi: Oxford University Press.

Rajaraman, Indira. 2005. Economics of brideprice and dowry. In *Dowry and inheritance*, ed. Srimati Basu, 42–55. New York: Zed Books.

Ram, Kalpana. 1991. *Mukkuvar women: Gender, hegemony, and capitalist transformation in a South Indian fishing community*. Atlantic Highlands: Zed Books.

Rawat, Basant Rawat. VHP crown for Gujarat mob leader. *The Telegraph*, February 28, 2004.

Rawls, John. 1996. *Political liberalism*. New York: Columbia University Press.

Ray, Raka. 1999. *Fields of protest: Women's movements in India*. New Delhi: Kali for Women.

Ray, Raka and Mary Katzenstein, ed. 2005. *Social movements in India: Poverty, power and politics*. Lanham: Rowman and Littlefield.

Resnik, J. 2003. Many doors? Closing doors? Alternative dispute resolution and adjudication. *Ohio State Journal on Dispute Resolution* 10, no. 2: 211–265.

Reynell, Josephine. 2006. Religious practice and the creation of personhood among Svetambara Murtipujak Jain women in Jaipur. In *Studies in Jaina history and culture: Disputes and dialogues*, ed. Peter Flugel, 208–237. New York: Routledge.

Riho, Isaka. 2006. Gujarati elites and the construction of regional identity in the late nineteenth century. In *Beyond representation: Colonial and postcolonial constructions of Indian identity*, ed. Crispin Bates, 151–176. New Delhi: Oxford University Press.

Robinson, Rowena and Sathianathan Clarke, ed. 2003. *Religious conversion in India: Modes, motivations, and meanings*. New Delhi: Oxford University Press.

Rosen, Lawrence. 1980–1981. Equity and discretion in a modern Islamic legal system. *Law and Society Review* 15, no. 2: 217–246.

Rosen, Lawrence. 1984. *Bargaining for reality: The construction of social relations in a Muslim community*. Chicago: University of Chicago Press.

Rosen, Lawrence. 1989. Islamic "case law" and the logic of consequence. In *History and power in the study of law: New directions in anthropology*, ed. June Starr and Jane Collier, 302–319. Ithaca: Cornell University Press.

Rosenberg, Gerald N. 1991. *The hollow hope: Can courts bring about social change?* Chicago: University of Chicago Press.

Rosenblum, Nancy L., ed. 2000. *Obligations of citizenship and demands of faith: Religious accommodation in pluralist democracies.* Princeton: Princeton University Press.

Rudner, David W. 1994. *Caste and capitalism in colonial India: The Nattukottai Chettiars.* Berkeley: University of California Press.

Rudolph, Lloyd and Susanne Rudolph. 1967. *The modernity of tradition: Political development in India.* Chicago: University of Chicago Press.

Rudolph, Susanne and Lloyd Rudolph. 2001. Living with difference in India: Legal pluralism and legal universalism in historical context. In *Religion and personal law in secular India: A call to judgment*, ed. Gerald Larson, 36–68. Bloomington: Indiana University Press.

Rwezaura, B. 1994–1995. Tanzania: Building a new family law out of plural legal system. *University of Louisville Journal of Family Law* 33, no. 2: 523–540.

Sagade, Jaya. 1996. *Law of maintenance: An empirical study.* Pune: Indian Law Society.

Samasta Meghwal Gnati Bandharan. 1987. Unpublished document.

Sangari, Kumkum. 1995. Politics of diversity: Religious community and multiple patriarchies. *Economic and Political Weekly* 30, no. 52 (December): 3381–3389.

Sangari, Kumkum. 2003. Politics of diversity: Religious communities and multiple patriarchies. In *Communal identity in India: Its construction and articulation in the twentieth century*, ed. Bidyut Chakrabarty, 181–213. New Delhi: Oxford University Press.

Santos, Boaventura de Sousa. 1977. The law of the oppressed: The construction and reproduction of legality in Pasardaga. *Law and Society Review* 12, no. 1 (Autumn): 5–126.

Santos, Boaventura de Sousa. 1995. *Toward a new common sense: Law, science, and politics in paradigmatic transition.* New York: Routledge.

Santos, Boaventura de Sousa. 2006. The heterogeneous state and legal pluralism in Mozambique. *Law and Society Review* 40, no. 1 (March): 39–75.

Sanyal, Usha. 1995. Pir, shaikh and prophet: The personalisation of religious authority in Ahmed Riza Khan's life. In *Muslim communities of South Asia: Culture, society and power*, ed. T. N. Madan, 405–448. New Delhi: Manohar.

Sanyal, Usha. 1996. *Devotional Islam and politics in British India: Ahmad Riza Khan Barelwi and his movement, 1870–1920.* Delhi: Oxford University Press.

Sapiro, Virginia. 1993. Engendering cultural differences. In *The rising tide of cultural pluralism: The nation state at bay?*, ed. Crawford Young, 36–54. Madison: University of Wisconsin Press.

Sarkar, Tanika. 2001. *Hindu wife, Hindu nation, community, religion and cultural nationalism.* Bloomington: Indiana University Press.

Sarkar, Tanika and Urvashi Butalia, ed. 1995. *Women and right-wing movements: Indian experiences.* Atlantic Highlands: Zed Books.

Satter, R. 1990. *Doing justice: A trial judge at work.* New York: Simon and Schuster.

Scalia, A. 1989. The rule of law as a law of rules. *University of Chicago Law Review* 56, no. 4 (Autumn): 1175–1188.

Schauer, Frederick. 1987. Precedent. *Stanford Law Review* 39, no. 3 (February): 571–605.

Schlichte, Klaus, ed. 2005. *The dynamics of states: The formation and crises of state domination.* Aldershot: Ashgate.

Schultz, Dorothea. 2003. Political factions, ideological fictions: The controversy over family law reform in Mali. In *Islamic Law and Society, Special Volume* 10, no. 1: 132–164.

Schwartz, Barry. 1997. Collective memory and history: How Abraham Lincoln became a symbol of racial equality. *Sociological Quarterly* 38, no. 3 (June): 469–496.

Schweickart, Patrocinio. 1995. What are we doing? What do we want? Who are we? Comprehending the subject of feminism. In *Provoking agents: Gender and agency in theory and practice*, ed. Judith Kegan Gardiner, 229–248. Chicago: University of Illinois Press.

Scott, David. 1999. *Refashioning futures: Criticism after postcoloniality.* Princeton: Princeton University Press.

Scott, James C. 1998. *Seeing like a state: How certain schemes to improve the human condition have failed.* New Haven: Yale University Press.

Searle-Chatterjee, Mary and Ursula Sharma. 1994. *Contextualising caste: Post-Dumontian approach.* Cambridge: Blackwell Publishers/Sociological Review.

Shachar, Ayelet. 1998. Group identity and women's rights in family law: The perils of multicultural accommodation. *The Journal of Political Philosophy* 6, no. 3 (September): 285–305.

Shachar, Ayelet. 2001. *Multicultural jurisdictions: Cultural difference and women's rights*. Cambridge: Cambridge University Press.

Shah, Chayanika. 2005. Marriage, family and community: A feminist dialogue. *Economic and Political Weekly* 40, no. 8 (February 19–25): 709–722.

Shah, Ghanshyam. 2001. The BJP's riddle in Gujarat: Caste, factionalism and Hindutva. In *The BJP and the compulsion of politics in India*, ed. Thomas Blom Hansen and Christophe Jaffrelot, 243–266. New York: Oxford University Press.

Shaheed, Farida. 2005. The cultural articulation of patriarchy: Legal systems, Islam and women. In *Women and Islam: Critical concepts in sociology, Vol. 1*, ed. Haideh Moghissi, 224–243. New York: Routledge.

Shankar, Shylashri. 2003. Dealing with religious freedom in India and Israel: Do courts follow an institutional logic? Unpublished paper.

Shanley, Mary Lyndon. 1989. *Feminism, marriage and the law in Victorian England, 1850–1895*. Princeton: Princeton University Press.

Sharma, Ursula. 1983. *Women, work and property in North-West India*. London: Tavistock.

Sharma, Ursula. 2005. Dowry in North India: Its consequences for women. In *Dowry and inheritance*, ed. Srimati Basu, 15–26. New York: Zed Books.

Sharma, Vijay. 1994. *Protection to women in matrimonial home*. New Delhi: Deep & Deep Publications.

Shastri, Amita and Jeyaratnam Wilson, ed. 2001. *Postcolonial states of South Asia: Democracy, identity, development, and security*. Richmond: Curzon.

Sheth, Dhirubhai. 1999. Secularization of caste and making of new middle class. *Economic and Political Weekly* 34, nos. 34–35 (August 21–September 3): 2502–2510.

Shinoda, Takashi. 2002. The structure of stagnancy: Sweepers in Ahmedabad district. In *Dalits and the State*, ed. Ghanshyam Shah, 241–271. New Delhi: Centre for Rural Studies, Concept Publications.

Shodhan, Amrita. 2001. *A question of community: Religious groups and colonial law*. Calcutta: Samya.

Sikand, Yoginder. "Listen to the women." *Outlook India*, Web edition. Available from http://www.outlookindia.com (accessed May 5, 2005).

Sikand, Yoginder. 2010. "Tolerable cruelty." *Tehelka* 7, no. 8, http://www.tehelka.com/story_main43.asp?filename=Ne270210proscons.asp (accessed February 27, 2010).

"Sikhs belong to Hindu Samaj." *The Indian Express*, May 2, 2007.
Singh, Shiv Sahai. 1993. *Unification of divorce laws in India*. With a foreword by Amit Sen. New Delhi: Deep & Deep Publications.
Singhi, N. K. 1991. A study of Jains in a Rajasthan town. In *The assembly of listeners: Jains in society*, ed. Michael Carrithers and Caroline Humphrey, 139–164. Cambridge: Cambridge University Press
Singha, Radhika. 1998. *A despotism of law: Crime and justice in early colonial India*. New York: Oxford University Press.
Sirsikar, V. M. 1995a. *Politics in Maharashtra: An overview*. Hyderabad: Orient Longman.
Sirsikar, V. M. 1995b. *The politics of modern Maharashtra*. Bombay: Orient Longman.
Smart, Carol. 1984. *The ties that bind: Law, marriage, and the reproduction of patriarchal relations*. Boston: Routledge, Kegan Paul.
Smart, Carol. 1990. Social relations in Guatemala over time and space. In *Guatemalan Indians and the state: 1540–1988*, ed. Carol Smith, 1–30. Austin: University of Texas Press.
Smith, A. 1983. *State and nation in the Third World: The Western State and African nationalism*. New York: St. Martin's Press.
Smith, Donald Eugene. 1963. *India as a secular state*. Princeton: Princeton University Press.
Smith, Mark J. 2000. *Rethinking state theory*. New York: Routledge.
Sonbol, Amira El Azhary, ed. 1996. *Women, the family, and divorce laws in Islamic history*. Syracuse: Syracuse University Press.
Song, Sarah. 2007. *Justice, gender, and the politics of multiculturalism*. Cambridge and New York: Cambridge University Press.
Spinner-Halev, Jeff. 1994. *The boundaries of citizenship: Race, ethnicity, and nationality in the liberal state*. Baltimore: John Hopkins University Press.
Sri Meghwal Gnati Bandharan. 1953. Unpublished document. Mumbai.
Sri Meghwal Gnati Bandharan. 1965. Unpublished document. Mumbai.
Sri Meghwal Gnati Bandharan. 1974–1975. Unpublished pamphlet. Mumbai.
Srinivas, M. N. 1954. A caste dispute among washermen of Mysore. *The Eastern Anthropologist* 6–7: 148–168.
Srinivas, M. N. 1962. *Caste in modern India and other essays*. London: Asia Publishing House.
Srinivas, M. N. 1987. *The dominant caste and other essays*. New York: Oxford University Press.

Srinivas, M. N. 1989. *The cohesive role of Sanskritization and other essays.* New York: Oxford University Press.
Starr, June. 1978. *Dispute and settlement in Turkey: An ethnography of law.* Leiden: Brill.
Starr, June. 1990. Islam and the struggle over state law in Turkey. In *Law and Islam in the Middle East*, ed. Daisy H. Dwyer, 77–98. New York: Bergin and Garvey.
Starr, June. 1992. *Law as metaphor: From Islamic courts to the palace of justice.* Albany: The State University of New York Press.
Starr, June and Jane F. Collier, ed. 1989. *History and power in the study of law: New directions in legal anthropology.* Ithaca: Cornell University Press.
Starr, June and Mark Goodale, ed. 2002. *Practicing ethnography in law: New dialogues, enduring methods.* New York: Palgrave Macmillan.
Steinmetz, George, ed. 1999. *State/culture: State-formation after the cultural turn.* Ithaca: Cornell University Press.
Stevens, Jacqueline. 1999. *Reproducing the state.* Princeton: Princeton University Press.
Sturman, Rachel. 2005. Property and attachments: Defining autonomy and the claims of family in nineteenth-century Western India. *Comparative Studies in Society and History* 47, no. 3 (July): 611–637.
Suad, Joseph. 1997. The public/private: The imagined boundary in the imagined nation/state/the community. *Feminist Review* 57, no. 1: 73–92.
Suad, Joseph and Susan Slyomovics, ed. 2001. *Gender and citizenship in the Middle East.* With a foreword by Deniz Kandiyoti. Syracuse: Syracuse University Press.
Subramanian, Narendra. 2004. The judiciary, the legislature, and the reform of Christian and Muslim law. Paper presented at the Annual Conference of the Association for Asian Studies, March 4–7.
Subramanian, Narendra. 2005. Legal change and gender inequality: Changes in Muslim family law in India. Paper presented at the Association for the Study of Nationalities Convention, New York, April 14–16.
Subramanian, Narendra. 2008. Legal change and gender inequality: Changes in Muslim family law in India. *Law and Social Inquiry* 33, no. 3 (Summer): 631–672.
Sugarman, David, ed. 1983. *Legality, ideology, and the state.* New York: Academic Press.

Sunder Rajan, Rajeswari. 2000. Women between community and state: Some implications of the uniform civil code debates in India. *Social Text* 18, no. 4 (Winter): 55–82.

Sunder Rajan, Rajeswari. 2003. *The scandal of the state: Women, law, citizenship in postcolonial India.* Durham: Duke University Press.

Swidler, Ann. 1986. Culture in action: Symbols and strategies. *American Sociological Review* 51, no. 2 (April): 273–286.

"Talaq woes worry prince." *The Statesman*, May 5, 2005.

Talib, Mohammad. 2003. Personalizing Islam in communicating divorce. In *Divorce and remarriage among Muslims in India*, ed. Imtiaz Ahmad, 179–206. Delhi: Manohar.

Tamanaha, Brian Z. 1993. The folly of "social scientific" concept of legal pluralism. *Journal of Law and Society* 20, no. 2 (Summer): 192–217.

Tamanaha, Brian Z. 1996. The internal/external distinction and the notion of "practice" in legal theory and sociolegal studies. *Law and Society Review* 30, no. 1: 163–204.

Tamanaha, Brian Z. 2001. *A general jurisprudence of law and society.* New York: Oxford University Press.

Tamanoi, Mariko Asano. 1991. Songs as weapons: The culture and history of Komori (nursemaids) in modern Japan. *Journal of Asian Studies* 50, no. 4 (November): 793–817.

Tan, Poh-Ling. Ed., 1997. *Asian legal systems: Law, society and pluralism in East Asia.* Sydney: Butterworths.

Teubner, Gunther. 1983. Substantive and reflexive elements in modern law. *Law and Society Review* 17, no. 2: 239–285.

Teubner, Gunther. 1986. After legal instrumentalism? Strategic models of post-regulatory law. In *Dilemmas of law in the welfare state*, ed. Gunther Teubner, 299–326. Berlin: Walter de Gryuter.

Teubner, Gunther. 1992. The two faces of Janus: Rethinking legal pluralism. *Cardozo Law Review* 13: 1443–1462.

Teubner, Gunther, ed. 1987. *Autopoietic law: A new approach to law and society.* Berlin: de Gruyter.

Thakkar, Usha. 1995. The commissioners and the corporators: Power politics at municipal level. In *Bombay: Metaphor for modern India*, ed. Sujata Patel and Alice Thorner, 248–267. Delhi: Oxford University Press.

Tilly, Charles. 1985. War making and state making as organized crime. In *Bringing the state back in*, ed. Peter B. Evans, Dietrich Rueschemeyer, and Theda Skocpol, 169–191. New York: Cambridge University Press.

Tilly, Charles, ed. 1975. *The formation of national states in Western Europe.* Princeton: Princeton University Press.

Tomasic, Roman and Malcolm Feeley, ed. 1982. *Neighborhood justice movement: An assessment of an emerging idea.* New York: Longman.

Toth, Katalin and Markus Kemmelmeier. 2009. Divorce attitudes around the world: Distinguishing the impact of culture on evaluations and attitude structures. *Cross-Cultural Research* 43, no. 280–297.

Trainor, Brian T. 1992. The state, marriage and divorce. *Journal of Applied Philosophy* 9, no. 2 (October): 135–148.

Tucker, Judith E. 1998. *In the house of law: Gender and Islamic law in Syria and Palestine.* Berkeley: University of California Press.

Tucker, Judith E. 2008. *Women, family, and gender in Islamic law.* Cambridge and New York: Cambridge University Press.

Tucker, Richard. 1976. Hindu traditionalism and nationalist ideologies in the 19th century Maharashtra. *Modern Asian Studies* 10, no. 3: 321–348.

Twining, William. 2005. Social science and diffusion of law. *Journal of Law and Society* 32, no. 2 (June): 203–240.

Uberoi, Patricia, ed. 1993. *Family, kinship and marriage in India.* Delhi: Oxford University Press.

Unnithan-Kumar, Maya. 1997. *Identity, gender and poverty: New perspectives on caste and tribe in Rajasthan.* Providence: Berghahn Books.

Upadhya, Carol. 2001. The concept of community in Indian social sciences: An anthropological perspective. In *Community and identities: Contemporary discourses on culture and politics in India*, ed. Surinder S. Jodhka, 32–58. New Delhi: Sage Publications.

Varshney, Ashutosh. 1993. Contested meanings: India's national identity, Hindu nationalism, and the politics of anxiety. *Daedalus* 122, no. 3 (Summer): 227–261.

Varshney, Ashutosh. 2001. Ethnic conflict and civil society: India and beyond. *World Politics* 53, no. 3 (April): 362–398.

Vatuk, Sylvia. 2001. "Where will she go? What'll she do?" Paternalism toward women in the administration of Muslim Personal Law in contemporary India. In *Religion and personal law in secular India: A call to judgment*, ed. Gerald Larson, 226–250. Bloomington: Indiana University Press.

Vatuk, Sylvia. 2003. Muslim women in the Indian family courts: A report from Chennai. In *Divorce and remarriage among Muslims in India*, ed. Imtiaz Ahmad, 137–160. Delhi: Manohar.

Vatuk, Sylvia. 2005. Moving the courts: Muslim women and personal law. In *The diversity of Muslim women's lives in India*, ed. Zoya Hasan and Ritu Menon, 18–58. New Brunswick: Rutgers University Press.

Vatuk, Sylvia. 2008. Divorce at the wife's initiative in Muslim Personal Law: What are the options and what are their implications for women's welfare? In *Redefining family law in India: Essays in honour of B. Sivaramayya*, ed. Archana Parashar and Amita Dhanda, 200–235. New Delhi: Routledge.

Verma, Krishna Kumar. 1979. *Changing role of caste associations*. New Delhi: National.

Viswanathan, Gauri. 1998. *Outside the fold: Conversion, modernity and belief*. Princeton: Princeton University Press.

Wadud, Amina. 1999. *Quran and Woman: Rereading the sacred text from a woman's perspective*. New York: Oxford University Press.

Walby, Kevin. 2007. Contributions to a post-sovereigntist understanding of law: Foucault, law as governance and legal pluralism. *Social and Legal Studies* 16, no. 4 (December): 551–571.

Waltman, Jerold L. and Kenneth M. Holland. 1988. *The political role of law courts in modern democracies*. New York: St. Martin's Press.

Wardle, Lynn D. 1995. International marriage and divorce regulation and recognition: A survey. *Family Law Quarterly* 29, no. 3: 497–499.

Warren, Mark E. 1996. Deliberative democracy and authority. *American Political Science Review* 90, no. 1 (March): 46–60.

Warren, Mark E. 2003. A second transformation of democracy? In *Democracy transformed? Expanding political opportunity in advanced industrial democracies*, ed. Bruce E. Cain, Russell J. Dalton, and Susan E. Scarrow, 223–249. Oxford: Oxford University Press.

Washbrook, David A. 1975. The development of caste organizations in South India. In *South India: Political institutions and political change, 1880–1940*, ed. Christopher John Baker and David Washbrook, 150–203. Delhi: MacMillan.

Washbrook, David A. 1981. Law, state and agrarian society in colonial India. *Modern Asian Studies* 15, no. 3: 649–721.

Weisbrod, Carol. 1999. Universals and particulars: A comment on women's human rights and religious marriage contract. *Southern California Review of Law and Women's Studies* 9, no. 1 (Fall): 77–100.

Welchman, Lynn. 2000. *Beyond the code: Muslim family law and the Shari'a judiciary in the Palestinian West Bank*. The Hague: Kluwer Law International.

Welchman, Lynn, ed. 2004. *Women's rights and Islamic family law: Perspectives on reform.* New York: Zed Books.

Welchman, Lynn. 2007. *Women and muslim family laws in Aran states: A comparative overview of textual development and advocacy.* Amsterdam: Amsterdam University Press.

"We will make our own *nikahnama*." *The Hindu*, May 7, 2005.

Wilkinson, Steven. 2004. *Votes and violence: Electoral competition and ethnic riots in India.* New York: Cambridge University Press.

Women's Crisis Centre. 2000. *Muslim women and access to justice: Historical, legal, and social experience in Malaysia.* Penang, Malaysia. Unpublished Report.

Woodman, Gordon R. 1999. The idea of legal pluralism. In *Legal pluralism in the Arab World*, ed. Baudouin Dupret, Maurits Berger, and Laila al-Zwaini, 3–20. Boston: Kluwer Law International.

Woods, Patricia. 2004. Gender and reproduction and maintenance of group boundaries: Why the "secular" state matters to religious authorities in Israel. In *Boundaries and belongings: States and societies in the struggle to shape identities and local practices*, ed. Joel S. Migdal, 226–248. Cambridge: Cambridge University Press.

Woods, Patricia. 2006. Cause lawyers and judicial community in Israel. In *Cause lawyers and social movements*, ed. Sarat, Austin and Stuart Scheingold, 307–348. Stanford: Stanford University Press.

Woods, Patricia. 2008. *Judicial power and national politics: Courts and gender in the religious-secular conflict in Israel.* Albany: State University of New York Press.

Working Group on Women's Rights. 1996. Reversing the option: Civil codes and personal laws. *Economic and Political Weekly* Vol. 31, no. 20: 1180–1183.

Yilmaz, Ihsan. 2002. Secular law and the emergence of unofficial Turkish Islamic law. *The Middle East Journal* 56, no. 1 (Winter): 113–131.

Yilmaz, Ihsan. 2005. *Muslim laws, politics and society in modern nation-states: Dynamic legal pluralisms in England, Turkey, and Pakistan.* Aldershot: Ashgate.

Young, Crawford. 1976. *The politics of cultural pluralism.* Madison: University of Wisconsin Press.

Young, Iris Marion. 1989. Polity and group difference: A critique of the ideal of universal citizenship. *Ethics* 99, no. 2 (January): 250–274.

Young, Iris Marion. 1990. *Justice and the politics of group difference.* Princeton: Princeton University Press.

Yuval-Davis, Nira. 1997. *Gender and nation*. Thousand Oaks: Sage Publications.

Zaman, Muhammad Qasim. 2002. *The Ulama in contemporary Islam: Custodians of change*. Princeton: Princeton University Press.

Zelliot, Eleanor. 1995. Learning the use of political means: The Mahars of Maharashtra. In *Caste in Indian* politics. 5th ed., ed. Rajni Kothari, 27–65. Hyderabad: Orient Longman.

Zelliot, Eleanor. 2001. Dalit traditions and Dalit consciousness. In *Democratic governance in India: Challenges of poverty, development and identity*, ed. Niraja Gopal Jayal and Sudha Pai, 232–252. New Delhi: Sage Publications.

Zemans, Frances Kahn. 1982. Framework for analysis of legal mobilization: A decision-making model. *American Bar Foundation Research Journal* 7, no. 4 (Autumn): 989–1071.

Index

Accountability of state and societal legal orders, 56–59
Adultery, 123, 208
Aga Khan (Ismaili leader), 179, 292–295
Agarwal, Bina, 78, 315
Agency and women's rights
 collective socio-legal process, in, 82–87
 feminism and, 78
 individual legal actors and, 79–82
 litigation and, 78–82
 Muslim Personal Law, in, 312–315
Agnes, Flavia, 93, 156, 162–163
Ahl i Hadiths (Muslim sect), 279, 305–306, 313
Ahmed, Israr, 275–276, 305
AIMPLB. *See* All India Muslim Personal Law Board (AIMPLB)
Akhtar, Niloufar, 317
Alam, Arshad, 320
Alexander, P.C., 295
Algeria, Muslim law in, 344
Ali (son-in-law of Prophet), 293
Ali, Abdulla Yusuf, 134
Ali, Ameer, 134
Ali, Maulana Mohamed, 134
Ali, Zeenat Shaukat, 317
Alimony. *See* Maintenance
All India Democratic Women's Association, 264, 319
All India Muslim Personal Law Board (AIMPLB)
 accommodationist stance of, 316
 Barlevis and, 300–301
 Criminal Procedure Code 1973 and, 300
 Dar ul Qazas and, 302–303
 Deobandis and, 279
 generally, 83, 85
 historical background, 300
 Indian Women's Movement and, 285–286
 legal reform and, 318–320
 Muslim Personal Law and, 285–286
 nikahnama and, 319
 representation of community by, 300–301
 sharia law and, 311
 stridhan and, 311
 "triple *talaq*" and, 305
All India Muslim Personal Law Board Jabid, 300
All India Progressive Muslims Conference, 317–318
All India Servants of Untouchables Society, 182–183
All India Shia Personal Law Board, 75, 300
All India Women's Congress, 13
al Mustanasir (imam), 292
Ambedkar, B.R., 180–182
Ambedkarites (political movement), 182
Anveshi Legal Team (women's organization), 23
Association of Mumbai Tailors, 226
Attorneys
 Hindu Personal Law, role in, 260–261
 Muslim Personal Law, role in, 273–274
Authoritarianism, 15
Authority of state and societal legal orders, 56–59
Autopoiesis, 44–45, 346

387

Awaz e Niswan (women's organization)
    activities of, 286–288
    generally, 37, 59, 87, 315
    legal reform and, 286
    mehar and, 307
    Muslim Personal Law and, 286–288
    nikahnama and, 319

Babri Mosque, destruction of, 17, 192–193
Bahujan Samaj Party, 193–194, 220
Bajrangi, Babu, 19
Bangladesh, customary law in, 9
Barkat, Nazneen, 322
Barlevis (Muslim sect)
    AIMPLB and, 300–301
    Dar ul Qazas and, 303
    Deobandis compared, 279, 301
    divorce, 305–306
    nikahnama and, 318–319
    "triple *talaq*" and, 305–306
Barot caste, 178
Baxamusa, Ramla, 317
Benami Transaction Prohibition Act 1988, 166
Bhardwaj, Hansraj, 302
Bhartiya Janata Party (BJP) (rightist Hindu party)
    coalition governments, 17–18, 333
    consent to marriage and, 19
    Ithna Ashari Khojas and, 295
    Mumbai, in, 29
    riots and, 192–193
    "strongmen," 19
    uniform civil code, on, 18–19, 321, 333
Bhattacharya, Chandrima, 317–318
Birla, G.K., 183
BJP. *See* Bhartiya Janata Party (BJP) (rightist Hindu party)
Black Panthers, 189
BMC. *See* Mumbai
Bohras (Muslim sect), 268, 271, 305
Bombay. *See* Mumbai
Bombay Family Court
    cases filed in, 95–97
    consensual *versus* adversarial justice in, 94, 100–104
    disposition of cases in, 97–100
    divorce in, 125–126
    effectiveness of, 29, 51
    establishment of, 97
    feminist attorneys in, 102
    functioning of, 92–97
    generally, 327
    Indian Women's Movement, relationship with, 254–255
    maintenance in, 122, 125, 142–143, 159, 162–163
    mutual consent cases, 101–102
    procedure in, 62
    scope of study, 32–33
    settlement in, 102–104
    stridhan in, 169
Bombay Grain Dealers' Association, 238
Bombay High Court, 33, 98, 162
Bombay Kamaghar Sangh (Employees' Union), 184–185
Bombay Mill-Owners' Association, 183
Bombay Public Trusts Act, 52
Botswana, customary law in, 9
Bunsha, Dione, 19

Caste system. *See specific caste*
    Hindu Personal Law. *See* (Hindu Personal Law)
Caste violence, 15, 189–190
Centralization of law
    generally, 172
    informal legal organizations, in, 64–65
    shared adjudication model and, 326–327
    state courts, in, 61–62
Chamar caste, 178–180
Charles II (England), 178
Chatterjee, Partha, 5, 54, 336
Chawls (tenements), 180, 193, 282
Chiba, Masaji, 43
Child marriage, 106–107
Child Marriage Restraint Act 1929, 301
Chowdry, Prem, 25, 206, 208
Christians, 18
Church of Holy Cross, 179
Code of Civil Procedure 1908, 117, 162–163
Code of Criminal Procedure 1973
    AIMPLB and, 300
    contempt, 159–160
    generally, 92

INDEX

maintenance, 15–16, 133, 140, 146–147, 151–157, 167, 213, 218, 233–234, 270, 272, 274–275
mehar, recovery of, 169
Muslims, applicability to, 155–157
number of cases filed under, 96
polygyny, 119
restitution of conjugal rights, 115
stridhan, recovery of, 169
Collective socio-legal process
agency of, 82–87
everyday adjudication through, 85–87
lawmaking through, 84–85
College of Social Work (Mumbai), 94, 258
Communalism, 321–322
Communist Party of India, 86, 186, 193–194, 264
Community Outreach Programme (Dharavi), 163
Congress Party
Communist Party and, 186
Dalit Panthers and, 190–191
Ithna Ashari Khojas and, 295
legal reform and, 334
Meghwal caste and, 185, 190–194
Mumbai, in, 185
Mumbai Public Complaint Centre and, 284
MWA and, 16
uniform civil code, on, 321
women's rights, on, 13
Constitution of India, Directive Principles, 13
Contempt for nonpayment of maintenance, 159–160
Context of study, 24–29
Copts, 4
Cover, Robert, 69, 86
Criminal breach of trust, 82, 256–257
Customary divorce, 10, 14, 26, 121, 129–130, 155

Dalit caste, 181–182, 190, 199, 214
Dalit Panthers, 189–192
Daniel Latifi case, 146–148
Dar ul Qazas (Muslim religious courts)
AIMPLB and, 302–303
appellate procedure, 58
Barlevis and, 303
clergy and, 303

divorce, 281
generally, 48
historical background, 278–280
khula and, 280
Muslim Personal Law in, 278–281
Dar ul Uloom (Deobandi school), 302
Das, Deshbandhu Chitranjan, 183
Das, Rathin, 19
Dashavatar (Hindu text), 293
Data collection
informal courts, in, 35–37
state courts, in, 34–35
Dawoodbhai Fazalbhoy Muslim Education Trust, 296
Decentralization of law
shared adjudication model and, 326–327, 346
society, in, 65–66
state courts, in, 62–64, 172–173
Deferred *mehar*, 141
Delegation of right to divorce, 270–271
Deliberative democracy, 339–340
Democratic professionalism, 273
Deobandis (Muslim sect)
AIMPLB and, 300
Barlevis compared, 279, 301
Dar ul Qazas (*See* Dar ul Qazas (Muslim religious courts))
divorce and, 305–306
Muslim Personal Law and, 278–279, 302
"triple *talaq*" and, 305–306
Deoband seminary, 48, 58, 302
Deora, Murli, 295
Desai, A.R., 185
Deshpande, Swati, 93
Deveaux, Monique, 341
Dhasal, Namdeo, 189–190
Dher caste, 178–180, 182–184, 198
Directive Principles (Constitution of India), 13
Dissolution of Muslim Marriages Act 1939
divorce, 120, 137, 139, 166, 271, 274, 308–309, 327
enactment of, 14
generally, 119
maintenance, 140–141
polygyny, 310
transfer of cases filed under, 96, 98

Divorce
   adultery and, 123
   Barlevis and, 305–306
   Bombay Family Court, in, 125–126
   children and, 125–127
   contested cases, 122–125
   customary divorce, 10, 14, 26, 121, 129–130, 155
   delegation of right to divorce, 270–271
   Deobandis and, 305–306
   Dissolution of Muslim Marriages Act 1939, 120, 137, 139, 166, 271, 274, 308–309, 327
   ex parte divorce, 125–126
   Family Courts Act 1984, 120, 130–132
   faskh, 138, 280–281, 298, 306–307
   grounds for, 121
   Hindu and Muslim law compared, 328
   Hindu Personal Law, 120–131
   HMA, 120–121, 123–125, 129–130, 137, 139, 327
   irretrievable breakdown of marriage and, 130–131
   Ithna Ashari Khojas, among, 298–299
   (*khula See Khula* (divorce))
   KVOs, among, 243, 245–248
   Meghwal caste, in, 197, 209, 213–216
   mubaraat, 138
   mutual consent cases, 121–122, 127–128, 309
   MWA, 172
   negotiated divorce, 272–273
   "no fault" divorce, 215–216
   oral divorce, 269–270, 304–306
   Penal Code 1860, 99, 125, 127, 132
   private divorces, 46
   reconciliation and, 120–121
   reversal of, 209–210
   Sai Suthar caste, in, 234–237
   settlements, 128–129
   talaq ahsan, 131, 280
   talaq e tafwid, 71, 306
   talaq hasan, 131, 280
   talaqnama, 156
   talaq ul bidaat, 87, 131–137, 273, 280, 304–306
   "triple *talaq*," 87, 131–137, 273, 280, 304–306
   unilateral divorce, 102–103, 137–139, 166–167
Diwan, Paras, 150
Domestic violence
   KVOs, among, 248
   loss of marital property due to, 80
   Meghwal caste, in, 221–222
   Penal Code 1860, 221–222, 248, 255–258, 270, 308
Doorstep courts, 30, 37, 55, 87, 290–292, 305
Dower. *See* Maintenance; *Mehar* (Muslim dower); *Stridhan* (gifts received by women in marriage)
Dowry, 168–169
Dowry Prohibition Act 1961, 168

East India Company, 178
Eckert, Julia, 25, 27, 263
Egypt, Muslim law in, 4, 344
Ellis, Cottam, 237
Elopement, 205–206, 208–209, 211
Engineer, Asghar Ali, 304, 317
England
   customary law in, 336
   Sharia law in, 338–339
Ethiopia
   legal centralism in, 2
   uniform law in, 2
Ethnic violence, 17–18, 286, 333
Ex parte divorce, 125–126

Family courts, 51. *See also* Bombay Family Court
Family Courts Act 1984
   defining marriage, 108
   divorce, 120, 130–132
   enactment of, 92
   generally, 92–94, 327
   injunctions, 162–164, 166–167
   maintenance, 140, 154, 290
   matrimonial home, right to, 75, 80
   polygyny, 119
   reconciliation, 94, 120, 213
   restitution of conjugal rights, 114–115
   settlements, 94
   void and voidable marriages, 106, 111–114
Family laws, 11–12
Faskh (divorce), 138, 280–281, 298, 306–307

INDEX 391

Fatwas (religious judgments), 272–273, 285, 302, 307
Fazhalbhoy, Nasreen, 317
Feminism
  agency and, 78
  assumptions from, 31–32
  autonomy and, 343
  Bombay Family Court, feminist attorneys in, 102
  legal pluralism and, 7–8
  legal reform and, 23
  multiculturalism and, 7–8, 23, 332, 343–344
  Muslim Personal Law and, 17–21, 288–290
  MWA and, 74–75, 149
  objections to religious law, 6, 22, 343–344
Fineman, Martha Albertson, 88
Fiqh (schools of law), 268
Forcible marriage, 258–259
Formal legal organizations, 52–55
Forum Against Oppression of Women (women's organization), 23, 31, 83, 255, 319, 343
Forum-shopping, 79–80, 309, 313–314
Fragmentation of law
  generally, 172–173
  society, in, 65–66
  state courts, in, 62–64
Francis, Sugandhi, 86
Fundamentalism, 15–19, 333
Fyzee, Asaf Ali Asghar, 107

Gada, U., 245
Gala, N., 245
Gandhi, Mahatma, 181–183
"Gatekeeping" function of doorstep courts, 55
Ghildiyal, Subodh, 302
Giddens, Anthony, 77
Gohil, Bipin, 201
Gokhale, Sandhya, 255
Gowda, Veena, 319
Griffiths, Anne, 8
Group rights, 6–7, 13, 16–17, 22, 325–326
Gujarat, ethnic violence in, 16–17, 286
Gupta, Suchandana, 319

Habib Trust, 296
Hakk e Niswan (women's organization), 85
Hallaq, Wael B., 344–345
HAMA. *See* Hindu Adoption and Maintenance Act 1956 (HAMA)
Hamraz Mahila Mandal (doorstep court), 73, 87, 291, 305, 317–318
Hanafi (Muslim school of law), 268, 301, 308, 316
Hanbali (Muslim school of law), 268, 316
Hansen, Thomas Bloom, 261
Harijan caste, 184, 190
Harijan Sevak Sangh (Congress Party civic organization), 181–182, 185
Harijan Temple Entry Bill, 182
Hindu Adoption and Maintenance Act 1956 (HAMA)
  generally, 92
  maintenance, 118, 139–143, 158, 235
Hindu Marriage Act 1955 (HMA)
  applicability of, 105
  caste constitutions and, 198
  consent, 19, 107, 112
  customary divorce, 10, 14, 26, 121
  dissolution, 20
  divorce, 120–121, 123–125, 129–130, 137, 139, 327
  maintenance, 125, 140–143, 149–150
  marriage, 105–106
  MWA compared, 149–150
  polygyny, 116–117
  publication of records, 33
  void and voidable marriages, 109
Hindu Marriage (Amendment) Act 1976, 121
Hindu Personal Law
  attorneys, role of, 260–261
  comparison of castes, 252–254
  divorce, 120–131
  gender equality in, 74–77
  generally, 175–177, 265–266
  individual legal actors, role of, 259–261
  KVOs, among *See* (Kutchi Visa Oswal (KVO) caste)
  maintenance, 141–145
  Meghwal caste, in
    (*See* Meghwal caste)
  middlemen, role of, 259–260

Hindu Personal Law (*cont.*)
  Muslim Personal Law compared, 66–68, 104–105, 108, 111, 114–116, 120, 139–141, 172–173
  notaries, role of, 260–261
  political parties, role of, 261–263
  polygyny, 116–120
  restitution of conjugal rights, 114–116
  Sai Suthar caste, in *See* (Sai Suthar caste)
  "strongmen," role of, 261–263
  void and voidable marriages, 109–114
  women's organization, role of, 254–259
Hindu Succession (Amendment) Act 2005, 18
Historical background, 11–24
HMA. *See* Hindu Marriage Act 1955 (HMA)
Holden, Livia, 25, 46, 206, 214
Homosexuality, 34, 87, 106, 230, 322–323
Human Rights Law Network (legal organization), 93, 163, 255–256
Husain, Qadir, 294
Iddat (waiting period after divorce), 111, 146, 155, 311

Ideologically diverse actors, 59, 345
Ilyas, Muhamed, 283
Imarat e Sharia (Muslim religious organization), 275–276
Imprisonment for nonpayment of maintenance, 160–162
Independent Labour Party, 181–182
Indian Association of Women's Studies Conference, 83
Indian Penal Code 1860
  adultery, 208
  caste constitutions and, 198
  criminal breach of trust, 82, 256–257
  divorce, 99, 125, 127, 132
  domestic violence, 221–222, 248, 255–258, 270, 308
  dowry-related violence, 168, 221–222
  forcible marriage, 258–259
  homosexuality, 106
  polygyny, 116
  stridhan, recovery of, 82, 169, 223, 256–257
Indian Women's Movement
  agenda and influence of, 20–22

AIMPLB and, 285–286
Bombay Family Court, relationship with, 254–255
community elite, dialogue with, 84
dowry-related violence, on, 221–222
legal reform, on, 31, 285–286
marital reform, on, 85
MWA, on, 16
uniform civil code, on, 13, 21
Individual legal actors
  agency of, 79–82
  forum-shopping by, 79–80
  generally, 55
  Hindu Personal Law, role in, 259–261
  KVOs, role among, 259–261
  structural change through individual agency, 80–82
Indonesia
  Muslim law in, 4, 344
  religious law in, 9
Informal legal organizations
  centralization of law in, 64–65
  generally, 55
  Hindu Personal Law *See* (Hindu Personal Law)
  KVOs, among, 240–242
  legal reform in, 329
  Meghwal caste, in, 37, 194–195
  Muslim Personal Law *See* (Muslim Personal Law)
  panchayats (*See* Panchayats (caste councils))
Injunctions for maintenance, 162–168
Insistence, marriage by, 205
Interest-based organizations, 54–55, 71–72
Interim Constitutional Amendment Committee (Meghwal caste), 187
Interim maintenance, 141–142
Intermarriage, 108–109
Irregular marriages, 110–111
Irretrievable breakdown of marriage, 130–131
Ismail (imam), 292
Ismailis (Muslim sect), 268, 294
Ismailism, 292
Israel, religious law in, 9
Ithna Ashari Khojas
  BJP and, 295
  Congress Party and, 295

INDEX

Constitution of 1955, 297
divorce, 298
family law, 296–298
generally, 53
gharsansar committee, 297
historical background, 292–295
interaction with other legal forums, 298–299
jamaat, 58–59, 296–297, 299
jamatkhana, 296–298
khula and, 298
maintenance, 298
mehar and, 297–298
muta marriage, 307
polygyny, 64, 68, 298
Shiv Sena and, 295
sociopolitical change among, 295–296
stridhan and, 298
women's committees, 84
Ivanow, W., 292

Jagtap, Pratibha, 95, 258–259
Jain, Sonu, 18
Jainism, 237, 243
Jamaat e Islami (Muslim religious organization), 301
Jamaats (collectives), 55, 58–59
Jamal, Devjibhai, 294
Jamiat e Ulema e Maharashtra (Muslim religious organization), 85, 276, 279
Janata Party, 186
Joint governance model, 337
Jordan, prenuptial agreements in, 316
Joshi, Manohar, 295
Joshi, Vaijayanta, 317
Juristic diversity, 50–55

Kapila, Kriti, 25
Kelkar, Kunda, 81
Khan, Ahmad Raza, 301
Khan, Hasina, 286–287
Khan, Pir Anwar Raza, 301
Khoja Muslims. *See also* Ithna Ashari Khojas
divorce, 271, 305
historical background, 292–295
sect-based laws, 268
Khula (divorce)
Dar ul Qazas and, 280

forum-shopping, 309
generally, 138, 272, 309–310, 314
Ithna Ashari Khojas, among, 298
mehar and, 309
polygyny and, 313
stridhan and, 312
"strongmen" and, 276
talaq, conversion to, 271–272, 309
Kidwai, Rasheed, 319
Kutchi Visa Oswal (KVO) caste
adjudicative forums, 177
comparison with other castes, 252–254
denial of divorce, 245–247
divorce, 243, 245–248
domestic violence, 248
factionalism among, 241–242
family structure among, 242–243
formal legal organizations, role of, 254–259, 261–263
"gendered sphere" among, 244–245
generally, 53, 83, 237–238
historical background, 238–239
individual legal actors, role of, 259–261
informal legal organizations in, 240–242
maintenance, 243, 248–250
marriage, 243
panchayats, 239–242, 251–252
settlements, 247–250
social movement in response to state legal reforms, 251–252
village *mahajans*, 242
KVOs. *See* Kutchi Visa Oswal (KVO) caste
Kymlicka, Will, 6

LABIA (Lesbians and Bisexuals in Action), 258
Lakshmi Narain Temple, 183
Langer, Rosanna, 53
Lawyers Collective (legal organization), 255
Lebanon, legal pluralism in, 9
Legal centralism, 1–2, 325–326
Legal pluralism
adjudicative forums, centrality of, 47–48
constitutive aspect of law, 46–47
continuum of, 8
feminism and, 7–8
generally, 1–2

Legal pluralism (*cont.*)
  group rights and, 22
  interpretation of local, national, and global law, 43–44
  law *versus* customs and morality, 44–45
  legal centralism and, 325–326
  shared adjudication model and, 49, 326, 341–343, 345
  state laws as distinct from nonstate legal orders, 43
  typologies of, 9
  uniform civil code and, 325–326
Legal reform
  AIMPLB and, 318–320
  Awaz e Niswan and, 286
  Congress Party and, 334
  feminism and, 23
  Indian Women's Movement on, 31, 285–286
  informal legal organizations, in, 329
  KVO social movement in response to, 251–252
  lower courts, in, 328
  Meghwal caste, in, 195
  Muslim Personal Law, in, 320–321
  nikahnama and, 316–320
  shared adjudication model and, 328–329, 343–346
  state-centric family law and conditions for, 344–345
Lesbians, 258–259
Levirate, 210, 213
Litigation, 78
Location of study, 29
Lower courts
  generally, 51
  legal reform in, 75–76, 167–168, 172–174, 328
Madrasas (Muslim schools), 48, 278–279

Mahajan, Gurpreet, 22
Mahar caste, 178–180, 182, 190, 198
Mahila Aghadi (Shiv Sena women's affiliate), 263–264, 276–277
Maintenance. *See also Mehar* (Muslim dower); *Stridhan* (gifts received by women in marriage)
  amount of, 127, 129, 137–138, 143, 145–147, 151

bargaining re, 143–144
Bombay Family Court, in, 122, 125, 142–143, 159, 162–163
Code of Criminal Procedure 1973, 15–16, 133, 140, 146–147, 151–157, 167, 213, 218, 233–234, 270, 272, 274–275
collection of, 158–159
considerations in granting, 142
contempt for nonpayment, 159–160
Dar ul Qaza and, 280
Dissolution of Muslim Marriages Act 1939, 140–141
effectiveness of, 155
entitlement to, 141, 151–153
Family Courts Act 1984, 140, 154, 290
fault and, 142–143
HAMA, 118, 139–143, 158, 235
Hindu and Muslim law compared, 139–141, 147, 149–150, 328
Hindu Personal Law, in, 141–145
HMA, 125, 140–143, 149–150
implementation of orders, 158–162
imprisonment for nonpayment, 160–162
injunctions, 162–168
interim maintenance, 141–142
Ithna Ashari Khojas, among, 298
judicial discretion re, 167–168
KVOs, among, 243, 248–250
Meghwal caste, in, 198, 213, 216–218
mutual consent cases, 143–145
MWA, 145–151, 157, 273, 311, 328
remarriage and, 147–149
Sai Suthar caste, in, 233–237
socio-economics and, 153–154
state laws, 139–141
Majlis (women's legal resource center), 23, 93, 130, 163, 255–256, 343
Malaysia
  Muslim law in, 4, 35, 344
  religious law in, 9
Maliki (Muslim school of law), 268, 308, 316
Mang caste, 180
Maniar, Zakir, 317
Manzar ul Islam (Muslim school of law), 301
Marital property. *See* Maintenance
Maroo, P.K., 201
Marriage

INDEX

child marriage, 106–107
defining, 104–108
divorce (*See* Divorce)
elopement, 205–206, 208–209, 211
forcible marriage, 258–259
heterosexuality, privilege of, 106–107
HMA, 105–106
insistence, by, 205
intermarriage, 108–109
irregular marriages, 110–111
irretrievable breakdown of, 130–131
KVOs, among, 243
levirate, 210, 213
marital property *See* (Maintenance)
Meghwal caste, in (*See* Meghwal caste)
muta marriage, 285, 307, 330
nikahnama, 85, 316–320
polygyny *See* (Polygyny)
prenuptial agreements, 316
purposes of, 104–105
qazis, role of, 274–275
registration of, 105–108
restitution of conjugal rights, 114–116
void and voidable marriages, 109–114
Marriage Laws (Amendment) 2010, 130
Masselos, J.C., 293
Meghwal caste
adjudication and appeal in *panchayats*, 202–203
adjudicative forums, 177
appellate procedure, 48, 58
autonomy of women in, 206–207
children in, 197
comparison with other castes, 252–254
Congress Party and, 185, 190–194
consent to marriage, 205–206
constitutional provisions, 195–198
Constitution of 1953, 185
Constitution Rejuvenation Committee, 190
democratic participatory justice in *panchayats*, 53, 200–202, 328–329
demographics of, 192–193
depoliticization of *panchayats*, 187–189
divorce, 197, 209, 213–216
domestic violence, 221–222
elections, 58
elopement, 205–206, 208–209, 211
fluidity of marriage, 198, 209

formal legal organizations, role of, 220–223, 254–259, 261–263
"gendered sphere" among, 198–200
generally, 83, 177
Hinduism and, 181–184, 193–194, 203–205
historical background, 178–195
individual legal actors, role of, 218–220, 259–261
informal legal organizations in, 37, 194–195
Interim Constitutional Amendment Committee, 187
legal reforms, 195
levirate, 210, 213
maintenance, 198, 213, 216–218
marriage by insistence, 205
Mumbai, emigration to, 178–181
"no fault" divorce, 215–216
polygyny, 198, 210–211
religion among, 193–194, 203–205
repoliticization of *panchayats*, 189–192
reversal of divorce, 209–210
rise of *panch* system, 184–186
stridhan, recovery of, 222–223
structure and organization of *panchayats*, 200–202
"untouchability" question and, 181–184
validity of marriage, 211–213
wealth retention in, 207–208
women's committees, 84
Meghwal Hitvardhak Mandal (caste organization), 183
Meghwal Sudharak Sabha (caste organization), 183
Mehar (Muslim dower).
See also Maintenance
amount of, 140–141, 307–308
Awaz e Niswan and, 307
Code of Criminal Procedure, recovery under, 169
customary divorce and, 155
Dar ul Qazas and, 280
deferred *mehar*, 141
defined, 73, 131
Ithna Ashari Khojas, among, 297–298
khula and, 309
Muslim Personal Law, in, 73

Mehar (Muslim dower) (*cont.*)
  mutual consent cases, 137–138
  prompt *mehar*, 140–141
  recovery of, 277
Mehta, Bob, 181
Mehta, Navin, 259–260
Memons (Muslim sect), 271, 305
Menski, Werner, 105–106, 117, 124, 139, 212
Methodist Episcopal Church, 179
Methodology of study, 29–31
Metropolitan Magistrates' Court (Mumbai), 34, 96, 147, 157, 166
Middlemen, 259–260
Migdal, Joel, 47–48
Mody, Perveez, 206
Mohalla committees (local committees), 37, 55, 229, 233
Moore, Erin, 25, 79–80
Morocco
  divorce in, 132
  legal centralism in, 2, 9
  Muslim law in, 344
  prenuptial agreements in, 316
Morris, Morris, D., 183
Mozambique
  interaction between legal orders in, 48–49
  privatization of justice in, 27
Mubaraat (divorce), 138
Mukhopadhyay, Maitreyee, 17, 24–25
Mulla, Dinshah Fardunji, 107–108, 114, 134, 140–141, 316
Multiculturalism, 1–8, 69–70, 338–339, 343–344
Multiculturalism Without Culture (Phillips), 338
Mumbai
  BJP in, 29
  Congress Party in, 185
  Family Court. *See* Bombay Family Court
  location of study, as, 29
  Meghwals, emigration of, 178–181
  Metropolitan Magistrates' Court, 34, 96, 147, 157, 166
  Preferential Treatment Policy, 184, 193–194, 213
  Public Complaint Centre, 83, 284–285, 307
  Shiv Sena in, 29, 186

Musawalla, Haroun, 77
Muslim League, 295
Muslim Personal Law
  agency and women's rights in, 312–315
  AIMPLB and, 285–286
  attorneys, role of, 273–274
  Awaz e Niswan and, 286–288
  clergy, role of, 274
  communalism and, 321–322
  competing ideologies in, 321
  Dar ul Qazas, in, 278–281
  delegation of right to divorce, 270–271
  Deobandis and, 278–279, 302
  divorce, 120–139
  doorstep courts, 290–292
  feminism and, 288–290
  forum-shopping in, 313–314
  gender equality in, 74–77
  generally, 267–269, 323
  Hindu Personal Law compared, 66–68, 108, 111, 114–116, 120, 139–141, 172–173
  homosexuality and, 322–323
  Indian Women's Movement and, 22–23, 85–87, 285–286
  Ithna Ashari Khojas, among *See* (Ithna Ashari Khojas)
  legal reforms in, 320–321
  mehar, 73, 307–308
  Mumbai Public Complaint Centre and, 284–285
  negotiated divorce, 272–273
  nikahnama, legal reforms re, 316–320
  oral divorce, 269–270
  partial codification of, 14
  polygyny, 116–120, 310, 313, 318
  prenuptial agreements, 316
  qazis, role of, 274–275
  representation of community, 300–301
  residential committees, role of, 281–284
  restitution of conjugal rights, 114–116
  stridhan, 311–312
  "strongmen," role of, 276–278
  "triple *talaq*," 304–306
  void and voidable marriages, 109–114
  Women's Research and Action Group and, 288
Muslim Women's (Protection of Rights on Divorce) Act 1986 (MWA)

INDEX

beneficial nature of, 22, 74–75, 311
cases filed under, 34
Congress Party and, 16
criticism of, 74
divorce, 172
enactment of, 16
feminism and, 74–75, 149
generally, 92
HMA compared, 149–150
Indian Women's Movement on, 16
injunctions, 166
maintenance, 145–151, 157, 273, 311, 328
polygyny, 119
reluctance to file cases under, 274
Muslim Women's Rights Network, 85, 287–288, 301, 305, 317–318
Mustal (imam), 292
Muta marriage (temporary marriage), 285, 307, 330
MWA. *See* Muslim Women's (Protection of Rights on Divorce) Act 1986 (MWA)

Naheed, Uzma, 318
Naidu, Sarojini, 183
Nainar, Vahida, 317
Najifi, Abdul Qasim, 294
Napu, Velji, 239
Nat caste, 178
Negotiated divorce, 272–273
Newbigin, Eleanor, 173
Niaz, Noorjehan, 290–291, 311
Nigeria, Muslim law in, 4
Nikahnama (Muslim marriage contract), 85, 316–320
Nizar (imam), 292
"No fault" divorce, 215–216
Notaries, 46, 260–261

Oral divorce, 269–270
Other Backward Classes (OBC), 224, 226, 264
Overview of theoretical debates, xxi–5, 37–39, 49–50, 325–332

Palkar, A.B., 159
Panchayats (caste councils)
appellate procedure, 58
generally, 53, 64

historical background, 11–12
KVOs, among, 239–242, 251–252
Meghwal caste, in (*See* Meghwal caste)
public trusts, as, 52
Sai Suthar caste, in, 224–227, 229–230
state courts and, 57, 59
Pandey, Geeta, 320
Paradoxical movement between legal orders, 60–66, 326–327
Paranjpe, Lakshmi, 317
Parekh, Bhagyashree, 94
Parmar, Gitaben, 228–229
Parry, Jonathan P., 206
Parsis, 18
Patel, Vitthalbhai, 183
Paternalism, 344
The Path (KVO magazine), 239
Peletz, Michael G., 35
Phillips, Anne, 338–339, 341
Phule, Jyotiba, 182
Political parties. *See also specific party*
Hindu Personal Law, role in, 261–263
KVOs, role among, 261–263
Meghwal caste, role in, 261–263
Sai Suthar caste, role in, 261–263
Polygyny
Code of Criminal Procedure 1973, 119
Dissolution of Muslim Marriages Act 1939, 310
Family Courts Act 1984, 119
Hindu and Muslim law compared, 64–68, 116–120, 327
Hindu Personal Law, 116–120
HMA, 116–117
Ithna Ashari Khojas, among, 64, 68, 298
Khula and, 313
Meghwal caste, in, 198, 210–211
Muslim Personal Law, in, 116–120, 310, 313, 318
MWA, 119
Penal Code 1860, 116
sharia law, in, 310
Polyvocality, 30
Poona Pact of 1932, 181
Preferential Treatment Policy (Mumbai), 184, 193–194, 213
Prenuptial agreements, 316
Prince of Arcot, 320
Private divorces, 46

Prompt *mehar*, 140–141
Property of women, 80.
　See also Maintenance; *Mehar* (Muslim dower); *Stridhan* (Hindu dower)
Protection of Women from Domestic Violence Act 2005, 107, 130–132, 167, 291
Public Complaint Centre (Mumbai), 83, 284–285, 307
Public trusts, 52
Qazis (Muslim religious judges), 105, 107, 274–275, 309

Qazi's Act 1880, 105, 107, 274
Quran, 268, 279

Ramdeo Pir (Hindu saint), 194, 204
Rashtriya Swayamsevan Sangh (BJP cultural affiliate), 333
Rawat, Basant, 19
Rawls, John, 5–6
Reflexive law, 346
Residential committees, 281–284
Restitution of conjugal rights, 114–116
Restrained autonomy, 10–11
Reversal of divorce, 209–210
Riots, 192–193, 333
RSS (Hindu cultural organization), 19
Rudolph, Lloyd, 12, 325–326
Rudolph, Susanne, 12, 325–326
Ruhi, Nusrat Bano, 319
Runaway marriages. *See* Elopement

Sagade, Jaya, 24, 143, 150
Sai Suthar caste
　adjudicative forums, 177
　comparison with other castes, 252–254
　decentralization of *panchayats*, 229–230
　divorce, 234–237
　"dual patriarchy" in, 234–237
　extralegal justice, 232–233
　formal legal organizations, role of, 254–259, 261–263
　"gendered sphere" among, 227–229
　generally, 37, 53, 224
　historical background, 224–227
　homosexuality and, 230
　individual legal actors, role of, 259–261
　maintenance, 233–237
　panchayats, 224–227
　political parties, role of, 261–263
　public *versus* private justice, 231
　state courts, impact of, 232–234
Samajwadi Party, 18, 77, 193–194, 264, 321
Samjhauta Mahila Mandal (doorstep court), 292, 305
Sampling
　informal courts, in, 35–37
　state courts, in, 32–34
Samyukta Maharashtra Samiti (multiparty alliance), 185–186
Sanskritization, 200
Santos, Boaventure de Sousa, 27, 43–44, 48–49, 313
Saptapadi (Hindu marriage ritual), 110
Sathe, Satyaranjan, 317
Sawla, Harshi, 244
Scheduled Castes, 203, 207, 226, 235
Scholarly objections to religious law, 6
Scott, David, 5, 336–337
Separatist movements, 15
Sequeira, Irene, 119, 163
Servants of India Society, 182–183, 185
Shachar, Ayelet, 7–8, 337
Shafi (Muslim school of law), 268, 308, 316
Shah, Anup, 239
Shah Bano case, 15–16, 155–156, 300
Shared adjudication model
　adjudicative forums, centrality of, 47–48
　arguments for, 49–50
　balancing cultural accommodation and gender justice in, 68–74
　centralization of law in, 326–327
　conjugal family, flexibility re, 72–74
　decentralization of law in, 326–327, 346
　defined, 10
　deliberative democracy compared, 339–340
　dynamic nature of, 332
　equality, shift toward, 328
　factors causing change in, 333–335
　gender equality in, 74–77, 88–89
　generally, 41–42, 89–90, 325–326, 346–347
　Hindu and Muslim law compared, 327–328
　Hindu fundamentalism, effect of, 333
　interaction between legal orders and, 56–60, 330–332
　interpenetrative nature of strands, 48–49

INDEX 399

intersocietal dialog in, 71–72
intragroup accommodation in, 70–71
intrareligious negotiation, effect of, 334
joint governance model compared, 337
juristic diversity and, 50–55
legal pluralism and, 49, 326, 341–343, 345
legal reform and, 328–329, 343–346
multiculturalism compared, 338–339
normative heterogeneity in, 69
ossification of religious boundaries, preventing, 69–70
other models compared, 335–343
paradoxical movement between legal orders in, 60–66
society-centric family law and, 336
state-society distinction in, 326
strategically focused deliberation compared, 341
theoretical framework of, 42–49
uniform civil code, effect of, 333–336
women's organizations, role of, 330
Sharia law
AIMPLB and, 311
colonialism, effect of, 344–345
conservatives and, 316
England, in, 338–339
Indonesia, in, 4
Nigeria, in, 4
polygyny, 310
Tabligh i Jamaat and, 283
women's organizations and, 321
Shariat Act 1937, 14, 303–304
Sheikh, Khatoom Gafoor, 73, 87, 317–318
Sheikh, Nahida, 317
Sheikh, Yasmin, 233, 290
Shia Muslims, 268, 279, 285, 300, 303–305. *See also* Ismailism; Ithna Ashari Khojas
Shiv Sena (rightist Hindu party)
caste violence and, 189–190
Ithna Ashari Khojas and, 295
Maharashtra, in, 190
Mahila Aghadi, 263–264, 276–277
Mumbai, in, 29, 186
riots and, 192–193
Shodhan, Amrita, 293
Sikand, Yoginder, 75, 311
Singhi, N.K., 237
Societalization of law, 173

Society-centric multiculturalism
generally, 5
shared adjudication model and, 336
Society for Promotion of Vanza-Wearers, 226
Society of St. John, 179
Song, Sarah, 339–341
South Africa
customary law in, 9
Muslim law in, 4
women's rights in, 341
Special Cell for Women and Children (Mumbai), 31, 37, 171, 201, 258, 264
Special Marriage Act 1954, 13–14, 19, 95, 108, 111, 130
Spinner-Halev, Jeff, 7
Sri Lanka
customary law in, 9
ethnic conflict in, 5
State-centric multiculturalism
conditions for legal reform and, 344–345
generally, 5–6
State courts
centralization of law in, 61–62
data collection in, 34–35
decentralization of law in, 62–64
fragmentation of law in, 62–64
generally, 91, 172–174
panchayats and, 57, 59
Sai Suthar caste, impact on, 232–234
sampling in, 32–34
State formation in postcolonial states, 2–3
Strategically focused deliberation, 341
Stree Mukti Sanghatana (women's organization), 37, 81, 93
Stree Sangam (women's organization), 258
Stridhan (gifts received by women in marriage). *See also* Maintenance
AIMPLB and, 311
All India Muslim Personal Law Board and, 311
amount of, 127, 137–138, 143, 167
Code of Criminal Procedure 1973, recovery under, 169
Dar ul Qaza and, 280
domestic violence and, 75–76
entitlement to, 140
Ithna Ashari Khojas, among, 298
khula and, 312
Meghwal caste, recovery in, 222–223

Muslim Personal Law, in, 311–312
negotiating recovery of, 168–172
ownership of, 140
Penal Code 1860, recovery under, 82, 169, 223, 256–257
recovery of, 277, 281
women's organizations and, 170
"Strongmen"
BJP, in, 19
Hindu Personal Law, in, 261–263
khula and, 276
Muslim Personal Law, in, 276–278
Sturman, Rachel, 36
Subramanian, Narendra, 76
Sudan, Muslim law in, 4
Sugarman, David, 312–313
Sunna (Prophet's statements), 268
Sunni Muslims, 268, 275–276, 300, 304–306.
    See also Ithna Ashari Khojas
Syeds (Muslim sect), 296
Syria
    Muslim law in, 344
    prenuptial agreements in, 316

Tabligh i Jamaat (religious movement), 283–284
Talaq ahsan (divorce), 131, 280
Talaq e tafwid (delegated divorce), 71, 306
Talaq hasan (divorce), 131, 280
Talaqnama (deed of divorce), 156
Talaq ul bidaat (divorce), 87, 131–137, 273, 280, 304–306
Tamanaha, Brian Z., 46, 326
Tamboli, Shamsuddin, 317
Tamir e Millat (Muslim religious organization), 301
Tan, Poh-Ling, 43
Tanzania, legal centralism in, 2, 9
Tata Institute of Social Sciences, 94, 258
Teubner, Gunther, 44–46, 346
Thailand, legal centralism in, 2
"Triple *talaq*," 87, 131–137, 273, 280, 304–306
Tunisia
    legal centralism in, 2, 9
    Muslim law in, 344
Turi caste, 178
Turkey
    customary law in, 336

legal centralism in, 2
uniform law in, 2

Ulemas (Muslim clergy), 48, 278–279, 318–320
Uniform Adoption Bill, 300
Uniform civil code
    attempts to enact, 12–15, 18–20
    BJP on, 18–19, 321, 333
    Congress Party on, 321
    legal pluralism and, 325–326
    shared adjudication model, effect on, 333–336
Unilateral divorce, 102–103, 137–139, 166–167
United States, divorce in, 88

Vajpayee, A.B., 295
Vanakar caste, 178, 184
Vatuk, Sylvia, 25, 272
Vishnu (Hindu deity), 293
Vishwa Hindu Parishad (BJP cultural affiliate), 19
Viswanathan, Gauri, 204
Void and voidable marriages, 109–114

Waghela, Lalitbhai, 85–86
Washbrook, David A., 11
Weber, Max, 42
Women Living Under Muslim Laws Network, 288
Women's Centre, 255
Women's organizations. *See also specific organization*
    Hindu Personal Law, role in, 254–259
    KVOs, role among, 254–259
    Meghwal caste, role in, 220–223, 254–259
    Sai Suthar caste, role in, 254–259
    shared adjudication model, role in, 330
    sharia law and, 321
    stridhan and, 170
Women's Research and Action Group, 288, 290–291, 305, 321–322
Woods, Patricia, 47, 163

Yilmaz, Ihsan, 8, 43
Young, Iris, 6–7

CAMBRIDGE STUDIES IN LAW AND SOCIETY *(continued from page iii)*

Law and Globalization from Below: Towards a Cosmopolitan Legality
Edited by Boaventura de Sousa Santos and César A. Rodríguez-Garavito

Justice and Reconciliation in Post-Apartheid South Africa
Edited by François du Bois and Antje du Bois-Pedain

Judicial Review and Bureaucratic Impact: International and Interdisciplinary Perspectives
Edited by Marc Hertogh and Simon Halliday

Paths to International Justice: Social and Legal Perspectives
Edited by Marie-Bénédicte Dembour and Tobias Kelly

The Practice of Human Rights: Tracking Law between the Global and the Local
Edited by Mark Goodale and Sally Engle Merry

Public Accountability: Designs, Dilemmas and Experiences
Edited by Michael W. Dowdle

Autonomy and Ethnicity: Negotiating Competing Claims in Multi-Ethnic States
Edited by Yash Ghai

The Ritual of Rights in Japan: Law, Society, and Health Policy
Eric A. Feldman

Constituting Democracy: Law, Globalism and South Africa's Political Reconstruction
Heinz Klug

Planted Flags: Trees, Land, and Law in Israel/Palestine
Irus Braverman

Social Citizenship and Workfare in the United States and Western Europe: The Paradox of Inclusion
Joel F. Handler

Darfur and the Crime of Genocide
John Hagan and Wenona Rymond-Richmond

The Invention of the Passport: Surveillance, Citizenship and the State
John Torpey

Fictions of Justice: The International Criminal Court and the Challenge of Legal Pluralism in Sub-Sahara Africa
Kamari Maxine Clarke

Immigrants at the Margins: Law, Race, and Exclusion in Southern Europe
Kitty Calavita

Judges beyond Politics in Democracy and Dictatorship: Lessons from Chile
Lisa Hilbink

Diseases of the Will: Alcohol and the Dilemmas of Freedom
Mariana Valverde

Law and Society in Vietnam: The Transition from Socialism in Comparative Perspective
Mark Sidel

Militarization and Violence against Women in Conflict Zones in the Middle East: A Palestinian Case-Study
Nadera Shalhoub-Kevorkian

Lawyers and Regulation: The Politics of the Administrative Process
Patrick Schmidt

Modernism and the Grounds of Law
Peter Fitzpatrick

The Politics of Truth and Reconciliation in South Africa: Legitimizing the Post-Apartheid State
Richard A. Wilson

The Colonies of Law: Colonialism, Zionism and Law in Early Mandate Palestine
Ronen Shamir

Legal Reform and Administrative Detention Powers in China
Sarah Biddulph

After Abu Ghraib: Exploring Human Rights in America and the Middle East
Shadi Mokhtari

Conducting Law and Society Research: Reflections on Methods and Practices
Simon Halliday and Patrick Schmidt

Child Pornography and Sexual Grooming: Legal and Societal Responses
Suzanne Ost

Culture under Cross-Examination: International Justice and the Special Court for Sierra Leone
Tim Kelsall

Law, Violence and Sovereignty Among West Bank Palestinians
Tobias Kelly

Unemployment and Government: Genealogies of the Social
William Walters

Globalisation, Human Rights and Labour Law in Pacific Asia
Anthony Woodiwiss

The Gacaca Courts, Post-Genocide Justice and Reconciliation in Rwanda: Justice without Lawyers
Phil Clark

Courting Democracy in Bosnia and Herzegovina: The Hague Tribunal's Impact in a Postwar State
Lara J. Nettelfield

Cultures of Legality: Judicialization and Political Activism in Latin America
Javier Couso, Alexandra Huneeus, and Rachel Sieder